HURLING GIANTS

G000065516

BRENDAN FULLAM is a native of Ardagh, Co. Limerick, and a retired bank manager, who served in that capacity in Killorglin, Co. Kerry, the Crescent in Wexford, and New Ross. In his younger years his banking career took him to Killorglin, Kilrush, Clifden, Ballyshannon, Wexford and Tralee, and in each of these towns he played with the local hurling team. The game of hurling is his greatest interest, and his vision in meeting and interviewing the legends of the game over the past eighteen years has resulted in three unique and invaluable records of the game and its players — *Giants of the Ash*, *Hurling Giants* and the final book in the series, *Legends of the Ash* — treasures for all sports followers.

To my wife Mary
who brought the sunshine back into my life.

Had I the gold of England's King,
The wealth of France or Spain
Or all the jewels that the big ships bring
From o'er the Spanish Main;
I'd leave them all, the great and small
For a verdant Irish lawn,
My comrades all, the flying ball
And a stout-grained ash camán.

Phil O'Neill
'Sliabh Ruadh'

HURLING GIANTS

Brendan Fullam

WOLFHOUND PRESS

First published in paperback 1998
First published 1994
Wolfhound Press Ltd
68 Mountjoy Square
Dublin 1
Tel: (353-1) 8740354
Fax: (353-1) 8720207

British Library Cataloguing in Publication Data
A catalogue record for this book is available from the British Library

ISBN 0-86327-444-7 hb
ISBN 0-86327-666-0 pb

10 9 8 7 6 5 4 3 2 1

The author and publishers are grateful to hurlers and their families who supplied photographs and to all who assisted in research for this book, and wish to thank sports photographer Jim Connolly in particular.

Photograph on page 232 courtesy of Ed O'Shea, Thurles

Cover design and photograph: Jan de Fouw
Cover photographs, and cover photographs of players: Inpho
Typesetting: Wolfhound Press
Printed in the Republic of Ireland by Colour Books, Dublin

PREFACE

The story of hurling goes back into the twilight of fable. 'Carbery' the renowned sportswriter and hurling enthusiast had this to say about the great game: 'So long and so unsullied has the game been handed down from sire to son that the very parish soil is permeated with the hurling spirit'.

The modern game dates from 1884 — the year the GAA was founded, following a historic meeting in Thurles.

For over one hundred years now hurling men have thrilled and entertained countless thousands with many breathtaking displays of our ancient game.

This book tells the story of some of those men — a personal glimpse — an insight — a reflection of their inner thoughts and feelings, hopes and aspirations — dreams come true — dreams dashed — memories and nostalgia of other days. It combines the hurlers of modern times with those of distant days. All are household names in the hurling calendar — each a link, combining to produce a chain of sporting memories to be cherished.

Each name spells hurling magic — Semple, King, Phelan, Baston, Rackard and Gray, samples from the past — Clarke, Hartigan, Cregan, Skehan, Barry-Murphy, Jimmy Doyle and Doran, some of the modern vintage. And of course a further profile of Meagher, Mackey and Ring.

In my first book, *Giants of the Ash* I included 79 players — seventy six of those I personally interviewed: three who were dead before I began this work — John Keane of Waterford, Lory Meagher of Kilkenny and Christy Ring of Cork, I profiled.

Sadly thirty or so of those I met are no longer with us — those most recently departed include Kevin Armstrong of Antrim, Tommy Doyle of Tipperary, Joe Salmon of Galway, Jimmy Langton of Kilkenny, Jim Young of Cork, Sean Herbert and Jackie Power of Limerick. Í seilbh ghrámhar Dé go raibh siad anois agus í gconaí.

In this book I write about twenty one great personalities who belonged to the earlier years of the association together with contributions from forty five players that I interviewed and whose careers span the years from the historic three finals of 1931 right up to the present day. Also included is an article on the late Pat Carroll of Offaly.

For over half a century now people of the camogie world have demonstrated their hurling prowess at the highest level and produced many thrilling performances. It is therefore a matter of great pride to have interviewed for this book five of camogie's greatest exponents — Kathleen Mills and Una O'Connor of Dublin, Marian McCarthy of Cork and the Downey twins, Angela and Ann of Kilkenny.

The two books together, deal with one hundred and fifty one of hurling's greatest names — admittedly the tip of the iceberg, for there were so many — covering all the years from 1895 to date. Of that figure one hundred and twenty six were interviewed by me. The remaining twenty five were imithe ar shlí na fírinne before this work began. The names and fame of all will live forever in hurling folklore.

'Ar dhroim an domhain níl radharc is áille
Na tríocha fear ag bualadh báire'.

5

WORDS OF COMMENDATION

MICHEÁL Ó MUIRCHEARTAIGH

Is ceart agus is cóir go dtiocfadh scéal maith i gcomharbacht ar scéal a thug taitneamh thar na bearta do's na mílte ar fud na tíre — an sóiscéal a chraobhscaoil Breandán in *Giants of the Ash* i samhain na bliana 1991.

I know of no book which fostered so much joyful reminiscing as the 'Giants' did and the 'Leabhar' itself has now become a Giant. Number two is eagerly looked forward to and those chronicled in it are worthy of inclusion in any list of greats.

Comhgháirdeachas, a Bhreandáin agus gura mear chugainn uimhir a 3.

Beir bua agus beannacht.
Micheál Ó Muircheartaigh

TOM HUMPHRIES

My Grandfather was a football man. Long before too many Sweet Afton had yellowed his fingers and thickened his cough, he wore the green and white of the O'Tooles club in Dublin. His success may have been modest but he rubbed shoulders with giants and the memory of them was burned into him.

His time was the period from 1919 onwards when Dublin and Kildare won sixteen out of seventeen Leinster titles. A residual fondness for the Lillywhites and the deeds of Larry Stanley stayed with him all his life but his favourite topic of conversation was Dublin football and the three great teams the Seville Place parish produced St.Mary's, St.Joseph's and O'Tooles. Decades on he could describe the cut and style of any players; Johnny McDonnell and Paddy McDonnell, the impossibly glamorous Synott clan of whom Josie was the favourite.

He was a football man but he genuflected like all football lovers to the beauty of hurling. Lory Meagher was a firm favourite although the longevity of Tull Considine of Clare was often mulled over. Dublin's occasional dabblings in the late stages of hurling championships left him apparently unmoved.

He bought me my first hurley (or hurl as we say in Dublin) and hoped that I might put it to better use than I did. Still between the football and the hurling and his memories of both games and my bungling progress at them, we had enough conversation to pass the longest evenings.

His memories went with him. The great names with which he embroidered his conversations finally had their death when nobody was left to talk about them.

Talk is the lifeblood that courses through great games like football and hurling, talk is what transforms dusty statistics into social history and warm memory.

For a race which is supposedly pinioned down by its own history we are careless about its artefacts. Sport in particular has suffered from our neglect. The video archive of our great games is a hit and miss affair and the literary canon attached to football and hurling wouldn't fill a modest shelf.

The Americans for all their hunger for the thrill of the new have long since realised the value of sporting memories. Each of their major sports has instituted a Hall of Fame, massive museums where the jerseys and bats and balls of the great names are preserved, that following generations might look and wonder.

Gaelic games has no true Hall of Fame, no physical shrine to the sporting history but at least hurling now has Brendan Fullam and his wonderful books. Brendan has taken the care to capture the words and memories of the legends. He has captured whole headfuls of talk and memories and given them to us between two covers.

Reading through the testimonies of these names already mossed over with magic and myth it is impossible not to let the wonder grow. Through the tales runs a love of hurling, a devotion to the art which transcends and outlives the rivalries of the game. Brendan Fullam has stitched together all these memories and in so doing has done hurling a wonderful service. We all have the chance now to share in the past, to drift along the sidelines and haunt long vanished dressing rooms. The start of any true hall of fame will be Brendan's book of manuscripts.

Words are the sustenance of hurling history and Brendan has given another book's worth to treasure.

Go raibh maith agat.
Tom Humphries

JIMMY MAGEE

Hurling Giants do not have to be gargantuan in physique. They come in all shapes and sizes — tall, thin, short, stout. All of them are fleet of foot, quick of hand, eagle of eye and have the magical mixture that concocts to supreme artistry.

Brendan Fullam's new book pays homage to these remarkable people, amateur sports players who have entertained in a style of which professionals would be proud.

Brendan's first work *Giants of the Ash* was the quality and style of book I'd love to have written and I haven't changed my opinion with the arrival of Book Mark 2.

Are hurlers born not made? Yes. How can anybody be made to look and perform like Jimmy Doyle, Jimmy Barry-Murphy, Mick Roche, Eamon Cregan — and the wondermen Christy Ring, Mick Mackey and Lory Meagher, by any standards a great triumvirate.

I am writing this in the week of the 1994 All Ireland final — the unique pairing of Limerick and Offaly. The tempo of expectation is increasing — the previews in words and pictures excite just as they've done every year since I attained the age of reason — that's if I ever reached it.

Microphones, cameras, lights, pens, tape machines and notebooks will be familiar to every man engaged in next Sunday's battle. Every question asked, every answer given will be recorded forever — for another Brendan Fullam to cast in prose into the next century?

How many of '94's stars will have the gift to live in the mind as long as the heroes enshrined in *Hurling Giants*.

Brendan Fullam for his work on these books is himself a Hurling Giant.

Jimmy Magee

Contents

Brendan HENNESSY	1955-1976	Ballyduff, Kerry and New York	135
Joe HENNESSY	1976-1988	James Stephens & Kilkenny	141
Padraig HORAN	1970-1986	St Rynagh's & Offaly	146
Willie HOUGH	1913-1929	Newcastlewest & Limerick	150
Michael KEATING	1964-1975	Ballybacon-Grange & Tipperary	154
Jim KELLIHER	1900-1914	Dungourney & Cork	155
Jimmy KENNEDY	1946-1951	UCD & Kiladangan, Dublin & Tipperary	156
Mick KING	1923-1935	Castlegar, Galway & Galway	160
Paddy LALOR	1946-1956	Abbeyleix & Laois	162
Johnny LEAHY	1909-1929	Boherlahan & Tipperary	166
John LYONS	1946-1960	Glen Rovers & Cork	168
John 'Tyler' MACKEY	1901-1917	Castleconnell & Limerick	172
Mick MACKEY	1930-1947	Ahane & Limerick	173
P.J. MACKEY	1907-1916	New Ross & Wexford	175
Michael MAHER	1890-1900	Toberadora & Tipperary	177
Marian McCARTHY	1970-1991	SPPP, Éire Óg and Cork	178
Joe McDONAGH	1972-1983	Ballinderreen & Galway	180
John 'Jobber' McGRATH	1950-1965	Rickardstown & Westmeath	183
Oliver McGRATH	1956-1965	Faythe Harriers & Wexford	184
Joe McKENNA	1971-1985	South Liberties & Limerick	190
Lory MEAGHER	1926-1937	Tullaroan & Kilkenny	193
Kathleen MILLS	1941-1961	GSR & Dublin	195
Barney MOYLAN	1965-1976	St Rynagh's & Offaly	198

Below: This early 'How to Play' hurling drawing from Ilustrated Sporting & Dramatic News predates the founding of the GAA

The 1887 team, winners of the first All Ireland hurling championship (photographed about 1910)
Back Row: D. Maher, J. Sullivan, E. Murphy, J. Ryan, M. Maher, E. Leamy, T. Burke, C. Callinan, D. Davoren, M
Murphy. Centre Row: P. Ryan, D. Maher, J. Stapleton (captain), T. Maher, G. Leamy, J. Ryan, J. Dwyer. Front Row
M. Carroll, M. McNamara, T. Butler

Jim STAPLETON   c. 1887   Thurles & Tipperary

Born: 1863

Jim Stapleton of Thurles town, born in 1863, was a farmer and a man of great physique. He had the honour of being the first All Ireland Senior Hurling winning captain when he led Tipperary (Thurles) to victory over Galway (Meelick) in the 1887 championship.

On the occasion of the first GAA championship things we take for granted today were either unknown or in their infancy — television, radio, telephone, the motor car, electricity, the aeroplane. The famine was a horror of living memory. Its legacy of emigration had taken a huge toll as hundreds of thousands had fled across the Atlantic. The abortive Fenian Insurrection of 1867 was still talked about but the Fenian movement continued and was particularly strong in America.

It was the era of Michael Davitt and the Land League, of Parnell and Home Rule, of Rack Rents and evictions, of landlords and Land Acts, of Secret Societies and Coercion Bills. Many were poorly educated or illiterate. It was customary in parishes for locals to gather at the forge at evening time where one would read the paper and acquaint them with the happenings of the day.

A spirit of national pride prevailed. It found expression in part in the GAA.

Five teams contested the 1887 championship — Galway, Wexford, Clare, Tipperary and Kilkenny who received a walkover from Cork. On route to the final Tipperary beat Clare (Smyth O'Brien's) at Nenagh by 1:7 to 0:2. — although some records show the score as 1:8 to 0:4. They beat Kilkenny (Tullaroan) at Urlingford by 4:7 to 0:0.

The final took place at Birr on Easter Sunday, 1 April 1888. The teams lined out 21 a side and played in their stockinged feet. The pitch measured 200 yards by 100

11

yards. The final score read Tipperary 1 goal, 1 point and 1 forfeit point to nil. Tommy Healy scored the goal — the first goal ever in the All Ireland championships — from a pass by Jim Stapleton — and wrote himself into the record books. It wasn't the only time the losers failed to score in a final. It happened again in 1902 when London lost to a Cork side captained by the legendary Jim Kelliher. This report on the 1887 final is taken from *The Freeman's Journal* —

Birr, Monday: At last the hurling championship for 1887 has been decided, and the result will hardly create any surprise in Gaelic circles, for it has been anticipated for many a day. Six months ago the intercounty ties were reduced to the final, and after an inexplicable delay, this was played off at Birr yesterday. The town was central as well as neutral for both Meelick and Thurles, the champion hurling teams of Galway and Tipperary, respectively and which have earned great fame in the Gaelic world, Thurles having played over twenty matches to come to the final. There were good grounds, superb weather, orderly spectators and an efficient referee. Special trains carried crowds of people from Tipperary, Kings County and Queens County into Birr, and east Galway seemed to have turned out to a man to escort the Meelick hurlers to the scene of strife. The Thurles hurlers travelled by special train, and they were met at Birr Railway station by a large crowd including Mr P. White, Hon Sec, King's County GAA, Mr Patrick Ryan, Vice President, etc. When they made their appearance, they were warmly cheered by the Tipperary men. From the time the Thurles and Meelick men met, their intercourse was characterised by the utmost good feeling and good humour, and the defeat of the latter did not in the least change that, for they accepted it in the same spirit as they would victory. After a short delay the members of both teams dressed themselves in the Gaelic costume. They were then marshalled by Capt Lynam, Meelick, who in military fashion ordered them into line, the Tipperary men in front and the Galway men behind. He then gave 'right about,' and they were formed two deep, every Tipp man standing shoulder to shoulder with a Galway man. In this order, they marched through the town to the field, Messrs Hugh Ryan, Andrew Callanan and Capt Lynam being in front ...

At three o'clock the teams lined up and the ball was thrown up by Mr Patrick White, Birr, and for eleven minutes, it was whizzing up and down the field now threatening one goal, now another. At that time, Thurles made the first score, one of the whips scoring a point. During a scrimmage, one of the Thurles men received an accidental stroke of the hurley on the nose, giving that organ so severe a battering that he had to give up playing. A Galway man had to be put out at seventeen minutes past for tripping. From fifteen minutes past to half time, the play was simply fierce. At a crucial point of the play, just before half time, and when the Thurles whips were carrying the ball towards the Galway posts, the Galway hurler who had been put out, rushed in and struck the ball to one of his colleagues. The referee remonstrated, and said he had observed him doing that before also; if it occurred again, he would award the match to Tipperary. There was no person admitted to replace the Thurles player.

Shortly after the change of sides, the Thurles forwards carried the ball close to the Galway posts, and here, after a long struggle, during which it was several times in close to the goal, a Galway hurler touched it over the sideline, giving Thurles a forfeit point. Thurles succeeded soon after in placing a goal to their credit scored by Tommy Healy, Borris, and at the call of time the play stood thus: For Thurles, 1 goal 1 point and 1 forfeit point; to Galway nil. The enthusiasm of the Tipps seems to be unbounded when play was declared.

They took the plucky captain of the brave Thurles team on their shoulders and carried him through the field in triumph.

The winning team was: Jim Stapleton (captain) Matty Maher, Andy Maher, Tom Bourke, Ned Murphy, Tom Stapleton, Ger Dwyer, Mick Carroll, Tom Carroll, Tom Maher, John Leamy, Ned Lambe, Martin McNamara, Johnny Mockler, Ger Ryan, Danny Ryan, Tom Dwyer, Ned Bowe, Tommy Healy, Jim Leahy, Johnny Dunne.

But the great historic victory was not without its share of controversy. The absence of Thurles captain, Denis Maher and six others is explained by him in this letter to the *Tipperary Star* in January 1913:

Dear Sir. In your second last issue I read the names of the men who played in the '87 All Ireland hurling final; of these men I have nothing to say, but as Captain of the old hurling team of Thurles from 1887 to 1894 I think it is my duty to explain our absence in the final. After winning the county championship we were drawn against Clare in the first inter-county match. The match was fixed for Limerick, but as Clare did not travel it was refixed for Nenagh. Our selection to meet Clare was: Six men from Borris, one from the Ragg, and fourteen from Thurles, and though I cannot remember the exact score we won by a big majority. Kilkenny was our next match for the semi-final and it was fixed for Clonmel and we relied on the team that beat Clare with one change.

Both Tipperary and Kilkenny were on the ground but owing to an infringement of the rules, the match was declared off, and had to be refixed for the following Thursday in Urlingford, Co Kilkenny. The teams travelled as selected, but Kilkenny objected to five of the Borris players and we had to play nineteen from Thurles and two from Borris who were legal, namely John Mockler and Tom Stapleton. We beat Kilkenny by a big score to nil, although they were long odds against us, and everyone who saw the match witnessed how Thurles played with, what I might say, an individual team. Our next and final match was against Galway which was fixed for Birr. The old six from Borris and fifteen from Thurles were selected. Their names were as far as I can

remember; Tom Healy, D. Ryan, J. Ryan, Tim Dwyer, J. Mockler and Ned Bowe, Two-Mile Borris; Pat Ryan, Mallaunbrack; Con Callanan, Ardbawn; Dan Davern, Ballycahill; D. Maher (Red) Matt Maher, Jack Maher (Black), Tom Maher, Mattie Maher (Little), Ned Maher, Andy Maher and D. Maher (Killinan); Jim Stapleton, Tom Bourke (Rossestown), Ned Murphy, Martin McNamara, Dick Butler, J.Doran (Thurles), Ger Dwyer (Castlestown).

I was on the selection committee and my instructions from the Killinan players were that the Railway fares should be paid out of club funds, as they had already travelled against Clare and Galway at a good deal of expense. The meeting was on the Friday night before the match and the team above selected, but the committee were not unanimous to pay the fares.

In the meantime, owing to some misleading rumours, and though I or any of the men left behind were unaware of any change, there were men from Gortnahoe, Drombane and Moyne called in and their expenses paid and seven of the old hurlers left standing on the platform, namely: D. Maher, Jack Maher, Con Callanan, Pat Ryan, Mattie Maher, Ned Maher and myself. These were the backbone of the club at the time and who kept Tipperary to the front rank of the hurling field for years after. These are the circumstances which I think it my duty to ventilate. I may also add that for my part I do not expect or seek to get a medal, but I feel satisfied in explaining, as far as my memory helps me, the cause of our absence from the 1887 final.

It is unlikely after the triumph of 1887 that Jim Stapleton paused to reflect on what would have evolved in the Association one hundred years hence. After all he was looking at an acorn in its infancy. The oak tree that was nurtured in the decades ahead would almost certainly have been beyond his comprehension and his wildest dreams.

In victory in 1887 Jim Stapleton carved for himself a unique place of honour and distinction in the annals of the GAA.

Born: 1964

great players and mentors.

Finally, I would like to thank my parents for all their love and support. Without them I would not be the man I am.

Ciaran Barr   **99**

66

My introduction to Gaelic games came from a couple of De La Salle Brothers in St Finian's Primary School on the Lower Falls Road. They were both Kerrymen and the school colours were the Kerry colours. They were great football men and taught us the Kerry style of the day, and we all idolised the Kerry team of the seventies.

When I then moved up to Grammar School the Christian Brothers introduced me to hurling. But with two older brothers who were great players I was the water bottle carrier for quite some time.

Eventually I followed my brothers on to the O'Donovan Rossa teams and enjoyed the team spirit and friendship of my colleagues there.

I suppose with my move to Dublin I cannot leave out St Vincent's, who have shown me great warmth, and I hope to end my playing days there.

I have always enjoyed playing gaelic games, but my great passion is for hurling. There is no game like it and it has been a privilege to play the game and to meet the

He was Ulster's and Antrim's first hurling All Star. That was in 1988 when he was chosen at centre-half-forward. It represented another step forward in the progress of Antrim hurling. The tradition is deep-rooted. The heritage is rich. The paucity of trophies and awards — a mere intermediate title in 1970 — does scant justice to decades of diligent endeavour. And yet failure in this sphere has never diminished the ardour and passion with which the men of Antrim play and live and breathe the ancient game. They just keep plugging away — all the time hoping that they will some day, as Wexford and Offaly did, assemble a lineout that will match the best and take an All Ireland crown.

In the forties a flame of hope flickered for a while and then faded. Galway were defeated at Corrigan Park Belfast in the All Ireland quarter-final of 1943 — a surprise. At the same venue in the semi-final Kilkenny fell victims — a shock. Cork provided the next hurdle at Croke Park and this time David failed to slay Goliath. Cork with one of its finest combinations — stars in every position — outclassed Antrim. Many of the Antrim players froze in Croke Park. Cork might have found the going tougher in Corrigan Park Belfast. Antrim had another moment of glory in 1945 when Leinster was defeated in the Railway Cup semi final — the venue Corrigan Park Belfast, their happy hurling ground.

Ciaran remembers as a twelve-year-old playing in the Féile na nGael hurling competition in Waterford and enjoying every moment of it. At that tender age he played at corner-back. His brother Damien took all the sideline cuts with a Randall hurley that he purchased in Wexford. 'He loved that hurley — he used to sleep with it.'

Around the same time Ciaran was taken to his 'first real big game'. It was the All Ireland final between Wexford and Cork. 'Everyone was talking about Doran. But at the time I didn't know who he was. I was only a nipper. I still remember the vivid red and the purple and gold.' Little did he think then that he would one day play against Tony Doran in a club All Ireland final in Croke Park — a dozen years later on St Patrick's Day 1989.

He excelled at waterpolo and played for Ireland. He also played for British Universities and took part in the World Student games at Zagreb in the late eighties.

I asked Ciaran to describe as he saw it his attributes and his shortcomings as a hurler. 'I could catch the ball — opponents couldn't stop me catching. I had vision. I could see what was happening around me and decide what option was best. I also had physical strength. You don't normally find a player of fifteen stone weight playing at centre-forward in hurling. Weight can be a help. When you are pulling on a ball you can communicate to your opponent the extent of your strength. On the negative side I lacked real speed — I wish I had it — I never had it for the short run — that's what you need in hurling — apart from the midfielders, speed in a twenty yards radius combined with good anticipation is what you need in hurling. I lacked the finesse of players like Bill Hennessy and D.J. Carey of Kilkenny and Tom Cashman, Dermot McCurtain, John Fenton and Tomás Mulcahy of Cork. I was never able to do the things with the ball that they could.'

He has a special admiration for Cork and Kilkenny hurling — 'because of their pure skill' — and this is clearly reflected in his choice of team. Ciaran says that Jimmy Barry-Murphy used say that a corner-forward had to be patient — if he gets worried or excited he will lose concentration — and then when that one chance comes he will not be equipped to take it. Ciaran has visions of a priest saying to Jimmy Barry Murphy in his youth — 'have patience, have patience — your chance will come — and when it does take it.'

He would make a few small changes. 'Ban the kicked goal — remove the small square — introduce two referees. The speed of the modern game is too much for one referee.'

Ciaran is particularly encouraged by what he has seen in Antrim hurling in the past dozen years. Club performances in the All Ireland club championship have been remarkably good. Loughgeil Shamrocks won the title in 1983 when they beat St Rynagh's of Offaly in a replay. And he remembers the Sunday in February 1988 when his club O'Donovan Rossa went down to Kilmallock to play Patrickswell in the All Ireland club semi-final on a wet and miserable day. 'Nobody gave us a chance — they said we would be hammered. Playing with a fairly strong wind we were only a few points up at halftime. Our cornerback Sean Collins who was thirty-six years of age said in the dressing-room — we have this crowd — you think like that — and there won't be a bother for the rest of it. We won narrowly — it was the greatest club game I played in.'

Some performances of the county team would also suggest that Antrim hurling is going through its best ever phase. In 1986 in the All Ireland semi-final at Croke Park they lost by only five points to Cork in a game where they demonstrated exceptional scoring accuracy — Cork 7:11 Antrim 1:24. 'Jimmy Barry-Murphy did the damage that day.' In 1987 and 1988 they ran Kilkenny and Tipperary close on the scores 2:18 to 2:11 and 3:15 to 2:10 respectively. He remembers well the game against Tipperary. 'It was a very hot day. I caught every ball that day. I remember blasting it at goal on one occasion. It hit the crossbar — rebounded outfield — and in four moves was finished to the net by Pat Fox for Tipp. Instead of our score being a goal greater it was Tipp who had the additional score — the might have beens of hurling.'

He feels that Antrim's greatest performance of recent times was in the All Ireland semi-final of 1989 against Offaly. 'We really played as a team that day — showed our true potential — some of the players even played above themselves.' Everyone who saw that game will remember the magnanimous gesture of Offaly in their hour of defeat as they lined up to form a guard of honour for the Antrim players as they left the pitch — surely a wonderful sporting gesture and an example and ideal for all young hurlers to look up to and emulate.

In the current national hurling league (1993/94) Antrim have added immensely to their stature with home wins over Limerick and Waterford and away wins over Wexford and Galway. Bigger things could be on the horizon. But whatever the future holds they will always play hurling in Antrim and particularly in the Glens — in Loughgiel, Ballycastle, Cushendall and Dunloy.

This is the team Ciaran would have liked to captain.

Ger Cunningham (Cork)

'Fan' Larkin (Kilkenny)   Conor Hayes (Galway)   Dick O'Hara (Kilkenny)

Pete Finnerty (Galway)   Ger Henderson (Kilkenny)   Dermot McCurtain (Cork)

John Fenton (Cork)   Frank Cummins (Kilkenny)

Tony O'Sullivan (Cork)   Ciaran Barr (Antrim)   Tomás Mulcahy (Cork)

Jimmy Barry-Murphy (Cork)   Tony Doran (Wexford)   Seanie O'Leary (Cork)

Born: 1914

" "

Lovely meeting Brendan Fullam and his wife Mary. We went through many happy memories.

Good luck to all the old hurlers and long may they live. Those were marvellous days. Cheers.

Willie Barron

1938 represented a milestone in Waterford hurling. It was the year they broke the barrier in Munster and collected their first Munster crown after victories over Cork and Clare. Prior to that the county could look back on a very barren spell since the foundation of the GAA. They had contested five Munster finals and in the earlier ones in 1903 and 1925 they were decisively beaten by Cork and Tipperary respectively.

But as the thirties dawned there were signs that the seeds of decades were about to bear some fruit and bring reward to the dedicated men of the Decies. In 1929 Waterford won the All Ireland minor title. This was

followed in 1931 and 1934 by All Ireland junior victories. In 1931 Waterford lost the Munster senior title to Cork after a replay and those still alive who remember the drawn game will recall that it was with the last puck of the game — eight minutes into time added on — that Jim Hurley sent over the equaliser for Cork. In 1933 and 1934 they failed to Limerick in the Munster senior hurling final. It is interesting to note that the 1933 final was abandoned with Limerick leading by 3:7 to 1:2 — the match was awarded to Limerick — the last major contest in the Munster GAA calendar to end in such a manner. Waterford names were beginning to appear on the Munster Railway cup teams — most notably Charlie Ware, John Keane and Christy Moylan. And Waterford were putting it up to the leading teams in Munster. There were signs that the breakthrough was close.

When it came in 1938 Willie Barron was at right-half-forward — his favourite position — and he remembers the final against Dublin with a certain amount of regret. 'We suffered from nerves that day

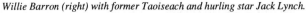

Willie Barron (right) with former Taoiseach and hurling star Jack Lynch.

1938 — first Waterford team to win a Munster Senior Hurling title. Back Row: J. Keane, J. O'Neill, C. Ware, W. Walsh, L. Byrne, J. Halpin, M. Hickey, D. Goode, C. Moylan, Con 'Sonny' Curley, S. Wyse. Middle: Davy Power, Tom Greaney, J. Fanning, Ned Daly, J. Feeney, T. Fitzgerald, J. Mountain. Front: J. Burke, W. Barron, J. Baston, Pa Sheehan, P. Greene

—Croke Park nerves. Many of the lads had never been to Dublin before, not to mind Croke Park. 'Twas a low scoring game — 11 points to 9 points (2:5 to 1:6) We got off to a good start but after about the first fifteen minutes it was obvious the "nerves" were affecting many of the players. John Keane was our best man — he scored four points — the best individual score of the day. We were a goal behind at halftime and, would you believe it, only five points were scored in the second half — two to Dublin and three to Waterford. What annoyed me most about losing was that we lost that day to the least accomplished of all the counties we met in the championship.'

Willie was 'fleet as deer' at half-forward. And he is still very lively on the feet. Every day — weather permitting — this seventy-nine-year-old plays his round of golf at Gold Coast Leisure Centre in Dungarvan. It was there I met him. He was like a two-year-old — lively, vivacious and happy-go-lucky. What's the secret Willie? 'Oh now I can't be telling that to everyone.' They tell me the recipe includes porridge, brown bread and raw eggs and a wee drop from the crater. He smiled. 'A man must stay fit you know.'

At present he trains the Dungarvan hurlers — 'they haven't won the county title since I captained them to victory over Mount Sion in 1941.' With Willie's system of training none of the players can keep up with him. He runs an inner circle while the players have to negotiate an outer circle of considerably larger radius. He has a very keen interest in Irish music and if there is a céilí within striking distance he is there to dance the Walls of Limerick and the Siege of Ennis. The man is indefatigable. Among the occasions he enjoys immensely are the ex-hurlers' golf outings. 'These are great occasions. You would never meet the hurling colleagues but for them.'

Four of these take place annually — the Captain's Prize, the Christy Ring Perpetual trophy, inter-county game at Thurles after the All Ireland final and a weekend in October at Clonea. At all these gatherings no fitter man swings a club than Willie.

He felt honoured to be on the victorious Railway Cup Munster team of 1942. 'I played on that great Kilkenny stylist Paddy Phelan. I had as my team mates names that live on in hurling history — John Keane and Christy Moylan of Waterford, Dick Stokes, Jackie Power, Peter Cregan and Jim McCarthy of Limerick, Jack Lynch, Johnny Quirke, Willie Murphy, Christy Ring and Batt Thornhill of Cork, Johnny Ryan, Dinny O'Gorman and Willie

O'Donnell of Tipperary.

The toughest game I played during my career was the All Ireland semi-final of 1938 against Galway at Ennis. It was won on the score 4:8 to 3:1. I got injured in that game but I didn't go off. I got the ball and as I was running past my man I didn't see a second man coming for me. I got sandwiched between them and after the game discovered that I had suffered injury to my shoulder blade, breast bone and ankle. Back in Dungarvan I went to a woman bonesetter — a Mrs Murphy — she was a great woman God bless her. "Willie," said she to me — "pack up the game — you're all broken up". She did what she had to do, bandaged me up and had me ready for the All Ireland final. She was some woman.'

Willie is stridently critical of some aspects of the modern game. 'They are nearly all picking the ball — solo running — getting nowhere — running into trouble. It's terrible watching them — sickening. Far more *hurling* was done in my day. When the ball came you didn't ask any questions — no such thing as putting up your hand — hard luck if you did. Hurling is a game of many skills — the fastest grass game in the world. What they are doing now slows it up. In my training days what you constantly heard was whip, whip, whip on the ball. It made for hurling skills.'

Around the mid-forties Willie who liked all games went to Waterford one day for what he described as 'a kind of a soccer trial kick-about.' The following Monday the national papers had it with headlines 'GAA star turns to soccer'. He was now *persona non grata* in GAA circles and for his alien activities he was dished out a two year suspension. But for it he would almost certainly have been in the lineout of 1948 that won Waterford a second Munster senior hurling title and went on to make history by defeating Dublin in the final — their first senior crown. To add to the joy of the 1948 occasion the minor team made it a unique double for the county.

He refereed matches and loves to recall a certain league game between Kilkenny and Dublin when he sent Mick Ryan of Dublin and Paddy Buggy of Kilkenny to the sideline. 'Sit down and enjoy the game from the sideline I told them. Whenever I meet Paddy Buggy he keeps reminding me of it and it gives me pleasure. I must be the only one to have ever sent off a President.'

Willie began life studying for the priesthood but a switch of direction took him into the leather business and to different locations around the country from time to time. As a result he played with St Aidan's Enniscorthy, Gorey, Ferns and a challenge game with Wexford against Kilkenny. In the mid-fifties he went to county Wicklow and won a county senior honours with Avoca — a team picked from a variety of clubs. After that he went to London and played initially with Brothers Pearse and later with Sean McDermotts — and won two senior London titles. He was picked to play with London and at the age of 47 played in the junior All Ireland hurling final at Tralee against Kerry. They lost but he still continued for some years to hurl in the London championship. Indefatigable!

Willie is a wonderful character and a great personality — amiable, affable, genial, and gentlemanly — full of zest and zeal. His approach to life is falstaffian.

Laugh and the world laughs with you
Sigh and you sigh alone.

His team was picked with speed and decisiveness. First he travelled down the centre — filling midfield on the way. The corners and wings were filled on the way back. A formidable bunch.

	Tony Reddin (Tipperary)	
Willie Murphy (Cork)	Nick O'Donnell (Wexford)	Andy Fleming (Waterford)
Dick Stokes (Limerick)	John Keane (Waterford)	Jackie Power (Limerick)
Jack Lynch (Cork)	Christy Moylan (Waterford)	
Willie Barron (Waterford)	Mick Mackey (Limerick)	Jimmy Doyle (Tipperary)
Christy Ring (Cork)	Joe McKenna (Limerick)	Johnny Quirke (Cork)

Born: 1928

"

Looking back from a distance at my career in hurling, let me put on record the great enjoyment that I got from playing the game at inter-county level.

It was my great privilege to have been on the same team as the greatest hurler of all time — Christy Ring (May he rest in peace). I played my first inter-county game in the National hurling league in 1947. I did not gain a regular place on the Cork championship team until 1952. From there until I retired in 1960 I was an ever present. That gave me fifteen years playing with Christy.

Until I got my place on the Cork team I was known to family and friends and parishioners of Glanmire parish as Pat. Mícheál O'Hehir christened me Paddy and it stuck to me since. As my club Sarsfields won the Cork Senior hurling championship in 1951 I had the honour of captaining Cork in 1952 to All Ireland success. I was one of the lucky ones to have won every honour in the game — three All Ireland medals — runner up in 1956 — two National hurling leagues — four Railway Cup medals — four Munster championships — two Cork County Senior hurling championships — one St Brendan's Cup medal — one

Fitzgibbon Cup medal (as a sub) — and two Cork County junior football championships.

It was nice to have won all these various championship medals but for this I must thank God that he saw fit to give me whatever skill I had. I was also lucky to be born a Corkman. Corkmen, Tipperary men and Kilkenny men have a greater chance of winning honours on the hurling scene. I realise how lucky I am when I recall all the great hurlers that have played with other counties — Wexford, Limerick, Offaly, Galway, Waterford, who have been known to win All Irelands and God knows should have won more between them.

Again there are many great hurlers in the three most successful counties who have not been lucky enough to get an All Ireland medal due to coming on the teams during the lean years.

I would like to express my thanks to all those who helped me in my career — my family, my clubmates in Glanmire and Sarsfields, my inter-county colleagues down through the years that I played with, with Cork. My thanks and my appreciation to all my opponents on the field of play. I hope I never made enemies from their ranks.

Finally, I must not forget to pay tribute to the greatest supporters in the game. I hope I have given pleasure to followers of the game in all counties.

My great regret was that my father Jim never lived to share my successes. Daddy was a founder member of the Carrigtwohill hurling club — a great GAA man. The hurling pitch in Carrigtwohill — Páirc Seamus de Barra — is dedicated to his memory and on behalf of my family and myself I would like to forever thank the Carrigtwohill club for bestowing this honour on him — ar dheis Dé go raibh a anam.

Paddy Barry **"**

Paddy Barry first played for Cork in an away National League game against Wexford in 1947. 'I was playing table tennis with my brother on Sunday morning when a car called looking for players. 'Twas a common enough occurrence. Some of the regulars would not want to travel so the mentors would look around for some young players.' Paddy was a sub against Waterford in 1948 when a Christy Ring shot for the equaliser in the closing moments was wide of the post in the Munster final.

He took part in the torrid 1949 first round replay against Tipperary in Limerick. After that he played in league and tournament games until he finally established himself as a regular in the Cork forward line in 1952. Paddy was an opportunist and a forward of vision. He was excellent with the ground ball — could cross it strategically — create openings — and add the finishing touch. He made many a score for Ring the maestro. And how did he perceive Ring?

'He was a fanatic for the game — fabulous really — way out on his own — a class apart. He could do anything with the ball in training — roll it up along the hurley — then up his arm — back down and on to the hurley again. He was great with youngsters and old people. I remember a training session when he went into goal. Josie Hartnett, Willie John Daly and myself couldn't get one past him. He had an incredible eye and reflexes. When the session ended we began to move away but Ring stayed in goal and the youngsters ran in and began to send in shots at him. He would leave the odd one in so that the youngsters would be able to say when they went home that Barry, Daly and Hartnett couldn't score against Ring but they did. That's the kind he was. He could of course read a game very well and he watched the referee's style too. After five minutes he might say to me — Paddy, you can carry the ball as far as you like with this ref.'

Paddy sees many changes in the game 'the third man tackle is gone — overhead striking is a rarity — the drop puck is almost extinct — some of the coaching is questionable — going out now backs are told to stop the ball. On the other hand the players are much fitter now as regards keeping going at speed over the full hour. Of course you can't touch the goalkeeper now. In the past the goalie had to watch man and ball and protect himself if the forward slipped the back.' That reminded Paddy of a story he heard about Micka Brennan of Cork and Paddy Scanlon the Limerick goalkeeper. 'Micka was good at taking the goalie and Paddy Scanlon was well aware of it. In the early stages of a particular game Scanlon called Brennan and asked him for a loan of his hurley to drive in a big nail that was sticking out of a hoop on the pole of his hurley. I knew well, said Brennan, that Scanlon was just letting me know it was there — and the size of it too.'

He sees less tolerance nowadays by referees towards dangerous or provocative play — and he welcomes this. 'There is no room on a hurling pitch for hatchet men. I blame the clubs for playing them in the first place and I blame selectors who pick them. They are no use to the game of hurling. I always believed in playing the ball and people often gave out to me for not hitting back when provoked.'

In the six years from 1949 to 1954 Cork and Tipperary met every year — 1949 in the first round that took two games and extra time to decide — and thereafter each year in the Munster final. The spoils were shared evenly. 'The games were tremendous — as were the occasions — but they were fierce and tough.' A deep rivalry built up. At times it reached unhealthy proportions and spilt over into conflict. It was good that they didn't meet in 1955 when Clare disposed of both of them. But when they met again in the finals of 1960 and 1961 there were further flare ups.

Paddy believes that the spoils of the years 1949 to 1954 were wrongly divided. He feels that they should have been in reverse — with Cork winning in 1949, 50 and 51 and Tipperary in 52, 53 and 54. The scoring was always very close and so it is interesting to look at:

1949	Tipperary 3:10 Cork 3:10	
Replay	Tipperary 2:9 Cork 1.9	*Tipp +3*
1950	Tipperary 2:17 Cork 3:11	*Tipp +3*
1951	Tipperary 2:11 Cork 2:9	*Tipp. +2*
		Total +8
1952	Cork 1:11 Tipperary 2:6	*Cork +2*
1953	Cork 3:10 Tipperary 1:11	*Cork +5*
1954	Cork 2:8 Tipperary 1:8	*Cork. +3*
		Total +10

Seven games and just two points between them — leaving spectators with memories of hurling thrills — splintering ash — spills — sparks — controversy — and blood and bandages. Practically every game had 'some incident of controversy in it — goals that were or weren't goals — advantage rule that should or shouldn't have been — frees given or not given — and all depending of course on what side you were on.' It is therefore understandable that an intense and passionate rivalry built up — reaching boiling point on occasions — and overflowed into exchanges that offended the canons of good sportsmanship.

He looks back on the All Ireland final of 1952 against Dublin as his most enjoyable game. It was of course his first All Ireland victory and to add to the glory of the occasion he was also captain. He played that day at left-full-forward — or as Mícheál O'Hehir would have described it — top of the left. On the day of the final Paddy's aunt, Sister Angela, a Presentation nun in Crosshaven was on a three day retreat. That meant silence and no reading of newspapers or listening to the radio. The priest giving the retreat knew she was Paddy's aunt and that she would be dying to know the result. She was sitting outside either praying or reading a spiritual book. He passed by praying — turned his head — and from the side of his mouth whispered 'they won'.

'The 1960 Munster final against Tipperary was one of my better games. It was a fierce tough game which we lost by two points. I was right-half-forward on John Doyle. In the course of this teak tough game we both dropped the hurleys — put up the fists to each other — and started sparring. My brother Michael said it was the best fight he ever saw. Gerry Fitzgerald the referee came over to us to sort things out. John Doyle told him we were doing nothing at all. We got a talking to but weren't sent off — mainly I think because we used fists rather than hurleys.

I think the best game I played was in 1956 against Wexford in the All Ireland final. Again we lost — though I feel we might have won. Whenever I think back on that game I recall an incident when we were playing into the canal goal. I was going through — Nick O'Donnell was in front of me — Ring was on O'Donnell's left. I passed the ball to Ring and I have often regretted it. I feel I took the wrong option. I believe if I kept going myself I would have scored.'

Paddy was one of nine boys in a family of eleven. Six of the boys played with Sarsfields senior hurling team. Paddy played with Sarsfields for a span of twenty three years — from 1946 to '68 — and 'never missed a championship match'. His mother took very little interest in the game. 'She would listen to the broadcasts. She would never praise if I scored but she would always remind me of the ones I missed. After the 1956 final against Wexford she said — pity you didn't win — Tommy had three the same as yourself.'

She was referring of course to Tom Barry, Paddy's uncle, who excelled with Cork in earlier days and won All Irelands in 1928, '29 and '31. 'I can only remember my mother going to two matches ever. On the day we were playing Glen Rovers in the second round of the 1947 championship at the Athletic Grounds she set off to Youghal for the day with my two aunts. Just before the throw-in I saw the three of them walking up the sideline — they had missed the train to Youghal. We won that day. We also won the second game she attended. It was the 1952 All Ireland final. I was glad she was there.'

Paddy retired in 1960 from inter-county hurling after the Munster final. But it proved to be a premature departure. In fact he made a comeback three times — (a record?) — in 1961, 1963 and 1964. Those were the years when Cork were desperately searching for a winning blend of experience and youth. Paddy was taken off in the Munster final of 1964. To this day he and his club Sarsfields feel it was both unnecessary and unfair. At the time Tipperary were coasting to victory in a game they won by 3:13 to 1:5.

Hanging on the wall of the sitting-room is a framed 'Address to Pat Barry' from the Committee and Members of Glanmire Recreation Club:

We, the Committee members of the Glanmire Recreation Club, wish to place on permanent record our pride and joy at the great achievement of our popular member Mr Pat Barry on captaining the Cork Senior Hurling team which won the All Ireland championship in Croke Park on Sept 7th 1952.

Pat Barry has long enjoyed the esteem of sportsmen in all parts of County Cork for his prowess on the hurling field. We recall with pride the big part he played in the great victory of Sarsfields Club which brought the County championship to Glanmire Parish for the first time ever.

We saw him lead the Corkmen to victory over Limerick and Tipperary in the Munster championship and over Galway in the All Ireland semi-final; and the great campaign was climaxed by the vanquishing of the Leinster champions, Dublin at Croke Park.

We now have the great privilege of seeing the All Ireland and Munster Cups reposing in Glanmire. We hope that Pat Barry — member of a family with a great hurling tradition — will have many another victory on the field of play.

Cork, All Ireland champions 1952, captained by Paddy Barry (fourth from left, front row) pictured before the Munster final.

Born: 1918

The name Vin Baston conjures up for me memories of long ago when all my world was young and he was one of my hurling heroes.

Vivid pictures of his style and greatness were implanted in my mind's eye through the magic voice of Mícheál O'Hehir. And if I close my eyes I can still hear that voice — an echo from the distant past, an echo from a Sunday afternoon. The style, the flow of words, the phrases — the great gift of painting instant images of action-packed hurling as the game swung from one end of the field to the other.

And the echoes? *Bail ó Dhia oraibh go léir a cháirde agus fáilte rómhaibh go — Hello everybody and welcome to — Both teams will play as selected and here are the lineouts. First of all Cork. In goal Tom Mulcahy of St Finbarr's — The Limerick team — full forward John Mackey of Ahane and top of the right Jackie Power of Ahane* (and if your own county was in action you felt a tingle of excitement run through you as he named those players and their parish clubs) — *The roll of the drum and the parade is on — backs go back to their positions* (now the excitement is really building within you*) — the players face the tricolour as the band plays Amhrán na bhFiann — everything is now ready for what promises to be a great game — the band scurries off the field — the referee looks at his watch, the whistle, the throw in and the game is on — first to break away is —.* And so it was Sunday after Sunday.

From the mid-forties on I used listen to all his broadcasts — glued to the wireless — and his vivid descriptions enabled me to follow the play — capture the excitement — get a feel for the positions of strength and weakness on either side and live a match I couldn't see. In an era when travel was difficult he brought entertainment and brightness to the lives of thousands on many a Sunday afternoon. It was an age of discretion too. When players were sent off by the referee you were never told their names — merely that two players, one from either side had been sidelined. But by careful listening you very soon deduced for yourself who had parted the scene.

Vin Baston excelled for Munster and Waterford. His hurling talents found full expression at centre-back and centre-field. A stylish, composed and sporting player, he won Munster, All Ireland and Railway cup honours. In 1947 when Connaught (all Galway) defeated Munster to take the Railway cup for the first time Vincent partnered fellow countyman Mick Hayes at centre-field in the Munster lineout. But the following three years brought Railway cup success. In 1948 and 1949 he was partnered at midfield by Mick Hayes of Waterford and Mick Ryan of Limerick respectively. In 1950 he manned the centre back berth.

In 1943 Waterford after victories over Tipperary and Limerick lost by two points to a great Cork team in the Munster final. Injury kept Vincent from playing that day. He may well have tipped the scales in favour of the Decies. He had to wait five years to achieve every hurler's ambition —

an All Ireland title. Cork were pipped by a point in the Munster final and Dublin fell at the last hurdle. In that year of triumph Vincent Baston played a key role at centre-back right through the championship.

In 1993 his native Passage reached the Waterford county senior hurling final for the first time ever. As a tribute to Vincent, Pat Fanning former GAA President wrote an article for the match programme. It is reproduced here with his kind permission.

It is particularly appropriate that a tribute be paid to Vin Baston on the occasion of Passage's first ever appearance in a Waterford senior hurling final. Through the generations, that little village of so much beauty has forged a tradition in hurling of which its people are justly proud. It is a tradition based not on heady success in County Finals, but on an unconquerable spirit of endurance and perseverance in face of adversity and, betimes seemingly disaster. In good times and bad, Passage has stood steadfast to its GAA, its hurling tradition. On and off the field, Passage hurling has been served by fine players and dedicated officials, men who never faltered in service of their club. That was, and remains, the Passage tradition. It is a proud tradition.

At the very heart of that tradition is the name and fame of Vincent Baston, hurler supreme, a hurling legend and a gentleman to the core. It was in Mount Sion CBS that I first encountered Vin Baston. Daily for five years he cycled from Passage to the Barrack St school, the hurley tied to the bar of the bike, an essential piece of equipment as the books on his back. He came to the school already a well known young hurler of considerable promise with a reputation gained in the colours of Passage at juvenile and minor level. With Mount Sion he played Munster colleges hurling, and was one of the brightest in the Harty Cup final of 1937, when Mount Sion lost to North Monastery CBS's team of all talent by a single point. Vin was twice picked for the Munster Colleges fifteen, the apex of every young hurler of school age in those days.

From school in Mount Sion, Vin went into the Army as a Cadet. Commissioned two years later, he eventually found himself posted to An Cath Gaelach — the first Irish speaking Batt., in Galway. Already a noted hurler with Waterford, his unique style marked him a man apart in the Galway of his day. There is little doubt that, had he thrown in his lot with Galway — and the pressure to do so was intense — Vincent would have provided that extra touch that would have guaranteed Galway All Ireland success. But, his loyalty to Waterford was total. He would not wear the colours of another county.

With Waterford throughout the forties Vin Baston was a giant in an era of hurling giants. His input into every game was considerable, and there were moments of sheer brilliance that won for the Passage stylist a place among the all time greats of hurling. Fitting it was that his unswerving loyalty to his native county should have its reward in 1948, when he saw Waterford to Munster and All Ireland triumph, through a campaign in which his personal contribution was considerable, if not, indeed decisive. For school and club, for county and province and for the Army, Vin Baston gave his all, bringing to everything he attempted a degree of sportsmanship and sense of fair play, that made him worthy of adulation accorded him by his peers and an admiring public. He was much more than a great hurler — he was a fine human being, a man who cherished friendship. I knew him well as a boy. I played hurling with him, and was privileged to visit him shortly before his untimely death. To know him was to be influenced by him. A quiet, almost self effacing man, he has left an indelible mark on the hurling scene he adorned, as man and boy. Passage may well be proud of its greatest hurling son. As the young men from that hurling village take the field today in quest of the only honour to elude Vin, they can find inspiration in the life of Vincent Baston, a hurling great, and, in the true sense of the words — An Officer and a Gentleman.'

Born: 1945

"

I started hurling at a very young age. With seven brothers in the family it was the thing to do. I lived in a lodge at the entrance to a big mansion. We spent a lot of time hurling a ball against the wall. Before we left for school in the mornings, lads passing would call in for a puck around. To me Tony O'Brien was a great hurler. I had great time for Vivian Cobb — Limerick dropped him years too soon. I admired Liam Devaney and Jimmy Doyle, (Tipperary) Eddie Keher and Pat Delaney (Kilkenny), Jimmy Cullinane & Pat Cronin (Clare) Tony Doran and Mick Jacob (Wexford), Gerald McCarthy and Jimmy Barry-Murphy (Cork).

Playing for Patrickswell was always tops for me. Wearing the Limerick jersey was a great honour. Winning my first championship with my club in 1965 as a full-back was mighty. Winning the All Ireland in 1973 was something special. The atmosphere in Croke Park as we ran onto the field will live with me forever. It is the best game in the world. You make great friends. It is great meeting hurlers you played against. Now I get great pleasure looking after the Patrickswell under-fifteens and under-sixteens. **"**

Richie Bennis

In top level hurling in finely balanced contests a team is unlikely to succeed unless it has a top quality goalkeeper and a first class marksman. In Richie Bennis Limerick had a marksman supreme. He proved it consistently and more importantly he demonstrated it under pressure. Three examples in particular illustrate this. In the National League final against Tipperary in 1971 at Cork the scores were level at 3:11 each with three minutes to go when Limerick was awarded a thirty yards free from an awkward angle. Richie sent over the winner — his eighth of the day, and he can still see Tony O'Brien emerging from defence with the ball in his hand and about to clear when the final whistle blew. In Thurles in 1973 in the Munster final against Tipperary he stood over a seventy with the teams level — the referee told him it was the last puck of the game and that he must score direct. The packed stadium held its breath. Richie steadied and looked, before sending the winner high over the bar and all Limerick erupted with delight. His total that day was 1:5. In the All Ireland final of the same year against Kilkenny he showed his class when scoring ten points, seven from frees. He had the ideal temperament — cool, calm, confident, nonchalant and philosophical. He headed the county scoring charts for six successive years from 1970 to 1975. Strangely enough, and unlike many great marksmen he didn't spend hours practising the art of taking frees. 'I never really practised frees — I never dwelt on it. I began taking them in a club game when our freetaker got injured. I was always fairly steady — had great confidence — it didn't worry me what people said if I missed.' He had always enjoyed watching a good western and this prompted one wag to suggest that that was why he was such a good sharpshooter.

Richie was one of a family of seven boys and six girls. When Patrickswell won the County senior hurling title in 1966 six

Bennis brothers shared the honours — Phil, Richie, Gerry, Pat, Peter and Thomas. A seventh brother Sean always played his hurling with Ballybrown, a half parish of Patrickswell. Richie was hurling from an early age and as a sixteen-year-old captained Limerick city to victory over Kilkenny in 1961 in the first All Ireland Vocational Schools final. He subsequently played minor, under 21 and senior with his native Limerick.

He was a sub on the 1966 Limerick team that defeated Tipperary — all conquering All Ireland champions of 1964 and 1965 — in the first round of the championship. An advantage rule, disallowed goal, cost them the semi-final against Cork who went on to win the All Ireland. Richie saw the 1966 team as 'one of much potential with a great set of backs' and from memory recalled it as follows: Jim Hogan / John McDonagh, J.J.Bresnihan, Ned Rea / Tony O'Brien, Kevin Long, Eddie Prendeville / Seamus Quaid, Bernie Hartigan / Eamon Grimes, Eamon Carey, Eamon Cregan / Andy Dunworth, Mick Savage, Tom Bluett.

'Brother Burke was associated with the team as trainer and many of the players had won Harty Cup medals. I was very disappointed not to be playing. Up to then I had played at full-back but in a game against Treaty Sarsfields I was centre forward and scored 3:4 from play. I thought I'd get on the team.'

For three great memories in his career he chose a Munster final, a club victory and an All Ireland final. The Munster final was that of 1973 against Tipperary when Limerick captured the title after a lapse of eighteen years. The drama of the final seconds has already been described. But Richie believes that the source of victory centred around a sideline throw-in some seconds before that. 'Liam O Donoghue lined up for the throw in. I stepped in, in place of Liam. I had decided with time running out and scores level that it was important to gain possession instead of pulling. I got the ball, soloed down the sideline and sent it to Frankie Nolan — his shot was blocked — eventually Eamon

Grimes first timed it — a seventy was signalled.' The rest is history. 'It compensated for the heart breaking one point defeat of 1971 at the hands of Tipp. I lay down in the mud of Killarney pitch that day when the final whistle blew and cried like an elephant. I didn't go home at all that week.'

His club won the Munster club title in 1989 — the first Limerick club to do so. 'We were ahead fourteen points at halftime after playing with a stormforce wind. Gradually in the second half Mount Sion came within striking distance. They had the ball in the net but were whistled back for a free in, which was driven wide. It was the hardest match I ever played — and I wasn't on the field at all. We held on to win by four points.' That recalled other club memories for Richie and he admitted to crying in the dressingroom after losing the 1991 All Ireland club final to Glenmore of Kilkenny. 'It was one we let slip. We did too much running with the ball.'

The All Ireland victory of 1973 was a special dream come true. Richie had a great game — a solo run in the second half chased by Liam O'Brien as he jinked and weaved his way into Kilkenny territory ending with him being fouled and Mícheál O'Hehir uttering 'Oh the absolute gall of the man and I mean that in the kindest possible way' — a sixty yards point from play that had class written all over it and will always be remembered by those who saw it — an all round performance of skill and endeavour which no doubt contributed to his All Star award of that year. The words of the late Jackie Power rang in his ears throughout the game — 'If you go on a solo run and it breaks down you'll be out here beside me — take your points from close in frees — make sure you don't let Liam O'Brien get between you and the goal whatever you do.' Liam gave Richie the slip at one stage and set off on a solo at great speed. Richie gave chase and it seemed a lost cause but he kept going and going and ended up dispossessing Liam and sending a long clearance upfield. It epitomised the Limerick spirit of the day.

Why did you go for a goal from a twenty

one yards free when the score stood 1:14 to 1:11 in Limerick's favour after Jackie Power's instructions? 'Well I did it against Clare and Tipperary and London and it worked. I had the confidence and I said I would have another belt at it. Jackie ate me afterwards but I reminded him he had said nothing when I did get the goals. He was a wonderful character and motivator — God rest him now.' Was it your best game? 'No. I feel my greatest match was against Clare in the first round of the championship that year. Clare had surprised us in Ennis the previous year and we knew it wasn't going to be easy. We won a torrid encounter by just two points. Clare were very good in the seventies.'

It was interesting to discuss with Richie the 1973 triumph over Kilkenny. Limerick had reason to be confident and not just because they were carrying the Tipperary scalp. Statistically and traditionally Limerick had a good record against Kilkenny and could always face them with a 50/50 chance of success. Limerick lost in 1933 by 1:7 to 0:6 — the day Johnny Dunne rounded Mickey Cross to write himself into hurling fame with a great goal. It came after a spell of intense Limerick pressure and the Kilkenny crowd on the sideline sprung to their feet to acclaim their hero and shouted 'Lovely, lovely, lovely Johnny Dunne'.

That did it. Forever after he was known in hurling circles as Lovely Johnny Dunne. Limerick lost again in 1935 when with time up and Kilkenny leading by 2:5 to 2:4 Mick Mackey stood over a twenty-one yards free on a rain soaked pitch and looked at a wet and sodden sliotar and then gazed goalwards. The crowd saw a draw and a replay. But Mick staked all as he went for the winner and failed.

In 1897 Limerick defeated Kilkenny to take their first title 3:4 to 2:4. They had further wins in 1936 and 1940, 5:6 to 1:5 and 3:7 to 1:7 respectively. In 1939 they had an Oireachtas victory over Kilkenny 4:4 to 2:5 in the final of the first such tournament. And in 1947 after a replay they won a National League thriller by 3:8 to 1:7. An excerpt from a newspaper report on the drawn game makes interesting reading.

The game was practically the same as the All Ireland final, except that Limerick wore green instead of red. Certainly the last ten minutes were every bit as exciting as when Kilkenny defeated Cork. For five minutes of this the ball never went out of play. The play swung from end to end but it was mainly in Kilkenny territory ... The half-back line of Sean Herbert, Jackie Power (a great defender) and Thomas O'Brien kept Limerick attacking.

The 1973 campaign was one where different individuals played a key role in each of the games. Richie agrees that goalkeeper Seamus Horgan is an oft forgotten hero of 1973. In the Munster final in Thurles entering the closing stages he saved at point blank range from Babs Keating. The rebound was met by John Flanagan and was again brilliantly saved. In the early stages of the second half against Kilkenny in the final he deflected over the bar a palmed shot from very close in from Mick Crotty. All were crucial saves at critical stages.

Richie had special words of praise for Cork hurlers and supporters whom he always found to be most sporting and gracious. He recalled a league game in Páirc Uí Chaoimh. He was awarded a free near the sideline and did an about turn inwards so as to improve the angle. The Cork crowd yelled and the referee sent him back. Incensed at the crowd he went right to the sideline and placed the ball thereon. He lifted and struck and watched with satisfaction as the ball sailed between the uprights — and then he heard the applause of appreciation from the Cork crowd.

Richie is essentially a clubman. He is very much part of Patrickswell. With a sense of pride he tells you that he has been associated with all the Patrickswell successes either in the capacity of player, trainer or mentor. Men like this are the foundation stone on which the GAA and its games flourish.

This is his team from the men he played against.

	Noel Skehan (Kilkenny)	
Fan Larkin (Kilkenny)	Pat McDonnell (Cork)	Tony Maher (Cork)
Jimmy Cullinane (Clare)	Mick Roche (Tipperary)	Ger McCarthy (Cork)
Richie Bennis (Limerick)	Frank Cummins (Kilkenny)	
Francis Loughnane (Tipperary)	Pat Delaney (Kilkenny)	Johnny Callinan (Clare)
Charlie McCarthy (Cork)	Tony Doran (Wexford)	Eddie Keher (Kilkenny)

"

Growing up in the 20's in Shandon Street we played every kind of outdoor game including hurling, rounders, handball, ball in the cap and cat and dog.

Our gear was very poor then including bits of timber, ragged ball and half hurleys. We also threw a few bowls up Fair Hill.

As students of North Mon we had to attend hurling and football practice in the Mon field every Tuesday halfday and if we failed to attend we got extra homework.

Denis J Buckley **"**

'To them was life a simple art
Of duties to be done,
A game where each man took his part
A race where all must run.'

From listening to people and hurling broadcasts and reading the sports writers I painted a picture in my childhood of Din Joe Buckley — fearless — unyielding and uncompromising — full of grit and tenacity — teak tough — that was Din Joe the

Born: 1919

hurling defender who played centre-back, left-half-back and left-full-back — the man who as he cleared the ball drew shouts of admiration from the fans 'Doubt you Din Joe boy' — the man who played on Mick Mackey and neither of them asked for any quarter as ash clashed on ash and body crunched on body in thundering exchanges as they flailed the sliotar with fury — and when 'twas all over they headed for a friendly drink. 'That was Mick. He loved the game. The harder you gave him the more he loved it. He relished the hard going. There was never any bitterness or rancour in him.'

When I visited Din Joe the picture had changed. The supple hands that swung the ash with glory were now afflicted with arthritis. The once sturdy frame was now less mobile, less agile. Timewise he was now heading for the mid-seventies. But the mind was fresh — the memories vivid — the recollections instant.

When Cork won the record-breaking four in a row 1941 to '44, nine players had the

Din Joe Buckley (centre) with brothers, Connie (left), and Jack (right).

honour of sharing all four successes — Willie Murphy, Batt Thornhill, Alan Lotty, Paddy O'Donovan, Christy Ring, Jim Young, Johnny Quirke, Jack Lynch and Din Joe. Apart from Din Joe the only other survivor is Jack Lynch — 'Time like an ever rolling stream bears all its sons away'. Imíonn na daoine ach fanann na cnoic.

You quit very young Din Joe? 'After the 1947 final when Kilkenny beat us by a point with the last puck of the game, I gave up county hurling but played with my club for three more years. I was recalled to the panel for the first round against Tipperary in 1949. They beat us after a replay and extra time. I gave up then — maybe I was getting stiff.'

But let's start at the very beginning. 'When we were very young we spent very little time indoors. We made our own fun and games and played every game. There was a handball alley not far away from Shandon Street which my father ran and we spent a lot of time there. Jack, Connie and myself all played for Cork in a National League game against Kilkenny in 1938 but Kilkenny beat us well. It was my first senior inter-county game — I was a sub on the minor team in 1937. Jack was on the panel from time to time but most of his hurling was with Glen Rovers. Connie played minor with Cork in 1933 and senior from 1934 to 1941 — Cork's lean years — Limerick were the masters then. He did however have the honour of captaining Cork to All Ireland victory in 1941 when he played at centre-forward. That was the year I joined the Army. I was there until 1945. Those years were called "The Emergency". The world war was on. We played every game — hurling, football, soccer, basketball. I was in the 31st battalion.'

Din Joe played in the 1939 League campaign but unfortunately missed out on the championship. 'I was suspended for playing soccer for a junior team. I could have got away with it but the club was too honest.' It was a pity he missed the championship. It saw the beginning of a Cork revival and some great games of hurling. Cork beat Munster champions Waterford in the first round 7:4 to 4:3 — a surprise. Next came the Munster final against Limerick at Thurles. A newspaper heading described it as follows 'Brilliant Camán Craft at Thurles: Hurling In Excelsis'. The report went on to place it beside the All Ireland finals of 1907 Kilkenny v Cork, 1922 Kilkenny v Tipperary, the second drawn game of the 1931 final Cork v Kilkenny and the first Railway Cup final played in 1927 Leinster v Munster. It described the hurling as 'grease lightning'.

Green Flag in his report on the game quoted the Cork trainer Jim Barry as telling his team. 'Get to the ball first and then pull on it. I knew that if our lads stood shoulder with the Limerickmen they would not be able to cope with the Shannonsiders craft. It was no use trying to beat them at their own game.' Green Flag went on — Cork's speed certainly paid a big part in their victory but the pull on the ball policy was the trump card. This is a good young Cork team that has grown more confident than it was at Fermoy and it will be a force for sometime in Munster (how prophetic). It has not the craft of Kilkenny or Limerick but it has dash in plenty which will be its strongest card in the final.

Carbery had this to say: 'That memorable second half was like an epic in an ancient Roman battle. The men were trained to the minute and played out their last ounce of reserve. We saw and heard splintering, quivering ash and heard the thud of strong hardy bodies as they crashed together in fearless rivalry.' Thomond in the *Limerick Leader* described it as 'the greatest Munster final since 1910'.

Then came the All Ireland final against Kilkenny and for the last twenty minutes rain fell in torrents — thunder pealed and lightning flashed and a thrilling game ended with Jimmy Kelly scoring the winning point in the dying moments following a seventy from Paddy Phelan. It was the first day of the second world war.

In 1940 Din Joe was back — back to stay this time — there would be no more soccer

Lost time was being played when spectators invaded the pitch at Thurles in the Munster final replay of 1940 betwe[en]
Limerick and Cork. It was cleared after 10 minutes and the remaining 2 minutes of the game were completed.

indiscretions. Cork opened the 1940 campaign with convincing victories of 6:3 to 2:6 and 7:6 to 3:5 over Tipperary and Clare respectively and faced Limerick in the Munster final at Thurles — and Din Joe at centre-back faced the mighty Mick Mackey. Here is an excerpt from a report on the game by Carbery in the *Cork Weekly Echo*. 'Many of us thought the 1939 Munster final had reached the hurling meridian. Best hurling game of the whole year it was. Yet last Sunday's vivid memories switch 1939 to "the limbo of forgotten things" and "battles long ago". Scribblers are bankrupt of phrases. Our vocabulary is exhausted — we must invent a new language to describe modern hurling ... 1940 was as like 1939 as two stacks of sound grain in adjoining harvest fields. But they were as different in flavour as wheat and oats; both wholesome; one richer than the other; last Sunday was the heart of wheat ... they started off like the crackling fire of Summer heath on a mountain ... Cork and Limerick keymen now manning every vital post with faces carved in marble — all pulling first time and not sparing ash and leather in around the house. Scanlon pulled

on flying balls and stopped all with charmed ease ... they meet again. Let us leave it at that, and we to our memories and expectations of gold in store.'

Well the replay produced gold aplenty — a game hectic and thrilling and breathtaking — with the final score Limerick 3:3 Cork 2:4. Cork's hour had not yet come. But the experience of 1939 and 1940 was knitting and moulding together a team destined to leave an indelible mark on hurling history.

And now to the famous four in a row. 'You know when I was going to Dublin for the 1944 final I didn't know we were going for a record at all. I just took it as another final.'

All four finals turned out to be mere formalities as the following scorelines indicate:

1941   Cork 5:11   Dublin 0:6
1942   Cork 2:14   Dublin 3:4
1943   Cork 5:16   Antrim 0:4
1944   Cork 2:13   Dublin 1:2

The few stumbling blocks that were, came chiefly in Munster. In 1942 in the first round Cork and Limerick produced another epic — according to the late Jim Young the best game he ever played in — when a game that seemed destined for a draw turned Cork's way in the final minutes to win by two points — 4:8 to 5:3. 'I didn't play in that game. I had a damaged wrist and was in hospital in Mallow.' As in 1939 and 1940 Jack Lynch was captain.

In 1943 it fell to Waterford to run Cork — under the captaincy of Mick Kennefick — close. Again it was a two points margin — 2:13 to 3:8. Jim Ware was brilliant in the Waterford goal and John Keane starred outfield. Waterford people who remember that day still bemoan a deflection from a defender that turned the ball passed Jim Ware into the net. 'I missed that game too — I was suspended — put off in an Army Game with Mick Mackey. Waterford were a most unlucky team. They were knocking at the door from the mid-thirties and didn't get the breaks until 1948. John Keane beat Cork that day — got the better of Paddy O'Donovan — he was great for a ball out of the air.'

In 1944 the year that Din Joe captained Glen Rovers to victory over St Finbarr's in the Cork county final the going got really tough in the championship. 'Tipp ran us close in the first game 1:9 to 1:6. And when we met Limerick in the Munster final that was drawn on the first day it was 1939 and 1940 all over again.'

These were games of indescribable thrills and excitement — of swaying fortunes and misfortunes — of glory for Cork and heartbreak for Limerick. In the drawn game Limerick came from eight or nine points down in the second half — had a two point lead going into broken time — a Johnny Quirke goal gave Cork a one point lead — and on the call of time Dick Stokes equalised for Limerick. 'Limerick led in the replay by one goal at halftime and in the last quarter were five points up. Mick Mackey got possession and headed for goal from 30/40 yards out. I hand tripped him — I was switched in the first half to mark him — he stumbled — the ref blew the whistle — Cork players stopped — Mackey continued and scored a goal — I know Mick's version was different and that the ball was in the net before the whistle blew

and that Limerick were denied the advantage. From the free Dick Stokes for once sent wide.' Lost time was being played and Cork were one point down — veteran Johnny Quirke sent over the equaliser. It looked another draw. 'I saw Ring gain possession outfield and go on a solo run up the right wing — he then let fly a low ball — backs and forwards pulled without connecting — Joe Kelly was in to harass Malone in the Limerick goal and the ball crossed the line for the winner.'

The semi-final against Galway in Ennis was another close affair 1:10 to 3:3. 'It was a controversial finish. Towards the end their captain Sean Condon, who had a great game was fouled — the referee blew — Condon went ahead and got a point which was allowed. Galway argued it should not have been allowed.'

Tipperary halted Cork in their bid for five in a row in 1945 but Cork were back again in 1946 and Din Joe won his fifth All Ireland medal.

In the article on Jim Stapleton, who captained Tipperary in 1887, we looked briefly at the Ireland of his day. It is interesting now to look at the Ireland of Din Joe's day — half a century after Jim Stapleton — half a century ago.

The scourge of landlordism was no more. The twenty-six county Free State had been established — Din Joe remembers British troops vacating the ports in 1938.

People still mourned their dead in the old tradition with women wearing black for a year after the death of a loved one and men wore a black tie and a black diamond on the coat sleeve. Pleasure activities were abandoned for a period of time. (John & Mick Mackey played with neither Limerick nor Ahane following the death of their brother in 1941).

The Economic War of the thirties had left its mark on a nation that was largely agricultural at the time.

The world was plunged in war, with Europe the battlefield. Wartime made frugal living the order of the day and many households lived on little more than bread and tea. Typhoid, diphtheria and TB were still killer diseases. Practically everything was rationed and every household had ration books with a supply of coupons for each member. Breach of rationing regulations could lead to fines — instance the following from the *Irish Times* of 3 April 1943.

Hotel Keeper Fined for Serving Butter.

What was described as the first case of its kind was heard at Ballyshannon District Court, when Elizabeth Hammond, Skene House Hotel, Bundoran, was charged with having served butter to persons taking meals consisting of two courses, and with failure to take steps to ensure that the words — 'it is illegal to serve butter at luncheons or dinners' were shown conspicuously on the bill of fare.

It was stated that butter had been served to three Department Inspectors who were staying at the Hotel. A fine of two pounds with ten shilling expenses, was imposed on the first charge, and the second was dismissed on the merits.

In farming circles compulsory tillage was the order of the day. There was strict censorship of films, books, papers, and magazines (many of them banned) apart altogether from the censorship associated with wartime.

People still greeted each other with blessings such as, God save all here; God bless the work; the Lord spare you the health; may God increase you.

But despite everything hurling was thriving in Cork. They were merely improving on what their ancestors had done fifty years earlier when in 1890 they won the All Ireland and after missing out in 1891 (it went to Kerry) they proceeded to record the first ever three in a row in 1892, '93 and '94.

Din Joe's admiration for the Limerick team of his era shone through and was reflected in his choice of team. Even though Cork were winning the All Ireland titles the calibre of the Limerick men was manifested in the Munster Railway Cup selections. In the six years from 1940 to '45 inclusive Munster won all apart from 1941. Of the ninety positions filled, Cork and Limerick accounted for sixty-four — Cork thirty-six. Limerick twenty-eight.

In close consultation with his brother Connie, he took some time to pick his team which finished up as a panel of twenty — he ran out of positions — oh for the days of twenty-one a side.

Paddy Scanlon (Limerick)

Dinny O'Gorman (Tipperary)   Tom McCarthy (Limerick)   Din Joe Buckley (Cork)

Jack Lynch (Cork)   Paddy Clohessy (Limerick)   Tommy Doyle (Tipperary)

Timmy Ryan (Limerick)   Christy Moylan (Waterford)

John Mackey (Limerick)   Mick Mackey (Limerick)   Christy Ring (Cork)

Johnny Quirke (Cork)   Willie O'Donnell (Tipperary)   Joe Gallagher (Galway)

Remainder of the panel: Jimmy Langton (Kilkenny), Jackie Power (Limerick), John Keane (Waterford), Vin Baston (Waterford) and Peter Cregan (Limerick).

Born: 1955

"

Hurling has been the most dominant factor in my life since I was able to play for the Quay Road (legally?) in the local street leagues. It would have been difficult to avoid hurling in Clarecastle. The whole sporting ethos was hurling, nurtured and maintained by the local 'master', John Hanley, a man I now know to be ahead of his time. As one got older it became even more difficult to avoid, given that St Flannan's was only up the road. As a seven-year-old I thought in my innocence in 1962 that the Harty Cup was a competition exclusive to the two secondary schools in Ennis.

Other pursuits such as school, exams, girls, work, all had to be accommodated to hurling — yes, even marriage dates. This madness contrasts somewhat with the demand for foreign holidays etc. on winning an All Ireland. I hope we are not losing our way. If sport reflects life as it is supposed to, hurling also of course gave its full quota of disappointments but we won't dwell on those. The great days training in Newman House and Belfield with UCD, in Tulla with Clare, in Lynchs or Devines fields with Clarecastle, the comradeship, the wins and even some of the defeats are, together with the friendships forged, the real memories. To have been privileged to play with and against the greatest hurlers will always be appreciated. This is what hurling has given me and I hope will give countless thousands into the future. Hurling must endure. It is, however, a delicate flower which needs a favourable environment and careful husbandry. Is it being given those things? We mustn't be sentimental about the game — but active, radical and thoughtful.

John Callinan "

John Callinan was seven years of age when his late father took him to Croke Park on All Ireland final day in 1962. That day Wexford and Tipperary seniors served up a game of breathtaking hurling. There were names in action that echo on through the decades. Yet of the sixty who lined out that day it was the Kilkenny minor centre-forward Tommy Walsh with the fair hair that caught the eye of John. He can still see Tommy in action. Everything else is a blur.

He talks about hurling with a passion and zeal that reflect his deep interest and commitment. To him the game is a national heritage. He wants it to grow and prosper and remain vibrant. He wants future generations to enjoy it as he has. His medals and trophies are relatively few but the memories of playing days suffice and no doubt will gather added lustre as the years roll on. Nowadays when he trains players — at present the Claughaun team — he tells them that they make their own luck and he tries to inculcate in them a positiveness that rejects excuses for defeat, such as the weather, the referee, the absence or loss of a player. And yet he admits to having been 'a terrible loser — I would brood on a defeat for a week afterwards.' He admits too to being a bad spectator. 'My elbows fly in all directions as I keep up with the ebb and flow of play. I am only learning to sit in the stand. I'm really out there playing.'

His hurling years were at a time when Clare produced some wonderful exponents of the game and some very fine teams. They were well represented in Munster Railway cup selections and were awarded thirteen All Stars — which John shared in, in '79 and '81. Some would say it was their finest era. Certainly, it at least matched the best of earlier days — the late twenties and early thirties, the early to mid-fifties.

They had two successive National League victories over Kilkenny, and the first in 1977 is one of John's cherished memories. At the time it looked like the gateway to greater things. But it wasn't to be. In '77 and '78 they contested the Munster finals with Cork. The former was lost by five points on a day when Clare lost their full-

back in the first half and played the rest of the game with fourteen men. In '78 they faced the second half supported by a strong wind and only a two-point deficit to make up. But they failed to capitalise on opportunities. The 0-13 to 0-11 defeat was even more galling when Clare reflected on the fact that John Horgan the Cork corner back was their highest scorer from long distance frees. Clare were favourites that day. 'There was a media expectation after our league victories. It was the tensest game I played in. Coming out the tunnel in Thurles that day I said to myself — this is different. The crowd was huge, about 55,000, one of the biggest ever for a Munster final. It was the second time in my career that I physically felt the presence of the crowd. The first was when I played with St Flannan's in a Harty Cup game against Ennis CBS in Tulla in 1971 before a crowd of 8-10,000 students, teachers and parents — Flannan's with players from Tipp, Limerick and Clare — Ennis CBS with all local players. You could feel the tension — the partisanship.'

1981 was the year that his hurling expectations and aspirations struck a nadir. 'Having lost to Waterford in the latter stages of the league we defeated them in the first round of the championship. Cork fell in the next round. I think I played my best game ever at right-half-forward that day. In terms of physical power I was at my peak. Playing well and being beaten can be a bit hollow. Beating Cork was great. It was the only time I played on a Clare team that beat Cork in the championship. Our hopes were high.' There followed the greatest disappointment of his career when they lost to Limerick in the Munster final 3:12 to 2:9. 'I felt deflated at the final whistle. Outfield the exchanges seemed so close. Joe McKenna destroyed us that day. He scored 3:3 and had a further 1:1 disallowed. When I look back now I feel that a very good Clare team was unfortunate to come up against the very talented Cork three-in-a-row team of '76 to '78 and an equally talented Limerick team of the early eighties.' The Oireachtas wins of '82 and '83 over Limerick and Kilkenny respectively were indicators of the strength of Clare hurling but such triumphs would pale in the face of a Munster or All Ireland crown.

John played at left and right-half-forward and also at midfield. The players he encountered? 'I met some great ones. I had a few good battles with Pat Lawlor of Kilkenny. He was very tight and very tidy — sticky too — if he got the ball you didn't have much chance getting it back. Joe Hennessy of Kilkenny had the same attributes backed up by first touch mastery and long clearances. Iggy Clarke of Galway was fantastic. We played against each other in Fitzgibbon Cup matches. He was very dynamic — an athlete — could murder you — he'd take off and score a point. He had the ability to play his own game and that of course was bad for the forward marking him. Sean Foley of Limerick was an outstanding hurler. He hit long clearances of up to 80-90 yards — that took your own half-back line out of the game and set up Cregan and McKenna for scores. Liam O'Donoghue of Limerick was a superb defender — kept pushing you upfield — difficult to dispossess — great positional sense. Dermot McCurtain and Tom Cashman of Cork were very classy players. If you were on your game and marked them close it was OK. But if they were beating you it would be devastating not only for you but also for your team. Frank Cummins of Kilkenny — well what can I say about him. His very physical presence was frightening.'

John recalls that in 1972 he played Dean Ryan and Harty Cup Colleges hurling — also minor, under 21 and senior for Clare. 'My club career followed — it must be kind of unique — and it took until 1968 before I won a county title with Clarecastle.' With UCD he won a Dublin under 21 title.

He says he could never talk about hurling without mentioning Justin McCarthy, 'the best coach I ever trained under' — Fr Harry Bohan, 'who made such an outstanding contribution to the game in Clare', Jackie O'Gorman, 'the best Clareman I ever played with, a ferocious competitor.'

Up to 1993 Clare contested 20 Munster finals. They were victorious on three occasions and advanced each time to the All Ireland final. In 1889 they lost to Dublin 5:1 to 1:6 but even if they had scored fourteen points that day it wouldn't have won them the title because under the rules of the time no number of points equalled a goal. The 1889 campaign was not without controversy — such being common in the early days of the association. Clare defeated Limerick in the first round 5:1 to 2:2. They lost to Tipperary in the semi-final but won the game on an objection. They then faced Kerry represented by a Kenmare selection in the Munster final. The game was fixed for Rathkeale. It seems that Kenmare were not in a position to fund the travelling expenses and Clare were awarded the game and so advanced to the All Ireland final.

In 1914 they defeated Laois to take their only title to date. In 1932 a Kilkenny team on the ascendancy beat them by one goal and that was Clare's last appearance in Croke Park on final day. In the past sixty years fortune has failed to favour Clare on quite a few occasions. In short they have often been unlucky. Yet John believes that as a general rule a team makes its own luck. That may be so, but the absence of medals and trophies from the Clare sideboard does scant justice to the valiant performances of her hurlers and the County's immense dedication and contribution to the game.

This is John's team selected from the men he played against.

Noel Skehan (Kilkenny)

Brian Murphy (Cork)	Leonard Enright (Limerick)	Joe Hennessy (Kilkenny)
Liam O'Donoghue (Limerick)	Ger Henderson (Kilkenny)	Iggy Clarke (Galway)
Frank Cummins (Kilkenny)	Tom Cashman (Cork)	
John Callinan (Clare)	Pat Delaney (Kilkenny)	Billy Fitzpatrick (Kilkenny)
Seanie O'Leary (Cork)	Joe McKenna (Limerick)	Eamon Cregan (Limerick)

Born: 1956

The emergence of Offaly as a hurling power in 1980 brought many fine exponents of the game to the forefront. Among them was the late Pat Carroll whose childhood hero was Kilkenny's Eddie Keher. An outstanding forward he was one of Offaly's finest hurling sons.

Damien Martin, Offaly's superb and long serving goalkeeper remembers seeing Pat playing a game in goal in Birr in his early teens and being very impressed. The red head stood out. Pat's father had played in goal for Offaly and served his county well.

Damien admits not having adjectives to adequately describe the dedication and commitment of Pat to the game he loved and adorned. He had immense hurling ability and it earned him All Star awards in 1980 and 1981. He was stylish, determined and tenacious. His accuracy at point taking from far out and from different angles together with his never-say-die spirit posed a major threat to all opposing teams. He did the basic things well. It was his forte. Despite the heavy demands of successfully managing his dairy farm he never missed a training session and was an example to all in this regard.

His death at the age of thirty stunned his colleagues. Damien and many Offaly folk are now looking forward to the day when Pat's son Brian will line out in the Coolderry jersey and then progress to wearing the green white and gold of Offaly — there to display again some of the deft hurling touches of his late father.

In August 1985 Offaly travelled to Armagh to play Antrim in the All Ireland semi-final. Pat was unwell but his immense love for the game made him determined to play. He took tablets to ease the pain in his head and staggered slightly going out from the dressingroom. He didn't finish the game — his hurling days were over — it was his swansong. He was now gripped by illness from which there would be no road back. On St Patrick's Day 1986 the pain and suffering was no more.

Bhí sé faoi shuaimheas go brách.

This is the Offaly team with whom Pat won his first All-Ireland in 1981.

Damien Martin

Tom Donoghue   Eugene Coughlan   Pat Fleury

Aidan Fogarty   Pat Delaney   Ger Coughlan

Joachim Kelly   Liam Currams

Paddy Kirwan   Brendan Bermingham   Mark Corrigan

Pat Carroll   Padraig Horan   Johnny Flaherty

Subs: Brendan Keeson and Danny Owens

Born: 1952

"

I am a native of Mullagh, Loughrea and it was there I gained my love for games and in particular hurling. My brothers were all keen on hurling and my brother Joe also lined out for Galway. My other brother Tony who died at an early age showed great potential. My older brother Tom was a handy corner-forward. After a day working on the farm all of us with our neighbours the Cahalans, Coens and Morgans gathered in our front lawn to play hurling. It was there we grew to love the game and learned all the skills between ourselves.

As young players we had a fair bit of success with Mullagh winning a county under 21 title with two intermediate titles. One of my great memories as a young player is being carried off the field shoulder high by a neighbour Pat Joe Garvey. It was an extremely wet evening and I was wearing a short pants. Playing hurling for the parish gave us a great sense of pride and it became for the parish a uniting force. It was and is a strong force behind any country parish. It was and is a medium that makes conversation easy and the whole social fabric of the parish is enhanced. It gives the parish a focal point of which they can be proud and all, young and old, usually give their full support.

I went to college in Garbally, Ballinasloe, better known for rugby than hurling perhaps. I played rugby as a schoolboy and represented Connaught schoolboys. There I also played football and soccer and took part in athletic competitions. I came in contact with other players like Andy Fenton, Sean Silke and Ciaran Fitzgerald. Garbally has many happy memories for me and as well as broadening my education it introduced me to a wide variety of other sports.

During this time I was called for my first minor trial. I was sowing potatoes with my father Joe when Padraic Donohue called and invited me to go. I said 'why me — the other lads are better than me — are they going.' Eventually I went and things took off from there. It was a Good Friday but I did not know then that religion and hurling would be so big in my life.

After Garbally I went to Maynooth to study for the priesthood and looking at it now I consider myself very lucky. I was able to continue to play for Galway at under 21 and senior level and that was something that many great players before me were not able to do. I am thinking of players like Fr Paddy Gantly, Fr Jack Solon, Fr Tom Keyes and many others who had to sacrifice their best years on account of their studies. Thank God the rules were relaxed on that because I could continue what I enjoyed and loved.

1980 was a historic year in Galway and I was thrilled to be part of it. I do not think I fully realised what hurling meant to the people of Galway until then. After winning the league in 1975 we got a taste for it and vowed to ourselves we would break the alleged curse and carry the McCarthy Cup across the Shannon. To have achieved that is a very cherished memory. Even though I was injured for the final it was an unbelievable thrill to be able to raise the McCarthy Cup aloft on that historic day when the

West was truly awake.

I will always be grateful to the Maynooth authorities for their flexibility. After Ordination I was appointed to Loughrea in 1978 and I later transferred to play with Loughrea which was a very painful decision. Playing on the field as a priest made no difference. It was open competition and profession was irrelevant. It was a great joy and a constant challenge.

Hurling is one of the greatest field games that I know and thank God it has not changed much over the years. In our day Tony Doran could palm the ball into the net and Jimmy Barry-Murphy could kick it to the net and it's good that the latter is still permissible.

Looking at the GAA authorities I would like if they were more open to other games — there is nothing to fear — if anything both hurling and football will thrive with open competition.

To any young person starting off I would say practise every day. I do not mean physical training. Enjoy it, for time passes quickly. I hope they will have as many happy memories as I had over the years.

fr Iggy Clarke. "

Iggy Clarke was ordained to the priesthood in 1978. Ordination however did not confer on him any indulgence or immunity from the rigours of battle on the hurling field. And he was to discover this before very long.

The pain was excruciating. He was positioned against the X-ray machine in the Mater Hospital and felt he might faint any minute. A nurse attempted to remove the maroon jersey. It was unbearable. 'Oh for God's sake cut if off' said Iggy. 'Twas done.

How did all this come about? 'A high ball came in falling between the half-back and full-back line which I retreated to gather. I gained possession from Mark Corrigan and dodged his tackle. Out of the corner of my eye I saw an inside-forward coming to tackle me and I avoided him — what I didn't see was a third Offaly man whose tackle from behind drove up my shoulder blade and broke the clavicle. As I went down I could feel the heat of the rush of blood. I knew I was in trouble. I waited for the free that never came. Sean Silke was beside me saying "Iggy let go of the ball" and louder "Iggy let go of the ball." I opened my hand and he cleared it down the field. I was removed on a stretcher — a hospital case. On that stretcher journey on that August Sunday in 1980 I faintly heard the applause of the crowd in my ears but in my mind I clearly saw my prospects of playing against Limerick in the All Ireland final recede and disappear. It was six months before I could hurl again.'

Looking back now Iggy feels that 1972 represented a turning point in the history of Galway hurling. Since 1923 the County had been living with a litany of near misses that had their followers demented with frustration. The Railway Cup success of 1947 was meagre reward for a county that had produced some fine teams and many excellent individuals.

'We won the under 21 All Ireland title in 1972 and I had the honour of being captain — beating Tipperary in the semi-final and Dublin in the final on the score 2:9 to 1:10. It was Galway's first All Ireland victory since 1923. We felt we had achieved something special and that more success lay ahead. In 1975 we won the league — the third in all — the first since 1951. We beat Kilkenny in the semi-final by 1:9 to 1:6 and had a sweet victory over Tipperary in the final 4:9 to 4:6.'

Iggy had earlier tasted a double success in the Fitzgibbon Cup with victories with Maynooth in 1973 and '74 — the only occasions to date that Maynooth have won the cup. Others who shared the success were Willie Fitzmaurice and Paudie Fitzmaurice of Limerick, Paddy Barry of Cork, Andy Fenton, Joe Clarke and Sean Silke of Galway. 'It was terrible hard to win — very stiff competition. I'll never forget our first victory. It was hosted by Queen's University Belfast and we defeated UCD at

Ballycastle — great celebrations.'

So by 1975 Galway and Galway players were beginning to taste victory. Confidence and morale were growing. Instead of losing by small margins as had been Galway's wont they were now winning by slender margins — winning under pressure — winning against the leading hurling counties. The pendulum was swinging in their favour. In Joe McDonagh, Sean Silke and Iggy Clarke they had found a quality half-back line. 'A strong half-back line is vital to a team. If you're weak there you are in trouble. With the puckout landing close to the half-back line you have the opportunity to place the ball towards the forwards to good advantage. Look at the impact the halfback line of Finnerty, Keady and McInerney made in the recent past. Despite the advances made in coaching, there is still great scope for individuals to practise the many skills of hurling themselves. As a player I found that a lot of what you do is an instinctive reaction. It's important to retain that — to have the freedom to have a go — to take a sortie up the field.'

He found Cork teams 'very gracious in defeat — fine skilful hurlers who played a lovely open game — very sporting and at the same time very competitive. The 1980 final between Galway and Limerick was of course exceptional for its sportsmanship. In defeat we knew exactly how Limerick felt — we had been there so often ourselves.'

Iggy Clarke might have won three All Ireland medals. The team of 1979 to 1981 was capable and worthy of three in a row. Yet he won none. Each final left him with a different type of disappointment.

In 1979 there seemed no reason at all why Galway shouldn't record their first All Ireland victory since 1923 — and their second in all. Cork fell at the semi-final stage and Galway looked impressive. Seven of the 1975 team were still there including the formidable half-back line of McDonagh, Silke and Clarke. They were facing the master craftsmen from Kilkenny but it looked as if they had a slight edge. But when the final whistle blew it was Kilkenny 2:12 Galway 1:8. It was a moment of dejection. It mattered not that both Kilkenny goals — one in each half — were of a freakish nature; that a Galway penalty was not converted; that Liam 'Chunky' O'Brien scored 1:7 of the Kilkenny total. It mattered not. 'There is a photograph as I am walking off the field — disconsolate and downhearted — and Eddie Keher saying to me — "you'll be there again next year". But I am not even looking at him — just dejected thinking to myself that we should have won this one — that we could have won this one.'

In 1980 he knew with the steel pins in the clavicle that there was no way he was going to take his place in the half-back line in the final against Limerick. 'People were coming up to me and saying you'll be OK. They meant well but really it was only adding to my inner torment as I battled to cope with the disappointment of not being able to play — it was very difficult. During the second half of the game I came out from the dugout and went by the back of the goal up to the Hogan Stand. I was conscious of meeting people with my shoulder in a sling — and I had to mind that shoulder. As I left the dugout I had an inner feeling — a premonition — we were going to win even though the game wasn't yet over. On my way to the Hogan Stand people kept asking me if we were going to win — was I praying. After Joe Connolly's great victory speech in Irish he turned to me and gave me the cup — made me part of the whole victory. It gave me the greatest satisfaction to hold the McCarthy Cup in front of the celebrating crowd and all the Galway maroon flags. There was a tremendous sense of the breakthrough — so huge — so historical — the barrier was gone — we had proved we could do it.'

For Iggy it was the disappointment of being on the outside when it all happened. It was a kind of contradictory disappointment — the agony of being outside — the ecstasy of the breakthrough and being an integral part of it. It brought him a medal as a substitute who had been part of the '80 campaign.

Now to 1981. 'I was grappling with injury — lots of problems and hamstring. At halftime it looked as if we were coasting even allowing for John Connolly's disallowed goal. We looked so much like winning until Johnny Flaherty's goal and even then I thought we were good enough to come back.' Strangely enough 1981 was not as big a disappointment for Iggy as 1979. 'In 1979 we had not won an All Ireland and I was conscious of the alleged curse that was on Galway hurlers — a curse that said we would never win an All Ireland. As a priest I wanted to disprove this rubbish — and that was done in 1980.'

The curtain came down on his intercounty career after the All Ireland semi-final defeat by Offaly in 1984 — 'not a happy memory' — the final score Offaly 4:15 Galway 1:10. It was a career that began in a game against Waterford in 1972 'when I felt lost in the midst of big men' but he made up for it in the next game against Antrim 'when everything went well' and as time went on he won four All Star awards in a career adorned with flair, skilful half-back play and sportsmanship. Did you retire a little early? 'Some said I did but I felt the dynamo was dying after fourteen years hurling. I didn't feel right anymore at half-back and the thought of going into the corner-back didn't appeal to me.'

But his love for the game is still very real — and finds expression at corner-forward where he now plays for Loughrea.

His team from the men of his time reads as follows.

Noel Skehan (Kilkenny)

Fan Larkin (Kilkenny)   Pat Hartigan (Limerick)   John Horgan (Cork)

Joe McDonagh (Galway)   Sean Silke (Galway)   Iggy Clarke (Galway)

John Connolly (Galway)   Frank Cummins (Kilkenny)

Jimmy Barry-Murphy (Cork)   Pat Delaney (Kilkenny)   Martin Quigley (Wexford)

Noel Lane (Galway)   Ray Cummins (Cork)   Eddie Keher (Kilkenny)

Born: 1931

"

I was born into the cauldron of hurling between the first and second replays — Cork v Kilkenny in 1931. I was reared on tales of great players and their deeds — Sim Walton, Dick Grace, Jack Keoghan. I often wondered about the style of play which prevailed during the period 1900-1925. My father was a strong robust player in his own right and was often selected to counteract Limerick's 'Tyler' Mackey who apparently was not known to take prisoners.

I practised the skills constantly and tried to copy the craft of idols such as Lory Meagher, Paddy Phelan and Jim Langton. Any spare moment would find hurleys in our hands and I frequently brought in the cows for milking by slapping a sponge ball at their rear ends. My father was a hard task master and the only relief from farming duties would be to play hurling. Many balls were lost in the course of learning the arts of the game. My older brother Jimmy (RIP) was the ball provider and I think he sometimes pretended to be angrier about ball losses than he really was in truth.

I played minor for Kilkenny in 1948 and 1949 (1st round). I was posted to Killorglin by my bank in May 1949. The Kilkenny County Board decided that I was either expendable or too expensive to bring back for matches. I played my first Senior County Championship with Tullaroan in 1952 and made adequate impression to merit a position on the Kilkenny team in 1953. We lost to Galway in the semi-final. The Kilkenny car neglected to collect me for this match and I had to press gang a friend to drive me to Croke Park from New-bridge. I left an electric ring on in my digs in the tension of the occasion and when I got home from the semi-final I had to face the wrath of the landlord. Having been substituted during the game it was not an auspicious first championship.

I was privileged to have played in the fifties and early sixties in the great Wexford /Waterford era. I met many worthy opponents in that time and Billy Rackard, Jimmy Finn and Seamus Power spring to mind instantly. It was a very exciting time in hurling — Wexford swashbuckling and fair — Waterford fast and fluid. I won two All Irelands in 1957 and 1963 and retired on a high note after the 1963 All Ireland. I was pleased to have been selected at mid-field, my favourite position. The ultimate laxative was to pass the Cathedral in Thurles to play Tipperary in Thurles Sportsfield (now Semple Stadium). One learned to adapt one's game to the Tipperary manner or you may as well stay at home. One of the great pleasures of the modern era is to see the emphasis on skill portrayed by the current Tipperary team, though this should hardly be surprising given the coaching input by Babs Keating and Donie Nealon.

I captained a rest of Ireland team in 1960 of which Christy Ring was a member. However, Christy took over the job from me but was gracious enough to pay tribute post match saying 'young fellow you might make a hurler yet'.

Hurling must be strictly controlled. Any habitual purveyor of physical injury should be banned from playing. The game is much faster now though not as skilful. There was a tremendous pride in the craft of the game in my time and hand passing the ball would have been considered a blasphemy. We all wanted to ape Ring and Langton and in Kilkenny at least an artful player was more admired than a 'hard man'.

The advantage rule is good in theory but in my view is often applied incorrectly. A scoring forward is frequently fouled and granted advantage. He has however, lost his scoring position in the meantime and the gain goes to the defending team.

I worry a little about the future of the game — our great national treasure. Injuries must be kept to an absolute minimum as jobs are often endangered by absence from work in the current economic climate. There is a danger that even parents who are strong devotees may not encourage their children to play. Helmets with facial guard should be obligatory from an early age.

Among my regrets are having to retire before availing of more years to exploit Eddie Keher's extraordinary score taking ability — we seldom discussed strategy but seemed to know each other's intentions instinctively — and failure to captain a winning Kilkenny All Ireland team.

Sean Clohosey. "

The birth of Sean Clohosey on 27 October 1931 — between replays of the historic 1931 hurling decider — ensured the continuity of Kilkenny's tradition of hurling stylists and for Tullaroan a worthy successor to Lory Meagher.

From 1953-1963 in the Kilkenny and Leinster jersey Sean demonstrated the skills of a hurler who loved to meet opponents who would play the ball with him. He had no time for 'schemozzles' or bunching or mullicking. His father Pat had a different mentality. 'He was on the Kilkenny selections around 1904 to 1916 — Kilkenny's first golden era. He was on the team that got a walkover from Limerick in 1911 but didn't take part in the other All Ireland victories. On the basis of horses for courses he was always selected to cope

with the fire and aggression and forcefulness of the likes of 'Tyler' Mackey. The way my father used to talk often made me wonder just what kind of game they played in those days.'

He was Sean's greatest critic. Sean can never recall words of praise but deep down in his father's heart there was a hidden pride that rarely surfaced. 'I would have loved to have been praised and openly admired by him but he wasn't that kind of man. But I did hear once when he had a few drinks taken that the pride and the glory surfaced.' The words Sean recalls hearing most from his father were — 'If I see you turning your back on him ...' This grim gutsyness is probably well reflected in the fact that he won his first county title with Tullaroan in 1904 and was still there to win his last in 1924.

Sean revelled in the centrefield position even though he gave some superlative displays as a forward: 'At midfield I found it possible to mentally relax. As long as you were able to read the game you could create space for yourself. In the forwards you were expected to score but at midfield scoring was a bonus. There was a freedom at midfield that enabled you to contribute to strategy and bring key players into the game. I played at full-forward against Cork in our league triumph in 1962 — I wasn't fit enough to play in any other position.

My hurling philosophy was to play the ball always — beat my man — but if beaten to pursue, harass, block, or hook.' Sean was well equipped for this. He had a very good pair of hands, was generally masterly with the first touch, was an accurate striker from all distances, conserved energy, preferring to use it on the ball rather than jostling with his man. Kevin Cashman in *The Sunday Tribune* included Sean Clohosey among those with a full repertoire of the games skills when he wrote: 'compared to the individual virtuosity which is — or seems — common place at the top level of say tennis or soccer, hurling skill is in the infancy of its development and distribution. The present writer in thirty five years of scrutiny has seen only Ring, Cregan,

Sean Clohosey, second from right, in action against Dublin

Stakelum, Clohosey, Cleere, Roche, John Connolly, Salmon, Cashman, Père et fils, Stack, Keher, Fitzelle, Iggy Clarke and at most another half dozen, attain mastery of the game's full repertoire of skills. And more than a few of that lot had flaws of the spirit. Consistent first touch control always was and remains a rarity. So was and is consistent length and accuracy of first time striking, though opportunity for the overhead variety is rare nowadays'.

Sean Clohosey's display at midfield in the All Ireland final of 1963 against Waterford carried the stamp of class. In the *Sunday Press* on the day of the game Mick Mackey, the legendary Limerick hurler said — 'Waterford will win the All Ireland hurling final. Of that I have no doubt — still I have one warning — should Sean Clohosey at centrefield strike top form, his "sweet" pucking and accurate opportunist shooting could sway the result'. The words were prophetic. Sean told me that when the Kilkenny selectors sat down to pick the team for the final they were in a quandary about midfield. While deliberations were going on the players were having a meal and the late Tom Waldron came to Sean, tapped him on the shoulder and requested a private word with him. 'Could you last 25 minutes at midfield?' He didn't say which 25 minutes. Sean reflected briefly — 'Inwardly I was smarting — could I last 25 minutes.' His reply was emphatic. 'I'll go the hour.'

He drew on all his experience in that final to turn in a class performance — all the skills were used — all the cunning and experience of a decade in top class hurling. One of my lasting memories of that game is that of Sean at midfield in open space — the ball coming towards him overhead — plenty of time to handle it — but he chose differently — a lovely overhead stroke that sent the ball onwards on its journey towards the Waterford goal. 'That day I had the pleasure of feeding Eddie Keher and watch him display his hurling genius.'

The final score saw Kilkenny win by three points — 4:17 to 6:8. It was a fitting note for Sean on which to retire.

This is his team from the men of his era that he would like to have captained.

	Ollie Walsh (Kilkenny)	
Fan Larkin (Kilkenny)	Nick O'Donnell (Wexford)	Jim Treacy (Kilkenny)
Jimmy Finn (Tipperary)	Pat Stakelum (Tipperary)	Billy Rackard (Wexford)
Sean Clohosey (Kilkenny)	Joe Salmon (Galway)	
Jimmy Doyle (Tipperary)	Pat Delaney (Kilkenny)	Eddie Keher (Kilkenny)
Jimmy Smyth (Clare)	Nicky Rackard (Wexford)	Christy Ring (Cork)

45

Jimmy 'Butler' Coffey (left) with Johnny Ryan (right) in O'Connell St, Dublin on 18/3/1938, the day after the Railway Cup final.

"

I was one of a family of eight — four boys and four girls. I was the second youngest of the family. My brother Paddy was sacristan in the Catholic Church for 70 years. My father used to carry me to see the hurlers training on Sunday afternoon. My greatest wish was to wear the Newport jersey one day. We had a 'cuairtiocht' house. My mother used to sit under the kitchen lamp and read the papers as all the men sat around the kitchen fire.The game of hurling was the main topic as the family sat around the kitchen fire. Jack and myself won the minor championship in 1926. Mike won the junior championship of 1924. The three of us won the North Tipp senior title in 1932 and 1935. Jack and myself won a minor All Ireland in 1930. Mikey won a junior All Ireland in 1926.

Newport played a famous game with Ahane in 1931 — Newport won by two goals. The memories of the games and the

Born: 1909

friends we made are the things we cherish most. Sad to say the numbers are getting thin on the ground. I'd like to thank Thurles, Moycarkey and Toomevara for selecting me on the county teams.

"

Jimmie Butler Coffey

Dates, details, data, names, memories and incidents roll off the tongue of Jimmy Coffey just as if they all happened a few hours ago — even though we were travelling back decades to more than half a century ago. His capacity for vivid recall is remarkable. He swings from decade to decade — year to year — from one epic encounter to another with such effortless ease that one is reminded of Goldsmith's 'Village Schoolmaster'.

And still they gazed, and still the wonder grew

That one small head could carry all he knew

So let's start at the beginning and travel through time and space with this affable and amiable eighty three year old, switching as he did from decade to decade in the course of the journey.

He was born in 1909 in Newport, Co Tipperary. He was about five years old, and with his brother who was about one year younger, was sitting on the floor of the kitchen between the legs of two of the many men who had gathered to hear his mother reading from the newspaper. 'We were play acting and upsetting the listeners and were told to stop the "kafflin" or go out and fight outside. As we rose my brother hit me on the nose and as I complained I sounded as if I was talking through my nose. Now said one of those gathered you sound like Phil Butler — a tall white bearded agent who was employed by the gentry of those days and who constantly spoke through his nose. Since that moment I became known in Newport as "Butler" Coffey.

I played a tournament game — my first senior one — with Tipperary in 1932 — having already won All Ireland minor honours with them in 1930 — the year they completed the triple, senior, junior and minor. I was selected for the replay against Waterford in the championship of 1933. We lost on the score 5:5 to 5:2. Individually as distinct from a team unit, it must have been one of the best fifteen ever to leave the county.'

Those names are carved with pride in his memory — the christian name, the surname, the position of each, the Club. He reels them off like a well learned poem:

Tommy O'Meara (Toomevara) / John Maher (Thurles) Jack Stapleton (Thurles) Phil Purcell (Moycarkey) / Jim Lanigan (Thurles) Tom Teehan (Army Metro) Bill Kennedy (Moycarkey) / Tommy Treacy (Young Irelands) Mick Daniels (Army Metro) / Phil Cahill (Moycarkey) Michael Cronin (Lorrha) Jimmy 'B' Coffey (Newport) / Tommy Leahy (Boherlahan) Martin Kennedy (Kiladangan) Jimmy Heeney

(Thurles) — 'Great men all.'

Jimmy now turned back the clock for a story about a very young Martin Kennedy.

'There was a cup called the O'Callaghan Cup that was played for between the champions of Cork and Limerick. In this particular year the contest was between Blackrock and Claughaun of Limerick. Claughaun felt they hadn't a great team. It was decided to take a sidecar to Toomevara and bring back a handful of hurlers for the game — among them a young Martin Kennedy — as yet unknown in the big time, and wearing a cap. Opposing him was the renowned Cork fullback Sean Óg Murphy. Martin performed very well and Claughaun won the game. In the following years championship Cork met Tipp and Sean Óg and Martin were marking each other — Martin complete with cap. The game wasn't long in progress when the ball came flying into the Cork goalmouth and suddenly it is in the net — via Martin. Sean Óg looks at him and says — "Did I come across you somewhere before?" "No Sir," replied Martin.'

Jimmy's childhood heroes were Martin Kennedy and Phil Cahill described by 'Carbery' as 'the fastest man in Ireland to lift, turn and score'. In his early hurling days Paddy Clohessy, the Limerick centre-half-back made an 'awful impression on me — he was rocklike at centre-back and in his playing days with Limerick CBS he was known as "the schoolboy wonder" and "Carbery" once labelled him "the Fedamore fire brand".'

Touring through the thirties and other decades Jimmy recalled to mind the following — 'in the Cork versus Limerick Munster championship game of 1934, I saw Jackie O'Connell of Limerick score a magnificent goal off no less a defender than George Garrett and I said to myself, I'll never again see one like it. Three minutes later, Jackie scored another equally brilliant one.

In the first replay of the 1931 All Ireland final between Cork and Kilkenny, Dinny Barry Murphy of Cork said that the ball was moving so fast that his mind got a little

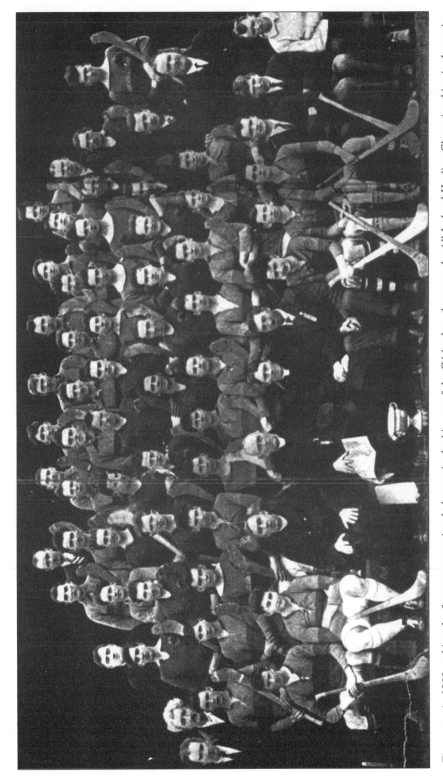

Tipperary, in 1930, achieved a feat never previously known in the history of the GAA when they won the All Ireland Hurling Championships in the senior, junior and minor grades. This remarkable photograph of the three teams was taken at Thurles sportsfield.

confused — it was no place for handymen.

I will always remember the oustanding display of Liam O'Neill, the Laois left-full-back in the minor All Ireland final of 1934 between Tipperary and Laois.'

Research I have done reveals that Tipperary brought on eight subs that day and the game was eight minutes into extra time when Tipperary got the winning goal scored by one of the subs with half a hurley, even though the referee had five minutes earlier told Liam O'Neill as he came up to take a seventy that it was all over. In the semi-final of that year Laois must surely have recorded the highest ever score in championship hurling. They beat Down in the semi-final by 17:10 to 2:7.

In 1934 Newport won the North Tipperary intermediate title. Being the Jubilee year of the GAA, it was a good year to win any medal. The one in question has a bust of Thomas MacDonagh — born in Clough-jordan in 1878, poet and one of the 1916 signatories to the Proclamation — super-imposed upon it.

I was associated with the Limerick team in 1955 when they won the Munster title against Clare and Dermot Kelly and Seamus Ryan were outstanding at centre-forward and centre-back respectively. We were leading in the semi-final at halftime at Croke Park against Wexford — and confident. But a couple of things contrib-uted to our defeat. The dressing-room was full of well wishers and it was impossible to clear it and talk with the team; the team had eleven selectors which made communication impossible; and Wexford made a master switch. They brought Ned Wheeler to centre-forward on Seamus Ryan where his height and size and weight told. They also brought on Paddy Kehoe and he thundered through for a great goal — although some say he carried it in his hand while pretending to the referee it was on the hurley — echoes of Mick Mackey?

In 1950 I drove a truck to Kilkenny to see Kilkenny and Wexford in a Leinster final that Wexford lost by one goal. Langton scored a great goal that day for Kilkenny

from a forty yards free — he spotted a gap. Wexford were still in the infancy of great-ness but even then they struck me as very glamorous. In the early stages of that game the first three balls that went in between Nicky Rackard and the "Diamond" Hayden resulted in three frees out to Kilkenny as the "Diamond" stood solid behind Nicky with the hurley against his back — (which you could do in those days). I thought the decisions were harsh.

I cycled to Birr from Newport and my wife cycled from Cappamore to see Galway and Kilkenny play in the All Ireland semi-final of 1947. A great game had a sensa-tional ending with confusion reigning regarding a mistaken final whistle. There must have been hundreds of spectators on the pitch when Jimmy Langton sent over the last point — a winning one in fact — although some Kilkenny players thought it was the equaliser. I was struck that day by the centrefield performance of the Galway duo, Paddy Gantly and John Killeen.

The three best games of hurling I saw were — the 1935 National League final between Limerick and Kilkenny at Nowlan Park when two of the greatest teams in hurling served up an unforgettable hours' entertainment. — The 1947 All Ireland final between Cork and Kilkenny when a superb second half ended in a welter of excitement as the magic of Terry Leahy stole the honours for Kilkenny. — The Munster colleges Harty Cup final of 1954 between Thurles CBS and St Flannan's — a hurling spectacle won by St Flannan's with Donie Nealon of future Tipperary stardom out-standing for St Flannan's.

Jimmy has seen the game evolve over several decades now. The thirties produced ground hurling in an abundance and was a delight to watch. The ball was despatched with speed and first time pulling was the order of the day. Great goals were witnessed — 'goals rouse the crowd — you see some lovely points nowadays but it's goals and the green flag waving that really thrill the crowd. In the three Munster finals of 1935, '36 and '37 between Limerick and Tipperary the aggregate score reveals that more goals than points were scored — 28 goals as against 26 points. It dosen't happen like that nowadays.' He is glad to see the late charging disallowed and likes the rule that gives a free from where the ball lands after such a foul. He considers that there is too much handling of the ball at present and that this can lead to frees — 'remember there were only nine frees in the 1937 final.' He has seen players pull on the flying ball in modern hurling and a free awarded against them because an opponent put up his hand and got hit — 'it inhibits the game, it needs to be re-examined.' He has great sympathy for referees 'the speed of the game makes their task very difficult. There is need to actively involve umpires and linesmen in highlighting offences.' He regrets the demise of the Thomond Feis tournament which took place each spring in Limerick and in which Limerick, Cork, Tipperary and Clare competed. 'It was a splendid occasion and produced some great games.' No wonder he is nostalgic about the tournament. After all it led to his selection on the Tipperary senior team and here is how he recalls it. 'I cycled to the tournament and on my way through the city Johnny Leahy, the renowned Tipp mentor spotted me and told me to tog out as they had no subs. The game between Tipp and Limerick wasn't five minutes old when Michael Cronin had to go off injured. Go in on Paddy Clohessy said Johnny Leahy to me — a tall order remarked Pat Stakelum to me years later as I related the story to him. I did as instructed and after a while switched to the wing on Mickey Cross. I must have done well for I never lost my place on the panel after that.'

The thirties were a time of austerity and frugality for the people of an infant nation struggling to grow and establish itself. It found inspiration in its traditions, history, ballads and hurling men. It was a decade that produced numerous outstanding games and a multitude of superb hurlers. It was dominated by Limerick in Munster and

Kilkenny in Leinster. Waterford, Clare, Tipperary, Cork, Galway and Dublin also made a big contribution. But Limerick were the glamour team. By 1937 they were heading for a fifth Munster title in a row and a similar number of All Ireland appearances. They seemed invincible. Let Jimmy tell the tale.

'In the dressing-room before the game Tom Semple spoke out. Now lads I want the team and myself in another room by ourselves. He was a powerfully built man — six foot three — wore a big hat. We all deeply respected him and listened intently. Now lads, you're going out today to play the best team that ever wore jerseys. You're fit and well. So are they. The game will be won in the last quarter of an hour. They will be tired. So will you. The man with the greater willpower will win. Let it be the Tipperary men. Well the game was of titanic proportions — the rivalry intense — the exchanges fierce — no quarters — and yet there wasn't one substitution in the entire hour. It was shortly before half time that Tipp got their only goal of the first half. Here is how Carbery described it in the *Cork Examiner*. "Coffey from Newport with hair the colour of ripe wheat flicked a ball from wing to square and 'Sweeper' Ryan turned it to the net." It was level at half time on 1:2 each. Then we got a brace of quick goals. Tommy Treacy got the first and Carbery described it as follows — "It cut a daisy on the way to the net and but for the net, would have hit Blackrock Castle two miles away." Limerick replied with a goal and we got a further brace. Boy did they fight back. In the end it was 6:3 to 4:3 and the two goal difference makes a mockery of just how close it was.'

Tipperary confirmed their Munster final form by defeating Kilkenny 3:11 to 0:3 in the All Ireland final at Killarney. Here is an excerpt from a Press report on the game. 'The halfline however, composed of Doyle, Treacy and Coffey was outstanding. The Newport man, assuredly one of the best forwards to don county colours for several years, was the best of the three. Opposed by Paddy Phelan, who made an entire Tipp forward line look like novices in the league game at Carrick, he careered around — a bundle of energy. As a resolute and determined hurler possessed of great stamina and dash, he has few equals. On Sunday, when slipped by Phelan on one occasion he kept "hell for leather" after his rival for fifty yards. Most hurlers would have given up — but not Coffey. He not alone overtook his opponent but dispossessed him and sent the ball flying goalwards with a great delivery.'

And so to 1938 — another All Ireland for Tipperary? Well, fate played a part and so of course did the Jimmy Cooney case. It all began when Jimmy Cooney attended an international rugby match in early 1938 — (under the rules of the time such an action would lead to suspension). Jimmy now takes up the story.

'We faced Clare in Limerick on the last Sunday in June. Coming on to the pitch Tom Hayes who had played with Limerick around the 1910 era, called me aside and said — Are you playing Cooney? — Play him today and you'll win today but you'll lose in the council chamber. Don't play him today and you'll win the match and you'll go on to win the All Ireland'. What happened was prophetic. Tipperary won 3:10 to 2:3 and lost in the council chamber.'

It is fitting to end with the last memorable game that Jimmy Coffey played. It was a club game for a church tournament and was played in his native Newport in May 1947. The contestants were Ahane and Thurles Sarsfields. Jimmy was now wearing the Ahane colours — (being resident in Cappamore Co Limerick made him eligible). A Press report described it as 'a struggle devoid of mercy and compassion' but Jimmy described it as an encounter in the classical mould with first time ground hurling the order of the day — victory snatched from their grasp in the dying moments after leading at halftime by four points — and 'nothing at stake but parish prestige.'

And now as Jimmy looks back from the vantage point of a very fresh eighty three he remembers with relish and fondness the fury, fire, fierceness and ferocity of the exchanges on the field and the bond of friendship that was woven in those clashes of ash — and which endures and manifests itself in a variety of wonderful ways.

Dul siar ar m'aistear
Le solas mo chroi.

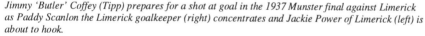

Jimmy 'Butler' Coffey (Tipp) prepares for a shot at goal in the 1937 Munster final against Limerick as Paddy Scanlon the Limerick goalkeeper (right) concentrates and Jackie Power of Limerick (left) is about to hook.

Born: c.1897

Turlough Considine better known as Tull came from a great sporting Clare family. He was one of seven brothers — all of whom distinguished themselves on the sports field. Two of them, Brendan and Willie, won Munster and All Ireland senior hurling honours with Clare in 1914. Brendan subsequently played with Dublin, Cork and Waterford.

Tull played in the full-forward line in the All Ireland final of 1932 against Kilkenny and with hindsight it was felt that he might have been better deployed in the half-line. A final assault by Tull on the Kilkenny goal failed to bring a vital score. It was felt by many that he had been fouled en route — but no free was awarded. Clare lost by one goal.

Earlier that year in the All Ireland semi-final at Limerick Tull had what was perhaps his greatest day. He went on a second half scoring spree against Galway. At halftime Galway led by thirteen points and seemed well on the road to victory. Gloom surrounded the Clare followers. The Clare gloom deepened early in the second half as Galway increased their lead to sixteen points. Many Clare supporters headed for home. They had seen enough humiliation. Some Galway fans left to celebrate. With less than ten minutes of the second half gone Tull swung into action. His rampage yielded seven goals and one point and turned the huge deficit of sixteen points into a five points winning margin. The final score in an absolutely amazing game was Clare 9:4 Galway 4:14. Of the Clare total Tull has been accredited with 8:1 — an incredible contribution. The supporters of both sides who had left the grounds early in the second half heard the final result with disbelief. Rumours began to circulate that some premature celebrations in the Galway dressing room at the interval may have been a key contributory factor to the eventual defeat.

The Clare team that contested the final of 1932 contained many household names and wonderful hurlers. It lined out as follows: Tommy Daly / 'Jumbo' Higgins, Pa 'Fowler' McInerney, John Joe Doyle / Jim Houlihan, Jim Hogan, Larry Blake / Jack Gleeson, Mick Falvey / Tom McInerney, Jim Mullane, Mick Connery / Tom Burnell, Tull Considine, Mick O'Rourke.

Tull was chosen by the Munster hurling selectors from 1928-1931 inclusive and won four Railway Cup medals. He was also on the Tailteann Games team of 1928.

He was a formidable footballer too and played in the All Ireland final of 1917 when Clare failed to Wexford on the score 0:9 to 0:5. Wexford were outstanding at that period. It was their third successive All Ireland victory in their great four in a row success of 1915-1918. Eleven years later in 1928 Tull was still considered good enough by the Munster football selectors to be chosen on the Railway Cup team. He opted however to line out with the Munster hurlers with whom he was also chosen.

Tull as a player, coach and trainer, was a man of great vision and foresight. His native Clare will always remember him with pride.

Born: 1940

(Bishop) Owens, for their great work with the underage players.

Like every chap in Comer at that time I too went down the pit and spent two years mining anthracite. It was a tough life.

I played with the local minor team and were it not for the efforts of the late Billy Treacy and Paddy Dunphy of greyhound fame, John Dwyer and John (Barber) Walsh, I would neither have got on the trial panel nor the county minor team. Thank you Paddy for driving me to the trial. I played county minor at centre-forward but Galway beat us in the All Ireland semi-final by a goal.

1958 was a thrilling year for Erin's Own when we won the County junior final against Knocktopher. I played senior for Erin's Own for twenty six years — 1959 to 1985 and although we went near on a few occasions, we never won the championship. Even one victory would have gladened my heart — been great for the club — and would have thrilled the late Fr John Kearns who was Mr Hurling himself in Castlecomer.

Again like every chap born in Kilkenny, I had a longing in my heart to wear the black and amber and play for Kilkenny. I always felt I would fulfil that ambition. I was overjoyed when I got my first call. I was on a Kilkenny team to play against a Kilkenny All Star selection. I played at centrefield. How did I play? The following story tells the tale. Next morning I was at my work in the local hospital when Fr Kearns appeared. 'Coogan you were useless yesterday,' he said. I don't need you to tell me that Father — I know it myself — I answered. We discussed the game. As a result I became a better player. That one game taught me what was necessary to reach county standard. From there on I trained like never before.

In the years that followed I trained with the county team in Nowlan Park — came home — togged out again and went to the

"

I am proud to be a Comer man. I was born there in a place called The Spike in 1940. From the time I was old enough to hold a hurl my brother Seamus and myself spent every evening until darkness fell hurling in the schoolyard. It was there I learned most of the skills of hurling that came easy to me as I grew up. As I grew older and the school yard seemed to get smaller we changed our venue to The Spike road. The hurling there was hard, fast and furious and I cherish memories of Martin Brennan (Goggie) and the late Hughie Cullen and Paddy (Swack) Brennan.

Whenever Kilkenny won we replayed the match that evening on the road, pretending we were the Kilkenny heroes of that day. Another reason why I am proud of our road is for the honour and fame brought to it by my great friend and neighbour Mick Dowling, the boxer. Mick was a good hurler too.

I hurled for my school in the under 14 championship and reached the under 16 final two years later but we lost. A word of thanks here to Fr Liam Carrigan and Tom

Prince grounds in Castlecomer and continued training until I was satisfied that I was fit. I would not play if I felt I wasn't fully fit. I also practised the skills I had learned long ago in the school yard and on our own road until I perfected the line ball, and my own favourite — the lift and strike without handling the ball. I spent hours every evening at that.

The Kilkenny selectors saw something in me and I played with Kilkenny from 1960 until 1972 — two years at centrefield and the rest at left-half-back. I am a natural left-handed hurler and I played right hand below. This made it difficult for opponents to hook me or block down the ball. In my years with Kilkenny I played against almost every hurling county in Ireland and I felt honoured to have played with some of the greatest hurlers and teams that Kilkenny ever produced. I would like to name all the Kilkenny players I played with but a few outstanding ones come to my mind like Ollie Walsh, Eddie Keher, Seamus Cleere, Jim Treacy, Pat Henderson and Ted Carroll.

I remember great players from the other counties too, like Jimmy Doyle (Tipp) who was very difficult to pin down as he played all over the field — Jimmy O'Brien and Phil Wilson of Wexford, Liam Devaney of Tipp and Mick Flannelly of Waterford.

I had the honour of playing against but not on Christy Ring. I had heard all the stories about Christy's fame and hurling artistry. On the day of the league final of 1962, I saw the king of hurlers as he displayed the great skill of flicking the ball or doubling on it as it came flying in about two feet off the ground and sending it bullet-like towards the goal. He never missed. I had played on the same field as my hero and I'll never forget it.

We won that league.

My advice to youngsters today is to practise the skills first, get fit and above all to play the game.

I like the new rules but I feel that the umpires and linesmen should take more action and help the referee with his difficult task. I also think that no player should be penalised as a result of what is seen later on video. There are enough officials watching to take action during the game. No player at county level should get himself sent off. He should be able to discipline himself at that level and always put his team first. In my day the pressure was a bit less. We all headed off with the boots stuffed with stockings and togs and tied to the hurl. I liked that.

The GAA, my local club and the black and amber meant everything to me and were good to me. I still train teams and at present am training Clara seniors. Playing the game is important. Winning is not always important but it is necessary to win now and again. I would love to start all over again.

Martin Coogan ”

Martin Coogan was a right hand under natural left-handed hurler. He arrived on the scene in 1961 and played against Wexford in a Walsh cup game in New Ross — Kilkenny winning 3:11 to 0:11. For the first two years he played at midfield but thereafter until he retired he 'owned' the left half back position on the Kilkenny team. There he gave some superlative displays reminiscent of Paddy Phelan of the thirties in the same position. Hurling ran freely in his blood. After the 1969 All Ireland victory over Cork he received the 'Man of the Match' award — thus adding a well deserved personal award to his many medals and trophies. This was followed in 1971 by his selection on the first ever All Star team.

Martin always placed tremendous emphasis on fitness and good sportsmanship. In this regard he was a shining example to youth. The disciplines he placed upon himself were quite remarkable — extra running after coming home from a training session — bed at nine thirty from the Wednesday night before an important match — no change in food patterns for days before a big match — meticulous attention to the basics of the game — total

When asked to pick a team Martin said he'd have been happy to captain any Kilkenny 15 from 1960 to '72 to play against the following opposition from other counties of the same era.

Damien Martin (Offaly)

Tony Maher (Cork)   Pat Hartigan (Limerick)   Tom Neville (Wexford)

Mick Jacob (Wexford)   Tony Wall (Tipperary)   Paddy Molloy (Offaly)

Phil Wilson (Wexford)   Mick Roche (Tipperary)

Jimmy Doyle (Tipperary)   John Connolly (Galway)   Liam Devaney (Tipperary)

Jimmy Cullinane (Clare)   Tony Doran (Wexford)   Mick Bermingham (Dublin)

'I could easily have picked many more opposition teams that would also have been a pleasure to play against.'

dedication to practice and training. Surely a coach's dream.

He was a model of sportsmanship and speaks with affection about his colleagues and opponents. 'I was sent off once — myself and Noel O'Dwyer of Tipp — a snig and a snig back — nothing really'. A stroke in the head saw him taken off with concussion after twenty minutes of the first half against Tipperary in 1964. Martin has a kind word for everyone and injuries he got, he puts down to — 'it was my ould style.'

His heart was in hurling and he loved to train. Self effacing and modest, it seemed to me that in some respects playing the game and training for it meant more to him than medals won. These were hidden away in a box until a Tipperary friend called to see his collection. Taken aback by the way they were stored, he returned one month later with a beautiful showcase in which Martin now displays the medals.

He made hurling look easy but he put countless hours into developing the skills and correcting the faults that manifested themselves during matches. He is a great admirer of overhead striking and loves to see players lift and strike in the one movement without handling the ball — 'it's terrific, I love watching it.' He believes in letting the ball do the work and loves to see players getting rid of it quickly.

The game that gives him most regret is the 1966 All Ireland final. 'We were red hot favourites — we had a very good team with plenty of experience — but we made a lot of mistakes that day. Cork won 3:9 to 1:10 and played no nonsense hurling. We were over confident. When it was all over there was even talk about us taking pills. There were lots of post mortems.'

Three All Ireland wins stand out. 'In 1963 we defeated a fine Waterford team. It was an unusual score 4:17 to 6:8. It was my first All Ireland win. Firsts are always special. In 1967 we met Tipp in the final. Tradition was against us as Kilkenny hadn't beaten Tipp in a final since 1922. Tipp were honours laden and star studded. They swept all before them in 1964 and 1965. The odds were against us but we scored a great victory — a victory however that was somewhat overshadowed by an accident on the field that caused our centre-forward Tommy Walsh to lose an eye. In 1972 I was a sub. It was an honour to come on in the second half and take part in a half that produced some wonderful hurling. 'Believe it or not I played that day at right-full-back.'

In Martin's young days money was very scarce. He and his brother Seamus would cut ash trees in the ditch and get 'Brussels' Kelly to make hurleys for them. Another way was to get broken hurleys at a match — especially of 'heroes' and again 'Brussels' converted the half hurley into a juvenile one.

Martin also excelled at other games — squash, tennis, handball and golf. It wasn't surprising then that in 1980 the Castlecomer Tennis Club arranged under great secrecy a surprise and presented Martin with a magnificent 'This is Your Life' book. Here are two excerpts —

'As a youngster in Castlecomer, his enthusiasm saw him train by candlelight for the game of hurling he loved. Later his efforts in the dark were to be rewarded when he received National acclaim, and when he eventually decided to step down from the inter-county scene, he left to cries of a "lost gentleman from hurling" ... The curtain came down on his magnificent inter-county hurling career in 1973 but he left memories that will stand the test of time and be forever among the best.'

An admirer Joe O'Neill made this poetic tribute to Martin:

No man will ever take his place.
For more than twenty years he's graced
this hurling game.
When he leaves and plays no more
We all know in our hearts
It will never be the same.
His style was like the breeze,
Crisp and free.
The ball went eighty yards
That stroke now legendary.

John (Ballyhea) Coughlan, taken in 1926.

M any family names have etched their fame on the hurling calendar. Coughlan (pronounced Call-on in Cork) of Blackrock — known as the cradle of Cork hurling — was among the first.

Five brothers played and starred with Blackrock. They were Patrick (Parson), Denis (Lyonsie), Dan (Big Dan), Jeremiah (Big Jur) and Tom (Honest man). All were strong athletic men and only Patrick and Tom fell short of the six foot mark. Collectively they won eight All Ireland medals between the years 1892 and 1903. Indeed, they might have won more but for the fact that Denis when training with Redmonds for the All Ireland final of 1892 accidentally hit a fatal blow to a friend and colleague while pulling on a dropping ball. He was so upset by the tragedy that he just pined away and died.

John (Ballyhea) Coughlan — they all had nicknames — who was born in 1898 was the oldest son of Patrick (Parson) whom

Born: 1898

'Carbery' described as 'a master of strategy, a strong fearless man, he revelled in the close hard clashes of the period'. On his mother's side Michael and William Dorney also played with Cork. John, regarded as one of the leading goalkeepers of his era, was overshadowed by his more famous brother Eudi, who played with Cork from 1920 to 1931 — winning four All Ireland medals and captaining them to glory on the historic occasion that was 1931.

But John had his moments too. He was in goal for Cork when they defeated Kilkenny in the All Ireland final of 1926 — decisively enough 4:6 to 2:0. He was there again when they faced the same opposition in 1931 but this time it took three attempts. On September 6th it ended at 1:6 each. In the replay on October 11th, hurling history was made when it ended in another draw 2:5 each. It seems that the officials wanted extra time but Eudi Coughlan, the Cork captain wasn't having any of it. He was reading well the signs of the times. 'We were going out and they were coming in.' How right he was as the thirties were to prove. And so to the third historic meeting on November 1st — victory and glory for Cork on the score 5:8 to 3:4.

In 1926 the Cork lineout included ten Blackrock players and in 1931 if you include George Garret who came on a sub in both replays, there were nine.

John also won seven County senior hurling medals with Blackrock and two National League titles with Cork.

A very shy and unassuming man, he always shunned publicity. Physically he wasn't as robust as Eudi. He was a fisherman on the River Lee like all his ancestors who in their day, had their own fleet of fishing boats. However in the late forties he joined the Staff of the Cork Harbour Commissioners from which he retired in 1960.

He died on his birthday in August 1965.

"

The highlight of my career is without doubt the All Ireland win of 1973. I always believed that this would happen and that I would be part of it. It was an unforgettable year. Limerick had been threatening for a number of years. It all started to happen when Jim Hogan, Tony O'Brien (RIP) and others went to the County Board and asked that we do winter training. The County Board to their credit agreed to do this.

But '73 happened many years before and it all goes back to primary school hurling which was very strong at the time, teams like St John's, St Munchin's, St Patrick's, Leamys, Model School, all participated — famous names like Eamon, Joe and Mikey Grimes, Walter Shanahan, Leonard Enright, Colm Tucker, Christy Campbell, Fr Pat O'Brien, Sean Foley, Bernie Hartigan, and Michael Cregan, to mention but a few.

Add to those Doon CBS, Adare CBS, and Charleville CBS which had Willie Moore, Jim Hogan, Jim O'Brien, Frankie Nolan and many more who formed the nucleus for the future. Without the schools we would have got nowhere and this is a lesson which must be kept in mind always.

The progression was then to secondary

Born: 1945

school — Sexton St, St Munchin's, Doon, Charleville — again schools the one common factor. Munchin's had Ned Rea and Fr Pat O'Brien but because of strict rules in the Church, Pat never realised his potential.

Sexton St. had a glorious five years in Harty Cup from 1964 to 1968 — beaten the last year.

Those wins gave Limerick confidence to go out and do battle against very good opposition. And this was mainly due to two people — Brother Burke (RIP) a Tipperary man and Jim Hennessy, a Waterford man. They made us believe in ourselves. In 1963 we had beaten Tipperary in the Munster minor final and this gave us confidence for future years that we had the beating of Tipperary.

After our win in '73 Limerick County Board made a bad mistake. We never capitalised on our win to promote hurling everywhere in Limerick. We had not the vision to see beyond '73. A golden opportunity was lost.

Pride was back with Limerick again. Our great rivals at the time were Tipperary, Cork, Clare and Kilkenny. Clare because of their closeness were always capable of beating us which they did to our dismay in 1972. The Kilkenny team of the early seventies was a fabulous team with Keher, Purcell, Delaney, Cummins, Skehan (a great keeper) Pat Henderson and Larkin. They played a tremendous game — skilful and effective. I also thought that the Tipperary team of the sixties was a great team — their strength was in the quality of their players. Waterford were also a fine side.

My hope for Limerick is that we can consistently compete against every other county at the highest level and win. In order to do this we must change our style back to a more basic style of game and in order to do this we must change the structure and coaching. Mick Tynan had the right idea but where is that now?

Two All Irelands in 53 years! Are we happy with that? If not, let us do something about it.

Eamon Cregan **"**

Eamon Cregan speaks with pride about his native city Limerick in whose history he is deeply interested; his club Claughaun which was founded in 1902 following a breakaway from St Patrick's and which had no pitch of its own until 1967; his school Sexton St (Limerick CBS) where his hurling brilliance blossomed; and finally his lifetime in hurling.

He can trace his ancestry back to the early 1700's and in the process of so doing he came across in the Land Registry Tenancy Agreements which were executed in the 1800's between his relations Michael Cregan and Con Cregan and Lord Devon, who by all accounts was a benevolent and 'improving' landlord.

His father Ned lived in Monagea and hurled with Newcastlewest before moving to Limerick City. Ned played in a junior All Ireland final with Limerick against Meath in 1927 but the Royal County were victorious. From there he progressed to the Senior team and won National League, Munster and All Ireland honours with the great Limerick team of the thirties. He played in the All Ireland finals of 1933, 1934, 1935 and was a sub in 1936. His moment of All Ireland glory came in 1934 when a very talented Dublin team was beaten after a replay. Both games produced thrill-packed contests of brilliant hurling, played at terrific pace and incredibly close man to man marking. Ned lined out at right fullback.

Did he ever compare the hurlers and hurling of the different decades? 'No, he never made comparisons. He very seldom spoke about the twenties and thirties. But he would observe Mick and myself. He would never say that the fellows of his day were better. He would offer us advice —

set us thinking. One day as he watched me strike continuously with the left he just said — have you got any right side. It put me thinking. There was one thing he always told me — never stick your hand up if you can stick up your hurley.'

Eamon talks about hurling as if he was pouring forth a series of theses.

The flow of words and thoughts is effortless. His views are definite and positive. His passion and love for the game radiate as he speaks. 'Hurling is a simple game but people complicate it. Players are the most important people in the GAA — without them the GAA would be dead. The players must be cared for. I can remember the old sheds that passed for dressing-rooms in the fifties at the Gaelic Grounds in Limerick.'

Since retiring Eamon has coached Limerick and Clare and is at present with Offaly who this year (1993) gave a superb account of themselves against Kilkenny in the Leinster championship and were a little unfortunate not to have won. I enquired about his tactical philosophy as he set about shaping and moulding a team. 'It's quite simple. The basics must be done well and done quickly. You must of course have a supply line and this is where the schools come in. If hurling is to thrive and prosper young lads must be taught the basics and parents must be satisfied that it is a safe game for their children to play. The present Kilkenny style is fabulous — so simple — so direct — backs very tight — the high ball is batted out — the ball on the ground is always covered by the defenders who sweep it out in front of them. Great credit is due to Fr Maher who changed the Kilkenny style in the sixties. Cork play a lovely style of hurling — it depends on skill for successful execution. I can get frustrated on the sideline when I see players giving away stupid frees — or showing poor anticipation — or sending in high balls that go wide when the low ball would put the defence under pressure — not that there isn't a time and a place for the high ball — see the way Kilkenny and Cork use the low fast ground ball and convert it. Of course I still play every stroke when I am sitting on the sideline and those beside me get elbowed and shouldered.'

While on the subject of Kilkenny he spoke in glowing terms of the outstanding goalkeeping qualities of Noel Skehan and the number of matches that his performances won for Kilkenny.

He then talked about the 'diamond' that incorporates the positions of centre-back, centre-field and centre-forward. 'If you're strong in these departments — if you can dominate these positions — then you will win matches because you are going to pressurise the opposition. You must have a centre-forward that will penetrate and upset a defence.' He instances John Power of Kilkenny — 'remember how he tortured and tormented Wexford in the 1992 and 1993 Leinster finals, Gerald McCarthy of Cork and his role against Wexford in the All Ireland final of 1977, Brendan Lynsky of Galway and the way he could draw defenders towards him and in so doing create loose colleagues, John Flanagan of Limerick whose agressive hurling paved the way for Limerick's successes over Cork and Clare in the Munster finals of 1980 and 1981 respectively.'

He laughs when he thinks of the ban and how long it lasted. 'I went to rugby and soccer matches regularly when the ban existed. When it was lifted I didn't bother much going. The ban was a farce in Limerick city where every game was seen as a sport and the same supporters were to be seen at the rugby and soccer and hurling matches. The ones with their heads down at the rugby matches (when they saw photographs being taken) were the GAA players.'

Eamon made his inter-county debut in a National League game against Dublin in the autumn of 1964 having turned down indirect approaches to join the panel in 1963 and 1964. 'I felt I was too young and I had seen others go to that level too early and fail.' The curtain came down on a brilliant and action filled hurling career when he came on a sub against Cork in the 1983 Munster championship.

Eamon won three All Star awards in the full-forward line. 'It is the last line of attack where you have to have a conversion rate mentality. There is no room for mistakes or lost opportunities. You have to be able to pounce on half chances or defensive blunders. In the course of an hour relatively few balls may come your way. When they do come you must be able to score yourself or make a score for a colleague. You must

1934 – Jubilee year of GAA. Limerick, All-Ireland winners. Back Row: Paddy Clohossey, Jackie O'Connell, Paddy Scanlon, Garret Howard, Ned Cregan, John Mackey, Jim Roche, Mick Ryan. Centre: Tom McCarthy, Timmy Ryan, Jimmy Close, Mickey Cross. Front Row: Mick Kennedy, Dave Clohessy, Mick Mackey.

think, concentrate and be alert the whole time.'

He was a highly accomplished thinking forward worthy of a place in modern hurling beside Eddie Keher of Kilkenny, Jimmy Doyle of Tipperary, Jimmy Smyth of Clare and Jimmy Barry Murphy of Cork. Mick Mackey rated him highly and saw him as capable of commanding a place on the great Limerick teams of the period from 1933 to 1945. No higher reference is possible.

He got many great scores. In a tense dour, dogged encounter against Cork in the Munster final of 1980 he scored a great first half goal at the town end. It was the score of a seasoned master — displaying coolness — taking the right option.

Against Galway in the All Ireland final of 1980 with Limerick stunned by an opening two goal burst, he rose to an incoming high ball and with a deft onward hand flick he had the ball in the Galway net before defence or spectators realised what had happened. There followed a truly magnificent point from well out the field on the Hogan Stand side when with his back to the goal and under pressure, he feigned to strike one way and then swivelled to the other side and swung to send the sliotar sailing over the Railway goal.

The Irish Press ran an editorial on the match on the following Monday. Here is an excerpt from it —

'Yesterday's All Ireland hurling final, apart from being one of the best, most thrilling, and most sporting played at Croke Park, will also go down in the annals of the GAA as triggering off one of the greatest celebratory outbursts that Galway or the West has ever witnessed.

And so Limerick, the almost universal favourites, lost. It's too bad there had to be a loser and a winner, because although the men from the West undeniably got the drop on the Shannonsiders, Limerick played fine hurling, and on almost any other day against any other side would certainly give a better account for themselves.

In such a game it is almost invidious to single out individuals, but if skill and heart

Eamon Cregan, Limerick, right, and Niall McInerney, Galway, in the 1980 All Ireland final.

could have done it Eamon Cregan, the top scorer of the match, would have single handedly won the trophy.'

One of Eamon's greatest displays was at centre-back for Limerick on a very wet Sunday afternoon in September 1973 against the reigning champions Kilkenny in the All Ireland final. He had the ideal temperament for the task — a temperament laced with steel, skill and stamina.

He minimised the threat of ace Kilkenny centreforward Pat Delaney — sealed effectively the road to goal through the centre — was the springboard from which Limerick successfully warded off the Kilkenny challenge. There was confidence, discipline and class in his display, and he was flanked that day by Sean Foley who gave a superlative display and Phil Bennis who with his uncompromising approach didn't give an inch. 'No way was I going to let Pat Delaney pass me and hop the ball on the ground and thunder through for scores as I had seen him do in other games. The decision to transfer me to centre-back for the final gave me a certain phychological advantage in the position. Kilkenny had never seen me play at centre-back and were unfamiliar with my style of play and approach to the game in that position. I had of course played most of my club hurling at centre-back so I was no stranger to the defensive role.'

His display against Tipperary in the opening round of the championship in 1966 heralded what lay ahead from Eamon Cregan the hurler. Tipperary had comprehensively defeated Kilkenny and Wexford in the All Ireland finals of 1964 and 1965 respectively and looked odds on to make it three in a row in 1966. But a scintillating display from Cregan whose speed and skill saw him score a total of 3:5 toppled Tipperary from the hurling pedestal.

He was sent off once in a game against Clare after scoring a great goal that was immediately followed by a flare up. When the tangle was unravelled he was incorrectly singled out by the referee as the culprit and sidelined. Eamon makes no secret of the fact that there are many occasions when action in around the goalmouth is no tea-party. It reminded me of the story I was told about Mick Mackey and a Limerick county final when a Clare referee called Quane was brought in to take charge. It seems that in the very early stages an Ahane attack saw Mick Mackey and John Mackey and the two defenders marking them embroiled in heated exchanges that didn't impress the referee. He called all four aside and announced he was sending them off and set about taking their names. Then Mick intervened — he could be a great diplomat if the occasion required diplomacy. Said Mick 'Why would you do that — what will the crowd think — they came to see a county final — this is a county final you know — not a lawn tennis tournament.' Diplomacy won or was it gentle persuasion. No one was sent off.

I wondered how he saw the future of Limerick hurling and queried too why such fine teams and players in the period from 1971 to 1984 didn't win a few more titles. 'Limerick will have to change their style of hurling and revert to playing effective ground hurling. They will have to overcome and cast aside living with the "might have beens". In this regard Wexford and Galway and to a lesser extent Clare must

do the same. The schools, the County Board and coaching can play a major part. Answering why we didn't win more is not easy. It is of course one of my regrets. We played some wonderful hurling that enriched the game — a style that was marvellously entertaining and very exciting — but we didn't have the depth of talent available to Cork and Kilkenny and in recent times in Galway — probably lacked balance in our team at times — had some very hard luck — the advantage rule often worked against us as did some refereeing decisions — and there were occasions when we conceded soft goals which you can't do at top level.'

But he does see hope for the future even if it is based partly on omen and portents. 'Sexton St CBS won the Harty Cup in 1932 — there followed a golden era in Limerick hurling. They won it again in the period 1964 to '67 — Limerick were once again a hurling power to match the best and give wonderful entertainment.

This year 1993 has seen another Harty Cup success at Sexton St. Maybe there are good days ahead.

Three occasions stand out as memorable in a hurling career that was filled with memories.

The first goes back to when he was eleven years of age. He won his first County juvenile medal in the under sixteen category. He played in goal.

Next comes the Harty Cup success of 1964 when he captained Sexton St CBS. 'We lived and died for Harty Cup success and took a tremendous pride in it. You had to be in Sexton St to understand what it meant to the school to win the Harty Cup.' Our trainers were Jim Hennessy and Br Michael Burke. They knew their hurling. They insisted that we play the game at high speed and to concentrate mainly on ground hurling. We used the wings and fast ground balls to open up defences'.

And finally there is the success of 1973 — Munster champions — All Ireland champions 'We did unbelievable training for that championship. We never came off the pitch tired. We could have played for two hours.'

Did your Dad witness the glory of 1973? I had touched a tender cord. It showed in the expression and in the downcast eyes. It was a moment of emotion and poignancy as he suppressed the sadness that had surfaced within him. After a short silent pause which I observed in empathy with him, he responded.

'Its twenty years now but it still hurts. He died in August 1972. He stopped going to matches in 1964. He used get too excited and that was bad for him. In 1967 he got ill. After a match I would go up to the room to talk to him in bed. I would analyse for him what happened and tell him what went on. That's how he learned about the games and stayed in touch.'

On the way back from Croke Park after the All Ireland victory of 1973 there was great rejoicing. It had been a sweet victory over Kilkenny. It was a time for celebration — and mirth and laughter and song. The train stopped at Castleconnell and the team travelled from there to Limerick by road — open vehicle. 'The crowd was enormous. It took two hours to travel from three miles out, to Honan's Quay in the city. On the way we passed our house. Mick Herbert, Limerick full-back of the late forties said to me — you are very quiet.' His thoughts were with his father.

Shelley expressed it well:

We look before and after,
And pine for what is not:
Our sincerest laughter
With some pain is fraught;
Our sweetest songs are those that tell of
saddest thought.

The victorious Limerick team of 1973

Seamus Horgan

Willie Moore   Pat Hartigan   Jim O'Brien

Phil Bennis   Eamon Cregan   Sean Foley

Richie Bennis   Eamon Grimes (capt)

Bernie Hartigan   Moss Dowling   Liam O'Donoghue

Frankie Nolan   Ned Rea   Joe McKenna

Born: 1947

my family life. My wife Madeleine was a great enthusiast and enjoyed all the games and after-match celebrations. My family were also fortunate to see me play with Blackrock and Kilkenny and share the successes with me. I can still remember the Monday night after the '82 All Ireland travelling back to Kilkenny with my wife, son Alan and daughter Deirdre carrying the cup. Alan is playing with Blackrock and maybe some day he might wear the red and white of Cork. Gerard's preference is for rugby. Jennifer who is five years old might play camogie. I got a lot out of the game during my career and sometime I would like to put something back into it — maybe coaching or training the youngsters.

Hurling in my opinion is the greatest field sport of all and I would advise all young people to play the game for the games sake and to play it sportingly.

Frank Cummins.

"

66

On Sunday April 12th at 3pm I was delighted to meet Brendan and Mary Fullam at my home. It was a great evening of chat about hurling present and past. Brendan asked me to write a few words about my career. Where will I begin?

I began to play at the age of five in the Stoneyford National School with my brothers and school pals. I then went to Belcamp College in Dublin and while a student there I was very lucky to have Father Connellan and Father Scully as coaches. Both priests had a big influence on my career. While attending Belcamp College I probably played more football than hurling and the team reached the Colleges Final in 1965.

My first outing with Kilkenny was in the Oireachtas final in November '66 and from then on I was more or less a regular with the team. I have played with and against many players during my playing days and to me the most important thing above all else is the friendship. Playing the game meant more to me than victory or defeat. Hurling and the GAA played a large part in

W hen Frank Cummins was growing up the talk in Kilkenny would have been about the 1947 All Ireland victory and to a lesser extent about the 1939 triumph — both against Cork and won coincidentally on each occasion by a point scored in the dying seconds. Jimmy Kelly was the hero in '39. Terry Leahy stole the limelight in '47. 'We heard about Terry Leahy morning, noon and night. But we also heard about Paddy Grace and Jack Mulcahy and Mark Marnell.'

The 1957 team is better remembered by Frank. He was ten and Denis Heaslip from the local club was a great favourite of his. 'I remember going to the local village for a wet battery for the radio to listen to the final. Ollie Walsh was my hero. I used wear a badge of Ollie made from a paper cutting on my coat going to school. My teacher was mad about Ollie too.' Both were able to celebrate on All Ireland day as Kilkenny defeated Waterford by one point — again a closing stages victory. It was the fourth successive time that Kilkenny took the title by one point. It started with victory over Limerick in 1935.

Frank's senior career began in 1966 with an Oireachtas game and he was a sub on the team that beat Tipperary the following year. He didn't establish himself on the team until the All Ireland final of 1969 when Cork were defeated and from then until he retired he operated at midfield for his county. Timmy Ryan of Limerick covered a similar span at midfield from 1930 to 1945. What a combination the two would have made.

Frank's career coincided with what was probably Kilkenny's greatest hurling era. He won major honours with county, province and his Cork club Blackrock. They include eight All Ireland medals counting his first as a sub in 1967, six Railway Cup victories and six county titles. He also won five Munster club titles with Blackrock and three of those were converted to All Ireland club victories in 1972, '74 and '79. He was part of Leinster's best ever run in the Railway cup when winning five in a row from 1971 to '75. His All Irelands were won in three different decades and he became the fifth Kilkenny man to win seven All Ireland medals on the field of play.

The sacrifice involved for a player so active as Frank for over such a long spell is quite enormous. Fortunately for him his wife Madeleine — a Cork woman — was a great enthusiast. All games Frank played in were seen as a family outing. As we talked Madeleine joined in and it was very clear she had a deep knowledge of the game and the players and when Frank set about picking his team Madeleine was able to remind him of the options for the different positions and the relative value of various players. She had come a long way since the day he first took her to Wexford Park to see a match he was playing. He drove the car into the embankment and positioned it so she would have a good view. To his con-

sternation she asked him who had won when the game was over.

I decided to ask Madeleine what in her estimation were his greatest moments because by now I had discovered she was Frank's greatest critic. She selected two. 'He played a league game in Nowlan Park against Tipperary in 1971. He was at centre-back. He hit everything that came his way and cleaned up all before him. Kilkenny won and he was awarded Sportstar of the Week in the *Irish Independent*. It was richly deserved. I think it was the finest game of hurling I ever saw him play. My second choice would be the 1983 All Ireland final against Cork. A very strong wind blew into the Railway goal and Kilkenny faced this in the second half with a six point lead that hardly seemed adequate. Frank kept dropping back from midfield to be under the long Cork puckouts. Himself and Ger Henderson did trojan work as they kept putting the ball downfield again. It was the toughest game I ever went through on the stand. I remember at one stage in the second half when the pressure was really on and Frank dropped his hurley to handpass the ball — a free of course. I nearly died and said aloud O Sacred Heart of Jesus what's wrong with him. Seconds later a Cork back did the same so I felt that there must be shocking pressure out there.' Frank confirmed that it was a pressure game and reminded me that Kilkenny didn't score in the last eighteen minutes. 'We played a defensive game in the second half. Those were our instructions. Our centrefield fell back hoping to pick up the breaking ball. It worked like a dream.'

It was a good year for Frank. He won Leinster, All Ireland and National league titles. He was selected as Hurler of the Year and to these was added his fourth All Star award. Indeed, the previous year, hurling followers will recall that he was equally outstanding at centrefield in a different type of game against Cork. He went into that final with broken ribs without realising it and played the full hour conscious only of some discomfort. It was a good year too —

ship Frank came up to take a penalty for Blackrock and to the delight of Blackrock supporters shook the net. His son Alan who was about four at the time in a spontaneous outburst of admiration announced to all around him — 'That's my Dad.' So much for anonymity.

Frank was probably not a classical hurler in the strict sense. But he was a superb midfielder — extremely effective and always very fit. There was an attacking and defensive dimension attaching to his game. He had the capacity to pace his game — an essential element in a midfielder. And he could pick off long range points — the kind of hurling skill that breaks the heart of opposing defences — indeed whole teams.

He was a great striker of a ball and could deliver a huge work-rate. A man of high sporting standards, he was durable and had high levels of strength, steel and stamina. It was a combination that rattled many a sturdy opponent. Tim Crowley of Cork is light years away from being a weakling but in the All Ireland final of 1982 when he went down from a shoulder from Frank Cummins beside the sideline on the Hogan Stand side it shook every bone in his body. Frank was a man of bronze — immensely strong. Little wonder someone once said of him — 'Frank Cummins wasn't born — he was quarried.'

Leinster, All Ireland and National league titles followed by an All Star award to add to the two he had collected in 1971 and '72.

Madeleine told me that when the family went to a game they would in order to preserve a level of anonymity always shout 'Come on Frank' instead of 'Come on Dad'. One day in a Cork county champion-

This is Frank's team selected from the men he played against and therefore excluding fellow Kilkennymen.

Pat Nolan (Wexford)

Tom Neville (Wexford)   Pat Hartigan (Limerick)   Pat Fleury (Offaly)

Tom Cashman (Cork)   Mick Jacob (Wexford)   Iggy Clarke (Galway)

Frank Cummins (Kilkenny)   John Connolly (Galway)

Martin Quigley (Wexford)   Gerald McCarthy (Cork)   Jimmy Doyle (Tipperary)

Jimmy Barry Murphy (Cork)   Ray Cummins (Cork)   Michael Keating (Tipp)

Born: 1894

He was one of Clare's greatest hurling sons and where All Ireland success was concerned he was their most decorated hero.

He got his first taste of hurling glory with the Clare junior team when they convincingly defeated Laois on the score 6:5 to 1:1 in the 1914 final. Tommy was in goal. The county senior team under trainer Jim Hehir — father of Mícheál — completed the double that year when they too beat Laois. Nobody would have believed then that it would be seventy nine years before Clare would win another All Ireland hurling crown. That was in 1993 when they had a sweet junior victory over Kilkenny. Despite the appalling conditions caused by incessant rain, Clare played determined first time hurling and when the final whistle blew had satisfied their ever faithful supporters.

When Tommy Daly, later to become Dr Tommy Daly, took up residence in Dublin he couldn't under the rules of the day play for any county but Dublin. His ability as a goalkeeper was quickly spotted in Dublin and he was on the 1917 team that surprised many by defeating the reigning champions Tipperary — captained by the renowned Johnny Leahy. Also on the winning Dublin team was his fellow countyman Brendan Considine.

Further honours came Tommy's way when Dublin won All Ireland crowns in 1920, 1924 and 1927 at the expense of Cork, Galway and Cork respectively. He was on the losing side in 1919 when they went under to Cork and in 1921 when Limerick triumphed. The 1927 victory was somewhat like the 1917 one — rather unexpected. Even though Dublin had an extremely fit and powerful combination they were facing a Cork team of considerable talent who were reigning champions. Dublin had nine of the famous Garda team in their lineout — four of them from Clare — Pa 'Fowler' McInerney, Tom O'Rourke, Jack Gleeson and Ned Fahy. Add to that Tommy Daly and you have five Claremen bringing fame and honour to their adopted Dublin with a smashing 4:8 to 1:3 win over Cork captained by Sean Óg Murphy and parading other great names such as Eudi Coughlan, Jim Hurley, Dinny Barry Murphy, Jim O'Regan, Paddy Delea and Mick Leahy.

Tommy was selected in goal for Leinster on the Railway Cup team of 1927 — the inaugural year. They defeated Munster in a thrilling game of hurling. The following year he was on the losing side when Munster won by 2:2 to 1:2. In 1933 (now with his native Clare) he was selected in goal for Munster only to lose by that one goal margin again 4:6 to 3:6. He was also chosen on the Tailteann Games team of 1928 together with fellow Clareman Tull Considine.

By virtue of a new rule that allowed players declare for their native county Tommy Daly declared for Clare in 1928 and lined out in the blue and gold. Other Claremen followed suit. Between then and

1932 Clare threatened to breakthrough. They faced Cork in the Munster final of 1932. On paper the lineout looked strong and very experienced with men like Tommy Daly, Pa 'Fowler' McInerney, John Joe Doyle, Larry Blake, Tull Considine, Jim Houlihan, Mick Falvey and Jim Mullane. Yet the odds seemed stacked against them. Cork looked the form team. They were still enjoying the epic victory of 1931 when they accounted for Kilkenny in the All Ireland final after two draws and a replay. As well as that they had been All Ireland champions in 1926, 1928 and 1929. But Clare struck form and won a famous victory — the first since 1914 — on the score 5:2 to 4:1 and Tommy Daly proudly collected his first Munster senior hurling medal. Hopes were high in Clare of an All Ireland crown when Galway were beaten in the semi-final. Kilkenny now stood between Clare and glory and a fifth All Ireland senior medal for Tommy Daly. At the final whistle it was that one goal margin again with Kilkenny inspired by Lory Meagher coming out on top 3:3 to 2:3 — and it was generally agreed that over the hour fortune slightly favoured the Nore-siders.

Tommy Daly gave many inspired displays of goalkeeping and in hurling circles his name is synonymous with brilliance between the posts.

He was a prominent referee in his day and he had charge of the memorable All Ireland Final of 1935 between Kilkenny and Limerick. He died following a fatal car accident at Tuamgraney in East Clare in September 1936 aged 42.

In his native Tulla the local pitch is named after him. He is also remembered in ballad. These verses are from Bryan MacMahon's composition:

On the windswept Hill of Tulla,
Where the Claremen place their dead,
Four solemn yews stand sentinel,
Above a hurler's head,
And from the broken North lands
From Burren bleak and bare,
The dirge of Tommy Daly
Goes surging on through Clare.

To think that never once again
He'll don with lithesome air
The claret-gold of Tulla
Nor the blue and gold of Clare.
— Perhaps they'll pray when feasts are high
And healed the wounds of fight
God rest you Tommy Daly
On your windswept hill tonight.

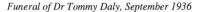

Funeral of Dr Tommy Daly, September 1936

Born: 1955

Offaly were outsiders in 1981 against Galway in the All Ireland final. Throughout most of the first half there was a fluency about Galway's hurling that threatened to turn to a torrent and engulf Offaly. The experience gained through the seventies was clearly evident in Galway. They had class players in several positions. It seemed as if they would win pulling up. And yet despite playing what at times looked like exhibition stuff they weren't reflecting their superiority on the scoreboard.

Each Offaly man was sticking grimly to his task — no frills — no fancy stuff — just total concentration on the basics. On every countenance there was resolve and determination. And none more so than on that of Pat Delaney. He played a key role in Offaly's historic win. At centreback he was cool and steadfast and inspired confidence. Within a minute of the start he pointed a seventy yards free and throughout the game demonstrated his accuracy from long distances. He finished the game as Offaly's top scorer with five points. At half time Offaly were in arrears 0:13 to 1:4 and spectators waited for the floodgates to open. But it didn't happen. The tenacity and doggedness that was to become a hallmark of Offaly hurling in the decade ahead manifested itself that day and proved to be a trump card.

In any close game it can be difficult to pinpoint a turning point but a number of factors can be identified as tilting the scales in Offaly's favour. From the outset and even when it seemed they might be outclassed they displayed a non-panic mentality. Galway had a goal disallowed at a crucial stage in the first half. Damien Martin was making superb saves in goal and inspiring his defenders — a crucial save from a shot by Noel Lane late in the second half probably lost the game for Galway. The introduction of Brendan Keeshan to the Offaly defence tightened it

"

    Where I lived in the Sliabh Bloom mountains the only pastime we had when we were young was the game of hurling. We listened to the broadcasts of Mícheál O'Hehir and played stormers after it. We became the John Doyles, Jimmy Doyle, Mackey McKenna, Liam Devaneys until dark. Tipp were the hurling power of that era 1964/65. Then at about the age of twelve my job in Kinnity hurling field was to puck the ball back from behind the goal to the senior players who won a championship in 1967 against Coolderry after thirty-seven years — ironically it was Coolderry they beat in 1930. It was the late Tom Mitchell from that team who brought me to my first All Ireland in 1969.

    Offaly's Paddy Molloy, a hurling genius, was my idol at that time. Little did I think myself that I would be playing in Croke Park in a Leinster minor championship semi-final in 1973 at centre-back. We lost by two points to a very good Wexford team who subsequently lost to Kilkenny and who won the All Ireland easily. There were a lot of disappointments between my first day hurling in Croke Park and 1980. "

Pat Delaney

up considerably and he made some fine first time clearances. Johnny Flaherty's goal that put Offaly into the lead came at a most psychological moment with only five minutes to go. And throughout the entire game Pat Delaney dominated at centreback — a key position on the hurling field. He deserved to be Hurler of the Year in 1981. How did you feel before the '81 final? 'I'd say we didn't realise what it was going to be like. Dermot Healy said to us that when we hit the tunnel we would hear a boom that would terrify us. The craic was now gone. This was serious stuff.'

Pat had his own views on training. 'I would puck a ball all day and love it but I detested physical training. I cycled three miles to National School and back. I cycled three miles to hurl. I thinned turnips and beet and saved hay. I never had hamstring trouble or broken bones. I didn't need physical training.' He recalled that in 1985 for the first round of the Leinster championship with Kilkenny he had done no physical training. 'I was down in Cork where I did the kind of training I loved — pucking the ball around. In the game against Kilkenny which ended in a draw I had my finest hour. I felt super fit. No matter where I went that day in Croke Park the ball followed me.' 1985 was a testing year for Offaly as they attempted to erase the memory of the Centenary year defeat by Cork. 'To lose two in a row would have been unthinkable. I can remember feeling a real sense of pressure in that All Ireland final. No matter what a mistake mustn't be made. It was going to be a case of concentrate and cover for the whole hour. We were cuter than in earlier years — we gave away less frees. I can still see Joe Cooney coming in with the ball — we kept going back — closed him down — baulked him and brought the ball to the ground.' At the final whistle it was victory for Offaly and a second All Ireland crown. For Pat it was a year that brought him his first All Star award.

In decades to come the memories that will remain vivid in Pat's mind all relate to occasions of defeat. His first day in Croke Park was for the Leinster final of 1969 between Kilkenny and Offaly. He was one of fourteen that a neighbour carried in a van to the match. However, in order to qualify for the free trip he had to assist with one man and two girls at the making of forty seven trams of hay on the Saturday before. He cried that day in Croke Park when the match was over. His heroes had come so near 3:9 to 0:16. 'Paddy Molloy was my idol. He scored the best point I ever saw that day. From his right corner forward position he crossed over and chased Ollie Walsh along the left wing to the corner of the Nally Stand — dispossessed him — and in full flight from an acute angle sent over a glorious point. My namesake on the Kilkenny team Pat Delaney of Johnstown got the three goals.' The Leinster final defeat of 1982 at the hands of Kilkenny still niggles. It was a game of very close man to man marking. Every score had to be earned. 'It was a marvellous game. The ball flew from end to end. Both sets of backs were exceptional. We had matured and improved vastly since 1980. It was probably the best Offaly team I played on. Yet we won nothing — made our exit in the Leinster final.' Both teams had twelve scores but Kilkenny got the only goal of the day — engineered by the quick thinking brain of Liam Fennelly — and it proved decisive. In the All Ireland semi-final of 1989 against Antrim Pat would have wished in the last quarter to see the ground open up and swallow them. The legs were giving up. 'When you were young you could cover off for colleagues. Now at thirty four I couldn't do it. And when Antrim put on the pressure and got vital scores in the final stages, we hadn't the reserves to respond and come back.' For Pat it was a defeat of deep disappointment. With a Leinster title at the expense of Kilkenny under their belt backed up by the vast experience gained in contesting ten successive Leinster finals — victorious in six — it was felt that the team had the necessary ingredients to take another All Ireland title. Ní mar a shíltear a bhítear.

One of his unfulfilled ambitions was the

failure of his club Kinnity to win either a Leinster or All Ireland club title. 'We played in three Leinster finals and on two of those occasions the team that defeated us went on to win the All Ireland title. To win a major title with your club is to win something for the very grassroots of the association — it is very special.'

Pat was a thoughtful player and he planned ahead. Every Christmas he purchased six Randall hurleys. Special attention was paid to the balance and the weight was paired down to one and a half pounds. He always took three of those hurleys to Croke Park. As a defender he was rock-like rather than stylish — composed rather than classy — calculating rather than flamboyant. In a distinguished career opponents learned that Pat was an extremely difficult player on which to excel.

Which way to go? Tony Doran grips the sliotar.

Born: 1946

"

I first started to play competitive hurling in the newly inaugurated Nicky Rackard Rural Schools league in 1956.

Attending National school in Boolavogue I played with Monageer-Boolavogue where my first coaches were Boolavogue Curate Fr Noel Hartley and Monageer teacher Mr Jim Doran. The highlight of that first years competition in which we eventually lost at the semi-final stage to Rathnure was when we played Bally-oughter in the quarter final and Nicky Rackard himself refereed.

In the years since then I have been lucky to have a number of high spots in my career with both club and county since I started with Buffers Alley in juvenile (under 16) in 1959 and Wexford minors in 1963.

Winning the All Ireland senior with Wexford in 1968 was a great honour and one of the highlights, while beating the all conquering Kilkenny of the first half of the seventies by seventeen points in the Leinster final was another great moment. Losing two All Irelands to Cork in 1976 and 1977 was very disappointing. In '76 we played well but were still beaten by four points in a great game and in '77, although I think we did not do ourselves justice on

the day, we were only denied a draw by a great Martin Coleman save from Christy Keogh in the dying moments. I think my greatest disappointment was losing to Offaly in the 1981 Leinster final. I was carried off in the early stages with a severe head injury and only heard the last few minutes on radio from a hospital bed.

Winning the 1989 All Ireland club championship with Buffers Alley, when we beat O'Donovan Rossa from Belfast in the final, was the real highlight of my career. Winning with a team from a small rural community and seeing the joy it brought to everyone — players, officials, supporters — was something words could not really describe. Coming as it did twenty one years after winning the All Ireland with Wexford made me appreciate it even more.

I think the rules, if they are properly interpreted by officials are fairly OK. I would never believe in changing rules for the sake of change, only if there is something positive to be gained. I did not agree with doing away with the palmed score, as I think the alternative of kicking scores is much more dangerous and untidy. Also I think it has reduced the number of goals scored, which means less excitement from a spectators point of view.

"

I take it Tony that you have at last retired? — was my opening question. He laughed. 'I didn't see it in the papers yet.' I posed the question because you never know with Tony: he just seems to go on forever. And then I discovered that this year (1992) he actually played junior club hurling — and he in his forty-seventh year.

He won his last major title in September 1991 when Wexford defeated Kildare in the over forties All Ireland Masters Hurling title. He played a captain's part in the 2:14

to 1:8 victory and had a personal tally of four points. I can't shake off the feeling that if there is an over fifties competition he'll be back — the strength, the fitness, the power and the stamina will all be there.

It all began for Tony in the big time when he played a tournament game with Wexford in New Ross in 1964 at the age of 18 — followed by league and Oireachtas games in 1965 and 1966. By 1967 he had established his claims to a permanent place on the panel and won his first league medal. His childhood hero and idol was Nicky Rackard. Still etched in Tony's memory is the day in 1956 when Nicky refereed a juvenile league quarter final. His young world took on an even brighter hue and they all felt six foot tall in the presence of their ero — a camán colossus.

He was chosen as Texaco Hurler of the Year in 1976 and his vast collection of medals and trophies include every major honour in the game. I therefore wondered if there had been any one particular moment of deep disappointment.

'If there was only one it wouldn't be too bad. There were many. One of the biggest was my departure from the 1981 Leinster final against Offaly. I was stretchered off after about 10 or 12 minutes — it was the only time I ever went off. The fact that I took so little part was very disappointing. I listened to the closing moments in hospital and it didn't help my morale to hear the final whistle announced with Wexford on the wrong side of a score of 3:12 to 2:13. I suppose after that the two in a row losses to Cork in 1976 and 1977 would be high on the list. You see we had beaten good Kilkenny teams in the Leinster finals of those years. We beat them well in 1976 — 2:20 to 1:6. It was closer in 1977 — 3:17 to 3:14. In the 1976 semi final we had two great games with Galway at Páirc Uí Chaoimh — winning the replay by one goal. Our scoring rate was high 5:14 to 2:23 in the drawn game and 3:14 to 2:14 in the replay. We were confident against Cork and went eight points up very early on. We faded somewhat in the last quarter. Half the team were over thirty — it had been a warm summer — the two games against Galway may have taken a toll. We played well enough to win but failed in the end by 2:21 to 4:11. In 1977 we didn't play well on the day — yet we came very close to snatching it — 1:17 to 3:8'.

Throughout the first half of the seventies Kilkenny were brilliant. Wexford faced them in every Leinster final from 1971 to 1975, providing some rousing performances and superb hurling. Did Tony think that Wexford were capable of capturing the McCarthy Cup in any of those years?

'Yes — I think 1974 — even though Kilkenny were probably at their peak. We were playing very well against them in the Leinster final of that year when misfortune struck. Just on the stroke of half time Phil Wilson was sent off.

We were down to fourteen men. We continued to play inspired hurling. Eddie Keher won it for Kilkenny by a point with the last puck of the game and Kilkenny went on to All Ireland success with decisive 12 point wins over Galway and Limerick.'

The parish is very dear to all hurlers. It's the cradle from which they emerge and grow into the big time. Victory for the parish is always memorable. You celebrate with your own and are feted by them. It's special. One of Tony's enduring moments will always be the victory over O'Donovan Rossa of Antrim in the All Ireland Club final of 1989 and the feelings of pride and elation felt by the entire locality after the great win. It was the first time a Wexford club had captured the trophy.

As a hurler I would describe Tony as inspirational rather than classical — stout hearted rather than stylish — brave rather than opportunist. He could absorb punishment with a smile: he never drew a foul stroke. The hand that clutched a thousand sliotars from the sky hasn't a mark on it — testimony to his skill at protecting it. There was a Matt the Thresher air about his style — his efforts were always herculean, the stuff of legend and folklore, readymade to be cast in the Táin — and possessing the charisma to match the role. He presented all fullbacks with problems and mentioned three in particular that he admired — Eugene Coughlan of Offaly, Pa Dillon of Kilkenny and Pat Hartigan of Limerick.

In 1968 Tipperary were still a formidable hurling force. They had comprehensive wins in 1964 and 1965 over Kilkenny and Wexford respectively and in 1971 they were still good enough to shade it over a quite talented Kilkenny fifteen.

So how could Wexford and Tony Doran in his first All Ireland final hope to do in 1968 against the men of Tipperary? Well, they produced a power packed second half that had the Munster champions reeling and Tony Doran in the forward line caused consternation in the Tipperary defence. 'I was centre forward in the first half — got a hurling lesson for twenty minutes from

Mick Roche — didn't see much of the ball — and moved to full forward before half time. We went in eight points down.' Wexford came out in the second half and set about getting back into the reckoning. Tony got a goal followed by further scores including a goal by Paul Lynch that levelled matters. There followed eight to nine minutes without a score. Then it began to happen for Wexford. 'I got my second goal — I will always remember that goal that put us in front. More scores and a goal by Jack Berry and we were eight points up and we were on our way to victory.'

Goodly news, goodly news, do I bring
Youth of Forth
Goodly news shall you hear Bargy man

I can still hear Mícheál O'Hehir describing Tony's goal that gave Wexford the lead. 'It's a goal, it's a goal — the red haired Tony Doran — the man from Boolavogue.' My father-in-law, the late Henry Armstrong — a great lover of history, Irish and folklore — taught Tony Doran — not hurling — just the three R's. He was extremely proud of his pupil's 1968 performance and rejoiced in Tony's All Ireland success and in his many gallant performances afterwards.

Tony was still doing gaisce when Wexford met Kilkenny in the Leinster semi-final of 1984. His goal with a left-handed stroke in the dying moments of Dick O'Hara after he had gained possession on the Hill 16 side of the Railway goal and moved towards the centre, put Wexford into the lead and sent their supporters delirious with excitement. Tony was no longer the nimble youth of 1968. But he was still deadly around goal and the old warrior celebrated his goal by taking a leap into the air as he came outfield. I thought the ground would shake with the thud when he came down.

1968 was a wonderful Wexford win. The celebrations that followed awakened memories of 1955, '56 and '60. The defeats of 1962 and 1965 at the hands of Tipperary were avenged. The pride of the fifties stirred again. They returned bearing victory amid great rejoicing throughtout Co Wexford. — in Enniscorthy, Rathnure and 'in Boolavogue as the sun was setting.'

Stiff flags flying in the night wind cold
In the gloom black purple
In the glint old gold

In the decades that followed Wexford produced as good if not better combinations. They deserved success — seemed capable of achieving it — were poised for glory on a number of occasions — but fate frowned on them.

In a career that spanned almost twenty years in top class hurling Tony has known all the joys of victory and the many disappointments of defeat. Now at forty-seven he is very philosophical about it all. 'Just to have played was wonderful.'

Tony selected a team from the men of his era after a lot of thought — sifting through three or four candidates for each position. The credentials of each was carefully considered and weighed on the balance. This is what emerged.

Noel Skehan (Kilkenny)

Fan Larkin (Kilkenny) Pat Hartigan (Limerick) Dan Quigley (Wexford)

Ger Henderson (Kilkenny) Mick Roche (Tipperary) Iggy Clarke (Galway)

Phil Wilson (Wexford) Frank Cummins (Kilkenny)

Jimmy Doyle (Tipperary) Pat Delaney (Kilkenny) Eddie Keher (Kilkenny)

Ray Cummins (Cork) Tony Doran (Wexford) Eamon Cregan (Limerick)

"

I played in my first Senior All Ireland final with Kilkenny in 1972 against Cork when I was fifteen. I can't remember the score but we were beaten. However, it was the only defeat Kilkenny suffered in an All Ireland final. My sister Ann has been a team mate on every occasion since and is also the holder of eleven All Irelands. Throughout those twenty odd years it's impossible to describe the enjoyment and pinpoint memorable occasions but I would have to say that my most memorable recollection is winning my eleventh All Ireland with Kilkenny in 1991 against Cork. I had the additional enjoyment of captaining a winning All Ireland team for the third occasion, on President Mary Robinson's first official visit to a camogie All Ireland final. Having said that some of my greatest memories are from club championship games played with the legendary St Paul's and later with Lisdowney.

Throughout all those years we played against some great players such as Margaret Lacey, Elsie Cody, Catherine Murphy, Orla Ni Siochain, Marian Sweeney, Mary O'Leary, Pat Moloney, Hanna Dineen and Sheila Murray.

Some of the greatest Kilkenny players I admired and played with when as many titles didn't flow Kilkenny's way, include Mary Conway, Phil and Carmel O'Shea, Helena & Teresa O'Neill, Nuala Duncan and the greatest of all camogie players Liz Neary — who has a record number of colleges, club and inter-county All Irelands which in my opinion will never be equalled.

It was fantastic being part of the great seven in a row team of the eighties under the guidance of Tom Ryan. He instilled that great determination and will to win in each and every player which is so vital if one is to be successful.

Angela Downey "

Born: 1957

Since the Senior Camogie Championship began in 1932 only five counties have succeeded in winning the title — Dublin, Cork, Kilkenny, Antrim and Wexford — while a total of thirteen counties have contested the finals. Kilkenny have been the dominant power in recent times and completed a run of seven in a row in 1991.

A key figure in those victories was Angela Downey — Camogie Player of the Year in 1977. Indeed, since she came on the scene in 1972 she has grown in stature yearly and is now a household name. She is without doubt the Lory Meagher of Kilkenny camogie — matchlessly talented and endowed with a vast repetoire of hurling skills.

Kilkenny won their first title in 1974 when they beat Cork after a replay. To date they have won eleven titles and Angela has participated in all of them. She has also won National League titles and has been successful at inter-provincial level. On the club front she has won All Ireland titles and numerous county titles. Throughout her career she has always displayed remarkably high levels of dedication, fitness, courage, resolve and leadership. Her's was a never-say-die spirit. Her skills and attributes on the pitch must on many occasions have made her the envy of many less talented county senior hurling male mortals.

Daughter of Shem, who played with Kilkenny from 1946 to 1954 and who took part in the memorable final of 1947 against Cork, she has failed, despite her fame, to shake off the tag of being Shem Downey's daughter. It leaves her with a double identity with the person of Angela Downey being on occasions subordinated to that of Shem Downey's daughter. This was brought home to her on a visit to the west of Ireland when she was introduced to the late 'Inky' Flaherty of Galway. They shook hands. In the course of conversation it was revealed she was Shem's daughter — result, another handshake.

When Angela started her camogie career the established outfit for camogie players was the gymslip and blouse and Kilkenny wore saffron and white. Angela recalled how warm one tended to get in the gymslip and how uncomfortable it could be. In 1974 Kilkenny broke with tradition and produced a new outfit consisting of a skirt and jersey — and the colours — black and amber of course.

It is sad to record that her great club St Paul's which was established in 1973 has ceased to exist since 1990. 'It disbanded as we had no junior team and there were no new players coming along.' Under camogie rules one has to play with a club in order to be eligible to play at county level. So Angela and her twin sister Ann threw in their lot with Lisdowney and the club proceeded to capture two county titles.

I asked her if she regarded the game as safe to play. 'It's like any other game — if you are fit and properly coached — if you have the skills and understand the game then it is safe.' Angela has escaped serious injury but has had her front teeth damaged on a number of occasions.

Many camogie games have served up outstanding fare and great entertainment — the kind of stuff that banishes or staves off for just a while the world's intrusions. Such a game was the 1986 All Ireland club final between Glen Rovers of Cork and St Paul's of Kilkenny played at Pairc an Gleanna and won by Glen Rovers on the score 4:11 to 5:7 — a mere point. In an article on the game in the *Sunday Tribune* of 18 January, 1987 Kevin Cashman described some of the many talents of Angela — the wonder girl of the camogie world.

The best and most passionate hurling of all of 1986 was served up, that afternoon in deepest Blackpool ... And scores born of rare and profound artistry — and enslavement to art — abounded ... And so a few minutes from the end, the Glen were two goals clear. Then Angela Downey took a hand. St Paul's made three or perhaps four incursions into Glen Rovers territory in those minutes and twice she drove the sliotar to the net ... That day in October she scored four goals and five points. Four of the points were object lessons in close-in free-taking: driven with full power a few feet above the crossbar. Her third goal came when her team's cause looked hopeless. She stole a breaking ball some twenty yards from Glen Rovers goal and to the left. Expertly shepherded by two Glen defenders she seemed to have nowhere to go. But she shielded it and got to the fifteen yards line a little to the right. And then, with no room for a full swing she dropped it towards her toes and clipped it half pace across the keeper and off a post to the net. Shortly before halftime she sprinted on to a ball bounding fast and awkwardly away to the left from the Glen goalmouth. She brought it to hand with one touch; and without checking, she struck lefthanded on the very next stride and a point bisected the crossbar. Of the twelve forwards who played in the All Ireland senior hurling final nine could not attempt, never mind execute, that brace of scores.

The essence of greatness is that it consistently proves itself and intermittently surpasses itself. So it is with Angela Downey.

gela and Ann Downey, Kilkenny's camogie twins.

"

Won my first Senior All Ireland as a sub in 1974. Played in thirteen finals (two replays) and won eleven. Started my camogie with primary school Ballyragget. Joined St Paul's when a very good friend of the family Paddy Conway persuaded his daughter Mary to take us on board. Won every county final from our first year 1973 to the time St Paul's disbanded in 1990.

Biggest thrill was to be the winning captain in 1990 with a great win over Cork.

Most memorable game was the success of St Paul's against Glenamaddy in the club All Ireland in 1988. My memories are not because the game was a classic, but because it was one game that just had to be won against all the odds. Twenty hours before the final was due to be played the game was called off. The following Saturday, Central Council held a meeting and put Angela out of the game for six months. Never was a club so united in that great win in Glenamaddy on 4th December, 1988. To make the victory even sweeter we won by just one point with the last puck of the ball.

Biggest disappointment was the treatment of Angela by Central Council and some of her self professed friends who suspended her in 1988. No loss of any game could ever come near the profound disappointment and sorrow I felt for one of the greatest players I'll ever have the privilege to play along side.

Players I admired — Pat Maloney, Marion Sweeney (Cork), Catherine Murphy, Elsie Coady, Margaret O'Leary, Ann Reddy (Wexford), Liz Neary, Helena O'Neill, Carmel O'Shea and Marie Fitzpatrick (Kilkenny).

Biggest influence — My father Shem, my sister Angela and Tom Ryan (trainer).

"

Ann Downey

Born: 1957

Ann has a triple identity, and some times she thinks that her real identity comes third. For she is generally either Angela's twin sister or Shem's daughter.

Ann plays in the backs and defenders rarely hit the headlines compared to scoring forwards. For this reason she tends to be overshadowed by her prolific scoring twin

Even in the days when she helped her father in the family butcher's shop she had to cope with the public perception of comparative ability. 'Is this the good one or the bad one' some customers would say Little did they realise that a defender's scope for error is very limited and often severly punished whereas a forward need only convert a fraction of opportunities and still prove quite devastating. Ann was stout-hearted, tenacious and very skilled — a highly accomplished defender.

She arrived on the camogie scene a year after her twin sister Angela and has shared with her the same major honours — eleven All Ireland medals, five All Ireland club medals, and six National league titles. The only scar of battle was a belt under the right eye that necessitated eighteen stitches. A superb job done by a plastic surgeon in Kilkenny has completely removed the evidence. Among her cherished possessions is a 1946 Junior All Ireland medal won by her father Shem which she wears as a pendant. It is a lovely medal and reflects the status of the junior game at that time.

Ann is a versatile sportswoman. She also plays hockey — which she took up three years ago — at inter-provincial level and recalled a recent very satisfactory victory over Ulster who are the kingpins of hockey 'We had on our team eight players who had camogie experience and the impact of the skills told in our favour. I don't regard myself as very skilled at hockey. When I started first I had problems with the offside rule and the fact that you can only hit with one side of the stick. I decided I would hit the ball hard instead of moving it around and that worked well for me.' Ann has mastered squash to a high degree and has been capped three times for Ireland.

Among the ingredients of her success is a disciplined approach to training and fitness. Playing for club and county involves four nights training each week and as well as that she would do a one hour fitness workout at a Kilkenny leisure centre.

She is extremely proud of the seven in a row run of All Ireland successes from 1985 to 1991 inclusive. She attributes much of the credit to their trainer Tom Ryan who also very successfully trained the Shamrock's hurling team. 'We did an awful lot of running in our training for the seven in a row and overall I'd say forty percent of the time was given to hurling. There is little point in being able to hurl if you can't last the pace. You can feel so nervous on All Ireland day that you need to be one hundred and twenty per cent fit.'

She would like to see the following changes: — more coverage and publicity for the game so that it might spread and progress. — The major matches played at Croke Park on one of the big occasions. She acknowledges that in order to attract media coverage and capture the imagination of the public that the fare served up, would have to be of a high standard. — Courses for referees and higher refereeing standards. — An improvement in the quality of the medal.

Her sister Angela concurs with her regarding these changes.

She feels that the game is holding its own and that the approach and attitude towards it have become much more professional. Ann would see the leading counties at the moment as being Cork and Kilkenny followed by Wexford and Galway with Tipperary improving.

Do you enjoy it all? Ann spoke for both herself and Angela. 'It's part and parcel of our lives. Everything you do such as when you take holidays has to be geared to fit in with camogie. We couldn't imagine what life would be like without sport.'

Liz Neary, the Kilkenny captain, surrounded by her team-mates following the presentation of the cup in 1981, the year they beat Cork in the senior All Ireland final.

Jimmy Doyle, Captain , Tipperary with the McCarthy Cup in 1965

Born: 1940

"

Well Brendan, it is an honour to write in this book — all about the game of hurling — because I think that hurling is the greatest game in the world.

It started for me at an early age when I won my school awards with Thurles CBS in the early fifties, up to winning and losing games in the seventies and eighties.

I will start with my senior games. I was lucky to be with a great team of players in the 1960s when we won four All Irelands out of five and that tells a lot. They were a great army of players and yet when we were beaten you would have to say that those players that were on those losing teams, were great players also.

As far as the game is concerned I would love to see the goalmouth spills come back to the game and also the third man tackle.

Hurling — you meet lovely people following the game — that's what its all about. I have played on a lot of good players from every county and have great friends.

Jimmy Doyle

"

The array of medals and awards is quite staggering — in excess of 120 — Hurler of the Year 1965; a treasured street league silver medal won in his youth; Harty Cup and Munster colleges medals; multiple honours in Munster, All Ireland, Railway Cup, Oireachtas and National League titles. They represent the power and the glory of Jimmy Doyle and Tipperary hurling.

Jimmy Doyle (right) with Mick Mackey.

But they were won at a price — a broken collarbone — a double fracture of the ankle — a broken thumb — broken knuckles — discs put out fourteen times — broken fingers — a litany of sundry 'softeners' and now the threat of arthritis from the myriad of knocks he took as he played the game he loved and breathed from his very early youth. Regrets? 'None — I would do it all over again.'

What a panorama unfolds as one examines the career of Jimmy Doyle — a hurling gentleman from Thurles town.

A brilliant hurling career began when he played in goal for Tipperary minors in 1954 at the age of fourteen. They lost to Dublin in the final but the three succeeding years brought All Ireland honours. His potency as a forward was heralded in the finals of 1955 and 1956 when he scored 2:8 and 2:3 against Galway and Kilkenny respectively. He confirmed this form at senior level in the All Ireland semi-final against Kilkenny in 1958 when he contributed 1:8 to a Tipperary total of 1:13.

Among the great thrills of his early days was to hear a man shout 'Congratulations' to him as he walked back to school with his bag on his back. 'What for' said Jimmy and the reply was 'You have been selected on the Munster Railway Cup team.' He travelled to Belfast accompanied by Christy Ring. Coming off the train Ring donned a cap and pulled it down over his eyes. Jimmy was a bit baffled and asked Ring why he was wearing the cap in that manner. 'Ah,' said Christy, 'I don't want to be recognised.' There were occasions when Ring liked privacy and as time passed Jimmy was to learn and understand for himself the significance of Ring's feelings. Even to this day there are times when Jimmy wishes that he could operate incognito.

Hurling followers associate certain teams with specific decades. In the case of Tipperary the sixties belonged to them. Their hurlers gave some scintillating performances. In the years 1961, '64 and '65 they made a clean sweep of Munster, All Ireland, National League and Oireachtas titles. Jimmy added a county title to each of those years. In 1961 he also won a Railway cup medal and in 1965 he received the Texaco Hurler of the Year award. 'In my estimation the best team we had in that era was Michael Murphy's team of 1964. We had been building to that peak since 1958. Over confidence cost us the Munster title against Waterford in 1963 when we lost by eleven points to eight. After 1964 the graph turned downwards — even though we added All Irelands in 1965 and 1971. Into that 1964 team came two of a great under 21 side — Babs Keating and Mick Roche. They added class and power to the team.'

Jimmy would abolish the small square. 'Now that the third man tackle is gone and since you can hardly touch the goalkeeper, the small square really serves no purpose. Indeed, we see examples regularly of good goals being disallowed for very questionable technical offences.' I then posed the question of making a goal equal to four points. After all points can be scored from long distances and any angle and high scoring of points is becoming increasingly common. By comparison goals can be scarce and hard to get. Jimmy fell silent as he reflected. 'I never thought about it — it's a hard one to answer — No, I wouldn't change it. Point scoring is a great skill. I'm always advising teams to take points at every opportunity — let the goals come in their own time'.

Among the highlights of Jimmy's career were the trips to America and he had several of these. 'It was lovely to go. Each one was special but the first at the age of 17 after winning the National League was the thrill of a lifetime. It was always wonderful to meet your own people abroad and to entertain them with our National game. It created a great sense of comradeship.'

Talking about trips to America Jimmy recalled the recent unexpected death in the USA of Mick Morrissey, one of Wexford's sterling defenders of the fifties who emigrated to America. As a chap of seventeen Jimmy played an Oireachtas game against Wexford in New Ross. Through a comedy of errors Jimmy was left behind by the Tipperary mentors. He went to the Garda station to tell his tale of woe. They drove around town with him searching for a Tipperary registration — but in vain. Fortunately, they hit upon Mick Morrissey who was travelling to Limerick next morning. 'I'll put you up for the night Jimmy,' said Mick. The problem was solved.

Because 1958 was his first All Ireland win 'it will always stand out as special.' There was a touch of nostalgia about the 1971 win. Despite injury he came on in the last ten minutes and won his sixth All Ireland medal. But the All Ireland campaigns that Jimmy chose to speak about in detail were those of 1961 and 1964.

First of all 1961. 'I had injuries right through my careeer — every accident sets you back a little bit. In the Munster final against Cork my ankle was broken in two places. At the time I didn't realise it and played for the entire game. I was taken to the Regional Hospital in Limerick but the swelling was so bad that the x-ray did not show the fracture. I went home to Thurles and as the days passed I knew my ankle wasn't right and I said so to Pat Stakelum when he called up to see me. He took me to Nenagh Hospital where an x-ray showed a double fracture. Surgeon O'Donnell — a Corkman — said, "Jimmy, you've a problem — you won't make the All Ireland — I have to put the ankle in plaster." I said to the Surgeon, "If you won't take off the plaster three weeks before the All Ireland you're not putting it on." We agreed on that and the plaster was taken off four weeks before the All Ireland. Surgeon O'Donnell said to me "Jimmy you still won't make it." Well I didn't train one bit but I walked the bank of the hurling field morning, noon and night and every night I went for a four-mile walk. As the All Ireland approached I was walking with no limp. On the Friday before the match Tony Wall, Kieran Carey and myself went to Thurles pitch for a fitness test. We pucked the ball around for a while. Then we were told to drop the hurleys and trot around the field. The whistle blew for a sprint — I wasn't able to go.

' "Out to the line — you won't make it" was the instruction to me. I sat and cried by the sideline.'

Shuigh mé síos le machnamh lán.
Do ligeas mo lámh fám ghrua
Gur thit frasa diana déar
Om dhearcaibh ar féar anuas.

'I wasn't able to walk home. Dr Herlihy called to the house to console me.

' "I'm sorry Jimmy but if you play you're gambling your leg. I can give you injections to deaden your leg but it must be your decision — your responsibility." My father and mother were there as we talked and Dr Herlihy said he would go away and let the three of us talk about it and come back to hear the decision. There was no way I was going to miss that All Ireland final and when Dr Herlihy returned my father told him I was going to take the field in Croke Park.

'I travelled by car on Sunday morning to Dublin. Three or four minutes before the match I was given three injections — it numbed my leg from the knee down.

'At half time I was given three more. When the final whistle blew we had won by one point — 0-16 to 1-12 for Dublin — and we were lucky to win. I shouldn't really have played. I was back in plaster for six months after the game.'

And so with a leg that had to be deadened twice in the space of a half an hour he won his second All Ireland medal and the remarkable Jimmy Doyle contributed nine points to Tipperary's total of sixteen.

Now for 1964. Kilkenny were the reigning champions and provided the opposition. Tipperary were playing tremendously well as a unit and proved it with a convincing 3-13 to 1-5 victory over Cork in the Munster final. But against Kilkenny you could never be sure.

'On the eve of the All Ireland final we were all ushered to bed in the Lucan Spa hotel at 9pm Dr Maloney was giving out the sleeping tablets. I declined to take one saying I would sleep. Liam Devaney who was behind me and sharing a room with me muttered something about sleeping tablets and also declined. We lay on our beds chatting and suddenly I said to Liam that the beating of Kilkenny could depend on me switching wings because I felt the Kilkenny mentors would send Martin Coogan after me and I knew from a practise match we had in Castlecomer that if I got Martin over to right-half-back I'd have his measure. We talked about it for a while and I then decided to go down and make the suggestion to Paddy Leahy. "Ah Jimmy, are you not asleep yet — What are you doing down here — go back to bed." I have the move to win the All Ireland tomorrow — put me at left-half-forward and they'll send Coogan after me. "Can't you arrange that switch yourself — go back to bed".'

As things turned out Jimmy's ruse wasn't necessary. Martin Coogan retired injured after twenty minutes — Tipperary led 1-8 to 0-6 at half time — Kilkenny unwisely brought Seamus Cleere from half-back to half-forward to mark Tipperary captain Michael Murphy — and in the end Tipperary ran out very convincing winners on the score 5-13 to 2-8.

After retiring Jimmy continued to remain very close to the game. He had spectacular success with Portlaoise hurlers. His coaching took them to the final in 1981. They lost by one or two points following a goal from a mis-directed puckout just before the final whistle. But the following three years brought success. The scoring rate was good 2-13, 2-12, 3-10. The points tally reflected Jimmy's philosophy of going for points and being accurate in that facet of the game. After that he coached the Laois county team for one year.

And on the evening of my visit Jimmy had an appointment to travel to Cappawhite for a training session with the local team.

After reading *Giants of the Ash* a hurling fan from Co Antrim wrote to me and said 'Doyle won All Irelands in the fifties, sixties and seventies and gave more pleasure to me than any other hurler.' His letter is testimony to the immense popularity and appeal of this hurling artist. Jimmy had great speed and was technically brilliant. The countless hours he spent practising are evidence of his commitment and dedication to the great game. Hurling of course was in the genes. His father Gerry was sub goalkeeper on the victorious All Ireland Tipperary teams of 1937 and 1945. His uncle Tommy gave outstanding service to Tipperary over a sixteen year period that began in 1937 and in 1986 he was honoured with a Bank of Ireland All Star Special Award. Jimmy was the ultimate in class and skilful almost to the point of hurling perfection. In many ways and particularly in sportsmanship he was a shining example to youth. 'I always played the ball — I never hit anyone — I wouldn't hit a child.' No greater sportsman ever graced the hurling fields of Ireland. He had a vast range of hurling skills and his repertoire matched that of Mackey and Ring. He was a virtuoso. He drew from the crowd a different kind of admiration than the two supremos. The Antrim man who wrote to me echoed the feelings of many.

Jimmy called it a day and officially hung up his hurley after the Munster final of 1973 against Limerick when he was a sub. His last inter-county match was in goal against Waterford in the Munster championship of that year. 'I let in two but we still won.' So a great career finished as it had started in 1954 — in goal.

This model of dedication, hurling skill and sportsmanship captained Tipperary to All Ireland success in 1962 and 1965.

Here is Jimmy's team from the men of his era.

Ollie Walsh (Kilkenny)

Jimmy Brohan (Cork)	Michael Maher (Tipperary)	Willie Rackard (Wexford)
Tom McGarry (Limerick)	Tony Wall (Tipperary)	Martin Coogan (Kilkenny)
	Phil Grimes (Waterford) Theo English (Tipperary)	
Jimmy Doyle (Tipperary)	Christy Ring (Cork)	Eddie Keher (Kilkenny)
'Hopper' McGrath (Wexford)	Tony Doran (Wexford)	Eamon Cregan (Limerick)

Jim English collects the National League Cup, 1955-56

Born: 1932

"

I was born into a house of hurling and sport in Ballindoney where hurleys and ball were kept just outside the kitchen door. My father was a keen man on the game, having played for the Templeudigan team with many of the neighbours. Games were often replayed around the fire or on the crossroads on a summer's evening. I had older brothers playing the game with Rathnure. The yard was always the starting point with the door of the stable and cowhouse as goals. Then to the crossroads as a meeting place in the evening. When the numbers arrived you ended up in the field with a combination of hurling and camogie. My first memory of a real match was when Rathnure minors played Geraldine O'Hanrahan's in Palace East in the championship of 1942. As a young lad I had the opportunity of playing with the crossroads brigade in Donard, Rathgarogue and Drummond — Johnny Kehoe's and Joyce's field. After listening to a match on Sunday on the radio, it was followed by a session in the field with some trying to follow the deeds of Christy Ring, Jim Langton, Lory Meagher, Nick Rackard and others. My first championship was a minor championship against the Starlights at The Leap Davidstown in 1949. My first county jersey was in Kilkenny in the 1950 Leinster minor championship. My first medal was won with New Ross CBS under the guidance of Brother Egan, Mr Butler and Mr O'Brien.

At Rathnure I had about fifteen wonderful years and enjoyed every minute of it. To represent your county has to be the ambition of every player and I consider myself very lucky to have been able to play in putting Wexford to the forefront in the fifties and sixties. I enjoyed ten years in the one position at number 5. Having finished my hurling with Rathnure I transferred to Erin's Own in Muine Bheag. I became involved at juvenile level in Muine Bheag and was Chairman of that club for twelve years and Chairman of Erin's Own and St Andrew's for seven years. In 1972 I was elected Leinster Council delegate for Carlow and served in that position for twenty years until I was elected Chairman of the County Board.

Hurling is considered a dangerous game by some but I never had a broken bone and was stitched on only one occasion. The GAA has been a great part of my life and gave me wonderful enjoyment and helped me make some great friends. My greatest pleasure was to see the smile on the faces of the old folk after victory. I have to thank many people for my wonderful years especially my father, mother, brothers and sisters for their help and encouragement — the officers and mentors of Rathnure club for their guidance in the early years — the county board officials and selectors who made my time with them a pleasure.

My hope for the future is that counties like Carlow may find a more level playing pitch in the future — that Rathnure may once again become a hurling force in Wexford and produce players who will help their county to bring the McCarthy Cup back to the model county.

May the GAA continue to give enjoyment to many people in the future.

Jim English "

Hurling and the GAA are still a major part of Jim's life. He is deeply immersed in the affairs of Carlow hurling — says the players are the easiest bunch to manage that you could imagine — and his wish is to see the standard raised to a level that will enable Carlow to compete with the best in Leinster and to give a good account of themselves. He sees this as achievable and points to the fact that in the championship of 1993 they scored sixteen points against Kilkenny and through inexperience conceded some soft goals. 'Competition against the better teams will help remedy this.' There was tremendous rejoicing in the county when they won the All Ireland Senior B hurling final in 1992. The previous hurling success was in 1962 when they won the intermediate title with players of the calibre of Red Willie Walsh and Black Willie Walsh. If they could produce more players like them and like Paddy Quirke — who played on Leinster Railway Cup teams, was centrefield on the victorious side of 1979, was a replacement All Star — then they would certainly be a force. He is proud to have three sons associated with the present Carlow team — Thomas who plays full-back — James in the half-back line and Pat who is part of the panel.

Jim was a sub in 1951 and an established member of the Wexford team in 1954. In many respects 1955 was going to be make or break year for Wexford. Failure would almost certainly lead to despondency and possibly self doubt.

In 1951 they had demonstrated their hurling ability. Failure to Tipperary at the last hurdle was seen as a stepping stone to greater things rather than a defeat. There was plenty of evidence in their displays to show that the purple and gold could bring enrichment and enhancement to the ancient game. In 1952 they left their supporters shattered in Nowlan Park when an unfancied Dublin tore their defence to shreds to take the Leinster title. The following year they failed by two points to Kilkenny in the Leinster final, having lost to the same opposition at the same stage in 1950 by just one goal. That brings us to 1954 when defeat was once again Wexford's lot — this time in the All Ireland final against Cork. A low scoring game that they were well capable of winning was lost by three points. So when 1955 dawned Wexford's loyal supporters could look back and see that their hurlers had contested every Leinster final since 1950 — two of the five were won — the two All Irelands they contested were lost. The general belief was that the day of reckoning was at hand.

In Leinster near neighbours Kilkenny would be very difficult and the unexpected 1952 defeat by Dublin was still fresh in every Wexford memory. In the West, Galway had been giving displays that suggested they could challenge the best. In Munster Cork had won three All Irelands in a row and Tipperary were just as good as them. Clare had some fine hurlers and gave evidence of their hurling class in the Oireachtas games of 1953 and 1954 — losing to Wexford in 1953 and winning against the same opposition in 1954 after a replay — two thrilling games. Limerick and Waterford could be dark horses. So the path to All Ireland glory in 1955 was going to be tough and testing. For Wexford it was a question of would the sum of all the experience they had gained in recent years in National League, Oireachtas and championship games be sufficient to see them through. Time would tell.

In the Leinster final replay Wexford had their first ever Leinster final victory over a Kilkenny team on the score 5:6 to 3:9. In the All Ireland semi-final before a record semi-final crowd of 50,840 they met Munster champions Limerick — young, fast and talented. Two points behind at half time Wexford turned on the power in the second half winning by nine points. In hurling ability they may have been evenly matched but experience, familiarity with Croke Park and greater physical strength turned the tide in favour of the Slaneymen. On the first Sunday in September Galway fell and Wexford were All Ireland champions for the first time since 1910.

Jim English collected his first All Ireland medal. Wexford had won with victories over Kilkenny, Limerick and Galway — all strongholds of hurling — boasting tradition and great names. But some questioned — even detracted from — Wexford's credentials as champions. They hadn't beaten Tipperary or Cork they said and pointed to the failures to those counties in 1951 and 1954 respectively. Would Wexford under the captaincy of Jim English answer to the critics in 1956?

In the League final of that year they faced Tipperary. Jim English had to go off in the first half with an eye injury. By half time and playing against a strong wind Wexford were fifteen points down and morale had sunk low but an incredible second half transformation took them to a four points victory and Jim English accepted the League trophy for 'The Boys of Wexford'. In the Leinster final they defeated Kilkenny by one point 4:8 to 3:10. Reporting on the game John D. Hickey wrote in the *Irish Independent,* 'if ever a captain inspired his men to a victory effort it was Jim English. The Rathnure man has played many great games for his county but never one so good when it was desperately needed. Time and again he came to his side's rescue when Kilkenny were on the rampage, and it was fitting that he and his colleagues in the half-back line should have been the greatest bulwark against the challengers.'

They were now able to match Kilkenny — one of the three superpowers of hurling — in hurling ability, mental approach and close finishes. Galway were overwhelmed in the All Ireland semi-final. In an enthralling and titanic contest Cork were beaten in the final by six points. And for good measure Kilkenny were defeated in the Oireachtas final. 1956 truly silenced the critics. Earlier that year Leinster trounced Munster in the Railway cup final and finished the game with ten Wexford men.

All through his career Jim gave great service and many outstanding perform-ances at right-half-back. A measure of his ability and talents was his capacity to contain the Cork maestro Christy Ring and at the same time give an effective defence.

After a magnificent 1958 League final between Wexford and Limerick John D. Hickey of the *Irish Independent* reported 'For my own part Jim English was the man of the match. Although pitted against the elusive and most dangerous Vivian Cobbe, he gave a majestic display that made great colleagues suffer by comparison.'

On another occasion Joe Sherwood of the *Evening Press* wrote as follows. 'The more I see of Jim English the more I think of him as a wing-half to go down in hurling history among the greats. With his body swerves and twists even when caught at most awkward angles he managed to wriggle through leaving his opponent wondering how he was beaten.'

In 1961 Gael Linn conducted a national poll to select a best ever team. Jim was awarded the right-half-back position.

I asked Jim to select the four games which for one reason or another remained upper-most in his mind. The first was the 1954 final against Cork. 'Being my first final experience of Croke Park it had to be special and of course I was marking Christy Ring. A Tipperary man named Blake — a runner in his day — came to me in the dressing-room and asked if I was nervous. I said, "a bit". "Don't put on your boots until you are ready to go out," he replied. "Why?" said I. "Don't you know," he replied "that when you saddle a horse he begins to prance." Ever after I didn't put on my boots till all were ready to go out.'

The second game was the victory over Cork in 1956. 'To beat them in a final before the second largest attendance ever (the biggest was in 1954) was wonderful. And to be captain made it extra special. That day I had the job of marking one of Cork's all time great forwards, Paddy Barry.' Jim's third choice was his first Railway Cup victory over Munster in 1956 when he was opposed by Jimmy Smyth of Clare. Finally there was the beating of Tipperary in the 1960 All Ireland final. 'The odds were against us and Tipp were hot favourites. I was driving sheep on the Saturday afternoon before the game and a Carlow neighbour asked if we had a hope I said it was 50/50. He went off and said to another neighbour that he thought I was stone mad.' Stone mad! Just look at the score: Wexford 2:15 Tipp. 0:11. No wonder he likes to remember it.

His wife Margaret who had been present during our chat was leaving me out when I noticed a hurling portrait of Jim hanging on the wall. Its style was such that I remarked to Jim that I never saw him being hooked. Whereupon his wife with a glint in her eye and a smile of satisfaction said, 'he was only hooked once.'

Born: 1952

"

I first hurled for Patrickswell under sixteen — managed by Richard Bennis.

Richard Bennis would be my favourite clubman. Both for underage and senior Richard is prepared to do any kind of work for the club.

Sean Foley in my mind would be the greatest half-back I ever saw playing the game. The greatest example of his play was lift and strike in the same movement and send a fast ball to his forwards — the ideal ball for forwards.

Great full-forwards I played against — Ray Cummins, Tony Doran, P.J. Cuddy and Noel Casey.

My hurling days with Patrickswell and Limerick were great days. I wish I could live them all over again. If I got my chance again I would try to improve my game. The friendships I made will last forever. If hurling was for making enemies I would never have played the game.

"

Leonard Enright

Leonard was a talented all-round athlete and sportsman. Success came early in life. At the age of twelve he joined Redgate Athletic Club and won trophies for jumping, running, discus and javelin. In 1966 he won the County Limerick decathlon — a fiercely demanding ten event contest. He set a record for the Munster discus. He tried his hand at soccer too for a while — the club suspended him — the county warned him. He also played football for his club at all grades.

However, it is as a hurler that Leonard is best known. He played minor, under 21 and senior with his native Limerick. One of his first games at senior level was in 1971 when he played in goal in a vital League match against Wexford at Enniscorthy. He shared in the Limerick league and Oireachtas victories of that year.

For most of the seventies he played intermittently with the county senior team. Then in 1979 Limerick suffered a severe blow when shortly before the Munster final Pat Hartigan, their outstanding fullback, received a fatal eye injury and had to withdraw. Jim O'Brien came out of retirement to fill the gap for just one game and Limerick had to search for a successor to Pat. They found it in the person of Leonard Enright. And what a wonderful successor he proved to be. He was an outstanding fullback — one of the best of his era and comparable to any of the all time greats. He had a safe pair of hands — had first touch mastery — could read a game well and was quick to size up a situation — was mobile, tight and utterly dependable. He won three All Star awards at fullback bringing the Limerick total in that position to eight.

He has always admired the Cork style of hurling where they make the ball do the work. And he often noted that when their half-forward line send the ball goalwards they tend to follow up and add to the pressure on the opposing defence. He feels Limerick have always been at their best

playing ground hurling. 'We were told to always play ground hurling when possible. We would do this and then on occasions change half way through. I think we sometimes lost games because of this.'

His 'nightmare game' was the 1984 championship clash with Cork. It was the day Limerick gave away three gift goals and Leonard was one of the donors. 'I was clearing the ball close to goal. As I struck it my leg slipped — the ball hit off my leg and dribbled over the line. It was a bad day — it turned out a very bad day.' And what about John Fenton's goal from a sideline cut fifty yards out that went all the way to the net through Tommy Quaid's fingers? 'I remember that too. John had a great pair of wrists. Patrickswell played Midleton one day and John Fenton came up to take a twenty one yards free. It struck the crossbar and rebounded outfield. It was gathered by Richie Bennis who was playing that day at centre-back. Imagine the power in that shot'.

His most memorable win was the Munster title of 1980 when Cork were defeated. 'It was the biggest we got in my time. It was the one that gave me greatest satisfaction.' He puts it ahead of the league victories of 1984 and 1985. In many ways it is understandable for Limerick victories over Cork in the championship have been relatively few in the past fifty years. A glance back at some of the clashes is worthwhile. In 1940 after two epic encounters Limerick won the replay. In 1942 another thriller — the best game he played in according to the late Jim Young of Cork — ended with a two point Cork victory. 1944 saw the two sides in action again. As in 1940 a draw and replay that left spectators limp with excitement and drama — and victory going to Cork by a goal scored by Christy Ring in 'lost' time. A superior Limerick team lost by three points in 1947, 2:6 to 2:3. Wrote one reporter — 'if ever a better team lost it was Limerick.' Now to 1956 when Limerick looked to be on their way to retaining their Munster title as they outhurled Cork at Thurles. The game was entering the closing stages. And then it happened. In less than ten minutes Ring who up to then had been like a dormant volcano erupted and scored three goals. More misfortune in 1966 when they lost by two points — and the 'advantage' rule worked against them after they had the ball in the Cork net. But it's a long road that has no turning and it came in 1971 when Limerick dethroned All Ireland champions Cork at Thurles 2:16 to 2:14 in a game of thrills and changing fortunes. In the Munster finals of 1975, '76 and '79 Cork re-established their supremacy. And so to 1980. Cork were heading for a record six in a row in Munster. On paper the team looked invincible — hurling talent and experience in abundance. They had beaten Limerick earlier in the year in two great games — a league final that went to a replay. 'We were quietly confident that day — we went out to win. We knew if we got the breaks we would win.' For once Limerick did get the breaks. Victory hinged on a number of things — an early first half goal by Eamon Cregan — a great opportunist second half goal by Ollie

O'Connor — Cregan's deadly accuracy from frees — the switch of Liam O'Donoghue to right-half-back where he proceeded to give one of his many superb displays for Limerick — the hurling aggression of John Flanagan at centre-forward — and finally superb defensive play by Leonard Enright at full-back ably supported by his cornermen Donie Murray and Dom Punch. For Limerick and Leonard Enright it was a famous victory.

The one that got away — the game he would want to play all over again was the first round Munster championship game against Waterford in 1982. 'We had won the Munster title in 1980 and 1981 and were confident of making it three in a row. It was something Limerick hadn't done since the thirties. We felt we could go on to win the All Ireland. A lapse in concentration lost it for us.' A free flowing game in which only thirteen frees were awarded was won by Waterford by one point. Limerick began off as if they would outclass their opponents and after a quarter of an hour were 0:5 to 0:0 ahead. But then Waterford made switches and with John Galvin at full-back and Pat McGrath at centre-back hurling superbly, Waterford went ahead at half time. With three minutes to go Ollie O'Connor pointed to give Limerick the lead. It looked a winner. Then came the loss of concentration. From the puck out the ball went from Jim Green to Stephen Breen to the back of the net, 2:14 to 2:12. John Flanagan narrowed the gap for Limerick and then their Captain Joe McKenna with a final effort to save the day was just wide of the post. It was Leonard's greatest disappointment.

What changes does he see in the game? 'County hurling is now like your work. The demands are immense — on fitness, on time, on family. With so much emphasis on physical fitness the basic skills of hurling have suffered.'

He is generous in his praise of opponents and mentions in particular Ray Cummins of Cork — 'He was an ideal full-forward — kept you guessing'; Tony Doran of Wexford 'always a very big handful and hard to win the ball from him in the air'; P.J.Cuddy of Laois 'who was always a major handful for any full-back.'

Leonard has a good word to say for all hurling colleagues. That's Leonard Enright.

This is the team he captained to National League victory over Wexford in the Centenary year 1984.

		Tommy Quaid		
Paudie Fitzsimons		Leonard Enright		Pat Herbert
Mick Lonergan		Mossie Carroll		Pa Foley
	Jimmy Carroll		Brian Carroll	
Liam O Donoghue		Danny Fitzgerald		Paddy Kelly
Ollie O'Connor		Joe McKenna		Matt Rea

Above: Leanne and Jamie Fennelly proudly hold the McCarthy Cup

Above right: Liam Fennelly with the McCarthy Cups — the old and the new.

Below: Liam Fennelly palms a goal against Wexford

Born: 1958

"

My basic skills were built into my game at a very early age at home in Castlebanny, playing hurling up against the wall, in the paddock, and hunting cattle around the family farm. I suppose the greatest influence on my career was my father and older brother Michael who insisted on teaching us all the skills. Hurling was part of growing up and probably was the most important part of our school days. It was in school that we started getting used to playing fifteen aside under the close eyes of Peadar O'Neill and Joe Dunphy.

I suppose every child's dream in Kilkenny is to wear the black and amber and I was delighted to get that chance and it was a bonus to play alongside great names such as Frank Cummins and the rest of the 1982/83 teams. Really the game of hurling was born for small parish teams and I had that great luck to win championships with the Shamrocks and knock a great fifteen years of unbelievable satisfaction for our local area.

If I had to condense my life in hurling into one sentence and to say what I most achieved from the game I would have to say the friends I made and also the fact that it is the greatest way of all to start a conversation. To conclude, I suppose I will never forget the 1992 final — the sense of satisfaction and achievement I felt when the final whistle sounded and knowing that this was to be my last day to wear the black and amber jersey. I hope for the future that the GAA will remain close to the grassroots of rural Ireland and long may it continue to create enjoyment and surprises to all.

"

Liam Fennelly

There were seven brothers and listed alphabetically they read Brendan, Dermot, Ger, Kevin, Liam, Michael and Sean. You could call them the famous Fennellys or you could call them the fantastic Fennellys. On second thoughts call them both. For that's what they were — famous and fantastic. All at one time or another wore the county colours and for a twenty two year spell from 1971 to 1992 the name Fennelly appeared regularly on some Kilkenny county lineout. Sean, Ger, Kevin and Liam all played in the 1987 All Ireland final against Galway.

You cannot talk about the Fennellys without making reference to their late father Kevin. He was instrumental with others in 1972 in uniting the parish into one team under the title Ballyhale Shamrocks. 'He was trainer, selector and chairman and he never missed a night in the field. His love for the game was total even though his only county game was in a Walsh cup match in the forties.' For years the club had been putting money aside to buy its own parish pitch 'and the dream came true when the pitch was officially opened by Peter Quinn, President of the GAA on 17th May 1992.' For a small parish it has a remarkable hurling tradition — according to Liam nearly always had someone on the panel down the years — and in recent times dominated hurling in Kilkenny just as Bennettsbridge (another small parish) did in the fifties and sixties and Tullaroan did in the early days of the century.

Not surprisingly, Liam's greatest moment — 'the biggest moment in my lifetime — the biggest moment in the club' — was when Ballyhale Shamrocks won the All Ireland club hurling title in 1981 by defeating St Finbarr's of Cork on the score 1:15 to 1:11. Finbarr's were powered by men like Ger Cunningham, Donal O'Grady and Jimmy Barry-Murphy. 'It was our greatest performance ever. In the dressingroom before the game there was silent determination on every face. You could see the imprint of people on the wall. There was no shouting or speeches — just silent grim resolve. The game itself was a great one — probably the best ever club final. We were the first rural parish to win the title and the homecoming was indescribable.' But parish glory did not end there. In 1984 they captured the title for the second time when defeating Gort after a replay by 1:10 to 0:7 — 'two very tough games. I came on in the drawn game in the closing stages when we were four points down. I had broken a bone in my leg in a league game and removed the plaster myself the Wednesday before the match. In the replay I played for the full hour but the damage I did to my ankle lasted for a good while afterwards.' The club won the title for the third time when they defeated Ballybrown of Limerick in 1990 — 1:16 to 0:16 — and his brother Ger got a goal that day direct from a fifty yards free when he spotted a gap and loss of concentration in the Ballybrown defence. In victory Ballyhale Shamrocks shared the leader board with Blackrock of Cork and the Fennelly family created a record that is unlikely to be ever equalled. All seven brothers played on the three winning teams. In the 1984 lineout five Fennellys played in the forwards — each knowing what the other was thinking — and the full-forward line read Dermot, Kevin and Liam. Happily, their father was alive to celebrate all three victories and share in a great family triumph.

Liam captained Kilkenny to their 23rd and 24th All Ireland successes and a further glow was added to the glory of each occasion by an All Star award. There was a uniqueness about those captaincies that may never be repeated. In 1983 Liam brought home to Kilkenny the original McCarthy Cup — first won by Limerick, captained by Bob McConkey in 1921 and presented for the last time to Declan Carr of Tipperary in 1991. In 1992 a new McCarthy Cup arrived on the scene and Kilkenny and Liam Fennelly were back after a lapse of nine years to take it to the Noreside.

He remembers both occasions very well. 'In 1983 I couldn't help feeling to myself — who am I to lead out these great ones — men like Noel Skehan, Joe Hennessy, Ger Henderson, Frank Cummins and Billy Fitzpatrick — all more experienced than me. The occasion was emotional. I felt tears come down from my eyes running onto Croke Park that day. It was a horrible day for hurling — a very strong wind — an awful hard day to win a match.' Kilkenny played with the wind in the first half. A typical Liam Fennelly goal — the opportunist variety at which he was so adept — less than ten minutes to half time, stretched Kilkenny's lead at the interval to six points. At the final whistle the scoreboard read Kilkenny 2:14 Cork 2:12.

By 1992 he had become the elder statesman — the only survivor on the first fifteen from the 1983 winning side. In leading his county to more than one victory he became the twelfth man to join the select band of Mikey Maher (Tipperary), Tom Semple (Tipperary), 'Drug' Walsh (Kilkenny), Johnny Leahy (Tipperary), Sean Óg Murphy (Cork), Jimmy Walsh (Kilkenny), Mick Mackey (Limerick), Christy Ring (Cork), Nick O'Donnell (Wexford), Jimmy Doyle (Tipperary), and Conor Hayes (Galway). 'As I held the cup aloft to jubilant Kilkenny followers I took a good look around Croke Park. I was savouring the moment. I knew it would never come again for my mind was firmly fixed on retirement. When I was young it never dawned on me that I would play for Kilkenny and now here I was leading them to victory for the second time — a great honour.' In that final Cork failed to convert superiority into scores in the first half. Kilkenny's three goals could only be described as half chances, but in typical Kilkenny fashion D.J. Carey from a penalty, John Power and Liam McCarthy seized the half chance and found the net — 'and that's what wins All Irelands.'

Liam fears for the future of club hurling. He is concerned too that the top teams of the present Cork, Tipperary, Kilkenny and Galway appear to be pulling further away from the other counties. His solution is the open draw and he is in no doubt at all that

HURLING IMAGES

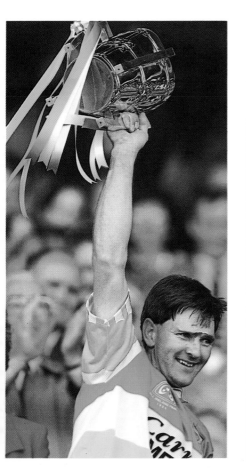

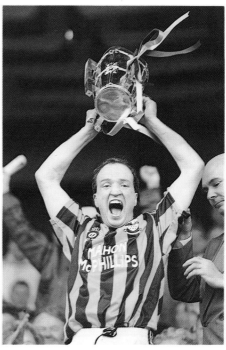

The ultimate winning goal — All Ireland victory. *Above left* (1994) Offaly captain Martin Hanamy, and *(right)* 1993 captain Kilkenny's Eddie O'Connor, celebrate victory. *Below:* Offaly, the winning team in 1994.

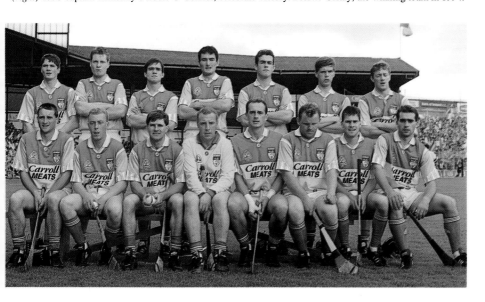

Sporting irony — Limerick Hurling Giant Eamon Cregan manages Offaly to a stunning victory over his home county in the 1994 All Ireland. *Below:* Action from the game — D. Clarke (Limerick) challenging Offaly's J. Dooley who has the sliotar well in hand.

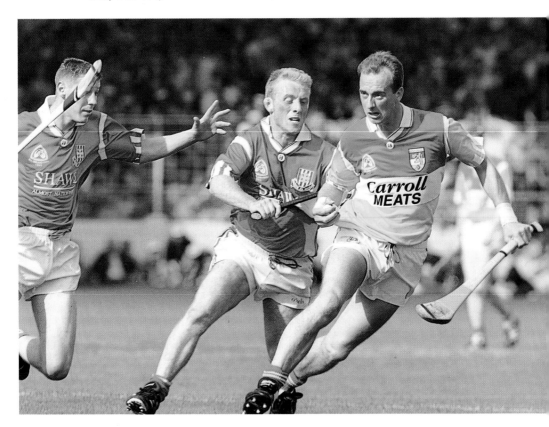

Babs Keating, another Hurling Giant turned manager, anxiously pleading with his team from the 1993 semi-final sidelines.

CAMOGIE IMAGES

Camogie too has produced its great players — five of whom are among the Hurling Giants in this book — Marion McCarthy of Cork *(below)* and Angela Downey of Kilkenny *(opposite top)* among them.

Opposite bottom: Action from the 1992 Camogie All Ireland final — J. O'Leary, Wexford and Colette O'Mahony of Cork

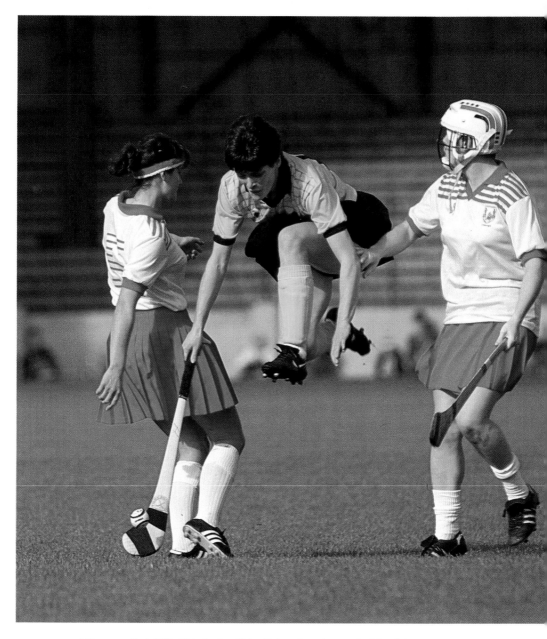

Kilkenny v. Cork 1988 All Ireland — Helen Holmes leaps in pursuit of the sliotar.

Up for the final — Tipperary and Galway fans, 1988

Iggy Clarke of Galway (1984) on the extreme left

Above: Conor Hayes of Galway and Bryan MacMahon of Dublin in the National Hurling League.

Left: John Fenton of Cork (1985)

hurling would greatly benefit.

The family has garnered a large collection of trophies and awards that includes seven All Ireland medals, five All Star awards, eleven National League titles, twenty one All Ireland club medals, several Leinster senior titles, a number of under age titles and in excess of fifty county medals. 'As the years pass it is not the medals — it is the memories that will mean most to me.'

Liam was a potent forward who operated mainly in the left corner and switched regularly to full forward during games. He was a worker and a forager who challenged for every ball. This together with a combination of skill, vision and positional sense enabled him to seize rare opportunities and steal snap scores.

When I visited the Fennelly home I was admitted by three vivacious children. There was Lorraine and Leanne and the eldest brother who was wearing the black and amber jersey. Jokingly I said, 'you must be Liam Fennelly.' 'No,' he replied, 'I'm Jamie.' Well it mightn't be long until Jamie will really wear the black and amber for as I spoke to Liam I learned that his wife Joan was a grandniece of the famous Doyles of Mooncoin. If blood has anything to do with it, Jamie must surely make the grade — and add further fame to the Fennelly name.

Liam picked a team from the men he played against.

Jim Troy (Offaly)

| Brian Murphy (Cork) | Conor Hayes (Galway) | Pat Fleury (Offaly) |
| Pete Finnerty (Galway) | Sean Silke (Galway) | Ger Loughnane (Clare) |

Tom Cashman (Cork)   Joe Cooney (Galway)

| Pat Carroll (Offaly) | Tony Doran (Wexford) | Johnny Callinan (Clare) |
| Pat Fox (Tipperary) | Joe McKenna (Limerick) | Liam Fennelly (Kilkenny) |

" "

Born: 1955

From my earliest days I always had an interest in sport particularly hurling and football but especially hurling. My father Dan, played with Carrigtwohill and the Cork junior team and he encouraged and helped me in every way. One of my great friends and mentors in later years, Willie John Daly played with my father on those teams and this was an inspiration to me to follow in their footsteps. Midleton CBS with Brother Moran was my first real introduction to the game. He spent many hours teaching us and were it not for his dedication and the dedication of other teachers the Midleton Club would not have attained the heights it has over the last fifteen years.

At club level it took us a number of years to make the big breakthrough in Cork senior hurling after winning the intermediate championship in 1978. When we finally succeeded on 9th October, 1983 in beating St Finbarr's in the final it was the culmination of all my hurling dreams. It was a fairytale ending to a story that nobody thought would ever be written. It was without doubt my greatest moment in sport and one which will always give me my fondest memory. The following twelve months were all go, with Midleton, Cork and Munster all being successful in what was a great year for the GAA — it being the Centenary year.

Looking back on my career I find that it helped me in a great way in developing my personality and character. The greatest memory I have is the friendship and comradeship I made with the players I played with and the players I played against. Today we can look back and enjoy our moments of glory and talk about the 'one that got away' and smile. We in Midleton and Cork gave it everything we had and win or lose, enjoyed every moment of it.

To young players of today I would say to practise the skills of the game as often as possible. I used to hit a tennis ball off the gable end wall of our house in Midleton and the countless hours spent in this way helped me in no small way in later years. Later on when playing with Midleton I often went to our local field to practise on my own, often to find one of my teammates there before me, or arrive shortly after me, and this work was well rewarded in later years.

There will always be disappointments in playing games but if you approach the game in a proper manner and play the game fairly it will always bring enjoyment and great memories to look back on when that final puck of the sliotar is struck.

John Fenton
" "

John Fenton began playing with Cork in 1975 but there was so much hurling talent in the county during the three in a row years of 1976— 1978 that it took John until the early eighties to firmly establish himself on the first fifteen. 'I was raw in those early days,' he said, as he attempted to bridge the considerable gap between intermediate club (which Midleton was at the time) hurling and county senior hurling. 'I had to learn fast and I needed space. I found that at midfield which was my favourite position.' The most disappointing moment in his career was when he was taken off in the second half of the All Ireland final of 1983 against Kilkenny. 'The temptation to quit the game altogether was very great.' Fortunately he didn't. The good days lay ahead in the centenary year of 1984 and thereafter. The spur to keep going came when his club Midleton won the 1983 County Cork Senior title. After that John captained Munster to Railway Cup honours in 1984. Under his captaincy Cork reached the Centenary final of 1984 and faced Offaly in Semple Stadium Thurles on a glorious first Sunday in September.

The path to the centenary final wasn't easy. In the Munster semi-final against Limerick, Cork had a very hard earned five point win in a game where Limerick conceded three goals — all of a freakish nature. John was involved in one of those. He took a sideline cut from fifty yards out on the stand side. As with all sideline cuts taken by John it travelled goalwards with laser precision. 'I watched the ball as it rose and sped goalwards. I saw Tommy Quaid put up his hand to catch it and glance outfield to see where he would place the clearance. It was that distraction that caused the ball to slip from his fingers into the net.'

In a great Munster final against Tipperary the game had to be pulled out of the fire in the closing moments. Cork led by 2:10 to 3:5 at half time. They had comprehensively outplayed Tipperary for almost twenty minutes of the first half but it wasn't being fully reflected on the scoreboard. A tenacious Tipperary kept plugging away and succeeded in getting three goals at crucial stages that steadied their confidence — one of those goals came at a psychological moment just before halftime. 'I think Tipp erred on the sideline. They played two unfit players and they moved Seamus Power from attack to defence. The winning of the game came with Denis Mulcahy's interception — as the seconds ticked away — of a Tipp handpass that had score written all over it. I can remember well the point scored by Noel O'Dwyer that put Tipp four points up with six minutes to go. The response from their enthusiastic supporters was such that I realised for the first time the meaning of the expression — lifting the roof off the stand.'

Apart altogether from the hurling side of matters the forward planning that went into the team schedule on the morning of the match was unique and psychologically clever. Let John tell the story. 'We left Cork by train on the morning of the match. On arrival in Thurles we all boarded a bus and as we took off a police escort preceded us. We had no idea where we were going. The next thing is we landed at the gate of the Ursuline Convent. What are we doing here we thought. In we went and met all the nuns. The Reverend Mother was from Cork and we discovered that our trainers Fr O'Brien and Justin McCarthy had arranged through the Ursuline Convent in Blackrock to base the team in the peace and tranquility of the Thurles Convent grounds on the morning of the match. Fr O'Brien said Mass. The nuns had arranged the hymns. There wasn't any doubt in any one of our minds what the central intention was. The last hymn was 'Faith of our Fathers'. It was sung with great gusto. Fellows sang who never sang before. We were all psyched up. Then there was a meal. The tablecloth was red and white. The napkins were red and white. After the meal we relaxed at the tennis courts and took photographs with the nuns. Meanwhile nobody knew where the Cork team was. A county board member came to the gates and was refused admission and told that 'there is no team here.' It was the best prematch preparation I ever encountered. The arrangement was a masterstroke. There was no hassle and we were all as happy as Larry leaving the convent grounds to go to Semple Stadium in the knowledge that the nuns would be praying for us and having promised them we would return the following morning — win or lose.'

Well Cork won — and decisively 3:16 to 1:12. Johnny Crowley at centre-back, Tim Crowley at centre-forward and the midfield pair of Pat Hartnett and John Fenton dominated in their positions and laid the foundations of a Cork victory. 'Thurles of course was worth four or five points to us — an advantage Leinster teams have when the final is in Croke Park. Tony O'Sullivan was declared Man of the Match and scored seven points from play. My recollection is that Cork made neither a substitution nor a positional switch that day.' John regrets that the team didn't make a visit through the Square — where so many Cork people would have gathered — at some stage that day. As promised the team with wives and girlfriends returned to the convent the following morning. Mass was celebrated again. But the quality of the singing didn't

match that of the previous day — the celebrations had taken their toll.

1984 wasn't of course the only year that Cork used links with the Divine in search of success. They did it in 1926 against Kilkenny when Fr Fitzgerald told the team that he had offered the Mass that they might win, whereupon a few of the team expressed the view that they would rather beat Kilkenny fair. Again in 1931 it seems that the Cork captain Eudi Coughlan offered thanks in the Messenger to the Sacred Heart following victory over Kilkenny. Now as everyone knows that All Ireland went to three games so Kilkenny may have been storming heaven through some other source of influence — a source that failed on the day but subsequently must have come good because of the nine All Ireland finals that Cork and Kilkenny have contested since 1931 Kilkenny has won

seven.

Further honours came John's way in the centenary year when he won an All Star and was also chosen as Hurler of the Year.

He played one of his greatest games ever in the replay of the League final of 1980 against Limerick. He missed the drawn game — which was brimful of superb hurling, drama and excitement — due to an eye injury sustained in a club game. Replays rarely live up to expectations when they succeed a great draw. But this was an exception. It was sparkling stuff watched by a crowd of almost thirty five thousand people. All through John Fenton was brilliant. In typical fashion he blazed a penalty to the net in the first half and in the second half scored a wonderful point from a sideline cut. He finished the day as Cork's leading scorer with 1:5 and Cork captured their eleventh league title.

101

Cork went into the All Ireland final of 1986 against Galway as complete underdogs and yet won decisively. I asked John why he went for a goal from a 21 yards free so early in the game — eight minutes after the throw-in. 'I remember saying to Ger Cunningham some days before the game that I was having a problem about Sunday's final as I couldn't make up my mind what I would do if we got a penalty in the first five minutes. If you get a penalty said Ger to me just stick it in the back of the net and then it will be their problem. If you had asked me two weeks before the 1982 final when we were red hot favourites against Kilkenny who would win, I could have told you Kilkenny because the mood was all wrong. But if you asked me two weeks before the '86 final I could have told you we would win. The mood was spot on. I felt in great mental and physical shape on the day of that final. No penalty came in the first five minutes but when the 21 yards free came after eight minutes I came up and stood over the ball and did what Ger Cunningham had advised.' That day John was the leading scorer with 1:4, jointly with Kevin Hennessy.

All who saw John's first half goal against Limerick in the replay of the Munster championship game of 1987 will never forget it. It came at a crucial time and sealed Limerick's fate. An attack on the Limerick goal was repulsed and play centred around the forty five yards mark and almost dead centre with the Limerick goal. John allowed a moving ball to position itself to his liking — then the swing — beautifully measured, timed and executed — goalward soared the sliotar — and before Tommy Quaid in the Limerick goal could react, the ball was in the top left hand corner of the net. It was undoubtedly one of the great goals of hurling. So dramatic was it that it subsequently became the background action for a farming advertisement. It was rated the Goal of the Year by RTE and won for John a magnificent Waterford Glass trophy appropriately enscribed.

John was one of the finest midfielders of his time and won five All Star awards in a row in that position from 1983 to 1987. He was excellent at the art of ground striking and a master of the sideline cut. He was a reliable long distance free taker and was deadly with frees in front of goal. All his attributes stemmed from perseverance and painstaking practise.

Nowadays he puts in a lot of work with underage players. He tries to instil into them a policy of ground hurling and a philosophy of letting the ball do the work — 'something which Fr Bertie Troy bred into us.' He discourages solo runs. At training sessions he picks out the fastest player and gives him a thirty yards start on a solo run. From where he took off another player strikes a ball which travels about sixty yards. 'No contest,' says John as he looks at his students and hopes he has driven the message home.

John's team from the men of his era is as follows.

Noel Skehan (Kilkenny)

Denis Mulcahy (Cork)   Pat Hartigan (Limerick)   Fan Larkin (Kilkenny)

Joe Hennessy (Kilkenny)   Johnny Crowley (Cork)   Tom Cashman (Cork)

John Fenton (Cork)   Gerald McCarthy (Cork)

Nicholas English (Tipperary)   Jimmy Barry Murphy (Cork)   Eddie Keher (Kilkenny)

Charlie McCarthy (Cork)   Ray Cummins (Cork)   Seanie O'Leary (Cork)

Born: 1933

"

I think that anybody who got as much out of hurling in Waterford as I did would be a fool not to acknowledge the good luck to be playing at a time when a magnificent bunch of hurlers was emerging in Waterford. Coupled with this was the fact that a small band of extraordinary people had the vision, the dream and the courage to suggest that maybe these hurlers could win an All Ireland title for Waterford.

But my good luck had started years earlier when I was born in Abbeyside, fifty yards from the village school where I came under the influence of a brilliant and dedicated teacher named Michael Foley who had in fact helped to train the 1948 successful All Ireland team. He it was who encouraged us to play hurling in front of the school and after school brought us to a small field near the church where we got special tuition playing backs and forwards.

At the age of ten the boys of the village became involved in the local scout troop and came under the influence of another extraordinary man — Liam Lanigan who inspired the troop from the small village to win the All Ireland trophy for scouting on a number of occasions. So growing up in Abbeyside one got a great sense of identity

and a deep pride in the 'Village'.

When I moved to secondary school at Dungarvan CBS (thanks to extra tuition after school from the aforementioned Mr Foley) I was immediately involved in school hurling under the guidance of Brother Murray who did great work for college hurling. Shortly after starting at the CBS I remember playing in a school final in Waterford when I learned a lot from an umpire at the match. The match was in progress for about ten minutes and I hadn't struck a ball. We were under great pressure and everytime the ball came my way the full-forward who was much bigger and stronger than I, was pushing and shoving and getting himself tangled up in me. I was really frustrated and did not know what to do. At this point the goalkeeper asked me to puck out the ball. I went back to pick it up and as I did so the umpire whispered 'keep away from your man until the ball arrives — he can't hurl.' Well I was open to suggestions. The next ball that came I pretended to go for it but left the full forward off. He was now dealing with a dropping ball but with nobody to tangle with, he did not know what to do. I just arrived at the right time (by accident) to gather the ball and clear. It was the first decent puck of the ball I got in the match and I remember thinking that this was a great idea. Afterwards whenever I had to mark anybody that was bigger or stronger than me I knew I had no business standing with him and I tried to implement this idea — not always with the same success however. The umpire was unknown to me then and little did I know of the influence he would have on my hurling career and that of Waterford hurling during the most glorious years (so far) from about 1956 to 1963. I later got to know him as Pat Fanning of Mount Sion.

In 1949 Abbeyside entered minor hurling and football teams and I played on both for three years. I remember meeting Tom

Cheasty for the first time when I played on him in a county final — I played at full-forward and Tom was full-back — no it wasn't hurling — it was a minor football final. Abbeyside won a number of minor football titles in a row but we lost minor hurling titles to Mount Sion. I was still in school in 1950 when I won a county junior hurling title playing at corner-back with Abbeyside. The following year I was selected to play on the Waterford junior hurling team against Clare in Waterford but the school principal advised against it as he felt I was not ready yet — so I withdrew. That year also I was captain of the school team which won the Dean Ryan cup for the first time by our school. We beat Thurles CBS in Clonmel in the final. Captain of Thurles CBS that day was Tony Wall.

Ten days previously I had played fullback on the Munster colleges team which beat Connaught in the final in Galway. Playing at centre-back that day was Tony Wall and I remember at left-half-forward Dermot Kelly of Limerick played a great game. The day before the match I had heard of Tony Wall for the first time when it was suggested to me that if an opportunity arose near the end of the match and assuming we were in front, then a tap on the ankle mightn't do Tony Wall any harm (he probably meant it *would* do him some harm).

I was amused by this suggestion and explained that I knew I would have more than enough to do coping with the full-forward besides watching for Tony Wall's ankles.

The following year 1952 I came on a sub in the first round of the senior hurling championship against Clare in Waterford. The match was a draw and we won the replay in Thurles (I was marking the famous Matt Nugent that day). We were well beaten by Tipperary in Limerick in the next round. For the next few years I played in the league but had not the same interest at that time at inter-county level as I had at club level. Things started to change around 1956 when we had a great game against Cork in the championship in Fermoy and another turning point came in a famous match in the league against the mighty Wexford team at Waterford. Things were now definitely changing and for the 1957 championship the panel was brought together in Dungarvan for collective training under John Keane as trainer and selector. Also present that evening were the other selectors, Jackie Good, Mickey Feeney, Seamus O'Brien (present Central Council delegate) and the Chairman Pat Fanning who made a famous address to the players which for me was the actual night it all started.

I remember the way he spelt out his firm belief in the capacity of this group to win an All Ireland for Waterford, the efforts the county board would make towards this goal and the total commitment, dedication and pride in the county that would be expected from the players. I didn't know most of the other players at that time and I remember thinking — this is serious stuff and I remember looking across at Seamus Power and Philly Grimes and thinking — my God am I out of my depth here — could I be in the same league as these fellows. Well in the years that followed lifelong friendships were forged between all present that night as well as all the replacements over the next seven or so glorious years.

Waterford played in 1957, '59 and 1963 All Irelands. We won in 1959 in the replay and many think we should have won more but we also won Oireachtas and National League titles. Many of us were in the Munster and Rest of Ireland teams. We travelled to New York as a team in 1960 and it was amazing how the visit brought so many Waterford people together in New York. In 1966 I was picked with Christy Ring, Bernie Hartigan, John Doyle and Pat Dunny to travel to New York for the Cardinal Cushing games. We played in New York and Chicago and had a visit to Robert Kennedy in his office in Washington. I became friendly with Christy during this visit and he often called to my house afterwards. Years earlier I remember walking down to the creamery to pass by his lorry to see the hurley in the cab while he offloaded heating oil and I was ashamed to

go over to talk to him.

Looking back now the team I admired most was the mighty Wexford team. The best hurler was Christy Ring. The club I admired most was Mount Sion with whom Abbeyside did battle on four occasions for the senior hurling final of Waterford but we never won. We were always up against it. As well as the six or seven county players they had six or seven more who were on the fringe of the county team so it would have been a great achievement for the village team to beat them. We went very close on a few occasions. So I never got a county medal but I got just as much satisfaction in trying for the one for Abbeyside as my friends on the Mount Sion side got in adding to their collection — so no regrets here.

The nicest hurler to watch I thought was Philly Grimes — to see him in full flight — he was so balanced and the picture of poetry in motion. For determination, true grit and never say die attitude (Pat Fanning would demand to give until it hurts and until you have nothing more left and you would dig a little deeper to find that little bit extra) — for the man who personified all this for me it has to be Seamus Power. For the inter-county player who was the least likely to be put off in a match I have no doubt that all the players of my time would name John Barron, so it has always been a great regret of mine that John was put off in the All Ireland final — John was everybody's No.1 gentleman.

Looking back now I got a great deal out of hurling but more important than any medals or trophies are the treasured memories and lifelong friendships with extraordinary people that could never have happened without the game of hurling.

The hurlers I admired, Christy Ring, Paddy Barry, Jimmy Brohan and Denis Riordan from Cork, Donie Nealon, Jimmy Doyle and Liam Devaney from Tipp, Dermot Kelly and Mick Tynan from Limerick, Denis Heaslip, Eddie Keher and Seamus Cleere from Kilkenny, Tim Flood, The Rackards and Jim English from Wexford.

Austin Flynn **"**

Abbeyside and everything associated with it has always had a very special attraction for Austin. He had no strong personal desire to move into hurling at the highest level. As a youth he enjoyed hurling at school and above all with his native Abbeyside. He was also very much involved in the Boy Scout movement and sailing. The lure of the sea was very strong — his father had been a seaman all his life.

In the full-back position at county and inter-provincial level Austin set high standards in clean play and good sportsmanship. Snippets from his hurling career unfold in no particular order as you talk to him. A vein of humour runs through many.

'Phil Grimes was my hurling hero and he was so modest about his performances. I will never forget his display when he moved to centre-back in the Munster final against Cork in Thurles in 1959. We had been under fierce pressure in the full-back line and were almost in a panic trying to contain the Cork attack. I must tell you a story about Grimes. We were playing Cork one day and suddenly Grimes's man is writhing on the ground and play up at the other end. No one saw anything. As the referee came down to investigate, Pat Fanning ran in to Grimes and said, "What happened Philly — what happened — move away — what happened?" "He threatened me," replied Philly. "He threatened me and I believed him."

I was a "stupid" hurler you know — I could only play at full-back. I never missed a match once I established myself — I was afraid they might find someone better.

I played on Nicky Rackard a few times towards the end of his career. I was always pleased with my performance. I never tried to hurl him close. I learned that lesson about big fellows in my schooldays.

We were playing Wexford one day and I ran from the full-back line to challenge Wexford half-forward Paddy Kehoe for a fifty-fifty ball. We clashed and crashed into each other. I didn't know where I was. I knew Nicky Rackard was unattended at full-forward. I jumped up and ran back. I couldn't breathe. I was deaf in my right ear and numb in my right side for about ten days. A year later we met Wexford again. A free into Wexford brought me face to face with Paddy Kehoe. He turned to me and said, "I don't want to bang into you again." I couldn't believe it. I knew then he had been affected too. I was delighted.

I remember the day before our championship match with Tipp in 1959 — reigning All Ireland champions. I had been out boating and as I came ashore two hurling fans approached me and enquired "how we would fare against Tipp?" So as to keep the discussion short I said we would beat the sugar out of them — end of conversation. We played with the wind in the first half and before long scored a goal. Devaney who was marking me let a swear out of him and looked at me but I said nothing. Then we got a second and third goal. Devaney kept watching me for reaction but I looked straight ahead as if it was to be expected. We were about eight goals up at half time and walked the match. The fans I met at the Harbour thought I was a prophet.

The day after the matches my mother used to clean away the clay from around the cogs of my boots into the geranium pots and used to say that she had a collection of clay from every county in Ireland.

A Christian brother at school used to ask us who won the All Ireland minor title in 1948. We would all say Waterford. And who should have won the All Ireland title in 1947? Waterford we would answer. And why didn't they win it? Because they all hadn't cogs on their boots.'

Time has not dimmed for Austin the scene in 1957 when the panel gathered in Dungarvan under the watchful eyes of trainer John Keane and County Chairman Pat Fanning. He remembers Pat's words of belief and exhortation 'As sure as God is my judge I believe in my heart and soul there is the winning of an All Ireland in you. I'll do everything I can to facilitate you. But I will expect you to give all you have. Tipp and Cork have tradition. We have a tradition too — a tradition of keeping going. But there is no great virtue in defeat. We can win an All Ireland.'

It was following a great league performance — which was either won or drawn — against Wexford in a packed Walsh Park in Waterford that Pat Fanning saw the potential that was there to be exploited. 'Pat was a leader of exceptional qualities and a man of total sincerity.'

Austin remembers the incredible hype that used precede each match and the level of excitement after each victory. 'It put the players under immense pressure. It was so different in a county like say Kilkenny where the real build up wouldn't start until before the All Ireland final. And then because they had such a winning tradition the players didn't feel anything like as pressurised as we did.

Following the All Ireland victory of 1959 we travelled as a team to New York in 1960. During the visit Pat Fanning addressed what would be the equivalent of a county convention in Ireland. He made us all feel proud — he made you feel proud of being from Waterford. He was a wonderful ambassador for the game.'

After a long barren patch Austin sees the future of Waterford hurling as getting brighter. The All Ireland under 21 victory and the Munster minor victory of 1992 could lead to greater things. 'Peter Power the juvenile hurling coach is doing great work with the schools. He has a great way with children. It augurs well for the future.'

His team selected from the men he played against is as follows.

Ollie Walsh (Kilkenny.)

Jimmy Brohan (Cork)	Nick O'Donnell (Wexford)	Bobby Rackard (Wexford)
Seamus Cleere (Kilkenny)	Tony Wall (Tipperary)	Jimmy Finn (Tipperary)
Joe Salmon (Galway)	Jim Morrissey (Wexford)	
Jimmy Doyle (Tipperary)	Donie Nealon (Tipperary)	Tim Flood (Wexford)
Christy Ring (Cork)	Nick Rackard (Wexford)	Jimmy Smyth (Clare)

Born: 1919

"

I was fortunate to have grown up where there was a long tradition for hurling of a good standard. Many of my near neighbours were men who had played for club and county when the GAA was in its infancy. They told tales of 'battles' long ago, of games won and lost in far off fields, and took a personal interest in those to whom they were handing on the torch. How difficult it must be to plant hurling in soil not nourished by tradition! But good coaches can do and are doing a lot.

Where the hurling tradition is strong, what is needed is the GAA structures to channel it; to provide well organised competition; to lead the youngsters along from one level to the next; from juvenile to minor, to senior club grade. Again I was lucky, and I remember with gratitude those who shepherded the youth of my time, taking us here and there for matches. One of the most remarkable features of the GAA is its ability to attract dedicated voluntary workers — thousands of them — all over the country, making the GAA the nation's largest youth movement. It is not always given the credit that is due to it. But so strong an organisation can expect to be

attacked. It is sufficiently mature and healthy to shrug off unjustified criticism and not to be too defensive or apologetic about the faults and mistakes of its officials or players. I was fortunate once more in coming on one of Galway's greatest ever hurling teams: the 1944/1954 team with which I played for a few years before going on the Missions in 1949. If there were an award for the greatest team never to win an All Ireland that team would be well in the running for it. The Cork/Kilkenny final of 1947 is the answer to the question about the rise in the standard of hurling in recent years. That final was regarded as the greatest up to that time and those who saw it have lived to see few that were its equal. One point separated the teams at the end of play, as one point had separated Galway and Kilkenny in the semi-final — three truly great teams that year. That same Galway team had already defeated, first the 'pick' of Leinster and then the Munster selection in the Railway Cup, when this competition ranked second in importance to the All Ireland championship.

To have taken part in games of that calibre, as in two well-remembered county championships with the Barrs in Cork and a Fitzgibbon with UCC leaves one with some cherished memories. And these, like good wine, improve with age. The sediment sinks.

Paddy Gantly   "

Paddy Gantly was ordained an SMA priest in Newry in the Summer of 1946. But in the days that I first remember him he was called Paddy Gardiner — in team line-outs and in newspaper photographs. That was how he lined out for Connaught in the Railway Cup against Munster in the finals of 1946 and 1947. The Church culture of

Paddy Gantly (black togs) of St Finbarrs awaits the throw in a Cork county final.

the times frowned on clergy taking part in games. Hence, the pseudonym or alias.

In 1946 Connaught (all Galway) lost by one point to Munster in the Railway Cup final at Croke Park on the score 3:12 to 4:8.

The following year Connaught (all Galway) went one step better. They beat Munster in the final by the score 2:5 to 1:1 and had earlier beaten Leinster by 2:6 to 2:5 — a game in which Paddy was opposed in the course of the hour by three very formidable opponents — Nicky Rackard of Wexford and Jack Mulcahy and Terry Leahy of Kilkenny.

The Munster team had household names such as Willie Murphy, Alan Lotty, Christy Ring and Jim Young of Cork — Jackie Power and Peter Cregan of Limerick — John Keane, Andy Fleming, Vin Baston and Mick Hayes of Waterford — and Tommy Doyle of Tipperary. Victory against such an array of talent reflected the ability and class of the Galway team. It lined out as follows - Sean Duggan, Donal Flynn, Paddy Forde, Willie Fahy, M.J.

'Inky' Flaherty, Jim Brophy, Bernie Power, John Killeen, Paddy Gantly, Josie Gallagher, Hubert Gordon, Paddy Jordan, Michael Nestor, Tadgh Kelly, Steve Gallagher.

Paddy Gantly excelled for Galway in all those games. The midfield combination of himself and John Killeen was one of the outstanding of the time.

1947 was the year of the severe snow and black frost. On St Patrick's Day the Croke Park pitch was considered fit for the football game only and the hurling was brought forward to Easter Sunday. Prior to the game Donal Flynn, a Cork man playing with Connaught went through both teams player by player with Paddy Gantly and declared — 'this Munster team will not beat us. In those days no Galway man would have said such a thing,' said Paddy.

Later that year Galway met Kilkenny in the All Ireland semi-final at Birr. In Galway hopes were high. Here is Paddy's account of a one point defeat that came about in 'lost' time.

109

1947 – Connacht (All-Galway) – first time to win the Railway Cup. Back Row: P. Forde, D. Flynn, P. Gantly, P. Diviney, T. Lyons, P. Barrett, P. Jordan, S. Duggan, S. Kennedy, H. Gordon. Centre: T. Kelly, B. Power, M.J. Flaherty, J. Killeen, W. Fahy, J. Callinan. Front: S. Gallagher, Jas Killeen, J. Brophy, J. Gallagher.

'The referee lost track of the score coming towards the end. He felt he hadn't performed well and was disappointed with the manner in which he had handled the game — so he made up his mind that a game which had been very close right through should end in a draw and that both sides should live to fight another day. He told me all this some months after the game. At one stage — Galway were ahead — he blew the whistle, which the crowd took to be the final one and rushed onto the pitch. He was confused about the score and restarted the game. Play continued with Kilkenny getting scores and when Terry Leahy pointed, the referee, believing that the sides were then level, blew full time.' It all added up to the exit from the championship of a fine Galway hurling combination.

After returning for a while from his African Missionary work in 1953, he trained the Galway hurling team and became very involved in hurling affairs — he was County chairman for a period — he was Galway's delegate to the Central Council — and in the mid fifties he was a member of the first coaching group set up by the GAA. 'Coaching has improved and television and video tapes are now a great support for coaching. They can be used to show basic errors to players and train and educate them to avoid such errors and take proper options. The competition for the interest of the youth is the greatest challenge to the GAA. More and more of its resources should be put into winning the interest and attention of the young. The great sums now being spent on giving semi-professional training to county teams can only be justified if large sums can also be spent on attracting the youth.'

Following the 1953 All Ireland defeat by Cork and bearing in mind the great hurling men and quality of the teams that Galway had produced in the decade from 1944, it was decided in Galway that some action had to be taken. 'You see we came so close so often and finished more than a decade with so little to show, that we had to take stock of our geographic location — in the hurling sense — and take some action.'

'An open draw was sought but the idea didn't receive favourable response. Galway then requested that they be allowed participate in Leinster. Agreement was reached and the draws were made but Wexford objected and that ended that line of approach. The concept of an artificial province was then mooted, involving Clare, Galway, Offaly and possibly Westmeath. It didn't find favour in Clare and was dropped. Finally, a delegation approached Munster and it was agreed that Munster would invite Galway to play in the Munster championship and that Munster would place the motion before congress.

The motion was carried and Galway were in Munster with effect from 1959. But they fell on lean times and had little success in the Senior championship during their term in Munster, 1959-1968. I believe they should have persevered and that they erred when they took the decision to withdraw from Munster.'

Paddy regards the under 21 competition as a superb innovation. 'It has been a blessing for Galway and is an ideal stepping stone to senior ranks.'

The best game he saw was the 1947 All Ireland final between Cork and Kilkenny. That was the day Terry Leahy added to his fame by scoring the winning point in dramatic fashion in the dying moments. Years later when he met Terry in New York the occasion was recalled and Terry told Paddy that when he grabbed the ball he turned to Alan Lotty and said 'Goodbye now Alan — this is it' — and it was.

In his student days in Cork, Paddy won two County titles with St Finbarr's — he became associated with St Finbarr's by virtue of the fact that in those days the club had no grounds and used to train at the SMA pitch in Wilton. In 1946 they defeated Glen Rovers. Paddy was at centre-field and opposed by Josie Hartnett but in the second half Ring was brought out to mark him. In 1947 against Sarsfields he played centre-forward on Alan Lotty. He played in the Fitzgibbon Cup with UCC. Stories abound about these games — especially those involving UCG who were allowed three outside players to strengthen their ranks — the reality was that on occasions more than three participated. There is the story about one individual who was asked by a doubting opponent what he was doing at the Uni and the replay was — 'Sums'. But the one I like most is Paddy Gantly's story about the fellow who was asked what *faculty* he was taking. His reply left his opponent in no doubt about his future safety — 'I think it's fight you're looking for.'

Paddy classified players into three categories for me —

— the hurler who is lacking in style and skill but very useful in making room for others. Most counties like to have at least one of those among the forwards.

— the hurler who is skilful, strong, determined, energetic and resourceful – a match winner. The hurler that every county is looking for.

— the hurler who is a stylist, a ball player, who waits for the opportunity and has every skill to take it, is not a forager, irritates a team manager and supporters but is a delight to watch — a Sean Clohosey of Kilkenny or a Martin Murphy of Claregalway.'

Father Paddy went to Nigeria in 1949 on board a cargo ship (he came home in 1953 — returned again to Nigeria in 1962, until 1966 — was in Rome from 1968 to 1973 — in London from 1973 to 1983 — and finally home to Ireland). They were sixteen days at sea. In those days Africa to the people of Ireland seemed worlds away. It was the Dark Continent, many parts of it the white man's grave, for some of its diseases particularly yellow fever, were killers.

As Father Paddy stood on deck leaving his native land and watching the shore recede he thought to himself 'this is the best day of my life' — 'you see the work of a Missionary and his sense of fulfilment isn't realised until he sets foot on his Mission field.' He literally stepped from one great love and calling of his life into another. For he went straight from Croke Park after playing with his native Galway in a challenge game against Dublin, to the cargo ship that was taking him to his mission work in Nigeria. As the shores of his native land receded, he gazed and bade farewell.

Mo chuig céad slán chun dúthaí m'athar
's chun an Oileáin ghrámhair.

Mick Gill in 1980 aged 81

Born: 1899

Mick Gill made his debut in championship hurling in 1922 when he played with his native Galway in the All Ireland semi-final against Kilkenny. Galway lost but Mick had made his mark. The following year he collected his first All Ireland medal when Galway defeated Limerick on the score 7:3 to 4:5 after the teams had been level at 2:3 to 3 goals for Galway at half time.

Interestingly, the 1923 All Ireland final was played on 14th September, 1924. Limerick failed to fulfil an original fixture in June of that year. The circumstances surrounding this were linked to the civil war and the matter of prisoners. Galway were awarded the match by the central council but declined to accept a walkover.

As a member of the Garda Síochána, Mick was based in Dublin for the 1924 championships and under the rules of the time could not declare for his native Galway. He threw in his lot with Dublin and three months to the day, after winning his 1923 All Ireland medal he lined out on the 14th December with his adopted Dublin to face his native Galway who were again contesting the final after beating Tipperary in the All Ireland semi-final. Dublin won on the score 5:3 to 2:6 and Mick Gill made a piece of hurling history by winning his second All Ireland hurling medal within the space of three months.

He grew in hurling stature and began to make a name for himself as a midfielder. In 1927 he won his third All Ireland medal when he captained a renowned and extremely fit Dublin Garda selection to victory over a highly vaunted Cork fifteen. That Dublin team contained many greats of the hurling world — Pa 'Fowler' McInerney of Clare, Garrett Howard of Limerick, Mattie Power of Kilkenny, Dinny O'Neill of Laois and Tommy Daly of Clare to mention but a few.

Mick Gill's hurling status was further enhanced in 1928 when the Tailteann games selectors chose him on the Irish team.

He played in his fourth All Ireland final in 1930 but on this occasion victory went to Tipperary. He played many times for Leinster in the Railway cup — captained them in 1928 and 1929 — and won his only medal in the inauguration game of 1927. He had two National League successes — with his adopted Dublin in 1929 when Cork were defeated — with Galway in 1932 when they triumphed over Tipperary.

He helped to build the Garda hurling team in Dublin and kept them on the peak of hurling for many years. It is said that his command of a falling ball was deadly and that he hit from either hand with equal freedom and confidence. In his time he was compared alongside Lory Meagher of Kilkenny, Jim Hurley of Cork and Bob Mockler of Tipperary.

He died in 1981 but not before he had the pleasure of seeing Galway defeat Limerick in the All Ireland final of that year — their first victory since 1923 — and coincidentally against the same opposition.

Mick will always rank with the immortals of the game.

Born: 1915

Down through the decades Laois produced many great hurling names. But Laois people would say not enough at any one time and this would partly answer the question as to why Laois has failed to figure prominently in the honours list.

They won their only All Ireland Senior Hurling title in 1915 when they defeated Cork on the score 6:2 to 4:1. The late Bob O'Keeffe who was part of that triumph returned to Ballybrophy by train and walked home to Borris-in-Ossory without anyone realising he had won an All Ireland medal — how times have changed. He was honoured with the office of President of the GAA from 1935 to 1938. He was the last of that Laois team to die and was laid to rest in Knockaroo graveyard. But his memory is preserved through the Leinster Senior hurling cup — the Bob O'Keeffe Cup.

The previous year 1914 Laois played Clare in the final and lost on the score 5:1 to 1 goal. Torrential rain marred the 1915 occasion and the Laois team came out in raincoats after the halftime break and took

them off just before the second half started.

Names like Tom Finlay, Bob O'Keeffe, Ned McEvoy, Dinny O'Neill, Ned Tobin, Joe Styles, Billy Bohane and Christy O'Brien will always be remembered in hurling history.

Few however, would argue with the suggestion that the late Harry Gray was in many ways Laois's greatest hurling son.

His senior hurling career began in 1934 with his native Laois — having played minor with the county in 1933. He retired from inter-county hurling in 1949 when Laois was defeated in the All Ireland final by Tipperary. That day Harry played at centre-forward.

In between those years Harry made his name as a midfielder in the Dublin and Leinster jerseys. When he won All Ireland honours with his adopted Dublin in 1938 — Waterford went under on the score 2:5 to 1:6 — he had as his team-mates such outstanding men as Mick Daniels (captain) Christy Forde, a most reliable goalkeeper, Tom Teehan, Charlie McMahon and Bill Loughnane.

He figured regularly on Leinster Railway Cup selections and won his only title in 1941 when he was partnered at midfield by Tipperary born Ned Wade.

According to Liam O'Neill who partnered Harry at midfield for Laois in the minor championship of 1933 Harry really first hit the limelight when he was switched in the 1937 Railway Cup final to curb Jimmy Cooney of Tipperary who was playing an absolute blinder for Munster.

Liam went on to describe this native of Rathdowney as a man of powerful physique and a wonderful stylist. As a midfielder, he saw him as being in the mould of the great Jim Hurley of Cork — and in appearance a larger edition of Alan Ladd the film star. In Dublin he played hurling with Faughs and won seven county titles. It wasn't only in Laois and Leinster that he

Above: Harry Grey receiving the Hall of Fame award from Seamus O'Riain. Below: On duty as the Gresham Hotel Porter

was rated highly — he was held in high esteem in Munster too. Limerick's versatile Sean Herbert and Prince of midfielders Timmy Ryan, named Harry Gray as one of their midfielders on the team they selected for me in *Giants of the Ash*. Jack Lynch of Cork named him among the men he particularly admired and Wexford's Padge Kehoe chose him on his team as one of his midfielders.

Harry was a drifter. He moved from job to job — often aided by Tommy Moore, the great Kilkennyman who had a pub in Dublin and who brought many a fine hurler to the capital and looked after them. Harry eventually found his real niche as a porter at the Gresham Hotel — a job ideally suited to his personality and temperament. Liam O'Neill told me a lovely story about Harry as porter — that truly reflects the charisma of the man.

'Liz Taylor and Richard Burton were filming in Ardmore and staying in a luxury suite at The Gresham. One evening Richard

Burton told The Gresham manager, Toddy Sullivan, that he would love to see the Dublin of Yeats and Sean O'Casey. No need for a second thought. Toddy knew he had the ideal man in Harry and assigned him to the job. The itinerary included a visit to the hurling drinking haunts. Harry who was of course well known in Dublin was greeted cordially everywhere he went and two drinks served up for himself and his friend. That evening neither Harry nor Richard had to pay for any drink — much to the amusement and bewilderment of Richard Burton. He was really enjoying the Dublin of Yeats and Sean O'Casey — and in particular the company of Harry and his numerous friends. The assignment lasted for a week. As they parted company Richard slipped a one hundred pound note into Harry's top pocket. Liz, who by now had heard a great deal about the kindly qualities of Harry, handed him a voucher for two bicycles from McHughs, for his two young daughters.'

Harry resumed his job as Porter with happy memories of two of the screens greatest celebrities.

Canon Sean Collier PP Borris-in-Ossory, a native of Camross, was a team mate of Harry's in 1948. Here are his momories:

'On my return to the dioceses of Ossory in December 1955, I was appointed CC in Rathdowney parish.

'Harry was born here in Mill Street in 1915. I had played with him on the Laois 1948 team. We played and beat Kilkenny in Portlaoise in the semi-final, but we were beaten by Dublin in the Leinster final in Tullamore.

'Harry was very supportive to us "young lads" and he called me over in the hotel where we togged out and with his big hand on my shoulder said, "you and Kevin (Molloy) can swing this one for us."

'As we (being clerical students) were banned from hurling we could not or were not allowed to play in 1949. Laois went on to contest the 1949 final against Tipperary, but alas were beaten and this was Harry's swan song at inter-county level.

'A school pal of Harry's, Michael Golden told me that Harry had a great love for the game and often spent hours pucking a ball against the wall. In fact, this is how he acquired his great skill of striking left and right. They had a great "street team" known as the "Flourbags" — their togs were made from them.

'When I came to Rathdowney in the mid-fifties it was obvious that the good work had continued on as Rathdowney produced some of the finest under-age teams you could ask for or see.

'Harry won his only Laois SH medal with his native parish Rathdowney in 1936. He had already won a Parish School's Cup medal in 1930 and a minor county championship in 1933. Despite his many great games for club and county he was lured to Dublin by Tommy Moore of Faughs (the friend of so many great Laois hurlers) in 1937. The policy then was you played for the county where you got your bread and butter. Perhaps this was fortunate for Harry as he succeeded in winning his only All Ireland medal with Dublin in 1938.

'It was ten years later when he returned to play for his native county. This was the twilight of his career and despite his best efforts, Tipperary proved too good and so Harry had to say farewell to the game he loved so well.

'Big in physique — he relied very much on his skill to "read the game" and make maximum use o f the least opportunity. His fine striking accuracy was tops and he could score from any angle.

'I found that the schoolboys could still say, "that's how Harry Gray did it" and indeed in another county many of those young lads would certainly have played in Croke Park. When I visited him in hospital shortly before his death, he still had high hopes for Laois hurlers — his witty comment was, "will they listen to you Fr Sean".'

He died in 1978. But he is not forgotten in his native Laois. His memory is commemorated through the Harry Gray Cup which is now presented each year to the Laois minor hurling champions.

Born: 1929

"

Having been born, bred and reared in Dublin, my father and mother coming from Longford, it may be wondered how I would have had any interest in hurling. However and strangely enough when I was growing up in Drumcondra the sports I took part in were hurling and soccer and both these games we played on the street. This combination was not at all unusual in Dublin and there was a standard of hurling then in the primary schools which was of the highest quality. Indeed an old soccer colleague of mine, Liam Whelan who tragically died in the Munich air crash when he was a Manchester United player, was an outstanding hurler and if I remember rightly he played for the Dublin primary schools against Belfast.

It was when I went to Colaiste Mhuire that my real interest developed and a Brother O'Coillean was a marvellous coach and I suppose from that point onwards my only interest was the game of hurling although I did play for Dublin in football for a few years.

There is no more satisfying game than the hurling and probably the nearest thing to the satisfaction of connecting right with a sliotar is to hit a good drive in golf, shot off the tee box.

There is no doubt but that hurlers are a special breed and whenever we meet, unfortunately usually at funerals, there is only one subject debated — many times over I suppose, but still only the one topic.

I had the great privilege of playing with and against marvellous players and indeed people. Paddy Grace always said that Des Foley was the best centrefield player he had ever seen since Lory Meagher. Achil Boothman was an artist and regretably Dublin did not sustain prominence long enough to illustrate the skills and courage that he had.

In my time Tim Flood, Christy Ring, Jimmy Doyle and Nicky Rackard put many a ball past me, and I'll never forgive Sean Clohessy for his last minute goal in the 1959 Leinster final. As to the best player that I have ever seen it has to be Eddie Keher.

I played in the 1961 All Ireland final in which Tipperary beat us by a point. Apart altogether from the personal disappointment, it was a tragedy from the point of view of the further development of the game in Dublin that we lost that game. I feel hurling nationally would have been much more universally played had we won that All Ireland.

Finally, I wouldn't trade any of my hurling experiences for all the rewards in the world.

Jimmy Gray **"**

If success alone is the measure of hurling progress then Dublin fares rather badly — the history graph is a downward one. Dublin struck a purple patch for the eleven years beginning 1917 during which time they won four All Ireland titles — albeit with a preponderance of players domiciled in Dublin from down the country. In the thirties they contested three All Irelands and won one — 1938 — their last success to date. Their captain that day was Tipperary born Mick Daniels — still going strong. Four finals were contested in the forties — all without success. In 1952 they won their only Leinster title of that decade and lost to Cork in the final. In that game the Down born Des Ferguson at right-half-back had a memorable first half on Christy Ring and over the hour acquitted himself with distinction and must have felt very pleased with his performance. Now to 1961 — the last time they won a Leinster title — the last time they appeared in an All Ireland final. Des Ferguson, one of Dublin's great dual players was the only link with the 1952 team. He was now at right-full-back.

Jimmy Gray was in goal. He remembers the occasion well. 'We had a very good team and had played well in the league so it was a question of getting it right on the day. Remember that in the Leinster final of 1959 we only lost by two points to Kilkenny and we beat All Ireland champions Wexford in the Leinster final of 1961. After our performance in the 1961 All Ireland Dublin had eight players on the Leinster Railway Cup team — the entire full-back line of Des Ferguson, Noel Drumgoole and Lar Foley — the two mid-fielders Des Foley and Mick Kennedy and three forwards Achil Boothman, Fran Whelan and Willie Jackson — and they beat Munster by two points in the final. So we certainly had the hurlers to compete with the best. We were quietly confident — without being too confident. Tipp had a lot of famous names and experienced hurlers in their lineout. It was a moderate first half at the end of which we were four points behind. Our lads gave an exhibition in the second half and played some great ground hurling. As the game wore on we began to realise that the men of Tipp were only human like ourselves. About midway through the second half we went a point ahead and even though we lost Lar Foley through sending off with Tom Ryan about

the same time, things began to look good. We were still a point ahead when I asked Maurice Hayes the umpire how much time there was to go. He reckoned three to four minutes. By this time Tipp had made a switch that proved masterly — Devaney to centre-back — he cleared everything.' When the final whistle blew it was Tipperary 0:16 Dublin 1:12. Jimmy had played a fine game and kept a clean goal. Dublin had played very well but they squandered chances. 'After the game a great sense of depression set in. A win would have meant so much to Dublin hurling. The youth would have been inspired and interest in the game would have multiplied. Hill 16 would have filled with hurling enthusiasts.'

I asked Jimmy if he thought they would have won a replay. 'I often thought about that. I think we would — especially after our performance. We had some excellent hurlers — Noel Drumgoole who it was a delight to play behind — Des Foley who was a majestic midfielder — Bernard Boothman who was a very intelligent player — Paddy Croke, a Tipperary man who was most loyal to Dublin hurling all his life and who could play in any position — Lar Foley, Des Ferguson, Willie Jackson, Fran Whelan and Achil Boothman who were all very experienced. It was really a question of taking our chances. We played Tipp afterwards in the Oireachtas in Carrick-on-Suir and even though short some players including Des Foley we lost by only a point. Yes, I would have given us a good chance in a replay.'

In most close encounters there are talking points and items of controversy. The 1961 final was no exception. Jimmy recalls that with Dublin leading by a point and the game well into the last quarter Donie Nealon sent in a shot that went about a yard wide of the upright but the umpire signalled a point. 'It was a body blow decision to a team like Dublin. I was very annoyed about it. My brother who was stewarding came running across because even from where he was it was an obvious wide.' After the publication of *Giants of the Ash*, a Christian

Brother who had seen every All Ireland from 1947 to 1961 wrote to me after he had read the book. The following excerpt relates to the 1961 final. 'You may recall the incident which lost the 1961 All Ireland final for Dublin. I believe the sending off of Lar Foley and Ryan (Tipp) turned the tide against Dublin. The Boothman brothers were flying at that stage and the writing was on the wall for Tipp. Two very doubtful frees against "Snitchy" Ferguson for picking the ball off the ground gave Tipp two golden points which made all the difference at the end ... my heart was with Dublin on that day.'

Jimmy's club, Na Fianna, only came into being in 1955 and during his playing days they were successful at junior and intermediate level. Jimmy was a talented footballer too. He came on as a sub in 1955 to help defeat Longford in the championship — 'much to my father's disappointment.' And Jimmy still wonders how they lost to Kerry in the 1955 football final — and why the selectors played a few who were unfit for the fray — and why the signs weren't read early on and corrective action taken.

After his playing days Jimmy remained very active in GAA affairs. He was Chairman of Dublin County Board from 1971 to 1980. For a three year term ending 1992 he was Chairman of the Leinster Council. He has just made an unsuccessful bid for the position of President of the Association. At present he is manager of the Dublin hurling team. He agrees that in this capacity his most difficult task is trying to identify players who have the combination of characteristics and talents that are required at county level. The fact that there are so

many clubs adds to the difficulty of his task. Jimmy feels that if there was a premier championship consisting of less clubs and incorporating perhaps divisional or district teams that it might lead to the selection of a better county fifteen.

Regarding the rules he would abolish the kicked goal — consider getting rid of the small square — and set up a rules committee akin to that in rugby, 'the present system of examining the rules is too cumbersome.'

His days on the playing field always evoke pleasant memories and the passage of time adds depth and glow to those bygone days.

This is his team from the men of his era.

Jimmy Gray (Dublin)

'Fan' Larkin (Kilkenny)	Noel Drumgoole (Dublin)	Jimmy Brohan (Cork)
Phil Grimes (Waterford)	Tony Wall (Tipperary)	Jimmy Finn (Tipperary)

Des Foley (Dublin)   Ned Wheeler (Wexford)

Achil Boothman (Dublin)	Christy Ring (Cork)	Donie Nealon (Tipperary)
Tim Flood (Wexford)	Nicky Rackard (Wexford)	Eddie Keher (Kilkenny)

Born: c.1872

Sean Óg hailed from Kilfinane. He has been described as 'the greatest hurler of his day'.

He was a giant among giants in the early days of hurling and he was the outstanding man on the field when Limerick (Kilfinane) defeated Kilkenny (Tullaroan) by 3:4 to 2:4 to take their first All Ireland title in 1897 — played on 20th November 1898. It was Kilkenny's third failure and Tullaroan's second since the championship began.

It was Limerick's first time contesting a final. In the Munster campaign Cork had an easy win over Tipperary. In the Southern final Limerick overcame Cork on the score 4:9 to 1:6. Hanley was the outstanding man of the match with two goals and a point to his credit.

The final against Kilkenny was played in Tipperary town. Limerick were captained by Denis Grimes and once again inspired by their star man Sean Óg Hanley. The 1897 victory was sandwiched in between five Tipperary All Ireland victories that began in 1895 with Tuberadoora the leading name of those days.

Sean Óg's real christian name was James but spectators of the day who watched him in action were reminded of the style and ability of his grandfather Sean — so they named him Sean Óg — and it stuck.

He was a ciotóg — holding his hurley right hand under — and was a natural left hander.

He was a man of great strength — over six feet one inch in height and weighed about fourteen stone. The length of his clearances was prodigious and another great asset was the speed with which he could lift and turn. So widespread was his fame and renown that when a young hurler on any team or in any county showed unusual promise he was referred to as 'a second Sean Óg'.

He emigrated to England and was associated with the London team which shocked Cork in the All Ireland final of 1901 — winning on the score 1:5 to 0:4 — and played on 2nd August, 1903.

In 1900 he played with London in the All Ireland final against Tipperary losing on the score 2:5 to 0:6. That game was played at Jones' Road on 26th October 1902.

When he died in his early fifties he was mourned by the hurling world but remembered long afterwards as the team selection hereunder shows. He is buried in Kensal Rise Cemetary and so great was the esteem in which he was held that the Gaels of Limerick and London subscribed to erect a memorial over his grave.

In the mid fifties P.D. Mehigan ('Carbery') picked a hurling fifteen titled 'The Best Men of My Time' for *The Gaelic Sportsman*.

He had seen more than fifty hurling finals. Here are excerpts from his introduction — excerpts that reflect very accurately the views of all those who have been asked to select a special fifteen.

When I went carefully through my file register I realised it was not fifteen men in hurling I would pick but fifteen hundred great men.

It is a pretty hard job to name the best fifteen in Ireland of any one year.'

Tomorrow or next day I could pick two

other teams very little behind the first. And so go on ad infinitum.

So here we go with an all-time, but rather lame effort:

CARBERY'S ALL-TIME FIFTEEN

John ('Skinny') O'Meara (Tipperary)

Dan Coughlan (Cork)   **Sean Óg Hanley (Limerick)**   Mick Derivan (Galway)

Pat Stakelum (Tipperary)   James Kelliher (Cork)   Dick Grace (Kilkenny)

Lory Meagher (Kilkenny)   Jim Hurley (Cork)

Eugene Coughlan (Cork)   Mick Mackey (Limerick)   Tom Semple (Tipperary)

Mattie Power (Kilkenny)   Martin Kennedy (Tipperary)   Christy Ring (Cork)

London-Irish — who defeated Cork — the 1901 All-Ireland Champions with whom Sean Óg Hanley was associated

Back row: W Douglas (Hon Sec), P King (Clare), J O'Connell (Limerick), Tim Doody (Limerick), T Redmond (Wexford), Dan Horgan (Cork), J McCarthy (Kilkenny), referee: L J O'Toole (Sec Central Council), J Shine (Galway). Second row: J Tobin (Hon Treas), J Lynch (Cork), Jack King (Clare), Ned Barrett (Kerry), C Crowley (Cork), J Fitzgerald (Limerick), M McMahon (Tipperary), M O'Brien, Wm McCarthy (President). Front row: M Horgan (Cork), Jim Barry (Cork), J O'Brien (Cork), J G Coughlin (Capt) (Clare), J Kelleher (Cork), Tom Barry (Cork), J O'Brien (Clare).

Born: 1950

"

Little did I think that growing up in Donoughmore, a hinterland of Limerick City, as a young lad during the fifties that it would provide me in the future with a culture that was to play a significant part in developing me through boyhood, to the present day.

The culture into which I was born, blessed me by creating a platform for me to grow, appreciate and enjoy the true values of rural Ireland. The culture which I refer to is one where I learned to strive for success both in mind and body where one's own ability to succeed was only surpassed by one's ability to be humble.

This culture was fashioned through school, work and play. All three were consistently tangible to one another, where play followed work, and work followed school. Without school and work there could be no play. With hindsight it was a marvellous way to utilise your playtime to the fullest.

Playtime was dominated by the game of hurling. During the 1950s one's aim was to be a John Doyle, a Christy Ring or indeed an Art Foley. These were the men most often spoken of by our forefathers and to dream of being one of these giants would

almost assure you a place in eternal folklore.

The mystique that surrounded such great players was awe-inspiring. Every 'three goals in' was adorned by these names or equally famous names of that era and it was always one's intention to carry out the skills of the game in a manner that would justify being called by one of the game's great names.

Donoughmore schoolyard, Butler's field and Hickey's closs, all carried the honour of being Croke Park from time to time. Often during the summer evenings these games were ended only by the fear of the dark.

Drombanna, along with the townlands of Donoughmore, Ballysheedy, Ballyneety and Knockea formed the backbone of the great South Liberties GAA club. It wasn't until I was fifteen years old that I had the honour of first wearing the famous 'green and gold'. The privilege and honour to play for South Liberties was never surpassed by any sporting achievement that came my way throughout my playing career. Even today every facet of my sporting life is dulled in comparison to the glorious memories I hold within myself from my playing days with South Liberties.

Today men like J.P. McManus, Joe McKenna and Eamon Grimes are strong personal friends, bonded together through their efforts and aspirations in steering South Liberties to greatness.

But the great names of South Liberties did not end there. We have had the brave Dooleys, the skilful Shanahans, the speedy Wades, the mighty Ryans, the fearless Crokers, the classy Butlers, just to mention a few. These were men who projected a glowing image throughout their playing days of all that is good in Irish manhood.

To bring the game of hurling back to its former glory days of whichever decade you wish, the club structure has to be revitalised and nurtured so that young ambitions can once again be kindled in order that the famous names of today can create the mystique for the youth of tomorrow.

Wouldn't it be great to be little boys again. **"**

It was 21 June 1979 and Pat was touring West Clare with friends from Los Angeles — friends he had stayed with on an All Stars visit to the States. At the same time he was looking forward to the Munster final against Cork. He was captain and he was hoping to emulate the deeds of 1973 — repeat its successes and relive all the joy and glory once again. He was confident. 'From the 1973 lineout there was myself, Eamon Grimes, Joe McKenna, Eamon Cregan, Liam O'Donoghue and Sean Foley still playing. I remember talking to Christy Ring in 1978 and he felt that after their four Munster titles and three All Irelands in a row that Cork's glory days were coming to an end. Indeed, in 1977 and 1978 fortune had favoured Cork when they twice beat a quite talented Clare team. In the quarter final of the 1978/79 league we played great hurling against Galway but a last minute goal gave them a one point victory. I felt in 1979 that we were the team more on the upswing than any other team'. And yet premonition and a strange foreboding was clouding in on top of Pat. He said to his friends he had a feeling that his 'hurling days were coming to an end.'

He had picked up a thigh injury in the game against Clare. It was responding slowly so when he went to the Gaelic grounds to train he began off doing some jogging. He then decided to tog out and play in a session of backs and forwards. He was marking Eamon Cregan but no play was coming their way. 'I suggested to Eamon that we move out but he said that if he moved out the selectors would be shout-ing at him to go back in. I moved towards midfield and a ball came my way. I hit it aside one handed — preparing to clear left handed. An incoming forward pulled against me — the ball flew up — I didn't get a chance to duck — the high ridge of the sliotar flicked off the eye centre and damaged the optic nerve.

I was removed to the Regional Hospital. What I had said to my Los Angeles friends flashed through my head when I got the belt of the ball. When they visited me in hospital they recalled my words with dis-belief.' It was now a battle against time if Pat was to play against Cork. Having been discharged from hospital he went to the Gaelic Grounds with Noel Drumgoole — the team manager — and they stood a dis-tance of fifty yards apart pucking the ball to each other. Pat was catching. Then Noel mishit one which dropped thirty yards away from Pat but he stood there waiting to catch it. That clarified and confirmed for Pat what the doctors had told him — he was going to have difficulty with distance and depth. He then went to the Handball Alley at St Munchin's College and began belting a ball against the wall. 'I found myself putting up my hand to catch it that split second late. I couldn't judge speed. I said to Noel — call this off — unless the eye improves I will have to withdraw from the Munster final. I kept my options open until forty eight hours before the game. I desper-ately wanted to play. It was a bad decision. It didn't give my understudy a chance to prepare.'

After the Munster final Pat travelled to the States to see if anything could be done to improve the eye. He went through a series of tests. The findings were the same as those back home. He returned with eye guards. His love for the game kept him hoping against hope. During 1980 he trained a bit — stayed part of the panel — didn't tog out with the team as he wasn't psychologically ready for this. The adjust-ment in his vision he was hoping for was not happening — the eye was not respond-ing. The level of vision in the damaged eye remained at ten percent.

Pat Hartigan about to take 'a wee deoch' during the Puck Fada competition.

In September 1980 he decided he would have another go at the game. He played full-forward for South Liberties against Patrickswell — 'I got a slight cut over the good eye — scored three goals — and Joe McKenna also scored three goals.' In the county final against Killeedy he moved out from full-forward to centre-forward and in the process of blocking down an opponent got hit in the good eye. It closed completely. In the anxious days that followed he had plenty of time to reach a definite and absolute conclusion on his hurling future. He used to lift up the eyelid of the closed eye and was grateful to discover that he could see. Pat now realised he had pushed his desire to play hurling to the very limits of common sense. Those days he spent in darkness made up his mind — his eyesight took precedence over his hurling.

So Pat, this warrior-like giant at the age of thirty — in superb physical shape and health — had to abandon at the height of his career the game he adored and adorned. He loved it so much he would certainly have given it another seven years at least. I think in the ordinary course of things Pat would never have decided to retire. 'If the selectors think you are good enough then you are never too old.' He wasn't yet twenty nine when the final curtain came down on his inter-county hurling career.

Happily, he had much to look back on — All Ireland, Railway Cup, Oireachtas, Provincial, National League and County title honours. He received five All Star awards in a row from 1971-75 in the full-back position — a remarkable record. He is especially proud of the 1973 All Star award. He was the only nominee and therefore an automatic choice. His school days brought many honours too — days when like every youngster he had his own selection of stars he admired and on occasions wondered in awe at — Jimmy Doyle and John Doyle of Tipperary, Nick O'Donnell and Ned Wheeler of Wexford and Ollie Walsh of Kilkenny. 'I used admire Ollie and I remember feeling after the drawn game against Waterford in the 1959 All Ireland final that he must be a real wizard altogether. Kilkenny scored 5:5 to Waterford's 1:17 and it was only in the final seconds that that lone goal passed Ollie.' With Limerick CBS he won Harty Cup honours in 1966 and 1967. The

Munster title of 1966 was converted into All Ireland honours. In 1967 St Peter's College Wexford defeated CBS in the All Ireland final after a replay — with Martin Quigley playing a key role in that victory. In 1968 CBS again reached the Munster final of the Harty cup and were opposed by Coláiste Chríost Rí of Cork. CBS were seeking a record five in a row. I reminded Pat how proud Brian Murphy of Cork was and still is of the Coláiste Chríost Rí win in 1968 — in Brian's words against the odds. 'Don't remind me of it. That's a sore one — it's a very sore one. We were favourites but by no means over confident. We had played basically against the same team in Dean Ryan cup games in earlier years and never found them easy. It's still a sore one — don't remind me of it.' He played minor hurling for Limerick for four years from 1965-1968 and he played in six successive years at under 21 level from 1966-71.

But it wasn't sufficient to be able to just look back. Pat now needed something to fill the vacuum. It came mainly in two forms. The first was athletics which he was always good at since his school days — especially the sixteen pound shot putt. In that competition he represented Ireland on four occasions — winning in Dublin in 1968 and taking second place in Spain in 1969. The second was the Puck Fada competition. It commemorates the legend of Setanta when he travelled from his father's house in Dundalk to his uncle's home in Armagh. So as to shorten the journey he took with him his hurley and ball — pucking it up into the sky and running with speed to meet it as it fell and by pulling on the dropping ball kept it airborne for the entire journey. The modern competition covers a three and a half mile course — starting near Carlingford and finishing at Corn na Madra. 'I entered the competition in 1981 and won. It brought me a huge element of compensation — to be able to handle a hurley again and puck the ball — to get an opportunity to compete. I beat Tommy Quaid. I defended the title the following year which threw up a surprise winner in Gerry Goodwin of Tyrone — a

win that resulted apparently from a counting error over the second half of the course. I finished in second place. I made my protest but accepted defeat. In 1983 I qualified in Munster with victory in Tipperary town. Ger Cunningham in second place went through with me. In the final I won again — Ger Cunningham was second — and Gerry Goodwin the 1982 winner finished in fifteenth place. The following year I was dethroned by Ger Cunningham, one of Cork's greatest goalkeepers.'

Without a doubt 1973 was the year of hurling highlights for Pat — the year of the breakthrough. It made up for 1971 when Limerick, the league champions, beat Cork in a thrilling Munster semi-final and then at Killarney failed to Tipperary by two points in another thriller — a game that left Limerick followers talking about the might have beens. It made up too for the surprising first round defeat at the hands of Clare in 1972 when Clare showed the kind of potential that made them a threat to the best all through the seventies.

1973 began with a narrow and hard earned win over Clare. Then to Thurles to face Tipperary — already carrying the Cork scalp — in the Munster final in their own back yard. 'We were based at the Anner Hotel. The trip to the pitch was slow moving because of the huge crowd. It was a mid-July day and the humidity was over powering. There were six of us in the car and we had to leave the windows open. People were putting books and slips of paper in the windows for autographs. It added to the excitement. At last we were in the dressing-room. The tension was incredible. This was Tipp's home ground — where they would be perceived by many as invincible. Even in the dressing-room the humidity was evident. I never saw so much water spilled in any dressing-room. It was approaching time to go out onto the pitch. Eamon Grimes spoke and I doubt if there was ever a better captain of any team. Facing Tipp brought out the best in him. Holding up his jersey he said — this is what it's about — today is the day — any man who thinks this isn't worth dying for —

stay here — we will go out without you. We all shared his feelings. We didn't need motivation going out to play Tipperary.

Running onto the pitch the roar of the crowd was deafening. Out on the pitch I got a feeling of claustrophobia — every exit was cut off — there was a feeling of no air — it was a cauldron of noise.' Now the toss of the coin — the parade — the pitch in perfect condition — the roar of the crowd increases — the tricolour is faced and the band strikes up Amhrán na Bhfiann — the crowd joins in and the players take deep breaths — the band scurries off the field — the throw in and the game is on. Limerick had eighty minutes to avenge '71. And they did it in a tense thriller. Hitchcock couldn't have written a better script. For it was with the last puck of the game — as indicated by the referee — that Richie Bennis sent over the winner from a seventy. And then he was engulfed. London were defeated in the semi-final and Limerick then faced the artists and stylists of Kilkenny in the final. Now to the dressing-room in Croke Park.

'Jackie Power, our coach — a warrior of great Limerick teams of the 30's and 40's gave us a pep talk. He spoke about 1940 when he was part of a Limerick team that defeated Kilkenny in the All Ireland final and said he wouldn't have believed then that it would take so long for Limerick to return again to Croke Park for All Ireland day. He was emotional. He told us he was a young man then but that he wasn't a young man now. Then the tears came. It sent a shiver through us. After a pause he just said — Go out and win it. I'll always remember Jackie's words. They remain with me to this day — more vivid than any aspect of the game. At half time we were two points ahead 0:12 to 1:7 and determined to win. Eamon Grimes spoke before going out again. In forty minutes I am going across for that cup and I want you all behind me. Here's my speech he said as he put it down inside his stocking.

We were six points ahead and the crowd was coming in over the Canal end and at the Nally Stand. Two further points sent us eight points clear. I didn't realise it was so near the end — the second half seemed to go very quickly. "Chunky" O'Brien got possession and sent over a Kilkenny point — we were now seven points ahead. The crowd was massing and increasing. I asked the umpire how much time was left. He waved his hands. I wasn't sure what it meant. Then I saw the referee Mick Slattery of Clare with his hand up. I still can't remember whether I pucked out the ball or not.' It didn't matter. It was over. They followed Eamon Grimes to the Hogan Stand. The crowd stood and chanted and cheered in glorious exhultation. The McCarthy Cup was on the way to the Shannonside for the first time in thirty three years.

Pat was a giant of the hurling arena — six foot three and fourteen stone ten — agile and athletic — dedicated and disciplined — a modern day Cuchulainn — a shining example to youth. He never used his strength unfairly. His sportsmanship was impeccable. It was an unwritten precept of Pat's never to act in a manner on the hurling field that would in any way sully the image of the great game. 'It would upset me to be remembered as a dirty player — or mean or dangerous. I was never sent off and never had my name taken for dirty play. I was booked once for a personal foul. From my early days at full-back I took a conscious decision to adopt and develop an open style plan of play — and it worked for me. Any high ball coming in within about thirty yards I believed in going for it and fetching it. That meant that instead of me marking the full-forward and playing him from behind, he had to adjust to the idea of marking me. Ray Cummins was the best full-forward I played on — a friendship was forged in those clashes on the pitch. Joe McKenna was the best full forward I never played on — nor would I have looked forward to opposing him.'

He has the highest of praise for the goal keeping brilliance of Noel Skehan of Kilkenny. 'The All Stars played Tipperary at Wembley. Going on to the pitch Noel said to me to let Roger Ryan the full forward hit any ball he got outside the twenty one yards line — adding I'll block it. If he gets it anyplace on or inside the fourteen yards hassle him and keep hassling him. It will slow up his shot and when he throws it up I'll be able to judge where he is shooting for and save it. On one occasion Roger slipped me and I chased him right into the goal line. He threw up the ball to palm it to the net and as he did so Skehan snatched it. He was a magnificent goalkeeper — he was supremely confident.'

Pat's older brother Bernie — just under six feet and over fourteen stone — was also a giant of the sporting scene; hurling, football, handball, discus, hammer, javelin and 16lb shot. He represented Ireland in 1969 and 1971 at hammer and discus throwing. He played senior hurling and senior football for Limerick and was selected on the Munster Railway Cup teams in both codes — hurling 1966, '67, '68, '70, '71 and football 1969. His hurling successes include a National League, Oireachtas and All Ireland title also two Munster titles and three Railway cup titles.

Looking back now Pat feels privileged and blessed to have been able to take part in the great game of hurling at the highest level — and as the years pass nostalgia adds glitter to those wonderful days.

Pat Hartigan (left) and Eamon Cregan (right) of Limerick in the 1973 All Ireland final.

Born: 1958

"

Hurling has always been in my life. Fr Jack Solan, RIP claimed that I was so young and small that he had to get a special short hurley made for me for the school's team. That would have been in the late sixties when Galway hurling at juvenile level was undergoing a revival that would have a major knock-on effect in later years.

Club hurling was played with Kiltormer who along with Laurencetown and Clantusbert won several minor and under 21 titles in the seventies along with making the breakthough to senior level in 1976 and winning the senior championship in 1976 and 1977.

Galway minor hurlers were well beaten in 1975 and 1976 but success was to follow at the under 21 final of 1978 when we beat Tipperary in a replay at Limerick. All Ireland senior success was more difficult to achieve but finally came in 1980 after fifty seven years waiting and having been beaten by Kilkenny the previous year. Offaly were to make the big breakthrough the following year at Galway's expense — a final for which I was injured. A few barren years followed up to the Farrell era of 85/90 when Galway contested a total of five All Ireland finals winning two '87 and '88 which I was

fortunate enough to be Captain of. Should have won more but that's the way it goes.

The team of '87 and '88 was by far the best that I have been involved with and won all that was to be won in hurling producing some of the most dedicated and skilful hurlers that I have ever played with. It also signified a major breakthrough for Galway defeating Kilkenny and Tipperary in All Ireland finals which would have been un-heard of twenty years before that.

A hurling career always seems short because of the enjoyment one gets from it and so 1990 saw me finished with the county scene to revert to the club and finish on an absolutely unbelievable note of two county championships and an All Ireland club championship before I called it a day.

There is no other game in the world that I enjoy playing or watching, and played at its best is unequalled for player and spectator.

To all those people who coached, trained and with whom I was associated as a player throughout the years at club, college, school and county level I can only say thanks and the memories will always be cherished and never forgotten.

Conor Hayes

"

It was the afternoon of the first Sunday in September 1980 and in a great game of hurling Galway had defeated Limerick by three points to take their first senior title since 1923. Conor Hayes at right fullback had played a significant part — in a full-back line that had to cope with the wiles and cunning of the Limerick full forward line of Ollie O'Connor, Joe McKenna and Eamon Cregan — in the historic victory and he too was relishing with his colleagues those early moments of celebration on the Hogan Stand. The long wait was over — the alleged 'curse' expunged.

The voice of Joe Connolly spoke — as

gaeilge — as he delivered a rousing victory speech to jubilant followers. The voice of Joe McDonagh spoke — in song — as he entertained the cheering fans with a rendering of 'The West's asleep'.

Conor remembers in his childhood, in the sixties when Galway had poor hurling teams, hearing his father who was a Clareman talking in awesome tones about Munster finals and in his youthful mind he used wonder what it was that was famous about them. And his father would come back from those finals and tell great stories about Christy Ring and Pat Stakelum and Vin Toomey and a host of others — deeds and daring and gallantry — misneach is teasbach is gaiscíocht. It seemed that there wasn't anyone in Galway like them and hopes in that barren decade of Galway winning an All Ireland title were a mere dream. But the dream became a reality in the days of Conor Hayes and his generation of Galway hurlers. 'There was a lot of confidence coming through at underage level during the seventies and most fellows believed an All Ireland would be won at some stage'.

In all close encounters a particular action at a critical juncture can sway the fortunes of battle. It was this that prompted me to ask Conor if he remembered the pass from Eamon Cregan to Joe McKenna that he intercepted late in the closing stages of the 1980 final when Limerick were pressing hard searching for what might be a winning goal and Galway were holding on to a slender lead. He had a vivid recollection and I then asked him if it was instinct or anticipation that brought about the crucial interception. 'It was anticipation. About five minutes earlier Cregan had done the same thing and I think it brought a point. I knew by the way he was holding the hurley and the way the hand holding the ball was positioned that he was going to pass rather than strike. Instead of going in to him I went back from him. I got the top of the hurley to the ball and hit it out over the sideline. At the time I didn't realise the extent of the significance of the interception. If it had gone to Joe McKenna there was nothing

between him and the goal'.

Conor's term in inter-county hurling coincided with Galway's greatest hurling decade. While he was winning three senior titles and a National league he was able to look at the supply line and the healthy picture it presented — eight Vocational school All Ireland titles in a row from 1980 to 1987 — a minor title in 1983 — under 21 titles in 1983 and 1986. It augured well for Galway hurling.

He played in six All Ireland finals — 1979 and 1980 and four in a row from 1985 to 1988. He can look back with satisfaction on the three victories against traditional strongholds. They were all won in close contests — Limerick in 1980 with three points to spare — Kilkenny in 1987 with six points to spare — Tipp. in 1988 with four points to spare. Offaly proved to be a bogey team beating them in 1981 and 1985 and 'we struck our lowest point in 1984 when they hammered us in Thurles in the All Ireland semi-final, and I was captain'. I suggested that Galway might well have won two sets of three in a row during his time. '1979 to 1981 was possible. It's strange that in those three finals we beat what was easily the best of the three teams — in the only one we won — when we beat Limerick in 1980'. The semi-final defeat at the hands of Tipp. in 1989 was his biggest disappointment — 'more so than the final defeat by Cork in '86 — we were fairly naive in '86, we should have known better in '89 — we had a lot under our belt — we had the luxury of a lot of good players coming through — three in a row was on'.

Great moments that will live in his memory and that time will not dim are the historic victory over Limerick in 1980 that brought so much joy to their followers, and the defeat of Kilkenny under his captaincy in 1987 in a hard tough game — it was a test of Galway mettle — when he had perhaps his most satisfying hour and there followed the second of his three successive All Star awards. The All Ireland victory of '87 was sealed following two great second half saves by goalkeeper John Commins and the scoring of the only goal of the game less than ten minutes from the end by Noel Lane. It was a year too when Galway won every league game they played and Conor captained them to league honours.

The winning of the All Ireland club title by Kiltormer in 1992 was another unforgettable moment. 'The club victory parallels anything I won during my career. It means so much to a rural club. Hurling is deep rooted in Kiltormer. Even in the sixties when Galway were winning three in a row in football it was hurling rather than football that was played in Kiltormer. We had three fantastic games in a saga with Cashel — the third at Croke Park. All three games could have gone either way. It was a sin that either team had to go out. Those games gave us great confidence and the experience gained stood to us in our victory in the final against Birr at Thurles'. It was

Conor's farewell to hurling.

In his young and impressionable years he was captivated by the hurling performances of Jimmy Doyle and Mick Roche of Tipperary, Pat Henderson and Eddie Keher of Kilkenny and he remembers watching the 1968 final between Wexford and Tipperary on television and 'being happy when the underdog Wexford won'.

Conor is the most recent of only three players ever to have captained his county to successive All Ireland victories. Mikey Maher of Tipperary did it in 1895 and 1896. Christy Ring led Cork to success in 1953 and 1954. The honour fell to Conor in 1987 and 1988. Indeed many would feel that but for a combination of unfortunate circumstances in 1989 he might well have led his native Galway to a unique and record breaking three in a row.

Conor Hayes of Galway with (behind) Eugene Coughlan, Offaly.

Born: 1943

"

I developed a love of hurling at a very early age when my father, who never played the game, used bring me as a small boy to games in Thurles, Kilkenny and Portlaoise. In those early days, late forties and early fifties, I remember seeing players like Ring, Langton and indeed Harry Gray of Laois in action. In those days I tried in the local national school to emulate the feats of those heroes of the time. In the early fifties I also watched the famous Rackard brothers of Wexford in action and when we played our own little games around the farmyard at home or in the schoolyard, we would assume the role of Rackard or Langton or Ring.

When I left national school and went to Thurles CBS in the mid fifties, I arrived in a real hot bed of hurling. This was where in years past several famous Tipp stars like the Doyles, Stakelum, Finn, Wall and many others had been to school. It was here the Brothers began to develop my skills and in my second year at college I won my first medal. In 1958 Tipp won the senior title and Tony Wall brought the McCarthy Cup to the school. John O'Grady, one of my teachers, was in fact the goalkeeper on that occasion. This occasion instilled a great desire in me to play in an All Ireland and represent my county.

In 1961 I first wore the black and amber at minor level and it was with this team I first came under the influence of Rev Fr Tommy Maher. He was to play a major part in the development of my career, particularly a few years later when I began to play on the senior team. The lessons learned from him on the training ground have been put to good use not just in my playing days but also in latter years when as a trainer or coach I have tried to pass on his knowledge.

I have been fortunate to have lived played and coached in a great era in Kilkenny hurling, to have won every honour in the game with my county. I have met and made lifelong friends with great men both from my own county and also the counties we played against Cork, Tipp Limerick, Wexford, Galway, Dublin, Offaly, Waterford, Clare. I also have fond memories of playing inter-provincial with some great men from Kildare, Westmeath, Laois and Carlow.

I would rate on a par with any of the great inter-county, the players and members of my own club 'Fenians Johnstown' who came together to form that club in the late sixties and in 1970 win the first senior title for the parish. I was honoured to have captained that team which went on to win four more senior titles between 1970 and 1977. In 1977 both John and Ger also played on the winning team and they both then went on to play inter-county with distinction.

I have been directly involved in the game over the past twenty five years and this has been possible because of the great interest and love of the game by all of my family, in particular Mary my wife and I am delighted to see my three sons so actively involved now as players and deriving much enjoyment from it.

"

Pat Henderson was one of hurling's most majestic centre-half-backs. A career that spanned fifteen years is dotted with numerous outstanding performances. No honour of the day eluded him. But even Homer nods and Pat knew what it was like to fall from grace and spend a session on the sideline. It happened after the 1971 All Ireland final against Tipperary — lost in a high scoring game by 5:17 to 5:14 — yet it might have been won. Pat was captain. 'Ollie Walsh and myself were made to shoulder most of the blame for the defeat. We sat together on the sideline for about six months after that. I can still see a ball hit by Noel O'Dwyer from far out travelling along the ground and beating Ollie in the goal in that final. He had given great service since 1956 — didn't make it back — Noel (Skehan) replaced him.'

In September 1971 Pat was heading for 29 years of age. It was a bad age at which to be dropped — especially in Kilkenny where so much young talent is always to hand. There might be no road back. 'About three weeks before the All Ireland I peaked in a county championship game against The Rower Inistioge. From then on I was going down. After the All Ireland I played in a league game against Limerick — wasn't feeling good, played terribly, and was taken off.' There followed months of watching from the sideline. But Pat was determined to come back. He was prepared to be patient and persevere. 'I wasn't going to give up. It was the stubbornness in me.'

He has fond memories of Thurles CBS and its Brothers where he learned a lot about hurling. In his native parish there was no club tradition at that time. It was only in the late sixties that Johnstown became a force in Kilkenny hurling and gave to the county such outstanding players as Pat Delaney, Billy Fitzpatrick, Nicky Orr and of course his two brothers Ger and John. 'I was the first from the parish to play on the county team since John Holohan in 1922.'

As a child he played in goal — then moved to full-back — won his first ever medal at left-full-forward — his second medal at centre-back and played centre-back as a minor. At county senior level he played right-half-back in 1964, right-full-back in 1966 and from 1967 onwards was at centre-back. It was his favourite position — he was happiest there. In that demanding berth he gave performances that made him comparable as a hurler to the elite centre-backs of the game — such as John Keane of Waterford, Jim Regan of Cork, Paddy Clohessy of Limerick, Billy and Bobby Rackard of Wexford and Pat Stakelum and Tony Wall of Tipperary.

Watching him perform on the field, there were occasions when one got the feeling that the man was indestructable. It is therefore hard to believe that in 1990 at the young age of 47 he had to undergo a quad-ruple by-pass. 'I suppose it is hard to reconcile both. I played a hurling match of sorts — Fenians Johnstown v Dicksboro — three weeks before the operation. I played squash the week before. It all came to light when I went for a check-up.' But his physical fitness stood to him and he was back at work within six weeks. He still pucks the ball about and continues to be deeply involved in coaching. Last year 1993 he coached Dicksboro who ironically defeated his native Johnstown — powered by his brothers Ger and John — in the final.

He finds it as energy sapping on the sideline as it was on the pitch. 'I play every ball. I should relax a bit but I can't.' He fell from grace in the coaching/training sphere too. 'Eddie Keher and myself shared the task in 1979 and we had a good win over Galway. We were beaten in 1980 by Offaly as they made their breakthrough. I was sacked at the end of that year. I got the job back in 1982 and was there for five years. We won All Ireland and League doubles in 1982 and 1983. As a matter of fact in 1982 we were in Division B of the League — won that — and then went on to win Division A.'

Pat arrived on the scene at a time when a golden era in Kilkenny hurling was dawning. Between 1964 and 1978 he played in ten All Ireland finals and was successful five times — 'and the butterflies rather than diminishing increased as time went on.' With these and so many other triumphs there was bound to be a lot of memorable moments. We decided therefore to concentrate on some of the unique ones. He chose four.

First of all there was 1967. 'I had lost in two All Ireland finals to Tipp and Cork in 1964 and 1966 respectively. I would have felt devastated to have lost a third. We were meeting Tipp for the fifth time since 1922 — the previous four had been lost. That together with the fact that it was my first All Ireland win made it very sweet. Kilkenny pulled off a master stroke that day by playing John Teehan at midfield on Tipperary's Mick Roche. 'It was a move the hurlers on the ditch didn't approve of but Fr Tommy Maher was a very shrewd

133

tactician — it was his move. That victory signalled the breakthrough. After that the team continued to improve and go from success to success.' In the second half of that game Tipp scored only one point. In a Kilkenny team that had many stars that day Pat Henderson was a stonewall at centre-back and in the course of the hour outhurled three different opponents.

Next comes 1972. In the All Ireland final against Cork we saw evidence of the magic and splendour of Kilkenny hurling. This was particularly so in the last quarter — when Kilkenny really took control to wipe out an eight point deficit and win by seven points — after what had been a moderate first half and exciting third quarter. 'We were dead — but we came back. I had a reasonably good game.' It was an under-statement. Pat rose to great heights in what was a famous victory.

In 1974 Pat was 'Hurler of the Year'. In a thrilling Leinster final against Wexford that produced forty five scores Kilkenny triumphed by one point 6:13 to 2:24. But neither of these was Pat's highlight of 1974. 'The only thing I remember about 1974 was that we avenged the 1973 defeat at the hands of Limerick. We had a point to prove. A lucky goal put us on the way.' It was a game in which Limerick opened up in great style — playing effective ground hurling — looking sharp and resolute — and leading by five points in less than ten minutes. But then Kilkenny moved into action and by half time were four points up. In a second half that they dominated they ran out easy winners. Opinions may vary but many hold that Pat gave his greatest ever display that day at centre-half-back.

Lastly, there was 1975. He chose it as a year rather than for any particular moment.

All-Ireland medal winners 1975: Pat Henderson (senior) and his brothers John (minor) and Ger (under-21)

It was his last All Ireland medal — his fifth But more especially it was a family year, a unique year for the Henderson family. As well as Pat winning a senior medal Ger won an under 21 and John won a minor. It was a unique triple for Kilkenny and the Henderson family. It may never be repeated.

For more than a quarter of a century the Henderson family has contributed greatly to Kilkenny and to hurling. Between the three brothers they have won eleven All Ireland senior hurling medals. Said Pat to me 'Ger succeeded me at centre-back — he got me dropped off the team.' Rarely if ever has one brother replaced another in the same position and performed with equal magnificence. The family tradition is carried on by Pat's son Ger who in recent years won an All Ireland minor medal and has also played at under 21 level.

Since his schooldays Pat has never been far removed from the game. He has played, coached, trained, represented his club as county board member for twenty-five years and still pucks the ball about when coaching. It is unlikely that he will ever really retire.

His team from the men he played against.

Peter O'Sulivan (Tipperary)

Tom Neville (Wexford)	Pat Hartigan (Limerick)	Padraig Horan (Offaly)
Mick Jacob (Wexford)	Pat Henderson (Kilkenny)	Con Roche (Cork)

John Connolly (Galway)   Mick Roche (Tipperary)

Jimmy Doyle (Tipperary)	Tony Doran (Wexford)	'Babs' Keating (Tipperary)
Mick Bermingham (Dublin)	Ray Cummins (Cork)	Eamon Cregan (Limerick)

Brendan Hennessy with his young son at his home in Florida.

❝

Our meeting has caused me some fond memories. I began the sport even before I remember with a stick in my hands at about three years old. The stick stayed in my hands for some thirty five years. Most of Kerry was an unlikely place for a hurler to grow up, but North Kerry and parts of South Kerry — Kilgarvan, Kenmare and Killarney — were all strongholds of the great game. My father and my brothers — the whole family except my mother — were part of the game and part of my growing up in it. Even my mother began to forget her worries about the bumps and bruises as we got more involved and more successful. My favourite Kerry hurlers when I was growing up were Tomaisin Nolan, Frank Kissane, Nicholas Scollard, Richie Purcell, John Joe O'Connell, Din Joe Galvin and Moss Kelly. The hurling gave me a chance to play against the best in the game; taught me that if you play at the top level you have to be in top shape mentally and physically; taught me to fear nobody but to respect everyone's ability. The bigger the names

Born: 1938

the better I played.

As far back as I remember the hurley and the ball were always with me. I spent countless hours hitting a sponge ball against the gable of the house. That developed my skills at a young age for the team play that came later. My older brothers Thomas, Teddy, Michael and Patrick were all outstanding hurlers and I wanted to be that good or better. The Principal of Ballyduff school was Master Lawlor who was a great hurling enthusiast. At lunch we played a match every day and if the game was good he always gave us an extra half hour. As juveniles in Ballyduff we won four North Kerry leagues in a row. Playing with me on those teams were J.O'Connor, R.McCarthy, M.J.Quinlan, E.O'Sullivan, P.Ross, P.O'Brien, M.Dunne, M.M.O'Connor, S.Rotchford, T.Sheehan, T.Kirby, D.Wynne and J.Wynne. And most of those players went on to win senior championships later.

I will never forget the men who gave their time training us — carried us to the games — and gave us moral support — Master Lawlor, John Gorman, Mossie Higgins, Mick Dowling and Gabe McKenna who is still involved with the Ballyduff club. In those days there were few cars around so most travel was done on bicycles, walking or sometimes in Peter Carbery's Morris Minor. I remember one time when eleven of us piled into Mr Carbery's little car.

I remember the day of confirmation in Ballyduff. After we were confirmed Richie McCarthy and myself went to Ignatius O'Brien's field in Rattoo practising. That's all we thought about — practice — practice — practice.

As juveniles we had a brown sliotar and when it ripped, up to Stephen Sullivan the harness maker to have it stitched. That sliotar must have had a hundred stitches.

When I was growing up in the forties and early fifties, Ballyduff had very good senior teams but they always seemed to get

135

beaten in finals or semi-finals. It was so disappointing. Crotta and Ardfert were the strong teams in those days. In 1955 at the age of sixteen I came on to the Ballyduff senior hurling team and played at midfield. We won the Kerry county championship for the first time since 1891 when Ballyduff representing Kerry won the All Ireland hurling title. It was the first breakthrough for the parish in 64 years and I was proud to be part of that historic team. I was so happy for some of my team-mates who tasted success for the first time and who had given great service to the club — Sonny Fitzgerald, Mike Joe Reagan, Stephen Sullivan, Gerry Fitzgerald, Harry Joe Connor, Tom O'Carroll and John Joe O'Connell. My brothers Teddy, Michael and Patrick were also on the team. The celebrations lasted for a week. We were beaten in the 1956 championship but we came back stronger than ever in 1957 and I captained the team to victory. We had a couple of new faces in 1957 — two of whom became household names in Kerry hurling for years — Mike Joe Quinlan and Eamon O'Sullivan.

I played with the Kerry hurling team from 1955 to 1957. In 1957 we beat Meath in the final of division 2 of the National League. That was probably the best hurling team that ever represented Kerry. I won a Munster junior championship with Kerry hurlers in 1956 and we were beaten by Kilkenny in the All Ireland final. We played against Galway in the National League of 1957. Michael and myself played midfield. I was on Joe Salmon — that's when I came of age. Joe was full of compliments to me after the match.

In 1953 I went to school in St Flannan's, Ennis. As a Kerryman I was expected to be a footballer — which I also played — but hurling was my first love. My friends that I made were very much surprised when I went to the hurling field on the first day of games. It was also the first and second year field. There were two teams picked and I think I was the last one chosen. Father Madden, who was the trainer of the senior hurling team happened to be passing by the

field and he watched the match. When it was all over he tapped me on the shoulder and told me to go to the senior field the following evening. I am happy and proud to say that I played on three Harty Cup teams. We beat North Mon in the final in 1957 and Kieran's beat us in the All Ireland colleges final. Eddie Keher and Ted Carroll starred on that Kieran's team. On the run of play we were the better team but you know what tradition means and they beat us. I won two All Ireland colleges medals — 1955 and 1956 when we beat Leinster. On those Munster colleges teams I played centrefield. Some of my team-mates were Ray Reidy, Jackie Rohan (Clare) — Jimmy Doyle, Tom McGarry, and Colm Madigan half forward line. On the full-forward line were Liam Moloney, Mick Tynan and Hubie Insko — all inter-county hurlers later on. What a team! I really enjoyed Flannan's. Not alone was it a great hurling nursery but it also got us ready for the real world when we graduated.

Father Madden from Clonakenny in Co Tipperary was our trainer in Flannan's.

I would say without a doubt he was one of the best that I ever played for. He knew everything there was to know about the game and he was also a marvellous tactician. It was under his tutelage that I really perfected the art of hurling and honed my skills to a fine point.

My career in Ireland came to an end in 1957 when I decided to emigrate to America. I was just a little over 19 when I left for America on 2 February 1958. Five of the Ballyduff team which won the 1957 championship emigrated with me — my brothers Michael and Thomas, Theo Carroll, J.Brosnan, M. Ross. It was very cold in New York when we landed. Of course there were no games that time of the year but I couldn't wait to see Gaelic Park. So after a couple of days my brother took me up there and it was then I met the legendary John Kerry O'Donnell.

In the New York championship Michael and myself played for Kilkenny. The first game we played was against Tipperary. I was playing on Sean O'Meara who had played with Tipp before he emigrated. After that game Michael and myself were picked for the New York All-Stars to play against All Ireland champions Kilkenny. There were some great hurlers in New York at the time and we hammered Kilkenny in both games. I was playing on Mick Brophy — by the way a true sportsman. Those games were played in the month of May. The first game was played in the Polo Grounds and the second one in Gaelic Park. We were scheduled to play in Ireland in September against the National League champions. We trained from July to September two nights a week and we were in great shape when we met Wexford for the St Brendan Cup final. In the pre-game write-up some of the writers wrote that the Hennessy brothers wouldn't have the experience to play on men like Wheeler and Jim Morrissey. But I guess we proved them wrong — the record speaks for itself — we were sportstars for the week for that game. It was the greatest birthday present I ever got. I was twenty years old the following day. I was on Ned Wheeler that day — a great hurler — a true sportsman — but I guess on the day he got a surprise. Kerrymen were not supposed to hurl like we did. Michael and myself were perfect partners — we knew each others moves — both of us good overhead — both of us good on the ground. I more or less travelled the field. Michael stayed around the middle of the field.

I played with New York All-Stars from 1958 to '74 and played on some of the best players who ever played the game — Cheasty, Roche, Theo English, Wheeler, Salmon, Devaney, P. Moran, Brophy, J. Condon, Flannelly. I also played centre-back and finished up playing full-forward on the likes of Pa Dillon. M. Considine (Clare), Jim Power, Pat McDonald (Cork). I swopped jerseys with all the great ones. Hurling in New York at the time was very good and the standard was very high. Some of the top players were, J .Carney, P. Dowling, S. Custy, H. McCabe, Brendan Kelleher, P. Philpott, J. Murphy, J. Firth and P. Kirby. I had some great duels with Jimmy Carney — he was a marvellous hurler — very clean. Paddy Dowling was another man who gave great service to New York. The three of us played together on New York teams for years. Gaelic Park was the number one meeting place for the Irish in New York. That's where the contacts were made for work and most of us met our wives there.

Brendan Hennessy 99

Beir beannacht óm chroí go tir na h-Éireann
Bánchnoic Éireann Óighe

These lines were written by the poet Donnchadh Rua Mac Conmara almost two hundred and fifty years ago during his time in Newfoundland. They expressed the sentiments of many an exile. Brendan Hennessy can identify with them.

When he emigrated to the United States on 2nd February, 1958 five of the Ballyduff Senior hurling team accompanied him. It reflects the social and economic conditions of the times. It was the raw material that inspired John B. Keane to write the play *Many Young Men of Twenty*.

In New York far from his native Ballyduff, hurling and his prowess at it proved to be a major trump card for Brendan. It was a social outlet — a link with home — an avenue through which work contacts were established — above all a medium through which relationships with fellow exiles were founded and fostered.

And yet mention Kerry or The Kingdom in the world of Gaelic Games and everyone immediately thinks of the fame and splendour of its many magnificent Gaelic footballers. It may therefore come as a surprise to many to learn that Kerry won its one and only hurling title in 1891, twelve years before it captured its first senior football crown. And yet, should it be a surprise? This extract from Leckey's *History of Ireland 1783 to 1850* carries this description of a game of hurling.

The great game in Kerry and indeed throughout the south is the game of

137

Brendan Hennessy in the New York jersey.

"Hurley" — a game rather rare, although not unknown in England. It is a fine manly exercise, with sufficient of danger to produce excitement; and is indeed, par excellence, the game of the peasantry of Ireland. To be an expert hurler, a man must possess athletic powers of no ordinary character; he must have a quick eye, a ready hand, and a strong arm; and he must be a good runner, a skilful wrestler, and withal, patient as well as resolute ...

The forms of the game are these: the players, sometimes to the number of fifty or sixty, being chosen for each side, they are arranged (usually bare-foot) in two opposing ranks, with their hurleys crossed, to await the tossing-up of the ball, the wickets or goals being previously fixed at the extremities of the hurling-green, which, from the nature of the play, is required to be a level extensive plain ... A person is chosen to throw up the ball, which is done as straight as possible, when the whole party, withdrawing their hurleys, stand with them elevated, to receive and strike it in its descent; now comes the crash of mimic war, hurleys rattle against hurleys — the ball is struck and restruck, often for several minutes,

without advancing much nearer to either goal; and when someone is lucky enough to get a clear "puck" at it, it is sent flying over the field. It is now followed by the entire party at their utmost speed; the men grapple, wrestle, and toss each other with amazing agility, neither victor nor vanquished waiting to take breath, but following the course of the rolling and flying prize; the best runners match each other, and keep almost shoulder to shoulder through the play, and the best wrestlers keep as close on them as possible to arrest or impede their progress. The ball must not be taken from the ground by the hand; and the tact and skill shown in taking it on the point of the hurley, and running with it half the length of the field, and when too closely pressed, striking it towards the goal, is a matter of astonishment to those who are but slightly acquainted with the play.

At the goal, is the chief brunt of the battle. The goal-keepers receive the prize, and are opposed by those set over them; the struggle is tremendous — every power of strength and skill is exerted; while the parties from opposite sides of the field run at full speed to support their men engaged in the conflict; then the tossing and straining is at its height; the men often lying in dozens side by side on the grass, while the ball is returned by some strong arm again, flying above their heads, towards the goal. Thus for hours has the contention been carried on, and frequently the darkness of night arrests the game without giving victory to either side. It is often attended with dangerous, and sometimes with fatal, results.

Matches are made, sometimes between different townlands or parishes, sometimes by barony against barony, and not unfrequently county against county; when the "crack men" from the most distant parts are selected, and the interest excited is proportionately great. About half a century ago, there was a great match played in the Phoenix Park, Dublin, between the Munstermen and the men of Leinster. It was got up by the then Lord

Lieutenant and other sporting noble men, and was attended by all the nobility and gentry belonging to the Vice- Regal Court, and the beauty and fashion of the Irish capital and its vicinity. The victory was contended for, a long time, with varied success; and at last it was decided in favour of the Munstermen, by one of that party, running with the ball on the point of his hurley and striking it through the open windows of the Vice-Regal carriage, and by that manoeuvre baffling the vigilance of the Leinster goalsmen, and driving it in triumph through the goal.

So now let us return to the 1891 All Ireland final. The game was played in Clonturk Park on 28 February 1892 when Ballyduff representing Kerry met Crossabeg representing Wexford. It has been described as a memorable final. One writer recalling the game said that 'these counties battled with Fianna fury and chivalry for ninety minutes.' It was level after an hour. An extra half hour was played. Kerry won with the last stroke on the score 2:3 to 1:5.

In the Munster final of that year Limerick defeated Kerry by 1:2 to 1:1 but following an objection on claims by Kerry that the game was over when Limerick scored the winning point, a replay was ordered and victory went to Kerry on the score 2:4 to 0:1. It was Kerry's first time contesting the Munster final. Subsequently, they contested but without success the finals of 1892 against Cork and 1900 against Tipperary. After that they faded as a power from the hurling scene. Football took over and hurling became the poor relation.

But the game still flourished in little pockets around Kenmare, Kilgarvan and Killarney — and particularly in North Kerry in the parishes of Ardfert, Crotta, Causeway, Kilmoyley, Abbeydorney, Lixnaw and Ballyduff where the young men were far more at home with the hurley and sliotar than the football. These parishes produced many outstanding hurlers and several of them would have walked onto the teams in the leading counties if they had been born in them.

The midfield pairing of the Hennessy

brothers — Brendan and Michael — from Ballyduff was as formidable as any of the great midfield combinations the game has known. They proved this in particular in 1958 in the St Brendan's Cup game when in the New York colours they played mighty Wexford and left that great Wexford midfield partnership of Ned Wheeler and Jim Morrissey playing second fiddle. Their display that day paved the way for a famous victory for the exiles on the score New York 3:8 Wexford 3:7.

I decided to contact Ned Wheeler. Do you remember the game Ned? 'Will I ever forget it. I went for a ground ball with Norman Allen and got a stroke on the ankle — broke a bone — and went to the altar to marry Kathleen on 6 October 1958 with the leg in plaster of paris.' His memories of Brendan Hennessy who was his immediate opponent? 'He was an athlete and a ball player — very fast off the mark — could hurl left and right — tended to pull first time — rarely caught the ball.' Surely the ingredients that go to make a class hurler.

When the 1959 All Ireland champions Waterford travelled to the US in 1960 they were beaten by New York and Brendan had an outstanding game at centre-back on no less a man than Tom Cheasty. His vast range of skills were again to the fore in 1963 when New York played Waterford in the league final at Croke Park. It ended in a draw 3:6 each. The same day Kerry played New York in football and scored 1:18. An Irish Press reporter the following week said that Kerry scored many fine points but the best point of all was kicked by Brendan Hennessy from around seventy yards after he had lost his hurley. New York lost the hurling replay at Nowlan Park 3:10 to 1:10.

In 1959 New York played Tipperary — the All Ireland champions of 1958 — in a challenge game at Gaelic Park, New York in sweltering heat before an attendance of six thousand spectators.

Here is an excerpt from a report on the match by the late John D.Hickey.

'This was the New York that we saw defeat Wexford in the St Brendan Cup final at Croke Park last year. Every man in the side hurled his weight, and Tipperary, mistakenly abandoning their customary ground game, were at sixes and sevens for most of the hour.

Star of the victorious side was Brendan Hennessy (Kerry) who gave an inspired display at centre-back. Not since Pat Stakelum was in his prime have I seen a better exhibition in the berth, and even when he was opposed by John Doyle he was still a most accomplished performer.'

A decade later he was still serving up first class performances. This time the game was against Kilkenny. After they had won their seventeenth All Ireland title by defeating Cork 2:15 to 2:9 in 1969 an invitation came from the Gaels in America. The late John D.Hickey wrote as follows.

'Despite the fact that some of them were in the veteran or near-veteran class, the New Yorker appeared to have great reserves of energy and stamina. Experts were bewildered by the splendid hurling produced by Custy, Dowling, Brendan Kelleher, Brendan Hennessy and Donal O'Brien, who proved that he was as good a forward as he had been a goalkeeper when helping Tipperary to two All Ireland successes in the early sixties.'

Brendan speaks with affection of his days in St Flannan's and the thrill of playing in the Harty Cup — and in particular the victory of 1957.

In the All Ireland final they met St Kieran's of Kilkenny and as a team mate of Brendan put it 'We didn't win — we didn't lose either — we just gave it away. Leading by eleven points at halftime we should not have lost.' But as Brendan put it 'they had Eddie Keher and he got three goals late in the game.'

They used to have 'money games' in St Flannan's. These were held on half days or free days. Thirty players would each pay sixpence (old pence). Two captains would select two teams on the field. If you were lucky enough to be on the victorious team you got a shilling (five new pence) from the captain.' Not much by today's standards but a lot of money in the early fifties.'

Brendan was an all rounder. He turned the scales at thirteen and a half stone. He was an accomplished footballer and won a National football league medal in 1964 when New York defeated Dublin. In his young days he was North Munster 880 yards and 440 yards champion. His greatest wish would be to have won an All Ireland hurling medal. The possibility was there. He qualified for admission to the Garda Síochána and in 1958 when New York beat Wexford in the St Brendan's cup final in Croke Park he was offered a location in Co Wexford and a place on the county hurling team. He however opted to return to America. We can only speculate as to what Wexford might have achieved on the hurling field with a man of his calibre.

Brendan was All Star material. In a later era with a leading hurling county he could have won many All Star awards.

'Seeing that most of my adult hurling was played in America this is the team that I would like to have captained.'

Paddy Fleming (Tipperary)

P.Dowling (Cork)	S.Custy (Clare)	P.Philpott (Cork)
J.Murphy (Tipperary)	B.Duffy (Galway)	K.Long (Limerick)
B.Hennessy (Kerry)	M.Hennessy (Kerry)	
R.Prendergast (Limerick)	B. Kelleher (Limerick)	J. Carney (Clare)
M. Furlong (Offaly)	S. O'Meara (Tipperary)	P. Kirby (Clare)

Born: 1956

"

I was born in the old Dean Street in 1956. There is none of the old street, houses or children left. It has all been replaced by modern buildings. I spent my early life there and for as far back as I can remember, I had a hurl in my hand just like most of the other children. We hurled and played in the Water Barracks. It passed many hours of fun for us.

Why did I hurl? I owe it all to my Dad, the late Paddy Hennessy. He had a love for the game that I never saw in anyone else. He organised street leagues that took in parishes adjoining the city and that included all grades from juvenile to senior. He refereed many of the matches and he brought truck loads of children to the matches on Sundays. I often went to two matches with him on Sunday afternoon and to another one in the evening. To him hurling was the greatest game in the world and his enthusiasm and spirit rubbed off on me. My Dad was my greatest hero.

We moved house to William Street and from then on I hurled in the Fair Green. When I was growing up children had nothing and many grown ups hadn't much more. There was no television so young and old headed for the Fair Green every

evening to pass away the time. Men up to fifty and children down to six hurled there. I often counted one hundred hurling. Two teams were picked. My father often refereed — the hurling was hard — no quarter given and none asked for. It was thrilling stuff. We hurled back the balls from behind the goals. On Friday evenings the men took out the girlfriends or went to the pictures in the Regent or the Savoy or else they headed for the pub. That was the only evening they had money and we had the Fair Green to ourselves. We hurled for hours. As time went by I went to the hand-ball alley called The Closh on all the evenings except Fridays by myself or with my brother Flor. It was there that I practised doubling on the ball, taking a ball off the back wall, cutting a ball off the floor and all kinds of overhead tricks using the hurley of course but never catching the ball. In time I became an expert at all the skills of ball playing. I had a deadly striking accuracy and a marvellous eye and years afterwards what I did on the great arenas around the country was the result of the hours of practice in the ball alley with the sponge ball.

In the CBS I continued to hurl and won under 12 and 14 County medals. I joined my club James Stephens and we won the county minor championship. James Stephens meant the world to me. I now hurled with the chaps I grew up with and I did that up to 1992. Here I have to thank especially Georgie Leahy who is over the club. He was a great motivator and drove us to heights beyond our wildest dreams.

I was picked at right-half-back on the county minor team of 1973 and we won the All Ireland against Galway. That match holds the happiest and dearest memories for me. My father and mother were there. They were overjoyed and I felt I had repaid a little of what my father had given to me. It was his last All Ireland. I played again in the minor All Ireland of 1974 but we lost to

141

Cork. My mother was there but she passed away in October to follow my father who had died earlier that year. He was fifty five and she was forty nine. I am forever grateful that we won in 1973 and I'm glad you were there, Dad.

In 1976 our club, James Stephens won the county senior hurling championship and from there we reached the All Ireland club final. This one will always be special to me. Blackrock, Cork were our opponents. Their record was great — three in a row and they were loaded with county players. I remember Dermot McCurtain, Tom Cashman, Pat Moylan, Ray Cummins, Eamon O'Donoghue, John Horgan, all of Cork and the great Frank Cummins of Kilkenny. They were five points up at the break but in a superb second half we won by 2:10 to 2:4. We were the first club outside of Munster to win the All Ireland club championship and we had beaten The Kings — Blackrock. We couldn't reach higher. It was like a dream to me but it all happened in Thurles. There was a surprise follow up. We had a great meal in Hayes Hotel and later Paddy Grace, County Board Secretary for years stopped me going up the street. 'Hey boy, there'll be a car to collect you next Sunday.'

He said no more. I was walking on air. I was a sub on a great Kilkenny team. It meant the world to me. I was among the greats of that time — Pat Henderson, Fan Larkin and Mick Crotty to name but a few. I came on a sub at corner-back against Wexford in 1976. We were skinned by seventeen points. Midfield in 1977 but it was Wexford again. Wexford lost both All Irelands to Cork but I think most people would agree that Wexford were un-fortunate not to win one of them. In 1979 I played at midfield against Wexford and after that we went on to win the All Ireland against Galway. 1982 and 1983 meant an awful lot to me as we defeated Cork in both All Irelands and what more could you ask for? The answer was simple for me. My wish was for 1984 All Ireland but it wasn't to be. Wexford put us out in the Leinster semi-final. For the record Cork beat Offaly

in the All Ireland. The greatest regret of my career was not winning the 1984 All Ireland. It was centenary year. We would have beaten Cork three times in a row and we would have had three All Irelands in a row. I'll never know why we failed but I have no excuses. I hurled up to 1989. I felt I had a great long run. I played with great players like Noel Skehan, Ger Henderson, Frank Cummins, Billy Fitzpatrick and many others who were dedicated to the game and the spirit of the game.

I must mention Pat Henderson here. He was one of the greats in charge of Kilkenny from 1982 to 1987. Looking back over the years I recall certain players who were so great that they were impossible to pin down. Pat Carroll (R.I.P.) Offaly, played all over the field and was a magnificent hurler. Johnny Murphy Wexford at mid-field was very fast and great in the air. Martin Quigley Wexford was a rare corner forward. Johnny Callinan Clare and Joe Cooney of Galway were beautiful ball players. John Fenton and Tom Cashman were the greatest of hurlers and outstanding sportsmen.

Talking about great players reminds me of great pitches. I loved Thurles as a pitch and for reasons already given. Croke Park is every players dream for the first Sunday in September. My own Nowlan Park is as good as any and I have a special liking for the Tulla pitch in Co Clare. It is very compact and you feel that the team is part of the crowd. We played Clare in a league game there. Having a huge Clare crowd made some difference to the home team and we felt a draw was a great result there. After the match the crowd was most friendly.

I also preferred the seventy minute game as I think it suits amateurs better. The game and the GAA meant everything to me. It was as important as going to Mass on a Sunday. The game and the weather were the main talking points. If it wasn't last Sunday's game then it was the next game we talked about. That kept me going. The game also provided me with hurling friends all over Ireland.

Having played for so many years I could write a whole book of incidents but here are two. In a Railway cup match, Leinster v Connaught, Sylvie Linnane and myself had one hell of a tussle for possession. Both of us eyed one another. We threw down the hurls and boxed. The referee sent both of us to the line. We walked off together, sat down on the sideline together, and talked during the rest of the match. We are still the best of friends.

The second incident happened in 1983. We were down eight points to Wexford at half time. We were in the dumps and were sure we were finished. The late Paddy Grace came in and sized up the situation immediately. 'Wexford have given their best. We have them now.' We believed him and his words gave us a great lift. We beat them by five points and went on to win the 1983 All Ireland final. Thanks Paddy. It was your All Ireland. You said the right words at the right time.

As a long playing back my advice to backs would be; train hard, get fit, be first to the ball and get rid of it fast.

In my day hurling was the fastest and best game in the world. It is still the same. I miss full-forwards like Ray Cummins, Tony Doran, Joe McKenna, Padraig Horan and Christy Heffernan who fielded the hurling ball out of the skies and were then almost impossible for any full-back to stop them lifting the net. For example everytime Tony Doran of Wexford fielded the ball, and he was a master at it, you could see the stands rising in anticipation of a goal. The crowds loved those fellows and so did the other players.

Referees are only amateurs like the players and they can make mistakes due to the split second decisions they have to make. A team should accept that decision as final. I think the media put referees under unnecessary pressure. I would have one referee for hurling because hurling is a very skilful and fast game that gives very little time to corner-forwards and backs to mess about. A ball can be pucked about ninety yards and due to the speed of the game I believe umpires and linesmen should make full use of their powers to aid the referee. At present they prefer to avoid the issues.

As I also played football I am convinced the game needs two referees. Football is slower, more physical and has more body contact. There are two many off the ball incidents at present. The second referee with the aid of umpires and linesmen could stamp out these incidents and so improve the game.

I conclude my story by dedicating it and all the enjoyment it brought me — all the friends I made — and the honour of wearing the black and amber for so many years, to my father, who made it all happen for me.

Joe Hennessy **99**

His calibre and consistency as a hurler is reflected in his All Star achievements. They are spread throughout his career — the first in 1978 — the last in 1987. In a County Senior playing life that spanned a dozen years, he was honoured with five All Star awards — a remarkably high success rate. It is interesting to note the diverse reasons given for his first four awards.

'For the admirable spirit of enterprise he exhibits in his half-back play, his coolness and self-assurance' in 1978.

'For the speed and skill he has displayed through the year' in 1979.

'For the stimulating way he performs his hurling with artistry' in 1983.

'For the marvellous dedication he gives to the game of hurling' in 1984.

He has been described as a 'lovable hurler' and was one of the black and amber's finest. One of his great fortes was his 'first touch' brilliance. Joe didn't have to mess about with the ball — he had an exceptional positional sense, got to the ball quickly, despatched it immediately, without fuss, even when under pressure. This made him a very formidable defender and posed all kinds of problems for his immediate opponent.

One of his ambitions was to win the Centenary All Ireland title of 1984. Fate had other plans. Wexford and Tony Doran ended Kilkenny hopes in the Leinster semi-final. Joe of course was aiming for three in a row All Ireland victories — something, strangely enough that Kilkenny has never achieved on the field. In spite of their wonderful tradition the three in a row honour

continues to elude them.

But Joe has many successes to look back on including the personal awards of Man of the Match when he played on Joe Cooney in Thurles in the All Ireland semi-final of 1986, and Kilkenny Hurler of the Year in 1987 — 'as hard to win as any All Star award because of the competition in Kilkenny.'

He enjoyed best the games against Galway. 'They have a passion for the game — play with zest and determination — it was real combat — I loved the intensity — they would give it everything.'

Right-half-back has always been his favourite position. 'I like to face the ball. Its easier to read the game. If you make a mistake in the half-back line there is room to recover if you have speed. In the full-back line the margin for error is small and there is very little space in which to recover'. Talking about the full-back line reminded him of Noel Skehan. 'He was tremendously dedicated. We would both arrive for training half an hour before the others. I would belt balls at him from every angle — impossible to score — the only places I had any chance were the top left and top right corners. He had an incredible eye and reflexes — he was of course a very talented squash player.'

Three events stand out as special in Joe's hurling life. We will deal with them in reverse order of importance. The third was Kilkenny's double-double of 1982 and 1983 when they captured All Ireland and National League titles — a rare achievement. The All Ireland results were achieved as follows: Kilkenny 3:18 Cork 1:13 and Kilkenny 2:14 Cork 2:12 respectively. The National League victories were

It was an era when Kilkenny had an abundance of first class hurlers. For that reason Joe decided to make his team selection from counties other than his native Kilkenny.

Seamus Durack (Clare)

Sylvie Linnane (Galway)   Pat Hartigan (Limerick)   John Horgan (Cork)
Joe Hennessy (Kilkenny)   Mick Jacob (Wexford)   Pat Delaney (Offaly)
John Fenton (Cork)   John Connolly (Galway)
Pat Carroll (Offaly)   Martin Quigley (Wexford)   JohnnyCallinan (Clare)
Jimmy Barry Murphy (Cork)   Tony Doran (Wexford)   Ray Cummins (Cork)

won on the scores Kilkenny 2:14 Wexford 1:11 and Kilkenny 2:14 Limerick 2:12 respectively.

Next came the All Ireland victory of 1979 against a talented Galway fifteen.

'It was my first All Ireland win — it's always a dream to win one — you look at the great hurlers winning — and then to win one yourself ...' he leaves the rest to your own imagination.

It has sometimes been said that the Kilkenny team of 1979 was not a good one. In many ways it is difficult to subscribe to that view. True, they might not have been the great power of the days from 1967 to 1975 but they had strength and hurling brilliance right down the centre — Noel Skehan, Paddy Prendergast, Ger Henderson, Joe Hennessy and Frank Cummins, Billy Fitzpatrick, Mick Crotty — and when you have that you are going to be very hard to beat.

Now we come to his most cherished hour and victory. The minor All Ireland success of 1973 against Galway. It was won the hard way. A sideline cut to Galway from their own twenty one yards line in the closing stages when they held a slender lead suggested they would lift the siege and hold out. But the cut was poorly hit and driven out over the sideline within yards of where it was taken. The resultant sideline cut to Kilkenny brought a goal and victory by one point — the score Kilkenny 4:5

Galway 3:7 What made it so special for Joe was the fact that his father and mother were present. There could be no repeat. A year later his father was dead. He was Joe's hero.

'It seem'd as if the hour were one
Sent from beyond the skies
Which scatter'd from above the sun
A light of Paradise'

His father had played hurling with Three-castles and got a run once or twice with the County team. But it was his work with youngsters that really sets him apart. He ranks with the unsung heroes of the GAA — men who give their time freely and in great quantities promoting the ancient game and encouraging the youth.

After the publication of *Giants of the Ash*, I got a letter from Fr P.J. Madden, a Columban Father in England — born in Belfast — who had spent his missionary life in Burma, USA and England. From a lovely letter I quote the following. 'When I was in the seminary in Navan, the Bursar was a Fr Tom Kennedy who played some games with Limerick just before the Mackey era. He loved to recall those matches and always lavished praise on Kilkenny. 'Sweet hurlers' he called them. A fine tribute to pay to opponents but typical of the spirit often found among the wielders of the ash'. 'Sweet hurlers' — a lovely tribute. Count Joe Hennessy among them.

Born: 1950

and 1966 brought the club their first Offaly senior success and the rest has now been written in history. For me the turning point came in 1971 when I decided to opt out of football and 'stick' with hurling. I believed that it would be in hurling that success would come and not as it turned out that year. But it was still great to be on the Hill in 1971 getting wet to the skin when Offaly won their first All Ireland — even if it was football — and I probably could have been out there playing.

I always loved Offaly and Offaly hurling and knew that some day Offaly would win an All Ireland. So while '81 was a long time coming, to me it was always on the way. Looking back I would say that winning was something I never got carried away with. But losing was something I hated. Hurling probably fits fourth into my life — after God, my family and work. When I think of the friends I have made through the game I am glad and always grateful that my father gave me that hurley for my sixth birthday.

Padraig Horan **"**

66

The first thing I can remember of hurling was my father buying me a new hurley for my birthday. The following Sunday my brothers and some friends were playing hurling out in the field at the front of our house. I was mad to show off my new stick but nobody could find it. The following morning my mother when making up my bed got the hurley under my pillow. And from that day on I probably never left a hurley out of my hand whether going for the cows or getting a bucket of water from the well.

Hurling was always my first love in sport and born into a hurling family always made things that bit special. Ballivor was the local junior club at the time and as a kid I always had the job of pucking the ball back to the older players. Hurling would start every Sunday at about 1pm. We broke for to listen to Mícheál O'Hehir at 3 or 3.30pm after which we would become Tony Wall, 'Link' Walsh or some other great player of that time.

In about 1962 St Rynagh's was formed and from there things started to move. 1965

P adraig Horan had a long and illustrious career in hurling that stretched over a period of almost seventeen years. He was extremely versatile — reflected in the fact that he played in every position except goal for his native Offaly.

In his very early days he was a dual player — tasted football success — but became convinced in 1970 that Offaly hurling had the ingredients and potential for success and decided to concentrate all his energies on that game.

I reminded him that Offaly had no tradition in 1970 outside of parish level on which to build hopes. 'That's true, but we made our own tradition right through the eighties. I thought after the Offaly performance against Kilkenny in 1968 when they played for most of the hour with only fourteen men coupled with the defeat of All Ireland champions Wexford in 1969 and following which the Leinster title was lost to Kilkenny by only two points (3:9 to 0:16), that the breakthrough was going to come earlier than it did.' Offaly had some great players then — among them Paddy Spellman, Barney Moylan, P.J. Whelehan, J.J. Healion, Padge Mulhaire, Paddy Molloy and Declan Hannify. A score of sixteen points was an indicator of possession and accuracy and quite an amount of supremacy outfield. But many of these were pushing on in years and the talent to replace them wasn't immediately available.

Padraig at the beginning of his career established a reputation as an outstanding and uncompromising defender. For four years from 1973 to 1976 he was full-back on the Leinster team and won three Railway Cup medals. He was in the company of stars. He did himself and Offaly proud. Later he was moved to the forwards and that happened somewhat by accident. 'We were playing Kilkenny in a league game and while we were doing very well we were getting few scores. Dick O'Hara was cleaning up at full-back for Kilkenny. I switched to full-forward in the second half and scored two goals. It was this that paved the way in due course for the switch of Eugene Coughlan from the forwards to full-back — and he turned out to be a terrific fullback'.

Centreback however, was Padraig's favourite position. 'I loved to play there. I found hurling easy at centre-back. I loved watching centre-backs in action — Pat Henderson, Ger Henderson, Dan Quigley, Jimmy Cullinane and Sean Stack. But my idol was Tony Wall of Tipperary. As a kid I used listen to radio broadcasts and then I would broadcast matches in my own mind. Tony Wall was always on my team. I was a better back than a forward and when playing in the centre — where I played my best hurling — I liked to play slightly behind my wing men. It's easy hurl that way.' That comment reminded me of

Paddy Clohessy of Limerick and his instructions to his wing-backs in the All Ireland final of 1940 against Kilkenny when he told Peter Cregan and Tommy Cooke to play on the outside of Jimmy Langton and Jack Gargan and that he would operate slightly behind them. It was a strategy that paid off.

It was as a forward that Padraig won his two All Ireland titles in 1981 and 1985. He had the honour of being captain in '81 when he led Offaly who were appearing in a final for the first time, to victory. In achieving that win against the odds many people overlooked the magnificent Offaly performance of the previous year when they beat Kilkenny by one point in the Leinster final and only lost by two points to Galway — a game they might well have won — in the All Ireland semi-final. 'Even if we had won I don't think we would have beaten Limerick that year in the final.' As a forward he was strong and forceful. He used his defensive experience to make life difficult for his opponent. He was crafty and difficult to mark and could score even with very little room to manoeuvre. After his performance in the '85 final he was nominated Man of the Match.

Our discussion then turned to 1984 — the centenary year — and Offaly's second appearance in an All Ireland final — staged in Thurles to commemorate the founding of the GAA there in 1884. While the Cork team relaxed in the tranquility of a convent grounds the Offaly players were in a hotel surrounded by supporters, well wishers and advisers. And when they went for a puck around as many gathered as when they were training. Padraig remembers it well. 'We let ourselves be made favourites and that was suicidal. Cork picked their team to hurl us. We didn't do likewise. It was a day I would love to have been at centre-back. I was worried from the moment we left in the bus from the hotel. It was like a carnival atmosphere and some were too confident. I knew we were in trouble. We didn't get the breaks. It was a game we might have won but then if we did we mightn't have won in '85 — these things tend to balance out.'

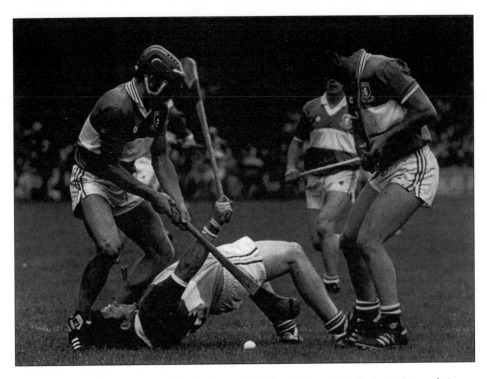

Padraig Horan, arched on the ground, has Laoismen John Bohane (left) and John Taylor (right) wondering what option to take in the Leinster final of 1985.

Do you remember the early moments when you gathered a ball that had goal written all over it and you sent it over the bar? 'I still dream about it. I think about it every morning. I gathered the ball behind Donal O'Grady's head and went to flick it over Ger Cunningham's head into the net — but it went over the bar. Later on another ball came in — Cunningham fell — I went to flick it under him — it rolled along the goal line and the chance was missed. Those scores would have settled us. I tend to remember the goals I missed rather than the ones I scored. I never stayed awake on an night before a match. When I did stay awake it was always the night after a match. I stayed in Cashel the night after the All Ireland. I didn't sleep. I kept waking up thinking of the ball that went over the bar.'

Reflecting in general over his long career he had the following to say. 'The 1969 team had great scoring power and was probably the best forward combination Offaly produced. In my seventeen years I played on better Offaly teams than those that won the All Irelands. Paddy Molloy was one of the best hurlers I saw. He had ferocious speed and tremendous skill. In the championship against Laois one year I sent a rasper of a shot from the edge of the square that made the umpire duck his head. The green flag waved. I was the only one that knew it had gone in between the outside of the goalpost and the net — it won the game for us. We had a great team in 1982 — probably our best team of the eighties. We came back after an All Star trip and beat a good Wexford team. We lost the Leinster title by two points to Kilkenny. It was the one year I felt we could have won another All Ireland title. We were a cleverer team in '85 than in '81. But we missed Johnny Flaherty. We knew Galway would probably be all over us at times but that if we kept in touch we'd be OK — and that's what happened.

I got my only All Star after the '85 win. I had a good year but I had had better years.

I question why All Ireland winners get so many All stars. Not enough consideration is given to League game performances. I sometimes think that players should nominate players other than from their own county. I still feel baffled as to why Jim Troy failed to get an All Star in 1985.'

The arrival of Offaly as a force widened the national hurling horizons and introduced many quality performers to the championship scene. A new power always brings a new dimension and a breath of fresh air. More importantly, it increases the level of competition. So it was with Offaly. They gave hurling lovers some wonderful exhibitions of hurling. They had their disappointments but with the help of players of the calibre and dedication of Padraig Horan and Damien Martin — 'he was more than a hurler, he was a great motivator and had an unshakeable belief in Offaly' — they harnessed their self belief from which a confidence blossomed that won for them the highest honour in the game.

He selected a team from the men he played against and as he perused it, lamented the fact that he had failed to find a place for Kieran Purcell, Joe McKenna, Ray Cummins, Tony Doran — 'better full-forwards than myself' — Mick Roche, Mick Jacob, Sean Stack and Niall McInerney. He held Paddy Molloy in such high regard that he felt compelled to include him in his team.

Noel Skehan (Kilkenny)

Fan Larkin (Kilkenny)   Pat Hartigan (Limerick)   Jim Treacy (Kilkenny)

Len Gaynor (Tipperary)   Ger Henderson (Kilkenny)   Iggy Clarke (Galway)

Frank Cummins (Kilkenny)   John Connolly (Galway)

Francis Loughnane (Tipperary)   Pat Delaney (Kilkenny)   Eddie Keher (Kilkenny)

Paddy Molloy (Offaly)   Padraig Horan (Offaly)   Eamon Cregan (Limerick)

149

Born: 1892

Willie Hough was born in 1892 in the parish of Monagea. He captained Limerick to All Ireland Senior Hurling honours in 1918.

The 1918 campaign was a strenuous one. The semi-final against Tipperary in the Markets field in Limerick was by all accounts a magnificent game. It ended level at 5:3 each. Limerick went into special training at Foynes for the replay at the Athletic Grounds in Cork on 18 August. In another thriller Limerick won on the score 3 goals to 2:2. Clare fell 11:3 to 1:2 in the Munster final and Galway were overcome in the All Ireland semi-final. In the final Limerick were offered a walkover — which they declined — from Wexford who were unable to field a team because of an outbreak of flu. The final was refixed for 26th January the following year when a very fit and talented Limerick outfit triumphed on the score 9:5 to 1:3.

He was on the victorious side again in 1921 when Bob McConkey, the Limerick captain became the first person to receive the McCarthy Cup. 'Carbery' named the Limerick half-back trio of that era, Jack Keane, Willie Hough and Dinny Lanigan as the greatest ever on the hurling field.

His prospects of winning a third All Ireland medal were dashed in 1923 when Galway beat Limerick to win their first title.

He played with Waterford in the 1913 Munster championship and was lauded for his outstanding leadership. The *Waterford Star* reported as follows — 'never was a team better captained and never did a commander infuse more hope and spirit by sheer example than Hough. He was here there and everywhere ... always on the ball ... now playing tig with his opponents and slapping shots into the forwards with a frequency and accuracy that charmed those who could appreciate hurling at its best.'

While teaching in Baltimore and hurling with UCC he was offered a place on the Cork team. It would have meant playing against Limerick so he declined.

His playing career with Limerick stretched from 1915 to 1926. During that period Limerick won two All Ireland titles — played in three and with a little luck might have taken four All Ireland crowns. They had a famous half-backline — Jack Keane, Hough and Lanigan — known as the Hindenburg line. Other famous names and colleagues of Willie at that time were Bob McConkey who played up to 1934, Paddy McInerney, captain of the 1923 team who subsequently emigrated to the USA, Jimmy Humphries one of the great small men of hurling, Mickey Cross who was still there in 1937, Mickey Fitzgibbon who captained Limerick in 1933, Garrett Howard the only Limerick man to win five All Ireland medals — two with Dublin in 1924 and 1927 and three with Limerick in 1921, 1934, and 1936, and John Joe Kinnane.

Five Limerick men were selected on the Tailteann Games team of 1924 — Jimmy Humphries (Capt.), Dave Murnane, Willie Ryan, Willie Gleeson and Garrett Howard.

Willie made a comeback to play at fullback against Waterford in 1929, but defeat was Limerick's lot.

On one occasion he cycled the twenty nine miles to Limerick to play a match against Tipperary in the Markets Field and they cycled home again. 'Carbery' has described Willie Hough as 'a Hercules of a man'. Weighing almost 14 stone he was famed for his long defensive clearances on the ground.

After retirement he became involved in the administrative side of the GAA and also served as a referee. In 1936 he was elected Treasurer of the Munster Council. When he resigned — after 26 years — the Munster Council showed their appreciation of his service by giving him a trip to the USA.

Willie Hough, a national teacher by profession, ranks among the immortals of the early days of the Association.

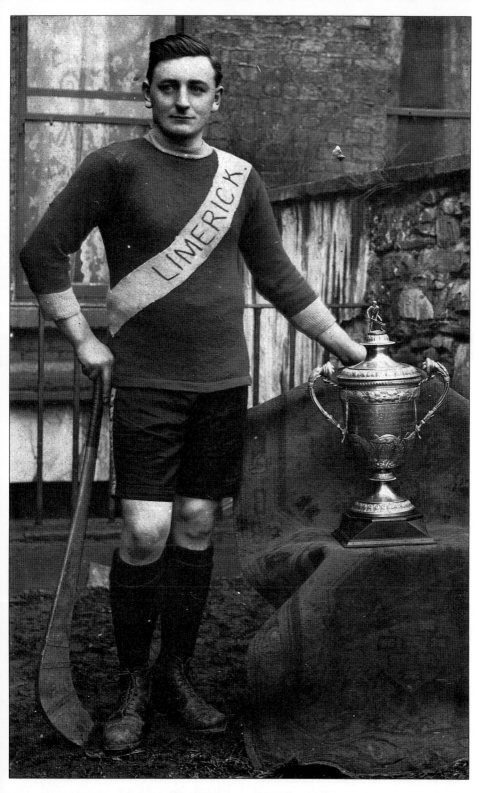

Willie Hough – Captain of Limerick in 1918 with the All-Ireland Cup.

Born: 1944

"

These few words are written two days after Ireland's defeat against Holland in the World Cup and as an out and out hurling man I feel very sorry for all those great fans who supported Ireland so well, that they never got the opportunity to enjoy a real hurling game — i.e. Killarney in '87, Cork and Thurles '91 and to go back much further the great Wexford team of '55/56; Kilkenny of '72/73; and I still think that I was privileged to have played in one of the great winning All Ireland teams — Tipperary 1964/65.

My wish is that parishes, schools and eventually counties will produce great hurlers and that our new Croke Park can be proud of the players that play on it. Best wishes.

Michael Keating "

How are you Michael? I enquired as he answered our pre-arranged phone call of Sunday night 29th May 1994. 'I have often felt better,' he replied. I understood. His fancied forces — recently crowned

League champions — had fallen to the men of Clare. It was unexpected. Tipperary were among the favourites for the '94 All Ireland crown and Michael was plotting and planning with that in mind. 'That's sport,' he said as we ended our conversation and arranged a meeting.

Michael hails from Ballybacon-Grange in South Tipperary — a football stronghold. 'I found it easier to play football than hurling. I had to train to play hurling but not football. I felt more confident at football. I was at it from my youth. As I went for the cows I would grab a football and kick it up the fields — from buachalán to buachalán as a test of judgement. I didn't prefer one above the other but looking back now I have to say there is no game in the world like hurling.' For ten years he was part of the Munster Railway cup football panel and won a medal in 1972 when Munster won the trophy for the first time in 23 years, after a replay. Football of course was in the blood. His granduncle Tommy Ryan — later to become Lt.Col. in the Irish Army — played football with Tipperary. He was playing in Croke Park on Bloody Sunday November 21st, 1920 and helped remove Michael Hogan from the pitch after he had been shot by the Black and Tans.

It is however as a hurler that Michael will be remembered in the years and decades ahead. He arrived on the inter-county scene in the early sixties. With Tipperary he could reasonably look forward to success. The records show that they won titles in every decade. They had a success rate that fostered tradition and bred confidence. For Michael success came immediately. An intermediate title was won in 1963. The following year he played under twenty one and senior and Tipperary won both titles. In senior ranks he was in the company of one of Tipperary's finest ever combinations and his presence in the forward line made that division a potent sector. He thought that in decades to come he would look back on 1964 as perhaps his most memorable year. He was only twenty and found himself Sports Star of the Week after the National League final, the Munster final and the All Ireland final. Did he appreciate it all then? — 'Perhaps it came too young.'

If Michael chose 1964 others might have chosen 1971 for him to remember. He was in devastating form. In the National League semi-final against Cork he scored 1:9. Against Galway in the All Ireland semi-final at Birr he amassed 2:12 — 'I got points that day from impossible angles including one from the end line.' He had seven points to his credit against Kilkenny in the All Ireland final. In the Munster final against Limerick at Killarney he left a lasting imprint. It was one of the great Southern deciders. In the first half, wave after wave of Limerick attacks swept in on the Tipperary goal. Limerick were ahead by two goals at half time and it could have been more. It augured well. But fortunes changed in the second half following a display of comhacht agus fuinneamh agus gaisciocht from Michael Keating. He scored three goals following precision clearances from Mick Roche. He finished the game with a personal tally of 3:4. Limerick matched Tipperary in fitness, skill and hurling ability. In a game that ended 4:16 to 3:18 Michael Keating was the difference — the big difference. Little wonder that he was nominated Hurler of the Year in 1971. He retired after defeat by Clare in the championship of 1974. In that game he broke his jaw in three places. The evidence is still there.

But he was back the following year and in the semi-final replay against Limerick he demonstrated — especially in the first half — his repertoire of skills and forceful forward play that suggested he might do a

1971 all over again and defeat Limerick on his own. But it wasn't to be.

In 1979 he coached Galway and they met Kilkenny in the final. 'I enjoyed it with the lads but my powers were restricted to coaching only.'

When he took over at the helm in Tipperary in 1986, Tipperary hurling had experienced its longest ever barren period. Since the All Ireland victory of 1971 only a National League title in 1979 helped to ease the pain of loss and the hurt of pride.

In taking office Michael cast the net far and wide just as had been done in 1949. In came players of youth and skill and potential. The building and renewal had begun. Time would add depth to the panel and depth would create a winning blend. He preached the gospel and hurling philosophy of Father J.J. Meagher who was Chairman of Tipperary County Board for many years from 1927 onwards. Fr Meagher's annual addresses — which were published in book form in 1938 — reflected the culture, aspirations and spirit of the day. The preface by Rev J.M. Hayes of Muintir na Tire fame noted some of the customs of the time. 'We have seen great crowds stand to attention whilst "Faith of our Fathers" echoed across the field, and we shall never forget the scene when the Angelus bell rang out — the ball was forgotten, and the hurleys lay idle, whilst players and spectators joined in silent prayer of homage.'

A key message among the many points in Fr Meagher's addresses was a request to play the game for the honour of the game. He pleaded for honour before honours. 'A healthy mind in a healthy body' was a principle he propounded.

Three brief excerpts from those addresses convey his views on good sportsmanship.

'— rough play should not be tolerated, and a spirit of friendly rivalry should pervade all our club matches.

— but it must be distinctly understood that deliberate rough play cannot and should not be tolerated by our referees, for such displays were ever the symbol of vulgarity and cowardice.

— there should be no half measures with a player who sets himself out to injure an opponent. In the dust of defeat as well as in the laurel of victory, there is glory to be found. Act well your part; there all the honour lies. Victory will be none the less sweet, and defeat will lose much of its bitterness, if each player is conscious of having contributed to the elevation of our games and pastimes.'

And so it was with Michael Keating — sportsmanship and clean play were paramount. And he demanded this side by side with a style of hurling that he wanted played with speed, skill, passion and aggression.

In training he preached the five S's — Speed and Stamina, Style and Skill, and from these four there should emerge Scores. 'Without scores you won't win anything. Take the points the goals will come themselves. An inter-county player should be able to stand up over a penalty and hit the back of the net — like D.J. Carey of Kilkenny for example. I had lunch with Ring one day and we were discussing 21 yard frees and penalties and he held the view that if the ball comes up right for you, you go for a goal — as he always did. If a man commits himself to go for a ball — especially a back — he must take it — he can't afford to fluff it. This was a golden rule I used when training.'

During Michael's time with Tipperary he guided them to five Munster titles — three in a row from '87 to '89 — two All Ireland crowns and two National Leagues. It was a good return in the space of eight years. 'I changed the face of hurling. I treated players well and gave them what they deserve. You must treat players well nowadays. To win an All Ireland it takes special ingredients — especially courage to play before sixty thousand people. You put on the jersey first for yourself and your family — next for the "little village" — lastly for your county. And when the game is over you must be able to say good luck — thanks.'

When Tipperary fell to Clare in the first round of the 1994 Munster championship Michael Keating immediately called it a day. The sudden parting was unexpected. He had contributed much. He strove unceasingly and with great intensity for hurling perfection, especially in forward play. He led Tipperary out of the desert. He restored their pride. He will be missed.

Oh how I long to travel back,
And tread again that ancient track!
That I might once more reach that plain,
Where first I left my glorious train.

Born: c.1880

In hurling circles, even today, the name Jim Kelliher of Dungourney, Co Cork is synonymous with hurling greatness. He would have been a must on a hurling team of the first quarter century of the GAA.

Of medium build at 5'8' he has been described as 'wide-shouldered and neatly built from head to ankle'. He was a magnificent defender, equally at home at full-back and centre-back. He was no stranger to the forward division either. Hurling was second nature to him. He used brain rather than brawn — was nimble and quick — and could turn on his tracks like a hare.

He won All Ireland honours with Cork when he captained them in 1902 and he won his second title the following year.

He was captain again in 1907. The Munster final of that year was Cork v Tipperary — it was Dungourney and Thurles Blues — it was the meeting of two hurling Giants, Jim Kelliher and Tom Semple — the clash of Titans. The game was played at Dungarvan. Close right through, it was anyone's game up to the final whistle when victory went to the men of Cork, Dungourney and Jim Kelliher on the score 1:6 to 1:4.

The All Ireland final against Kilkenny represented by a Mooncoin selection was not played until the 21st June 1908, again at Dungarvan. It was a thriller — the yardstick against which future finals would be measured — with household names in both camps — Gerry Desmond, Tom Mahony, Pats Leahy, Andy Buckley, Steve Riordan, Willie Hennessy, Jim Roynane, Tom Coughlan and Jim Kelliher of Cork — Jack Rochford, John T. Power, Jack Anthony, Sim Walton, Matt Gargan, Dan Kennedy, the three Doyle brothers and team captain 'Drug' Walsh of Kilkenny. The final score was Kilkenny 3:12 Cork 4:8 with the winning point coming as the dying seconds ticked away.

It wasn't the first time Kilkenny had a one point victory over Cork — in 1904 the score was 1:9 to 1:8. And it wasn't the last time — for they repeated the formula in 1912 and in 1939 and 1947 with time almost up the winning point was scored — compliments of Jimmy Kelly and Terry Leahy respectively.

Carbery described Jim Kelliher as 'perhaps the greatest Roman of them all' and went on to say, 'Kelliher had brains, skill, stamina and ash-craft in abundance. I saw him play in twenty six major matches and he never left the field without being the outstanding hurler of the hour.'

Twenty years or so after his retirement Jim described the hurlers of that time as 'hairoil hurlers' — not a patch on the men of his day. The way the human mind perceives the glories of the past changes very little from generation to generation.

Jim Kelliher was more than a hurler. He was also a superb horseman. His successes in that field are legendary too. His victory in a point to point race on a mare called 'Home Chat' against the leading gentry of the day was perhaps his greatest triumph. It was hailed as a feather in the cap of the common man.

Born: 1926

"

You have asked me, Brendan, what differences, if any, I see between the game as it is played today and as it was played in my time. Well, two differences immediately come to mind. The first is the rule change that eliminated the 'third man' tackle and the charge on the goalkeeper. I am in complete agreement with that rule change. The 'third man' tackle was the bane of my life. It was one thing to be floored by a fair man to man shoulder charge, when you saw it coming — were prepared for it — and the effects were minimal.

But it was another thing to be floored by a hefty charge from someone you were not aware of and at a time when your attention was focused on the ball and on your immediate opponent. To me it was the equivalent to running into a wall in the dark.

The second difference I see is the almost complete absence of first time striking. Players are obsessed with getting the ball into the hand — trying to lift it in the most unlikely situations — when a quick pull would send it forty or fifty yards. Similarly with the dropping ball — no attempt made to pull above head height but instead hands reaching for the ball and fielding it in football fashion. As a result of these tactics the two greatest skills in the game have vanished. If players were to revert to first time pulling there would be a lot less bunching and scrummaging around the ball and the game would be more flowing and a lot less energy sapping.

Another difference I see is the excessive use of the hand-pass today, and if I had any say in the matter I would ban it altogether. Of course exceptions would have to be made for the player whose hurley was broken or knocked from his grasp. The game of hurling is the most skilful game in the world and is all about propelling the ball with the hurley.

The above remarks are in no way meant to be critical of present day players — they continue to serve up thrilling encounters and continue to draw huge crowds. They are ten times fitter than ever we were and I would love to see them combine that superior fitness with the first time striking I have referred to above.

"

Jimmy Kennedy

I n 1949 Ireland was declared a Republic — Jimmy Kennedy declared for his native Tipperary — and on the first Sunday in September of that year Tipperary were declared All Ireland champions.

Jimmy had been at right half forward on the Dublin team that failed to a fine Waterford combination in the All Ireland final of 1948. His ability and class as a potent forward weren't lost on the shrewd mentors of Tipperary. So when they set out to select their 1949 team with a view to restoring Tipperary hurling glory he was very much on their minds. The circumstances surrounding the negotiations to get Jimmy to declare had all the ingredients of a Hitchcock thriller.

His impact in the Tipperary jersey was immediate. In his four games in the Munster championship he scored two goals and twenty seven points. One of those goals was crucial. Without it there might never have been the three in a row glory of 1949, 1950 and 1951. The goal came in the dying moments of the first round replay against Cork and here is how Jimmy remembers it. 'I think it was Mick Ryan that sent the ball in. It was going wide on the right corner. Sonny Maher ran out for it. Con Murphy, the Cork full-back was between me and the goal. Sonny Maher looked over his shoulder. He gave a quick flick back to me. It came hopping at right angles. I knew that Josie Hartnett couldn't be too far away from me and I was conscious that Con Murphy was in the line of flight. I pulled first time — connected — and the ball headed for inches inside the upright. Tom Mulcahy dived to his right — his anticipation was perfect — but he was fractionally short as he dived in an effort to save. I ran out towards midfield in anticipation of the puck out. As the ball dropped the referee blew the whistle. What's wrong I said and he replied — it's over. Well I couldn't believe it. I thought there should be about ten minutes to go. That's what happens when you're involved and totally engrossed in the hectic exchanges of a close tense encounter. Time flies and the game is over before you realise it.'

That equalising goal took the game into extra time and victory for Tipperary. There followed a difficult game against a good Clare team but Tipperary survived the challenge and went on to meet Limerick in the Munster final. It was a good Limerick team with an uncompromising defence. Limerick folk will never forget Jimmy Kennedy's contribution to Tipperary's 1:16 to 2:10 victory — and Jackie Power's great goal that was disallowed. Jimmy scored ten points that day — nine of them from frees from a variety of angles and distances. His scoring ability from play and frees was a feature of his sojourn in the Tipperary jersey. It led him to being a 'marked man' on occasions.

After the Limerick game Johnny Leahy the great Tipperary defender of earlier days paid tribute to Jimmy Kennedy at a meeting of the County Board. Here is how it was reported in a Tipperary newspaper. 'In a tribute to Jim Kennedy Mr Leahy said that Kennedy had given the greatest display of artistic hurling that they had ever seen in the county. He (Mr Leahy) had seen all the great hurlers — Tom Semple, Bob Mockler, Mick King of Galway, Willie Gleeson, Jim Hurley etc. — but never had he seen anything like the artistry shown by young Kennedy in this year's final. The artistry of Kennedy will be talked of for many a long day Mr Leahy declared and his feat of scoring ten or eleven points, some from almost impossible angles. His accuracy was such that the Limerick defenders could only look up and see the ball sailing through the uprights. His was a magnificent display and I think great credit is due to Jim Kennedy for bringing us so near to another All Ireland championship. Tipp supporters left the field on Sunday saying — "Knocknagow is not yet gone"!'

It is interesting to trace the elements and influences that shaped and moulded the hurling brilliance of this tall lightly built player from Kiladangan. It began in his native parish when he used to take a sponge ball or tennis ball and belt it up against the barn door and spend ages pulling on each rebound — sometimes lifting the returning ball with speed and letting fly again. And then he would put a ladder up against the haybarn — step back 21 yards — and shoot between the rungs, shifting his position so as to adjust the angle. 'It reached the stage when I could almost select which set of rungs I would drive the ball between. I also practised by placing three or four balls in a line at different angles from the ladder and took frees.'

His secondary education took him to St Flannan's College, Ennis — that great hurling nursery. Here he was fortunate to come in contact with Tull Considine — one of Clare's greatest hurling men. 'He was a great trainer — away ahead of his time. He turned a panel of St Flannan's no-hopers into world beaters.

He put fellows into positions we wouldn't dream of. My chance came in the Harty Cup game against Limerick CBS in 1944. I wasn't getting a puck in the half-forward line. Go into the corner said Tull — I had a blinder. Tull used insist on ground hurling — play the wings — cross the ball diagonally towards goal — or straight across the goals — the most effective way to open up any defence. It was the first Harty Cup. It was on an experimental basis and was so successful that it became an annual competition. We won the Munster and All Ireland Colleges title that year and I was also a member of the successful Munster Colleges team.'

Next we move to UCD. There he encountered Mick Darcy and Dick Stokes. Both made a lasting impression on him. Mick had hurled with Tipperary in the twenties and won All Ireland honours in 1925. He was President of the UCD Club. Hurling was his life and he was held in the highest regard by all the UCD players. 'Mick put polish to my free taking. I was pretty accurate but under Mick's tutelage I became even more accurate. As I practised he would say to me — look at the ball — look at the goalpost — don't move your feet — concentrate. The first evening I went to Belfield grounds in 1944 I saw Dick Stokes togged out on the field in the middle of young lads. I stayed in the background for a little while. I felt in awe of Dick — a highly talented hurler. I was aware of his brilliance with Limerick — his great scores — his Munster and All Ireland successes of 1940 — and of course his victories with Munster in the Railway Cup. I learned a lot from him. He was always so unassuming and led by example and encouragement.'

Jimmy first played for Dublin in a game against Antrim in Belfast and the first thing that struck him was the difference in the pace between county hurling and club hurling. He was a regular in the Dublin colours in 1947 and 1948 and had the honour of captaining the Leinster Railway Cup team of 1949.

His first game for his native Tipperary was in the Thomond Feis Tournament against Clare in May 1949. Among his most memorable games are the 150 minutes marathon encounter against Cork in Limerick in the first round of the championship in 1949. 'Each of those games and the extra time were tremendous tussles. Then there was the National League final against Kilkenny in 1950 when the prize was a trip to America — the treat of a lifetime in those days. It was a hellish game — one of the great games of hurling — a game that Shem Downey nearly won on his own for Kilkenny. After that National League victory it was imperative that we win the All Ireland so that we could go to America as champions — win we did — and travelled proudly as league and All Ireland champions.'

But there is one game and one episode that Jimmy prefers to forget. The game was the Munster final against Cork in 1951. 'I shouldn't have played. I had cracked my ribs in training. Dr Courtney strapped me up — I couldn't take a deep breath — I played against his advice. I didn't rate in the game. It was all too much of an ordeal. After the game I lost my place on the team but remained on the panel. I was a sub against Wexford in the All Ireland final — one of six. There were twenty medals — I received none.' That has always been a great disappointment with Jimmy. Three in a row hurling triumphs are rare enough and Jimmy would love to have three medals to show for his part in Tipperary's great three in a row of '49 to '51. It was the first time his native county had done it since 1900.

Jimmy had great admiration and praise for many of the hurling men he encountered during his hurling career. 'I saw Harry

Gray of Dublin and Laois towards the end of his hurling days but his great artistry was still in evidence. Joe Salmon of Galway was a beautiful hurler — there wasn't a wrong stroke in him. Jackie Power of Limerick was one of the great ones. I have to name Tony Reddin as tops among goal-keepers — he had it everyway. In saying this I know that Seanie Duggan of Galway and Paddy Scanlon of Limerick could run him close and perhaps be the first choice of others. Mick Ryan of Tipp was a superb centre-forward — Pat Stakelum a wonderful centre-back. I had special admiration for Con Murphy of Cork as a hurler and especially as a referee. In his capacity as referee he had an authoritative presence. He would issue the first warning before the ball was thrown in and after that if your conduct warranted it you headed for the line. Con pioneered the "cleaning-up" of the game. He was not prepared to tolerate charging the goalkeeper when the ball was gone and he was equally strict on the "third man"

tackle when the ball was gone.'

Jimmy's hurling days with Dublin evoke very happy memories. 'We were very well cared for at both club and county level. There was great comradeship and the Dublin sense of humour was marvellous.'

Jimmy believes that hurling will always survive but he does have certain fears and concerns. 'I don't like the win at all costs approach that has become so prevalent nowadays. I think that underage competition should be non-competitive — with players concentrating on enjoying the game and developing their natural skills. I would also be advocating a high level of ground hurling. If a player fails to lift the ball first time he shouldn't try again — simply pull on the ball.'

Jimmy's stay was relatively short. He retired at twenty-five. He shot across the sky like a meteor. He shone brightly and left a lasting imprint.

Beidh clú agus cáil agus iomrádh air go deo.

Jimmy Kennedy (third from right) in action against Limerick in 1950.

Born: 1905

faced Cork in the decider. It was a fateful day for Mick. An injury of severe proportions shattered his knee. It necessitated thirty-three stitches — three wire ones — around the whole kneecap. He spent a year in hospital. It seemed as if his hurling career was ended. But sheer willpower, determination and a love of the game saw him return to the playing pitch.

It was the Patrician Brothers in Lombard Street, Galway who instilled in him his early love of the game. There he was influenced by Tipperary man Brother Killian Hackett — a member of the same clan that gave Stephen Hackett to Tipperary hurling and Martin Hackett to Dublin. In the 1917 final when Tipperary and Dublin met the two brothers were on opposite sides. Mick did his club hurling with Castlegar and Galway City.

No rush of major honours came his way — yet he won fame. He excelled in Railway Cup games and gave masterly displays in the Tailteann games of 1928 and 1932. In one of those games he wore the number 13 jersey and scored (3:4) 13 points from all angles. In the 1928 series he scored the amazing total of 28 points. He was however well equipped for this. From his early days he practised assiduously. He used remove a stone from the gable of the house and practise aiming at the cavity from various angles of the garden. It became a ritual. Before a match he would test the wind's direction by throwing up a cluster of grass and then take a few shots at goal so as to get his eye in. In the 1932 League final against Tipperary his genius engineered a last gasp dramatic goal to give Galway their first League title on the score 4:5 to 4:4.

He was magnificent at midfield and centre-forward. Not only was he a brilliant hurler — he was also a true sportsman — over six feet tall — exceptionally clean — and he had speed and hurling instinct in abundance. One of his hurleys is now on display in a glass case in Liam Mellow's

Mick King was born in 1905 and at the relatively young age of fifty-six was called to Solas na bhFlaitheas on 15 March 1961.

I am indebted to his daughter Erna and nephew John Francis for much of the detail in this article.

He was one of the foremost hurlers of his day and remained close to it after his retirement and worked tirelessly for its promotion. He was also honoured with election to the post of County Chairman.

Mick's native Galway took part in five All Ireland finals in the twenties. Fame-wise he hadn't yet arrived when they won their first title in 1923 and failed to retain it when Dublin beat them in 1924. He was however according to John Francis, part of the panel. His first cousin Martin played on these teams and since the records merely state M. King in the lineout it has on occasions led to the cousins being understood to be one and the same person.

Mick really arrived on the scene in 1925 and despite losing to Tipperary his skills and potential were in evidence. Galway were back in the final again in 1928 and

Clubhouse in Galway.

He had great admiration for Martin Kennedy — famed Tipperary full-forward. Of Bobby Rackard he said, according to John Francis, that he was one of the greatest centre-half-backs he ever saw and then added — that's a hurler. Phil Purcell of Tipperary was a great friend — on and off the field. Whenever Mick talked about the Galway team of the Josie Gallagher era he used express the view that with just a few minor changes in position, it could have been a great team and even as it was, was worth an All Ireland or two.

He was a very shy man and loathe to talk about his hurling prowess. Such however, would have been common among the culture of his generation. The late John D. Hickey of the *Irish Independent* once visited him with a view to writing about him. He got a peremptory, but very gentlemanly dismissal whereupon he headed for Phil Purcell in Tipperary and got lots to write about. On discovering this Mick declared what he would and what he wouldn't do to Phil when he next met him. It was however a benign threat.

The late Jim Young of Cork ranked him among the greats. Limerick's outstanding midfielder Timmy Ryan said that one of the greatest individual displays he ever saw was given by Mick King at centre-forward in the 1932 All Ireland semi-final against Clare at Limerick — despite the fact that in scoring terms Tull Considine of Clare stole the limelight that day. Garrett Howard of Limerick who also played with Dublin and Tipperary named Mick as one of the great hurlers of his era.

A sportswriter of many decades ago had this to say, 'At Tailteann and Railway Cup, King was the Cuchulainn of the side and his endless work for the Gaels' games in Connaught has to some extent compensated for his physical injury now repaired ... he has played a big part in helping Galway's manly part in keeping the hurling standard flying west of the Shannon where competition is negligible and talent confined.'

To Mick hurling was a love — an art — a medium of expression. He was one of its noble ambassadors.

Born: 1926

glorious day is a wonderful memory which I have cherished all my life.

It was great to have been part of those golden days for Laois hurling in 1948/1949. The recurring question to which no Laois man has yet come up with a satisfactory answer is — where did we come from in 1948 and where did we disappear to after our All Ireland trouncing by Tipperary in 1949? There is no satisfactory answer. Our 1948/49 squad was a great one, but we clashed with greater. I can safely say that we in Laois annually look forward hopefully to being drawn against Kilkenny in the Leinster championship, but it seldom occurs. Playing Kilkenny invariably brings out the very best in Laois players, but fate doesn't provide us with that draw. Wexford on the other hand has a hoodoo over us. It started away back in 1950 and has remained since.

Meanwhile, our neighbours Offaly have emerged and stolen the show and shown us how to win All Irelands — both in hurling and football. We still can boast of having great exponents of hurling in Laois. We should now have transferred to us from the O'Connor to the O'Moore County, the mantle of the faithful county. It remains for some twenty of our Laois hurlers to get things all together at the same time. We are hungry for a return of the 1948/49 era, but more hungry for a repeat of the Great 1914/15 era. Maybe Clare hurlers will emulate their footballers before the end of the century and so encourage Laois to join them in Croke Park as they did in 1914 — for a replay of that game — and maybe then Laois would reproduce their 1915 form.

"

While 1949 was for Laois our All Ireland year, I must go back to the first round of the 1948 Leinster championship for my happiest playing day and my most pleasant recollection as a Laois player. In September 1947 I had sat enthralled on the Cusack Stand witnessing the greatest All Ireland I had seen up to then (or since) between the two greatest teams ever to come out of Cork and Kilkenny. Kilkenny won this battle of Gaelic Gladiators with a last second point from Terry Leahy. While I am a Laois man who is extremely proud to have worn the blue and white jersey, I would have smiled quite ruefully on that All Ireland Sunday evening if anyone had suggested that Laois might beat that Kilkenny team in the next championship match.

However, that is exactly what we did. Laois convincingly beat that same Kilkenny team (only Terry Leahy was missing) in O'Moore Park, Portlaoise in the first round of the 1948 Leinster championship and I had the wonderful satisfaction of contributing two goals to that historic Laois victory — our first over Kilkenny in Donkey's years. The ecstasy of the Laois supporters in O'Moore Park on that

"

Paddy Lalor

When you beat Kilkenny two years in succession in the championship, it has to reflect hurling progress in the county involved. So it was with Laois in 1948 and 1949. 'We began to feel we had their measure and could handle them. We looked forward with hope and expectations of success — real success. And what happened? We ran headlong into the rising power that was Wexford — losing the Leinster final of 1951 by 3:12 to 4:3 and Wexford continued — admittedly after lots of growing pains — to gain in stature and confidence and we faded.' It brought home to Paddy just how hard it is out there in the hurling world — first of all to reach the stage of being able to match the best — and then to stay at that level and move up a gear and beat the best.

Laois moments of glory in the hurling world have sadly been few and far between. They certainly produced the hurlers. Many Laois men starred on Dublin teams in the 20's and 30's when Dublin were a real hurling force. In the Railway Cup competition Laois men displayed their abilities and skills on Leinster teams. So often Laois have provided stern opposition for the best. But the breakthrough seems to elude them. Lack of tradition may be a factor. If it is then they should take a long hard look at Offaly and their remarkable achievements all through the 80's. Perhaps more outside guidance from men of the calibre of George Leahy might be the answer.

A glance through the records show that apart from walkovers given in 1889 and 1891 to Dublin and Wexford respectively, Laois have contested thirteen Leinster finals. They were successful on three occasions — 1914, 1915 and 1949. Only 1915 paved the way for All Ireland success when Cork fell on the score 6:2 to 4:1. Reproduced here (page 165) is a ticket of invitation to the Presentation of the All Ireland medals to the Laois team of 1915. Note in particular the title given to the team — 'Leix & Ossory'. Note too, that the ticket in question is designated a 'Lady's Ticket'.

And that brings us to Paddy Lalor and the late forties and early fifties when it seemed for fleeting moments that Laois might make the all important breakthrough. The mentors had cast the net wide in search of talent — in County Laois itself and in Dublin where Laois men were hurling with the clubs. Among those in the Laois lineout was that great veteran Harry Gray — 'a man who always praised and encouraged colleagues — never heard him criticise — no matter what blunder you might make. He was a great advocate of Mol an Óige and of course one of hurling's great artists.'

In the Leinster championship of 1948 Kilkenny the All Ireland champions were beaten by Laois at O'Moore Park, Portlaoise — and decisively at that 4:8 to 2:7. Paddy scored two of those Laois goals, first time ground striking, from passes from Harry Gray, off no less a defender than Mark Marnell, and was carried shoulder high like the rest of his team mates by jubilant supporters when the final whistle blew. 'I can still sense the excitement of the fans. There I was on their shoulders — heading for the sideline and the dressing-room. Barbed wire passed over the gateway from the sideline. I leaned back to avoid it and pass under — up I was pushed from behind again — the excitement intense. Seeing the looming danger I tilted sideways — the fans weren't having it — up I'm pushed again — and only at the last minute did I duck sufficiently to avoid the barbed wire and a nasty accident. That victory over All Ireland champions Kilkenny made me feel we might be going places. We fell to Dublin in the Leinster final but looked forward to the following year.'

Laois began the 1949 campaign with victories over Offaly and Dublin. When Kilkenny fell in the Leinster final by 3:8 to 3:6 the fans were ecstatic. Neutrals were pleased — this could only be good for hurling. This success story continued when Laois beat a very talented Galway team — a team that included great players like Sean Duggan, Willie Fahy, 'Inky' Flaherty, Colm Corless, Miko McInerney, John

Killeen, Hubert Gordon, Tadhg Kelly, and Josie Gallagher — in the All Ireland semifinal. And it is worth remembering that in the Railway Cup final the previous St Patrick's Day, Munster were hard pressed to beat the same Galway team. It was a narrow victory 5:3 to 2:9. This wasn't lost on Laois and it added to their confidence.

But it all went wrong on All Ireland day. 'We may have overdone the training — I don't know — I'm not sure. It was probably nerves and inexperience too. We were raw to the big time — raw too where training tactics were concerned. I felt stuck to the ground and didn't want to see the ball coming my way — a terrible mental approach. Paddy Kelly in the other corner felt the same way. Not a lot of ball came my way but the one chance I did get in the first half to score a goal, I missed. Timmy Fitzpatrick, our goalkeeper had a great game. And would you believe it so had Jackie Bergin our full-back. He did the least amount of training — he disliked training — he dodged as much of it as he could. Jimmy Murray in the half-back line had a first class game. Our midfielders Joe Styles and Billy Bohane held their own in the first half.'

The final score was 3:11 to 0:3 in Tipperary's favour, after a first half that was satisfactory from a Laois point of view — being only 1:5 to 0:3 in arrears at half time. It was a pity. It didn't do justice to Laois. It made recovery and the road forward very difficult. It wouldn't have mattered to an established county. Indeed it happened to Kilkenny in 1937 when coincidentally Tipperary beat them by the same score in the All Ireland final. But Kilkenny were back in 1939 to take the title at the expense of Cork. That's tradition at

work. Five Laois men were honoured by the Leinster selectors when the Railway cup team was picked. Timmy Fitzpatrick, Jimmy Murray, Tom Byrne, Joe Styles, and Andy Dunne. 'In our two midfielders Joe Styles and Billy Bohane, we had at that time a midfield combination capable of holding their own with the best in the country.'

Paddy enjoyed the short and fleeting glory days with his native Laois. He played Railway Cup for Leinster but without success as those were the days when Munster dominated that competition. After the All Ireland defeat Paddy was dropped for the Oireachtas semi-final against Cork. 'As if I were to blame for the whole thing.' However, his replacement didn't travel and Paddy was restored to the team and 'had the satisfaction of scoring the winning goal.' In the final Tipperary again provided the opposition. The final score was Tipperary 2:8 Laois 1:6 — probably a much fairer reflection of the ability of the Laois team of 1949.

His school days were spent at Knockbeg College where football was the leading game. His heroes in those days were Bill Delaney and Tommy Murphy of football renown. Indeed Paddy used to dream that future sporting glory lay for him in the football field. But Abbeyleix was a hurling parish with which he captured three Laois county titles in 1944, 1945 and 1949 and this led to county hurling recognition. He did however play some Senior football with the county team.

He was County Secretary for three years in the mid-fifties and is now President of the Supporters Club. Now as he prepares to retire from the positon of MEP, he is psyching himself up to tackle three

---

Here is his team — from the men of his period.

Sean Duggan (Galway)

| Bobby Rackard (Wexford) | Con Murphy (Cork) | John Doyle (Tipperary) |
| Seamus Cleere (Kilkenny) | Pat Stakelum(Tipperary) | Jim Young (Cork) |

Joe Salmon (Galway)   Vin Baston (Waterford)

| Christy Ring (Cork) | Harry Gray (Laois) | Jim Langton (Kilkenny) |
| Paddy Lalor (Laois) | Nick Rackard (Wexford) | Tim Flood (Wexford). |

ambitions he would like to see fulfilled before the turn of the century — 'a county senior title for Abbeyleix (they haven't won one since 1949) — a tidy towns victory for Abbeyleix — and an All Ireland success for his native Laois — Offaly did it — showed it can be done so why couldn't Laois with the right approach.'

Paddy's team is an interesting one. It contains three of his 'pet hurlers' — Vin Baston of Waterford, Seamus Cleere of Kilkenny and Tim Flood of Wexford.

He eulogises about them and as he talks shakes his head slowly as he reflects on their brilliance — 'their hurling class — their range of skills — above all their sportsmanship.' And having selected the team he wished it could have been a twenty one aside for he was looking for places for several others including Tom Walton of Kilkenny, Jimmy Doyle of Tipperary, Jimmy Smyth of Clare, 'Diamond' Hayden of Kilkenny and the Laois trio of Jimmy Murray, Billy Bohane and Joe Styles.

A 1915 'Lady's Ticket' to a GAA presentation in Abbeyleix.

Born: 1890

Johnny Leahy, a legendary figure in his native Tipperary, is affectionately referred to as 'Captain Johnny' in family circles.

A native of Boherlahan, he led Tipperary to victory over Kilkenny in the 1916 decider on the score 5:4 to 3:2 and he led them to success again in 1925 with a good win over Galway 5:6 to 1:5. In 1917 he was also captain but Tipperary went down to a surprise defeat at the hands of Dublin on the score 5:4 to 4:2. Johnny's nephew Seamus, told me it was one of those defeats often talked about in Tipperary — a might have been — a one Johnny felt was left behind — and in his final weeks as he lay ill when his mind occasionally rambled and wandered back to the past he was heard to talk about that 1917 lost final. In 1926 he toured America with his team where his leadership qualities earned him the title 'Captain Johnny Leahy'.

He was born on the 1st January, 1890 and in 1913 was one of the founder members of the Boherlahan hurling club. Prior to that he had made his senior club debut with Cashel in 1909. In 1930 at the age of 40 he played in the Tipperary County final — his last game.

He held the office of County Chairman while still a player. He also held the office of County Treasurer and was County Secretary from 1927 to 1948. He represented Tipperary on the Munster Council from 1920 to 1948. He filled all posts with distinction.

His three brothers Mick, Tommy and Paddy — who together with Joe Nagle missed the 1922 final against Kilkenny because both were on the run — all played at county level.

When Johnny died in November, 1949 he was laid to rest in the old Cistersian Abbey of Holycross. All Gaeldom mourned. The GAA had lost one of its great players and administrators. Father J.J. Meagher, one time Chairman of Tipperary County Board once spoke as follows of Johnny. 'No stauncher Gael or truer christian has ever trod this fertile land of our beloved Tipperary.'

A newspaper headline described him thus:

'A noble kindly character, a sincere friend and a lifetime worker for the GAA.'

The article went on to say — 'probably not since the funeral of that other son of this same parish of Boherlahan, who died for Ireland in Gloucester prison in 1919 — Pierce McCann — has there been such a great manifestation of public sorrow and respect. And he was worthy of it all.'

John D. Hickey of the *Irish Independent* once described him thus — 'As a captain he was unsurpassed and as a player he had few equals ... despite the esteem in which he was held and the many laurels showered upon him Johnny was always modest and unassuming, rather boyish in his ways and it was those qualities that endeared him to all.'

Here is an excerpt from an appreciation on his death:

Mr. John Leahy' we never knew. 'Captain Leahy' we heard on rare occasions.

But 'Johnny Leahy' we all knew and that speaks volumes in itself. Never again shall we feel his warm hearty hand clasp nor hear his merry voice in happy laughter and drole anecdote. His last bottle of holy water has been carried to the dressing-room 'to shake on the boys' before they take the field and when the last drops are sprinkled on his final resting place tomorrow, the prayers of countless friends and admirers will unite and mount to the Great White Throne of God that He Who so loved children and the meek and humble of heart may receive into the Heavenly Mansions this great little man who, in Peter Pan fashion never grew up but, 'lived in glory all his lovely days and is immortal, dead'.

In his book *A Lifetime in Hurling* Tommy Doyle, who featured in *Giants of the Ash* selected his best team in 1955. Not only did it include Johnny Leahy but Tommy also honoured him with the captaincy. It read:

	Tony Reddin (Tipperary)	
Johnny Leahy (Tipperary)	Sean Óg Murphy (Cork)	John Joe Doyle (Clare)
John Keane (Waterford)	Paddy Clohessy (Limerick)	Paddy Phelan (Kilkenny)
	Jim Hurley (Cork)	Lory Meagher (Kilkenny)	
Christy Ring (Cork)	Mick Mackey (Limerick)	Phil Cahill (Tipperary)
Eudi Coughlan (Cork)	Martin Kennedy (Tipperary)	Mattie Power (Kilkenny)

Born: 1924

"

Hurling to me is the greatest field game of all. I am a hurling purist and derive my greatest enjoyment from a good hurling game. When I first went to school in North Mon, that year the Mon were in the Harty Cup final with Limerick CBS. I can well recall Brother McConville coming around to the classrooms selling the rail tickets for the final in Mitchelstown. Two shillings was the fare — a lot of money in those days. The trip to Mitchelstown to me was wondrous. Blue and white colours — sweets and lemonade. The Mon won and I can remember the parade from the station, up McCurtain St, through Patrick St, North Main St, Shandon St, St Mary's Road to the school — Molly Owens bonfire in Shandon St and another at the front entrance to the school. My great hero of course, someone whom I had the great honour of playing with later, was the Mon captain Jack Lynch. From then on, while I played any kind of a game with a ball, hurling was my favourite game. I progressed through North Mon until I was wearing the famous blue and white versus our great rivals Farranferris in the under 17 final. My immediate opponent was Joe Kelly who later became Father Joe and won an All Ireland with

Cork in 1946. In the Mon Harty teams of those years we had Con Murphy, the late Gerry Riordan, his brother Mossy and Sean O'Brien.

From school I went straight into the Glen senior team and won the county championship of 1944. That team contained some of the all time greats in Cork hurling, Jack Lynch, D.J. Buckley, Paddy Donovan, Jim Young, Christy Ring and David Creedon. My years with Glen Rovers from 1944 to 1961 are studded with great memories of great matches and great friends — great rivalries with the Barrs, Blackrock, Sars — great friends such as Seamus O'Brien. Sean O'Brien, Donie O'Donovan, Jimmy Lynam. Great wins, many defeats but above all my memories from 1944 to '61 are of playing and enjoying to the fullest, hurling — The Beautiful Game.

John Lyons "

John Lyons established himself on a permanent basis at full-back in the Cork number 3 jersey in 1952. Prior to that he had been a sub in the 1946 panel and thereafter played in league and tournament games. It was only when Con Murphy — that great servant of the GAA and Cork hurling — retired in 1951 leaving the full-back position vacant that room was found for John.

He was however far from being a raw defender. Indeed, in many ways he was quite experienced and battle hardened. In his school days he played for four years with North Mon in the Harty Cup and captained them once. They were victorious on three occasions. He also played interprovincial colleges with Munster and was on the winning team three times. John recalls that on one of those Munster colleges teams in the early forties North Mon contributed twelve players and three subs. He won a Munster junior football medal with North Mon in the first year they entered the competition. 'We weren't really serious about football. We were hurlers playing football. Football was only a means to an end in North Mon.'

At the age of 20 he played senior hurling with The Glen and won a county title in 1944 — the first of ten. He was captain on three occasions — 1950, '58 and '59.

When he took his place at full-back in 1952 in the red jersey of Cork he had added to his college victories five county senior hurling medals. It was a background of considerable experience — a background that gave him a winning mentality — vital at county level when you go out to contest All Ireland matches. 'I never felt a sense of pressure. I was always cool about games — even when it was a Munster or All Ireland final. The Cork county championship games and finals could be as demanding and testing as many a Munster or All Ireland final.'

He remembers the first time he got an opportunity to play for Cork. 'It was a tournament game in Fermoy in 1945. Tony Brennan of Tipp who was later to become their staunch full-back was playing at full-forward on me. He gave me the greatest dressing down I ever got. He was too big and too strong for me. He was a tall, rangy, boney man. I got a baptism of fire — to put it mildly — and me captain of Cork for the day. My last game with Cork was in the Oireachtas against Tipperary in 1960. I had injured my knee previously and had to come off in that game.'

I asked John to pick two highlights from the great three in a row victory campaign of 1952-54. 'I suppose the Munster final of 1952 would have to stand out. Tipp had three in a row All Irelands under their belt and were going for a fourth. There was a very strong incentive there to stop them equalling Cork's unequalled four in a row of 1941-1944. But the odds looked very much against us. They had walked through Waterford — were hot favourites and on paper looked all over winners — maybe that is why we beat them. They had a very experienced team with players like Seamus Bannon, Tommy Doyle, Jimmy Finn, Pat Stakelum, Mickey Byrne, Paddy Kenny and the Ryans. I was playing on Sonny Maher. The excitement and tension was unbelievable. The Limerick pitch was packed to capacity. You got the feeling that the crowd was in on top of you. We played against the wind — a fairly strong breeze — in the first half. Early on in that half it seemed as if Tipp would run all over us but our backs did their job well and Tipp had misses. We were two goals down at half time but didn't feel the game was lost. It was a hectic second half. Ring was outstanding — he was bandaged. It was he who got the equalising point — the crowd went wild. Creedon and Reddin had been making great saves. In a bid to save the day Tipp released a fierce assault in the last ten minutes and camped in our half of the field. We defended and defended. At the final whistle we were just ahead 1:11 to 2:6 — a great win.' In Cork it was a lineout to remember with pride and here it is —

Dave Creedon, Gerry O'Riordan, John Lyons, Tony O'Shaughnessy, Willie J. Daly, Vin Toomey, Seanie O'Brien, Joe Toomey, Gerard Murphy, Mossie O'Riordan, Joe Hartnett, Christy Ring, Paddy Healy, Liam Dowling and Paddy Barry.

'My second choice would be the All Ireland final of 1954 against Wexford. Everyone was saying that the outcome depended on how Wexford would cope with Ring and how I would perform on Nick Rackard. I didn't feel any sense of pressure. I was always a cool character and took each game and each opponent as they came. I was walking down O'Connell Street the evening before the match with Seanie O'Brien when a man and his wife stopped to talk to Seanie. They didn't know who I was. The whole conversation was about the match and how English would perform on Ring and could Lyons hold Rackard. But of course there was more to it than that. I always took the view that a defence must function as a unit. If Nick slipped away from me someone else would pick him up. We had six good defenders. Gerry O'Riordan and Tony O'Shaughnessy were my flankers and in the half-line you had Mattie Fouhy, Vin Toomey and Derry Hayes. Dave Creedon was an excellent goalkeeper. In the three All Irelands of 1952, '53 and '54 he was beaten only once — and that was in the game against Wexford when Tom Ryan palmed the ball to the net shortly before halftime. It was a very low scoring game 1:9 to 1:6. I feel Wexford were a shade the better team. But they were still inexperienced and didn't convert their chances. The goal that gave us the lead and which proved to be a winner came from the hurley of Johnny Clifford with about four minutes to go.' So Cork in their twenty ninth All Ireland final and heading the honours list won their nineteenth All Ireland title. Christy Ring collected his eighth All Ireland medal in a game that enthralled Gaeldom. The record attendance of 84,856 still stands. The crowds had begun to queue at 9am that morning and half an hour before the start of the senior game the Croke Park gates were closed.

Any other memories that stand out? 'Only that Waterford were so good around that time I feel we would have won two more All Irelands in 1957 and 1959. In 1959 in the Munster final we played against the wind in the first half and were four points up at halftime. Normally I was a terrible pessimist on the field. No matter how much we were ahead I wouldn't be happy until the final whistle. That day at halftime I couldn't see us losing. But Phil Grimes who had switched to centre-back for Waterford dominated that Munster final and played a stormer and when the final whistle blew it was 3:9 to 2:9 in Water-

ford's favour.'

Your memories of Ring? 'He was there before me and continued after me. I played with him from 1944 to 1961 — at club, county, and inter-provincial level — and we were in the States together. I saw no one like him — he was on a plane of his own. If I had to pick one characteristic above any other it would be his courage. He saw no danger. If there was a ball there to be got he never drew back. At times Tipp didn't spare the hurleys but if there was a score to be got Ring wouldn't see them. I will always remember the 1956 Munster final against Limerick in Thurles. We were a beaten team well into the last quarter of the game. But in a five minute spell Ring scored three goals and one point to give Cork victory. It was a game Limerick let slip.'

John is extremely proud of his club Glen Rovers. 'When the club won its first county final in 1934 with a 3:2 to 0:6 victory over St Finbarr's — refereed incidentally by the legendary Clare goalkeeper Dr Tommy Daly — a great social uplift was given to the whole northside of Cork City. Up to then the Barrs and Sars and Blackrock were the clubs for good hurlers — all south of the river — no heroes north of the river. By 1941 the club had annexed an eighth successive county senior title. North of the city was always a great sporting area. People were involved with harrier dogs, greyhounds, ferreting, bowl playing and handball but there were no heroes — none that is until Glen Rovers became a hurling power and then there were heroes aplenty. And the whole population of the northside basked in the reflected glory of the hurling men and felt a sense of pride and importance and wellbeing. Hurling was a

Here is his team from the men of his era.

Tony Reddin (Tipperary)

| John Doyle (Tipperary) | John Lyons (Cork) | Din Joe Buckley (Cork) |
| Jimmy Finn (Tipperary) | Tony Wall (Tipperary) | Jim Young (Cork) |

Jack Lynch (Cork)   Joe Salmon (Galway)

| Jimmy Doyle (Tipperary) | Mick Mackey (Limerick) | Eddie Keher (Kilkenny) |
| Paddy Barry (Cork) | Nick Rackard (Wexford) | Christy Ring (Cork) |

topic for discussion and something to be argued and debated and discussed in the workplace and the pubs and any kind of social gathering.'

John was a student of full-back play. He thought about the game and realised that playing at full-back involved more than just hurling. 'The operative word was defender. You had to read the game — blend into the defence as a unit — protect your goalkeeper in my day — cover the goal and above all keep the ball out of the danger area.' John believes that the vast bulk of players will want to play the ball provided their opponents do likewise. John always played the ball. Little wonder he was known as 'the gentleman full-back' — a title any hurling man would be extremely proud of.

Action from the past: Jimmy Maher, Tipp with cap and behind him John Mackey of Limerick – son of 'Tyler' (see page 172).

John 'Tyler' MACKEY   1901-1917   Castleconnell & Limerick

Born: c.1883

J ohn Mackey better known in the hurling world as 'Tyler' Mackey — ever since the day he purchased a pair of new shoes in Tylers of Limerick — was father of Mick Mackey and John Mackey who starred with the great Limerick teams in the 1930's and 1940's.

'Tyler' played his hurling hard — very hard. He was immensely strong and fast, lion-hearted and fearless, tough and daring, and at times impetuous.

He captained Limerick in 1910 when they failed in controversial circumstances to Wexford in the All Ireland final on the score 7 goals to 6:2.

As the score would suggest it was a game of almost all ground hurling. It was the only occasion in the history of the GAA that the winning team failed to score a point in the final.

After the disappointment of 1910 'Tyler' had great hopes of All Ireland glory the following year when Limerick reached the final against Kilkenny. On the path to the final they beat Kerry in the first round — Clare in the Munster semi-final and Tipperary in the Munster final — staging a great late rally to win a very exciting game by 5:3 to 4:3.

The 1911 final was fixed for Cork on the 18th February 1912. Torrential rain fell and despite Limerick protestations the pitch was declared unplayable and the game was postponed. The match was refixed for Thurles on 3rd April but Limerick refused to travel to that venue — claiming that it would be Cork or nowhere. The matter then came before congress on Easter Sunday for which Limerick tabled a motion with a view to getting the venue changed. The motion was defeated and the game refixed for May 18th. Limerick refused to travel to Thurles and Kilkenny were awarded a walkover — the first and only walkover in the history of the game. So for the second successive year 'Tyler's' hopes of All Ireland glory were dashed.

His whole life centred around the GAA and in particular the game of hurling. So after a long career that lasted 17 years he must have felt robbed of an All Ireland medal when his native Limerick captured the All Ireland crown in 1918 — the year after his retirement.

But he did have the compensation of two Munster medals in 1910 and 1911 — the joy and pride of watching his two sons Mick and John give regal displays in the Limerick and Munster jerseys — and the reward and fulfillment that a lifetime in hurling and GAA can bring to its players, enthusiasts and promoters.

Mick MACKEY   1930-1947   Ahane & Limerick

Mick Mackey leads Limerick in a Munster final against Tipperary.

Born: 1912

He first wore the Limerick jersey in a National League game against Kilkenny at Limerick Gaelic Grounds on 16 November 1930. He donned the green and white for the last time on 22 June 1947 when he came on a substitute against Tipperary in the first round of the Munster championship at Cork. Between times he thrilled and entertained and dazzled tens of thousands of hurling enthusiasts with displays of rare magnificence that became a metaphor for excellence. He added new dimensions to the great game and made his name synonymous with it.

It was an era when Limerick played a brand of hurling that was a delight to watch. They drew the crowds, they set records, they entertained — whether League, Tournament or Championship, whether against Kilkenny, Cork, Tipperary, Dublin, Clare, Waterford or Galway. And Mick inspired his men — a list that reads like a litany of All Stars — Paddy Scanlon, John Mackey, Timmy Ryan, Dick Stokes, Tom McCarthy, Paddy O'Carroll, Ned Cregan, Mick Kennedy, Mickey Cross, Paddy Clohessy, Garrett Howard, Paddy McMahon, Jackie Power, Peter Cregan and Mick Ryan. They were the talk of the land and the stuff of folklore.

Mick's hurling feats are legion and legendary but we will select one of his finest from the twilight days of an action filled career. It was the Munster final of 1944 — the 'Bicycle Final'. Private cars were off the road due to the war. Every other mode of conveyance was used to get to Thurles — but mainly the bicycle — and they arrived in their thousands from all directions. Here is how some newspaper reports described Mick's performance, as Limerick attempted to halt Cork's bid for a record four in a row All Ireland titles.

'If any man could be said to have stood out head and shoulders over such a gathering of stars as both teams numbered that man is Mick Mackey. Quite true, he lacked the speed of the days when his famous solos were features of every game in which he played, but his scheming and strategy, from

173

which he notched two goals and three points should be an inspiration and example for all young forwards who aspire to reach the top.' ... 'The playboy, Mick Mackey, selling the dummy or cutting over a beauty of a point from the corner was again the hero of the crowd.' ... 'The game was an individual triumph for Mick Mackey, who led the Limerick rally, weaving his way through the Cork defence to obtain himself or make for others the scores that helped his side to share the honours.'

'Mick Mackey revealed all the artistry of his best years, and the points he scored from acute angles bore the hallmark of the master. It was hard to believe he had been hurling since 1931, for he still showed the pace and skill of his best years.'

Mick as captain, had the honour of leading his club, county and province to success. He always led by example and exhortation. With his club Ahane he had the rare distinction of winning five senior football county titles between 1935 and 1939 while in the same years capturing five of his fifteen county senior hurling medals. The score in the 1939 county senior football final in a game that was unfinished and awarded to Ahane must surely be rare if not unique. It read Ahane 0:1 Glin 0:0. Mick also played senior football with Limerick and in a Munster semi-final in 1945 playing at full-forward he scored 2:4 off no less a defender than the stonewall Paddy 'Bawn' Brosnan.

Mick has been described as 'probably the most colourful player that ever gripped a camán or graced the green sward of any hurling arena.' Carbery had this to say of him, 'Playboy of the Southern World — Munster's pride and Limerick's glory — the one and only Mick Mackey. From a combination of skill and power, of brains and brawn the Castleconnell man, son of the great Tyler Mackey brought joy and thrills galore to thousands.'

As a hurler he was supreme — skilful, daring, dashing and extremely strong. As a personality he was warm, gregarious, affable and generous hearted. Mick was the Laughing Cavalier — the Falstaff of the hurling arena. Many of the stories about him reveal this and none better than the opening moments of the Senior hurling game between Ahane and Thurles Sarsfields at Newport in May 1947.

It was customary in those days — even at All Ireland finals — for a prominent clergyman to throw in the ball to start the game. Sometimes it stood as the real throw-in and the game proceeded. But on occasions it merely served as a ceremonial throw-in. At the game in question the local PP threw in the ball. Mick, up to one of his tricks shouted 'take it easy now boys. This is not the real throw-in at all.' Some of the opposing team fell for the gambit and Mick gathered the ball — raced goalwards and scored the opening point. Those who knew Mick will picture him heartily laughing his way back to his position.

Mick won every honour in the game including the Hall of Fame award in 1962 and a Bank of Ireland Special All Star award in 1980. He belongs to a small select band of captains who were presented with the McCarthy Cup on more than one occasion. Mick had the honour in 1936 and 1940. In 1936 he captained one of hurling's greatest ever combinations. It read:

Paddy Scanlon / Paddy O'Carroll, Tom McCarthy, Mick Kennedy / Mickey Cross, Paddy Clohessey, Garrett Howard / Timmy Ryan, Mick Ryan / John Mackey, Mick Mackey, Jim Roche / Dave Clohessey, Paddy McMahon, Jackie Power.

He was selected as Limerick's representative on the Munster Council in 1950 and held the position for the record spell of 32 years. He died on 13 September 1982 having completed his seventieth year on the previous 12 July.

He was buried like a king. They came from all over Ireland. The funeral cortege was three miles long. The route was lined with mourners. It was the last farewell to a living legend — now dead.

Is glas an féar ar uaigh na laoch
A gcuimhne glas 'nár gcroí
Cé fada anois atáid faoin gcré
Go suaimhneach ina luí

The Mackey stand at Páirc na nGael Limerick perpetuates his memory.

Born: 1889

Down through the decades many outstanding dual performers have worn the Wexford jersey. Paddy Mackey is one of them and ranks among the greats.

The Rower in Co Kilkenny is only a stone's throw from New Ross. It was Paddy's native place. In his young days Tullaroan and Mooncoin were the Kilkenny hurling strongholds and between 1904 and 1913 they won seven All Ireland hurling titles. There was so much talent available that they probably either missed or weren't interested in Paddy's prowess with the camán.

It turned out to be Wexford's gain. He came to work in New Ross and so as to qualify to play for Wexford he was accommodated with sleeping quarters in New Ross town by Sean O'Kennedy, one of Wexford's greatest sportsmen.

Hurling fame first came Paddy's way. That was in 1910 when Wexford met Limerick in the final. It was Wexford's fourth appearance and Limerick's second. It was a game of two halves. Wexford dominated the first half and led at the interval by 6:0 to 3:1. Limerick's second half rallies failed to carry the day and the final score read Wexford 7:0 Limerick 6:2. Paddy Mackey was one of Wexford's outstanding players.

He had all the attributes of a good defender — a safe pair of hands — positional sense — anticipation and speed. He was ox-like and rarely shouldered to the ground. It is said that hurling followers who saw Paddy Phelan, the richly talented Kilkenny defender of the 30's in action, used to call to mind the displays of Paddy Mackey and make comparison. No greater hurling tribute could be paid to Paddy Mackey. His daughter Patricia Fleming is now the proud possessor of that cherished 1910 hurling medal.

Football fame followed shortly. In 1913 Paddy was superb in the overthrow of All Ireland champions Louth in the Leinster final on the score 2:3 to 2:2.

The following year they also beat Louth in the Leinster final. It was close again 0:3

to 0:1. In each of those years they failed to Kerry in the final.

But the foundations of success and glory had been laid. In the years 1915 to 1918 Wexford won four All Ireland titles in a row beating the best that Kerry, Mayo, Clare and Tipperary respectively could produce. Paddy Mackey played a major part in those great triumphs. No other county has so far appeared in six successive senior football finals and only Kerry subsequently equalled that great four in a row record in the eras 1929 to 1932 and 1978 to 1981.

By 1918 Paddy had added to his Leinster and All Ireland hurling medals of 1910, six successive Leinster football medals 1913-1918 and four successive All Ireland medals 1915-1918. It was a performance that is unlikely to be surpassed. New Ross and Wexford are still very proud of him.

Above: Jimmy Barry Murphy
of Cork

Right: Ciaran Barr, Antrim 1991

Above: Tony Doran takes a shot
for Wexford

Left: Johnny Callinan of Clare

Opposite page top: Joe McKenna of
Limerick

Opposite page bottom: Leonard Enright
of Limerick — holding the hurley right
hand under left, 1988.

Pat Delaney, Offaly, and Ger Fennelly, Kilkenny, rise for the ball in the Leinster Hurling Final 1989.

Born: 1870

Michael was the first man to lead a county team to more than one All Ireland victory. He was captain of a famed Tubberadora selection and led them to three All Ireland successes in the years 1895, 1896 and 1898. He won two further titles in 1899 and 1900. Here is how he was described in the programme of the Gaelic League Carnival of August 1911 'A huge man of soft kindly countenance, he had a quiet, commanding way with him that made his team respect him as no captain ever was respected. Never a beautiful hurler, he was the most dangerous man on the forty yards or midfield that a back ever was up against. He could tear down a stone wall, dashing into everything, had a powerful long shot off either left or right, and his ground drives sent terror into many a goalkeeper's heart. A big scoring balance against his team never made his heart quake. When things looked black for Tipp, Maher would suddenly rise, titan-like, dribble up the field, sweep down opposition as a scythe does hay in June, tear along and shoot. That score would change the whole aspect of the game.

Those Tipperary mens blood would boil, their virility would assert itself, they would drive into their men, reckless of life and limb, and actually walk over the stretched bodies of their opponents to victory.'

His nephew Michael Maher — son of Matty — carried on a proud family hurling tradition winning five All Ireland medals with his native Tipperary at full-back in the years 1958, 1961, 1962, 1964 and '65. A second nephew Sonny Maher — son of Jack — won three All Ireland medals with Tipperary in the 1949-51 period at full-forward. Interestingly, all were involved in back to back successes and between them they have shared in thirteen of Tipperary's All Ireland victories.

Only two other hurlers to date, the great Christy Ring of Cork, and the renowned 'Drug' Walsh of Kilkenny — captained three winning All Ireland teams.

Big Mikey, as he was always known was 25 when Tubberadora stormed onto the national hurling scene. He was revered by his team mates and was one of hurling's greatest captains.

In 1918 Big Mikey left his native place in Tipperary, where it was said he 'carried more weight than the Parish Priest' and settled in Galbally Co Limerick. In Boherlahan he was thereafter perceived as a King in exile.

Here is how Seamus Leahy in a lovely article described his funeral — 'When he died in 1947 many of them travelled there to help carry his giant frame to its last resting place in Tipperary's St Michael's cemetery. To his neighbours at Gleneffy (Galbally) he had been a big, soft spoken kindly man who worked hard and was a well liked neighbour. But to the men of his native place who knew him in his prime, he was Cúchulainn and Napoleon and Matt the Thresher. He was Big Mikey and there would never be his like again.'

177

Born: 1954

"

I won my first senior All Ireland as a sub for Cork in 1970, after playing for the junior team the same day. I can't remember playing with anything else when I was young only a hurley and ball, never a doll.

I have made many a good friend through camogie which I will always be grateful for. My one wish is to see Cork camogie have their own headquarters where all senior championship matches could be played.

I still do a lot of training with my club Eire Óg and I have to say I still enjoy it as much as ever. Maybe the legs are not as fast as they used to be but who knows Cork might need a goalie again and I'll be ready.

Marian McCarthy   **"**

Marian McCarthy is Cork's and Munster's most decorated camogie player. In addition to numerous personal awards she has won at senior level:

— Eight All Ireland titles counting her first as a sub in 1970.

— Three National League titles, and she had the honour of captaining the side to

victory in 1986.

— Three Gael Linn interprovincial titles.

— Twenty Munster titles.

— Two Munster club titles. (SPPP 1970 & Eire Óg 1985.)

— Five County titles. (Three with SPPP and two with Eire Óg.)

Cork has always been strong in the camogie world with sixteen titles to its credit — second to Dublin who lead with twenty-six titles. Cork has contested titles in every decade but failed to win any in the '50's and '60's when Dublin ruled.

Marian won three in a row — 1971 to '73 — titles outfield, operating mainly at centrefield. Then when Deirdre Sutton of the Glen retired Cork set about finding a goalkeeper. Having failed to find an established one, the selectors cast their eyes to the talent available to them in the outfield positions. Marian was chosen and amenable character that she is responded to the call and lined out for the 1978 championship in goal. A fruitful one it proved to be and Marian collected her fifth All Ireland medal when Dublin went under in the decider by 6:4 to 1:2. Coming up to half time in that game a high lobbing ball came goalwards. Marian advanced and pulling first time cleared to within thirty yards of the Dublin goal. I have been told that the language in the Cork dug out was atrocious. There were no marks for the brilliant timing, just undisguised dismay at what would have happened had she missed.

In 1980 she was nominated Camogie player of the year. They beat Limerick in the final. It was and still remains the only time that two Munster teams met in the final since the open draw was introduced in 1973. Marian felt sorry for Limerick. After Croagh-Kilfinny won the All Ireland senior club title in 1975/76 it seemed that Limerick might build a team to make the breakthrough and in 1980 they reached the final for the first time. Cork had the edge in experience, tradition and success and were the favourites. But Limerick produced a surprise performance and drew. 'We got it hard in the replay and were relieved to come away with a one goal victory. I felt sorry for them. It was the one time they got a chance of winning the title.'

Her most memorable game? 'I suppose they all have their own little bit of history. But there was something special about 1982. You see in 1981 we lost the final after a replay to Kilkenny. In the drawn game we were leading by nine points with six minutes to go. Then Kilkenny started scoring. With normal time up we were still ahead but we lost our concentration as we looked to the referee to blow fulltime. For some strange reason five minutes added on time was played and we felt robbed. So when we met Kilkenny in the semi-final of 1982 at Ballinlough we were all out to avenge the previous year. We won the game in extra time. It was a very hot day and it was Sandy Fitzgibbon's first game at senior level. She travelled all over the field like lightning. She won the game for us. In the final we beat Dublin by one point when Mary O'Leary sent over the bar with only ten seconds of play remaining. It was a difficult championship. It was great after the disappointment of '81. It was special.'

Her eighth and last medal was won in 1983. In the *Evening Press* Con Houlihan had this to say — 'It's a familiar axiom in camogie — if you have a good keeper and a good free taker you are in business. I dislike singling out individuals from two fine teams, but surely must give a metaphorical pat on the back to Cork's keeper; Marian McCarthy was as efficient as ever in winning her eighth senior All Ireland.'

She was also a talented badminton player. Her attitude to sport was very healthy and

positive. 'We celebrated in victory and we also celebrated in defeat. After all games are there to be enjoyed.'

She retired in 1991 and now watches from the sideline where on occasion she has seen games that produce the same excitement, tension, drama and rivalry, as hurling. One such game was the 1993 All Ireland semi-final at Nowlan Park between Cork and Kilkenny. It was the day that Colette O'Mahony got three goals from close in frees despite the herculean efforts of Ann Downey. It was the day Cork were trailing as the game went into lost time. And then Lyn Dunlea who had come on as a sub wrote glory across her name as she sent the ball to the net — and victory to Cork.

In a manner of speaking Marian's brother Sean has followed in her footsteps as he now does honour to the family name at midfield for Cork hurlers.

This is Marian's chosen team — an all-Cork lineout.

Marian McCarthy

Marie Costine

Mirian Higgins   Catherine Landers   Eileen Dineen

Liz Garvin   Pat Moloney   Sandy Fitzgibbon

Mary O'Leary   Marion Sweeney   Ann Comerford.

Mary Geaney

Born: 1953

``

Growing up in the heartland of South Galway, still under the charismatic influence of Michael Cusack since his soujourn there as a teacher, it was obvious I would become engaged in the only past-time of the area — hurling.

Once I began to attend the games of my local club, Ballinderreen, it became a ritual for me to spend hours by the gable-end re-enacting the deeds of my local heroes. There I learned the basic skills and once acquired the next step was my visits on summers' evenings to the 'turlough' where all of hurlers practised, young and old. We delighted in the task of pucking back the sliotar from behind the goals or a rare treat was to be asked to play between the stones when all the adults wished to play outfield.

I was very lucky that my involvement in the hurling coincided with the National Coiste Iomana drive of 1965. Here in Galway the administrative challenge was taken up by a pioneering and far-sighted board. Structures, both competitive and organisational were put in place and I began with the first under 14 bunch to compete for my club in 1965. Regular organised coaching sessions replaced the haphazard games in the 'Turlough' and

eventually we reached our first ever county final against mighty Castlegar in 1965. Though defeated, we learned a lot and the experience assisted us in winning divisional south board under-age titles in following years.

While attending Colaise Einde in Galway City, I came under the influence of Fr Enda Muldoon, now deceased, and though the college was not noted for its hurling, he encouraged me to practise constantly in the expansive handball alleys in the school.

By 1970 I had made the county minor team and we appeared in the All Ireland semi-final against Wexford in Páirc Chiaráin, Athlone. This was Galway's first competitive outing in the championship outside of Munster since 1959.

We created a big surprise in defeating Wexford and it was like a dream come true to be appearing in Croke Park in the minor final against Cork. Unfortunately a powerful Cork minor side defeated us comprehensively in the final but the experience left a lasting impression and a strong desire to return! I'll never forget the roar of the crowd as we came out from under the Cusack Stand tunnel.

The next major stepping stone was the All Ireland under 21 success of 1972. Having embarked on a student working visit to New York earlier that summer, I was enjoying the life in the Big Apple and playing hurling for Galway, when a sudden telegraph came through inviting me home to join the panel for the All Ireland final against Dublin. Galway had defeated Tipperary in the semi-final and were leaving no stone unturned in order to win the county its first title in this grade. I joined my colleagues in training and an unfortunate injury in a challenge against St Rynagh's left me struggling to regain fitness for the final. Though failing to make the first fifteen as a result, I was delighted to be able to come in as a substitute in the second half at midfield, and win my first

All Ireland medal.

Following that victory in 1972, a number of us were invited to join the senior panel and I remember being selected for my first senior game in the opening round of the National League against Offaly in Birr. I was selected at centre-half-forward and was marked by Padraig Horan. My second game was in the more familiar surrounds of left-half-back against Tipperary in Portumna when I marked the elusive Francis Loughnane. Obviously the step up to senior was a big one and it took us some time to adjust. However the longterm building programme undertaken by M.J. Flaherty our coach paid off some two years later when we coasted through Division 1B of the League and defeated Cork in the National-League quarter-final in Limerick. This victory shocked the nation and we progressed to defeat a lethargic Kilkenny in the semi-final before beating much vaunted Tipperary in an historic final in Limerick. At last the barrier was broken and we looked forward with relish to the championship.

Having qualified for the All Ireland semi-final against Cork we started the game in whirlwind fashion and created yet another sensation in qualifying for Galway's first senior final since 1958. It was heady stuff, and expectations were high, but in reality we were never a match for one of Kilkenny's greatest ever teams. My opponent that day was Kilkenny's young captain Billy Fitzpatrick. We have remained lifelong friends since.

On the club front, my club's underage policy of the sixties began to pay dividends when we qualified for the knock-out stages of the county senior championship in 1977 and 1978. Having been defeated in the county semi-final of 1977 by Athenry we went one better in 1978 . I was honoured to be captain but unfortunately, I did not prove to be a lucky captain for either club or county. Our great rivals and near neighbours Ardrahan defeated us in the '78 final after a replay and extra time. Following that club campaign, I was chosen to captain Galway the following season and finished up the losing captain again in the:

Oireachtas final v Wexford 1978,
Railway Cup final v Leinster 1979,
National League final v Tipperary 1979,
All Ireland final v Kilkenny 1979.

Undoubtedly, luck was not one of my major traits as captain.

Having suffered a long illness after the 1979 final, I was delighted to be asked to rejoin my colleagues for the 1980 campaign. Though not playing, I felt as much a part of the team as the players since we had struggled and suffered since 1975. The euphoria that attended the 1980 final had to be seen to be believed. The long wait was over and suddenly Galway's hurling passion exploded. We've been on a roller coaster ever since. All the curses and psychological barriers have been dispelled and due to a careful attention to administrative detail Galway's hurling successes of recent times have been carefully harvested. The future looks bright as hurling has become the major sporting interest within the county. I'm glad to have lived to participate in and witness such a happening.

Joe McDonagh

J oe McDonagh hails from the little parish of Ballindereen in South Co Galway. 'There are hardly two hundred houses in the parish.' It is the native place of Mick Gill, outstanding Galway midfielder of the twenties who also starred with Dublin. In more recent times the parish has given Noel Lane and Tom Helebert to Galway hurling.

Joe's first real awakening to hurling came when his father took him to the Railway Cup final of 1963. There for the first time he saw Ring — pointed out to him by his father — in action for the last time in a major engagement outside of club. In his youth his heroes were Joe Salmon and Jimmy Duggan and as he grew older his admiration centred on John Connolly — a man he would one day hurl with in the maroon of Galway. 'I have tremendous regard for John. I was delighted to hurl with him. He played an enormous role with

Galway in 1975 — much more than ordinary captaincy. We beat Cork by two points in the '75 semi-final. After that the euphoria in Galway was unbelievable. The county was on a roller coaster. But the expectations weren't based on reality. We were still unready to face a team of the calibre of Kilkenny and learned that in the final.

The following year we were a more potent force. We drew with Wexford at Páirc Uí Chaoimh in a great semi-final game and lost an equally great replay by a goal. It was an extremely hot summer. The two games were played within a week of each other and the replay was within two weeks of the All Ireland final. The game burned a lot of stamina. I believe if either ourselves or Wexford had won the first day, that Cork would have been defeated in the final.'

Joe was there at the dawn of what is now a golden era in Galway hurling. It began with the 1972 under 21 All Ireland victory and was followed by National League success at the expense of Tipperary in 1975 — 'the watershed and one of my hurling highlights for in those days the blue and gold jersey of Tipperary had for us a hue of invincibility attaching to it.' 1979 was a highlight too when Joe was honoured with the captaincy. As in 1975 Cork fell at the semi-final stage. Galway hurling was growing in confidence — an Oireachtas title in 1976, a second under 21 title in 1978 — all signs of strength in depth. But the 1979 final against Kilkenny when Galway looked the form team, turned into a nightmare for the men from the west. Two freakish goals — one in each half, among other things left the final score 2:12 to 1:8 It was a day of near despair for Galway supporters. 'We wasted a lot in the first half. I don't think the rain suited us. Kilkenny were spurred on by the defeat at the hands of Cork the previous year and didn't want a second successive defeat. Of course I shouldn't have been playing at all. I was ill but didn't realise it. Afterwards doctors were mystified that I had been able to play for 70 minutes with the complaint I had.'

Joe's greatest regret is without doubt the missing out on the 1980 campaign. It is surely ironic that when the great breakthrough came against Limerick on the first Sunday in September two of Galway's finest ever wing-backs — Joe McDonagh and Iggy Clarke — were absent from the lineout. They together with Sean Silke at centre-back had been there since 1972 — one of the great half-back lines of hurling history. Joe however was able to savour the ecstasy of victory. For despite his illness, he was still part of the Galway hurling fold. After the great victory speech in the gaelic tongue from captain Joe Connolly the McCarthy Cup was handed to Iggy Clarke and then Joe got the nod from Cyril Farrell. 'I was reluctant but we were used to taking orders from Cyril on the field — and obeying.' Joe broke into a rendering of 'The West's Awake' and all Croke Park was filled with emotion. There were tears too as the frustrations of years of near misses were buried and the psychological barrier breached. 'We sung that song as we came off the pitch after UCG had beaten Maynooth in the Fitzgibbon Cup final of 1977 — it was our victory anthem.'

Joe's playing days are now a thing of the past but he remains very involved with the GAA. An Officer of the Galway Co. Board since 1979 and Galway representative on the Central Council since 1988.

He is justifiably proud of Galway's contribution to modern hurling and his commitment to the great game — its spread and preservation — is total.

His team selection is as follows:-

Noel Skehan (Kilkenny)

Niall McInerney (Galway) Pat Hartigan (Limerick) Brian Murphy (Cork)

Joe McDonagh (Galway) Ger Henderson (Kilkenny) Iggy Clarke (Galway)

John Connolly (Galway) Frank Cummins (Kilkenny)

Billy Fitzpatrick (Kilkenny) Jimmy Barry Murphy (Cork) Eddie Keher (Kilkenny)

Francis Loughnane (Tipperary) Tony Doran (Wexford) Eamon Cregan (Limerick)

John 'Jobber' McGRATH   1950-1965   Rickardstown & Westmeath

Born: 1928

full the game he adored.

He was a big raw-boned man who never seemed to carry an ounce of spare flesh. He worked in England for a while and after coming home took up farming. He was always very fit. His lifestyle which included, being a non-smoker, non-drinker, would have led one to take a lease on his life so when death called, it was a great shock to all who knew him.

As a member of Rickardstown Hurling Club he won several county championships. The scourge of emigration took its inevitable toll on this rural club and it went out of existence. John was later instrumental in the formation of a new junior club — Lough Lein Gaels, Collinstown — in the late sixties. He retired after he had helped them win the junior championship in 1972/73.

He had an unorthrodox, but highly effective hurling style. He was extremely difficult to block when striking the ball because while he was basically right handed he seemed to have the ability to strike the ball from different angles and positions. He was well known for being able to hit the ball when seemingly bottled up by two or three opponents — he simply used his hurley one handed like a tennis racket and he could drive the ball fifty to sixty yards over his head backwards. This sometimes made life difficult for an opponent but never failed to raise a cheer from the spectators.

For a man of his build he was deceptively strong and while never using this feature unfairly he was well able to take care of himself in close exchanges.

When he retired from active participation he was one of the driving forces behind the Westmeath Past Hurlers Association. This had the dual affect of bringing together socially, many of the older long retired hurlers, and in addition helping many charitable organisations.

When he died hurling lost one of its unsung heroes.

It is a great pity that the Railway Cup competition has assumed a secondary importance. Time there was when it attracted crowds of up to 40,000 people.

It had a special glamour on St Patrick's Day and in its glory days Croke Park was the mecca of followers of Gaelic games.

It gave players like 'Jobber' McGrath the opportunity to show his skills and hurl with and against the elite of the game. He was often selected on the Leinster panel and made a winning Railway Cup final debut at centrefield for Leinster against Munster in 1956. His partner that day was the great Wexford midfielder Jim Morrissey. They were opposed by Pat Stakelum of Tipperary and Johnny O'Connor of Waterford. It speaks volumes for his ability that he was capable of being selected for Leinster in 1956, in an era when Wexford were great and Kilkenny were not far behind.

When 'Jobber' died suddenly at the age of 51 Westmeath hurling lost one of its greats — perhaps its greatest. He would have found favour in any county. Indeed inducements were held out to him. But he always declined. He was happy hurling with his native Westmeath where he enjoyed to the

Born: 1938

background was well and truly laid in football and I was brought up on the great Volunteers football teams of that period. The talk of these unbeatable combinations was the non stop subject of my early sporting life.

There was of course at that time no hurling to speak of in Wexford town. I can remember going to the county football final of 1945 on the bar of my father's bicycle. I remember this because of the pain of my leg each time I got off the bike when my father needed a rest or when a hill proved too steep. I can never recall the reason I took such an interest in hurling. I seemed always to have my precious hurl with me. This doubled as a gun when playing cowboys and indians as was the case with all my pals.

The Sunday broadcast from Mícheál O'Hehir was the highlight of our week. Names like Lory Meagher, Seanie Duggan. Paddy Kenny, Inky Flaherty, Peter McDermott, Paddy O'Brien, Christy Ring, Jimmy Langton, Corless, Doyle, Kennedy — all great players. We imitated all these players through the descriptions given by Mícheál O'Hehir. The Sundays were spent at the local championship in Wexford Park racing for the broken hurls. Our All Irelands were held on the Green at John Street on the Volunteer's training 'grounds'.

Enter the Christian Brothers and their love for the Gaelic heritage. While I was in the 'Boker' we were all shown the skills of our National game of hurling. Teachers like Bros. Perkins, Kennedy and Cullen and others spent hours teaching us the art of hurling. I have always thought that not enough credit is given to the Christian Brothers. They taught a love of all things Irish. Class leagues, street leagues, interschool leagues, were all promoted by these dedicated people. The discipline which they demanded is sadly lacking today in the youth, to a degree.

"

My early introduction to the GAA, was as I remember, my late father visiting his relations and parents in Hill Street, Wexford. I was usually brought with him on Sunday mornings. I shall always remember the thrill of seeing the array of medals at my great-uncles. He was of course the great Tom McGrath of the Wexford 1914-1918 football team. My

When I was seventeen I found myself on the county minor team. We were beaten by Kilkenny in the Leinster final after a draw. The following year we played Kilkenny in the Leinster final and lost by a goal. Late in 1956 I played my first senior inter-county game with Wexford against Cork. I was overwhelmed to be a member of this great All Ireland winning team. It was in the following National League at Nowlan Park that I really established myself on the team. We went on to win that League 1957/58. Everything seemed to develop from there. We were All Ireland champions in 1960. Beaten in the final of 1962 — this was what I thought to be the greatest game I played in.

It has been a source of comfort for the older players to see some progress in recent years on the hurling field by Wexford. Hopefully, it will not be too long before great victories will be achieved again.

Among the regrets I have is the failure of the national television station to give much more coverage to the national games. I consider it to be their duty to promote the Irish heritage. I also regret the direction Croke Park is heading in. That mecca of all Irish GAA people is being turned into a rich mans club. Corporate boxes, hospitality areas etc. are a long way from the ordinary clubman trying to raise funds to keep the Club going — looking after under 12 and under 14 etc. I hope I am wrong but it looks like going to Croke Park in the future will be out of the reach of the ordinary grass root GAA person.

Whenever I am asked about the best game you remember I always turn to the All Ireland final of 1962. We were six points down after five minutes — level with five minutes to go — narrowly behind and pressing at full-time. For sheer excitement this had everything. I have never seen supporters who were as happy in defeat. I think they were happy because they realised Wexford could compete with the best in Ireland — were as good as anyone and did not have to win to prove that.

The 1960 final was a special day — of that there is no doubt. Arriving back in town

and being the first native to achieve the distinction of having won an All Ireland senior hurling medal was great.

Asked about people who you admire most, always poses a question I find difficult to answer. When I was young and all this excitement of club victories and county games was happening, a lot of things went over my head. The constant practice, pressure, injuries, travelling etc., did not allow much pondering. When now I think of such things, I have to nominate my parents for the great understanding shown — to take my efforts seriously and to think that I might have the ability to graduate to senior inter-county class. I do think that young people need adults to take them seriously, for them to achieve their potential. This probably holds true more in weaker counties. My wife of course who is ever understanding and always has been, where GAA is concerned. I think people like these parents and wives are invaluable to our organization. I do not think this has always been recognised. They should be regarded as important cogs in a team effort. After all it is an amateur sport and the time required for participation is family time. The great Nick Rackard and Paddy Cullen were two people I admired to a great degree. Paddy Cullen the great secretary and father of the Faythe Harriers club had the drive and was the inspiration to take a street league winning team to senior hurling and senior football county champions in a space of eight or nine years — also Leinster Senior hurling club champions as well. This will always stand out as a great achievement. Of Nick Rackard, no more can be said — the inspiration and main figure in the Wexford hurling revival. Everything about him in those lean years was marvellous. His spirit never sagged — his fierce determination, mainly at county board, where he had to convince the sceptics of the value of his suggestions — then to lead the great hurling teams of the fifties — to position them as hurlers at the head of the list of greats. Long may his achievements be a source of hope for all the weaker counties in general and to Wexford men in particular.

Some rule changes I would like to see. I think the square needs to be made smaller. Since the rule change regarding the tackling of the goalman in the square, the scoring of goals has suffered. Too many frees for square infringements. I think that linesmen and umpires should have more input into the game. The 'sin bin' should be brought into play. Referees are reluctant to send off players. If they could send them off for ten minutes I think it would be of greater benefit. If the penalty was defined it would eliminate lobbying for leniency and canvassing the disciplinary officials to intercede on certain players behalf.

Players who are regularly sent off and known as hard men have no place in the games. I would like to see a record of their sending off offences referred to and more stringent action taken against them and their clubs. I would like to see the time keeping in our games looked after some other way. I think the referee should not have this extra responsibility. Perhaps a log-in clock could be used.

Oliver McGrath

W henever Wexford hurling is talked about the fifties and sixties immediately come to mind. These were the glory days — days of ecstasy and delight — but with a liberal sprinkling of disappointment and frustration. The Wexford men of those decades brought a new dimension to the hurling scene. The lingering memories of those days conjure up physically big men bedecked in purple and gold who played our ancient game with glamour and flair and above all great sportsmanship. Oliver McGrath played his part in some of those glorious years.

Few realise that Wexford made an impact and were quite prominent in the early years of the GAA. Before the turn of the century they had contested three All Ireland finals — all without success. Their first final was against Cork represented by Augha-bullogue in 1890. At the interval the Cork side led by 1:3 to 0:1 Early in the second half when the score stood Cork 1:6 Wexford 2:2 the game was abandoned — the first of two in the history of the Association — the second was in 1892 when Cork played Dublin and Dublin withdrew after fifty minutes play with Cork leading by 2:4 to 1:1. Rough play alleged on the part of the Wexford men, though never subsequently substantiated led to the abandonment of the 1890 final. Later Cork were awarded the match. It is interesting to note that under present day rules Cork were a point ahead when the game was abandoned — (nine points to eight points). However under the rules of the time Wexford were actually leading because no number of points equalled a goal.

The following year 1891 Wexford again contested the final. This time their opponents were Kerry represented by Ballyduff. Fortune again frowned on Wexford. The final score was Kerry 2:3 Wexford 1:5. It was the only time that extra time was played in a final. It was the last time that teams lined out 21 aside.The Kerry men played in their bare feet.

In 1899 Wexford contested the final with Tipperary but this time there were no disputes — there could be no arguing — the verdict was clear cut. The men of Tipperary represented by a Moycarkey selection won well on the score 3:12 to 1:4.

Oliver McGrath known affectionately to all hurling followers as 'Hopper' played like his fellow countymen before the turn of the century, in three All Ireland finals. But he reaped greater reward. His granduncle Tom McGrath played in goal in five All Ireland finals for the famous Wexford football team from 1914-1918 — losing to Kerry after a replay in 1914 and winning four in a row thereafter. His father too played football with Wexford at junior level. Oliver proved that football ability was still present in the McGrath blood when in 1960 he won a county senior football title with Faythe Harriers. This together with a senior hurling medal

completed a rare double in Wexford GAA history — only achieved once previously in 1903 by Slaney Harriers.

Oliver first came to the notice of the county selectors with great minor displays against Kilkenny in the Leinster finals of 1955 and 1956. 'I can remember the closing stages of the drawn minor final of 1955. We were a goal down. Croke Park was packed for the senior final between the same counties. I remember coming through with the ball — Ollie Walsh was in goal — as I struck I kind of stumbled and lost control — I was going for a point but the ball finished up in the net. Well all Croke Park seemed to rise — the stands erupted. It was my first real experience of the Croke Park roar. We lost the replay and the final of the following year by only one goal.'

He played in the 1956/57 National League campaign and likewise the following year when he excelled in games against Kilkenny — at Nowlan Park where he did remarkably well on Jim Hogan and relished the victory over the reigning All Ireland champions — Waterford and Antrim. And so to the final against Limerick where he came on as a sub in the first half. 'I was surprised I wasn't on from the start because I had been playing very well in earlier games.' It was his first taste of the big time and what a glorious occasion it was to be part of. Wexford won a breathtaking thriller by 5:7 to 4:8. It was Oliver's first major medal. The journalists ran out of superlatives as they attempted to describe this game of games. John D. Hickey in the *Irish Independent* said, 'The greatest game of hurling I have ever seen.' In the *Irish Press* Mick Dunne wrote, 'The hurling was superbly exciting, the pace bewilderingly fast, an enthralling struggle was waged with intense vigour, yet the exchanges were scrupulously fair and sportsmanlike.' Joe Sherwood writing in the *Evening Press* said, 'It was a gripping pulsating combat, but what a sporting game' and finally Mitchel Cogley in the *Irish Independent*, 'Here was a victory to be proud of; defeat with honour; in a game that was a privilege to see.'

Even though Wexford might have won three in a row from 1954-1956 Oliver feels that they had an even better opportunity to achieve three in a row between 1960 and 1962. 'Wexford were more experienced in the big time and had a greater depth of talent available. We showed our ability and potential in overwhelming Tipperary in 1960 by 2:15 to 0:11. The 1961 Leinster final against Dublin in Nowlan Park was an unnatural game. Early on we were coasting — all over Dublin — scoring well. Then the ball went down to the Dublin forwards and it was 1952 all over again. Before it came back again to us Dublin had scored four or five goals — the backs had caved in. We lost 7:5 to 4:8 — and we had played so well against Kilkenny with Andy Doyle at full-forward getting great goals and displaying knowledge of every facet of good full-forward play. The way we started in the 1962 final we set ourselves an almost impossible task — lost in the end by only two points and might have won. I remember when the ball was thrown in I headed for my position at corner-forward. By the time I got there and looked around the green flag was waving for a Tipperary goal. Then a bad puck out and the ball is in the net again — less than two minutes gone.'

Oliver had his own views about training methods and tactics. And where these were concerned he could be quite outspoken and vociferous. It didn't always endear him to the selectors.

Wexford surprised Kilkenny in the Leinster final of 1965. 'We weren't given a chance. Two points from Martin Byrne and a point from myself levelled matters in the closing stages. Then Martin Codd just seemed to amble out towards the sideline to gain possession. He hit the ball over his head — away up into the clouds — down, down it came — and we watched it as it landed on top of the net for the winner. In the early stages of that game I got a ball that some thought I should have buried in the net. But when I saw Ollie Walsh standing on his goal line with determination written all over him — I felt he was going to have one of those days when he was well nigh unbeatable — I decided to take the point. One of the selectors passed the remark that I had lost my nerve. In fact I was thinking. When the final whistle blew that point was worth gold. I had arranged my wedding for a week or so before the All Ireland final — never expecting to be in it — no one expected us to be in it. The selectors wanted me to postpone the wedding. That wasn't possible. On my way back from the honeymoon on the Wednesday before the final — cut short so as to play in the final — I heard the team being announced on the radio. I wasn't on — relegated to the subs. Wheeler and myself came on at half time but by then Tipp had the game taken out of our reach.'

Oliver trained with the panel in the early stages of the 1968 championship and played in a tournament game against Cork. After that he feels he was unlucky to have been dropped. 'I was very disappointed. I felt I still had something to contribute. I was only thirty.'

Oliver was the first hurler of prominence to come out of Wexford town — a town famed for football and boasting at the time three senior football teams — Volunteers, Dan O'Connell's and Sarsfields. He won all the major honours of his day and was selected on the rest of Ireland team to play the All Ireland champions in 1958 and 1962. Though small in stature this elusive and potent forward was a big handful for any corner-back. He was a thinking player with very good ball control and a deceptive turn of speed. He could jinx his way through a defence with a style that suggested he was floating through. From his earliest days his legs gave him considerable trouble and this no doubt partly contributed to the early departure from the county scene of this scrupulously clean and sporting hurler.

This is the Wexford team of 1960 — that surprised Tipperary — and with whom Oliver won his first All-Ireland medal.

Pat Nolan

John Mitchell   Nick O'Donnell (capt)   Tom Neville

Jim English   Billy Rackard   John Nolan

Ned Wheeler   Jim Morrissey

Jimmy O'Brien   Padge Kehoe   Seamus Quaid

Oliver McGrath   John Harding   Tim Flood

Born: 1951

"

I was educated at St Flannan's College and played Dean Ryan and Harty Cup, winning a Dean Ryan medal. I played minor and under 21 with Offaly for four years and played senior for two years before transferring to Limerick.

"

Joe McKenna was born in Shinrone, Co Offaly and is a first cousin of John 'Mackey' McKenna who starred in the forward line with the great Tipperary team of the sixties. Greyhound enthusiasts may be interested to learn that Joe is also a first cousin of Ger McKenna. The big Shinrone man — six foot two and fourteen stone — blended beautifully into the Limerick team of the period 1973 to 1985. He played in several positions but eventually settled into full-forward where his hurling talents blossomed and captured the imagination of the hurling world. It was the position to which he was best suited. 'I didn't have the stamina to last a full hour in the half-forward line. I also found that if I pushed my training beyond a certain point my

performance deteriorated. If I trained too hard in the summer my energy suffered.'

He was a superb full-forward — one of the all time greats — ranking in the modern game with Ray Cummins of Cork and Tony Doran of Wexford, though each had his own distinct style and method of approach. Joe used his height and strength to maximum advantage but always fairly. He loved the dropping ball. He would soar into the air and confidently grasp it. He was a master of the drop puck and often used it with great effect. Full-backs rarely mastered him although Niall McInerney of Galway always shadowed him well and gave little away. Some big men tend to be cumbersome and awkward but not Joe. He was a hurling athlete — agile, nimble and possessed of a deceptive turn of speed. Add to that an alert mind, consistency and a gifted sense of anticipation that enabled him to outfox many a fine full-back and you had a full-forward of rare potency.

In the late seventies he played with Clare in New York (all above board) and won three senior titles with them. How did it come about? 'I shared a house with Joe Firth, a Clareman, in my single days. One evening I got a phone call from his brother Pat in New York asking me to play with Clare. They were looking for a forward. I had relations in New York so I decided to go. We never lost a match.'

Joe believes that he played the best hurling of his career in 1981. It was a great year for him. He captained Munster to Railway Cup victory over Leinster on St Patrick's Day at Ennis 2:16 to 2:6. It was only the fourth time that a Limerick player captained Munster to victory. Timmy Ryan did it in 1934 and 1935 and Mick Mackey did it in 1937. The occasion was unique in that two Offaly men carried the mantle of captain — Joe McKenna leading Munster — Padraig Horan leading Leinster. And to add further to the uniqueness both played at full-forward. In the Munster championship against Tipperary he banged in 3:1 in the drawn game at Thurles. 'We were thirteen points down at an early stage in the second half and yet drew. If that was against Cork we were definitely gone. In my time we were never beaten in the championship by Tipperary. Cork were the bogey team.'

In the Munster final against Clare he scored 3:3. He beat Clare that day — great full-forward play. He was the leading scorer in 1981 with 7:12 from five games. A further accolade came his way when he received his sixth All Star award — the fourth in a row at full-forward.

He is an ardent supporter of the open draw. He believes it would increase the winning prospects of teams like Clare, Wexford, Laois and Limerick. 'You would definitely get some shock results every year. The game would benefit. It would open up the championship.'

The 'most gratifying win' of his career was the Munster final victory over Cork in 1980. He recalled how close they had come so many times both in league and championship and how decisively they had been beaten in the previous years Munster final by Cork. In 1975 when Limerick had high hopes — going for three in a row in Munster — Joe was at centrefield. For much of the hour it seemed as if Limerick would prevail but a Jimmy Barry Murphy goal — at a vital stage and not for the first time — turned the tables in Cork's favour who ran out comfortable winners 3:14 to 0:12. Tom Brown writing in the *Evening Press* after that game said that he had never seen such an exhibition of midfield play from any one man on a losing team. So of all the victories of his career the one over Cork in the Munster final of 1980 will always stand out — even more so than the 1973 All Ireland win over Kilkenny. That was the year he made his Limerick debut. He played in the first round against Clare — wasn't picked for the Munster final against Tipperary — wasn't even in Ennis for the All Ireland semi-final against London as he was sick — and when Limerick switched Eamon Cregan to centre-

half-back for the final against Kilkenny, Joe was back in the lineout at left-full-forward. When the teams went into action it was amusing to behold the diminutive Fan Larkin and the giant sized Joe do battle but the Mutt and Jeff scene didn't last long as Limerick switched Joe to centre-forward where he proceeded to minimise the effectiveness of Pat Henderson who had been an absolute colossus in the previous years final against Cork.

If Joe could go back in time he would want to play the 1983 and 1984 championship games against Cork all over again. 'We let them off the hook in both of those years. We were superior. We left it behind. We could never, never again concede three goals like the ones in 1984. If we had reached the All Ireland final that year we would have won. We always did well in Thurles.'

There is a lot of substance in what Joe has to say about 1983 and 1984. In the League final of 1983 in a thrilling exhibition of hurling Limerick lost to Kilkenny at Thurles by 2:14 to 2:12 — a Kilkenny team that had won the All Ireland and National League double in 1982 and 1983. In 1984 Limerick beat Wexford in convincing fashion in the League final at Thurles 3:15 to 1:9. Earlier that year Munster had beaten Leinster in the Railway cup final at Ennis with a team that had six Limerick men in the lineout. And again on the 14th April 1985 at Thurles in the League final of that year, Limerick gave further evidence of their hurling ability when beating Clare 3:12 to 1:7. The talent was there for All Ireland victories but fate and misfortune and the bogey team Cork barred the way. Those games against Cork were full of drama, excitement and some delightful hurling. After the drawn game of 1983 Mícheál O'Hehir in his radio broadcast finished by saying — Thank God for the hurlers of Cork — Thank God for the hurlers of Limerick — Thank God for the game of hurling.

It reminded me of a story a friend of mine from Tipperary used to tell. In his youth he used travel with his father and a friend to the Munster championship games between Limerick and Cork. After each game his father would turn to the friend and say 'Well what do you think'. The reply was always the same 'Thirty great men'. There was never a word of criticism — just profound appreciation of the entertainment provided by thirty hurlers playing our ancient game.

Joe would like to see Limerick win another senior title in the near future. He is critical of inconsistencies that are evident in refereeing. He wonders if there is an appreciation of the key role that players play in the GAA. 'To play at top level nowadays — club and county — with the demands for training and exceptional fitness levels, you would need to have no job to do. It was because of this that I quit at thirty-three. I went before my time.'

'A GIANT AMONG GIANTS'

Born: 1899

Lory from Tullaroan was a hurling stylist — a stylist supreme.

His name was a household word in Kilkenny and his fame as a hurler spread throughout the land for his performances with great Kilkenny teams during the ten years ending 1935.

In an era of close marking when scores were hard to come by, he would unexpectedly steal one from far out. It was a forte of his. It was no wonder then, that the young generation of Kilkenny men that succeeded Lory used to proudly chant 'Over the bar said Lory Meagher' as they themselves swung the ash in the practice fields or cheered on their heroes in the black and amber.

Lory was their king and in his playing days he was surrounded by princes — each of them a hurling artist. They brought glory to Kilkenny and honour to hurling — Paddy Phelan, Paddy Larkin, Padge and Ned Byrne, Mattie Power, Martin White, Peter O'Reilly, Jimmy Walsh, Jimmy O'Connell, Peter Blanchfield, Tommy Leahy and Ned Doyle. They were famed in song and live on in legend.

An admirer who signed himself 'A Limerick Gael' wrote an eleven verse ballad about Lory to the air of 'Boolavogue'. I liked the third and fifth verses.

I've seen him out with the best in Ireland
No one can beat him in all-round play.
For he's deadly-sure with his left and right
*　　hand*
A lovely striker on any day.

One ball he hits high above his shoulder,
Then again he will drop one upon the ground.
On his varied strokes his opponents wonder,
And him in vain they will circle round.

Lory shunned the limelight. It was as if it weighed heavily upon him. It is therefore easy to understand the story about the journalist who met Lory by the roadside one day and enquired — where he might find Lory Meagher — only to be told — 'you've just missed him, he passed up this way about five minutes ago — if you hurry you might catch him.'

Lory was in many ways a very private person. But he always felt at ease with the camán. The game of hurling remained very dear to his heart. So in 1971 when an over forty game was arranged between a Tullaroan selection and a Kilkenny selection it is no real surprise to learn that Lory togged out for the occasion. The photograph in this article shows Lory on the right at seventy two years of age accompanied by that other great stylist Paddy Phelan then aged 61. Both are wearing the protective headgear of their halcyon days — the peak cap.

In a beautiful article on Lory, Padraig Puirseal described the funeral of this shy hurling star thus, 'And, on a spring evening in 1973, Kilkenny gave him a funeral befitting a prince. As steel blue clouds spread like a mourning pall across the evening sky, hundreds, young and old, filed through the mortuary chapel of St Luke's Hospital for a last glimpse of one of the greatest craftsmen of the camán. Then, the heavens themselves wept without restraint and the funeral procession wound its slow way through the narrow streets of Irishtown, old world streets silent now, but streets that had so often re-echoed the thundering cheers of victory for returning heroes garlanded with hurling glory.'

Tullaroan and District Heritage Committee have paid honour to Lory through their memorial project of 1991 to restore, decorate and furnish to the 1884 period the house in which he lived. This project was officially opened by President Mary

Lory Meagher with Paddy Phelan on his left.

Robinson on 24 May 1994 before a large gathering that included hurling enthusiasts from many counties — among them John Joe Doyle of Clare, Martin White of Kilkenny and Jimmy Coffey of Tipperary — three contemporaries of Lory.

The Lory Meagher Heritage Centre is a GAA museum with a particular emphasis on Kilkenny. Lory Meagher lived here and the house has been restored to the way it would have been in 1884.

194

Born: 1923

66

When I was five years old I first held a hurley and from that day to 1961 I never left it out of my hand. I also took part in racing, table-tennis and gymnastics. Camogie was my whole life.

Mary Mills **99**

The Camogie Association was established in 1904. Its early activities were confined to club level. It wasn't until 1932 that the first Senior All Ireland camogie championship took place. Each year the winners are presented with the Sean O'Duffy cup, a man who all his life was closely associated with camogie. Dublin won the first title with victory over Galway 3:2 to 0:2.

Kathleen Mills was then nine years old — born a Dub of a Dublin mother and Cork father — but she had been swinging a hurley since she was five. Her mother died when she was only eighteen months old and Kathleen was reared by her maternal grandmother. She had a natural aptitude for sport and athletics. As well as camogie she played table-tennis, was a very good runner and won many trophies at gymnastics. 'After school I would go out on the Green every evening practising. On Sunday I would go to ten o'clock Mass — play a match at 12 noon — stay practising after the match — come home at 6pm and get the works over the state my dinner would be in by that hour.' She was and still is an avid soccer fan. In her day the 'ban' was in operation — anyone caught playing or attending rugby, hockey, cricket, or soccer matches would be suspended. But this didn't deter Kathleen. She regularly went to matches and remembers one day going to Dalymount to see Jackie Carey playing. As she made her way in she heard a voice shout — 'Hey Mills, I'll report you to the Board.' The threat was never carried out.

Kathleen made her debut with her club GSR — later to become known as CIE — in 1938. From then until she retired in 1961 she was in the limelight and set the incredible record of winning twenty Leinster titles and fifteen All Ireland medals in an era when Dublin dominated the camogie scene and produced some outstanding combinations. Indeed, her All Ireland medal collection would have been greater but for the fact that she didn't play in 1949 and dispute within the organisation led to Dublin not taking any further part in the championship after winning the Leinster titles of 1945 and 1946.

She first played at county level in 1941 when Dublin lost the final to Cork. Because Kathleen was the only one selected from the GSR club they presented her with a lovely medal bearing the emblem of the old railway steam engine. Throughout her entire career Kathleen only played in one position — left wing — and she was devastating there. She was a natural lefthander, right hand under — could strike left and right — could even take frees left or right. She had many deft touches including a capacity to send sideline cuts over the

195

bar. She was a speed merchant — to use her own words, 'I could fly along. I could rise the ball and strike in the one motion. I could also grab a ball and strike.' Add to this her long striking — accurate distribution — excellent wrist work and you had a player with a mix of skills rare in the hurling world. She was a prolific scorer and was well known for her ability to send in a high dropping ball that would on occasions dip in under the crossbar. Her hurleys were always purchased from Hanleys at Clonee, Co Meath.

It is interesting to take a look at some of her All Ireland victories and what she remembers about them. In 1942 they travelled to Cork to play Cork in the final. She will never forget the train journey. They left Kingsbridge Station at 10am and didn't arrive in Cork until 9.30pm. It was wartime and coal was either scarce or unavailable. 'The train had to stop three times on the journey to pick up logs of timber to keep the engine going. But we got a great meal in The Metropole — a mixed grill — we were starving. The trip included a visit

to a cinema. Before the programme they played "The Banks Of My Own Lovely Lee" followed by "Cockles and Mussels". Then they flashed little snippets about some of the players on the screen.' The final was a draw 1:2 each but Dublin won the replay in Croke Park 4:1 to 2:2. Kathleen collected her first All Ireland medal. She was expecting gold but to her disappointment it turned out to be silver.

Victories in 1943 and 1944 made it three in a row and the medals were now a gold product. After the excitement of the 1942 final and replay an attendance of 10,000 turned out to cheer Dublin and Cork at Croke Park in 1943. The medal won in 1944 is probably her most prized possession. It is a beautiful pin-broach depicting a map of Ireland — 'the best medal of all.'

In 1947, the year she got married, her club GSR affiliated to the Central Council. They won their way to the All Ireland final and lost an exciting game to a great Antrim combination. But the following year the club won all before it and overwhelmed Down in the final. Forty years later in 1988

t was decided to have a reunion to elebrate the 1948 victory. Happily, ten of he twelve were alive to celebrate.

The Jubilee year was 1954 — Derry were eaten in the final — a special medal was truck and a special inter-provincial ompetition was played. In 1958 Kathleen vas captain. She led Dublin to victory over Tipperary and collected her twelfth All reland medal. There will always be something special about her fifteenth All Ireland medal. It was in 1961 — won on her birthday — the year she retired, 'and I was playing as good as ever.'

On the pitch she cut a tall, blonde, lithe figure. Her grandmother never saw her play in the All Ireland finals. But she was listening in one day to a final broadcast by Mícheál O'Hehir. She heard him say — and Kathleen Mills is going down the wing like a blonde streak of lightning.' 'Gran was delighted and proud. It was better than if she had been at the match.'

Her career overlapped with that of the great Christy Ring. In 1954 when Christy vas collecting his record eighth All Ireland medal Kathleen was collecting her ninth and two years later when Wexford denied Christy his ninth, Kathleen had accumulated ten. While she was a naturally fit person — she was as dedicated to training as Christy — the training schedules were quite exacting — running backwards and forwards across the width of the field — swinging the arms in various drill formations — tipping the toes. Kathleen described the game of her day as stylish and spectacular with a minimum of physical contact.

The game had its lighter moments too. And one of those occured when they played a game against Kildare. 'They had a player I was a bit suspicious of. I thought the legs weren't right — and the way she pulled on the ball on a couple of occasions. I knew she was wearing a wig. I whispered to my colleague — that's a man you're marking.' Did you beat them? 'We didn't beat them — we annihilated them. She disappeared very quick after the match — a soldier from the Curragh I believe.'

As well as her Leinster and All Ireland medals Kathleen also has the following awards. Several club medals; two Gael-Linn inter-provincial medals in 1956 and 1958; first camogie player to win Sports Star of the Week in the *Irish Independent*; Certificate in 1961 from Basketball Association of Ireland in appreciation of her outstanding performances in camogie; Cuchulainn award 1957 presented by Nuachtan Gael; replica of the O'Duffy All Ireland cup presented by the Camogie Board in 1961; Club na nGael trophy 1957.

Kathleen who is now seventy one is light-hearted and vivacious. She has a great sense of humour and has a warm and welcoming personality. When I asked her if I could call her Kathleen she replied, 'Do, it will make me feel young.'

This is the team from her era which she would like to captain.

	Peg Hogg (Cork)	
	Rose Martin (Dublin)	
Pat Kenny (Dublin)	Mary Fitzgerald (Cork)	Rose Fletcher (Dublin)
T.Griffin (Tipperary)	Kay Cody (Dublin)	Kay Mills (Dublin)
Una O'Connor (Dublin)	Annette Corrigan (Dublin)	Ide O'Kiely (Dublin)
	Sophie Brack (Dublin)	

Born: 1943

Barney wasn't on the playing pitch to reap the benefits of the harvest when the breakthrough came for Offaly in the '80's but he did see the seeds being sown and nurtured.

He believes that the All Ireland club championship did great things for Offaly hurling. It proved they could compete with the leading clubs of the established counties. It improved their game and generated confidence. In his time they played in Leinster club finals against Buffer's Alley and Rathnure of Wexford and The Fenians of Kilkenny. They came up against players of the calibre of Pat Henderson, Nicky Orr, Pat Delaney, Teddy O'Connor & Tony Doran. 'The experience gained was invaluable. You must play against top class class teams and players if you are to improve.'

In his youth he was captivated by the skills of Tim Flood of Wexford. Greats that he played against and admired included Eddie Keher, Pat Henderson, Seamus Cleere and Martin Coogan of Kilkenny, Phil Wilson, Dan Quigley and Tony Doran of Wexford, Jimmy Doyle and Mick Roche of Tipperary, Charlie McCarthy and Gerald McCarthy of Cork and Eamon Cregan of Limerick. He mentioned in particular the quality of the Kilkenny half-back line of Seamus Cleere, Pat Henderson and Martin Coogan and their superb performance in the All Ireland final of 1967.

Barney is a quiet and unassuming man who talks about hurling with a passion and sincerity that shows hurling was far more than just a game to him. It was the centre of his universe and he was willing to give it everything — every spare moment with a view to developing its many skills and aiming to be an artist of the game. 'I loved the old game — I lived for it.' That sentence dominated our interview — it was repeated many times. 'Medals didn't bother me. I played for the love of the game. I didn't like being beaten but it didn't kill my love for

"

My hurling days were extra special — right from the time my father got me my first hurley.

I have a lot of lovely memories of playing with St Rynagh's. I enjoyed every game whether with club, county or province.

When I was in Canada for almost two years I played a game every Sunday during the hurling season and practised every evening. Hurling in America was very hard and physical.

"

Barney Moylan

he game and that's for sure. I didn't care what position I played in. I didn't give a damn as long as I was out there. I played at half-back and half-forward — preferred half forward and would like to play there in the present day game — better protection for the forwards now under the rules.

From an early age I was encouraged by my father who played with St Rynagh's (Banagher). I can't say at what age I first handled the camán, probably about four years old and from the start I lived for hurling. I played before, at and after school and I won my first medal with Bollivar — a juvenile medal in 1959. The following year I was back with St Rynagh's with whom I won minor, junior and nine senior medals. We played Roscrea and Glen Rovers in two All Ireland club finals but unfortunately were beaten in both but we did our club proud.'

I asked him why a club like St Rynagh's could make it to the All Ireland club finals and yet Offaly was not considered a hurling force in Leinster. 'We didn't come together to train. It was only when the famous Tony Reddin of Tipp came to live in Banagher and took it on himself to train the local team that we had our first introduction to organised training. We looked up to him. I cycled four miles to train and togged out under the ditch. There was no dressing-room that time. I loved hurling and lived for the game.

The main problem with Offaly hurling in the '60s was that although we had some great individual hurlers on the team, the local club scene was still considered all important. There was fierce rivalry between the clubs and I don't think we blended into as good a county team as we should have been.'

And yet Offaly almost made it. In 1968 they showed signs that they could be a real force. They met reigning All Ireland champions Kilkenny in the Leinster semi-final. After ten minutes of the first half they were down to fourteen men. At half-time they were level and in the end lost by only four points. The following year they continued to show their ability. Barney who emigrated to Toronto, Canada, very early

in 1968 'came back for a holiday in the summer of 1969 and didn't go back any more.' Laois were beaten in the first round and Barney was called into action in the game against All Ireland champions Wexford in the semi-final. Barney played on Phil Wilson in that game that saw the All Ireland champions dethroned and Offaly advanced to the Leinster final against Kilkenny. 'It was the nearest we came to winning anything. I played with a broken bone in my hand — sure you'd play no matter what. I remember well in the second half a high lobbing ball went into the Kilkenny goalmouth — it hopped three times on the crossbar — most unusual — and went over. It might have gone into the net but it didn't. I was marking Eddie Keher that day. Sadly we were beaten by two points.' What Barney did not tell me was that the legendary Keher scored something like only two points from play. That by any standard was a remarkable piece of good marking by Barney. It was a key reflection of his hurling ability.

'By then too many of that team were pushing on in years and we had to await the arrival of Brother Denis and Dermot Healy who would coach and mould new names that would bring fame to Offaly. Star hurlers on the Offaly teams of the late sixties were Paddy Molloy, Johnny Flaherty, Damien Martin, Padge Whelehan, J.J. Healion and Paddy Spellman — a great bit of stuff who played with Faughs in Dublin.

I played for Offaly in New York in 1968/69 and we hurled against the best teams of that time. I worked in Toronto and had to get a plane on Saturday to New York. We played our match on Sunday — got a flight back to Toronto after the match and was back at work on Monday morning. I was often sore but I wouldn't have missed it for the world. There was a fanaticism for the game in the States.' That is surely the type of dedication that great sporting stars are made of.

'That same year I was picked to go on a World tour with the Offaly (USA) team but I couldn't leave the job in Toronto. It was really a great pity because I would have had the opportunity of playing against Tipperary in Birr. In my days in Toronto there were about six hurling teams.'

I wondered if there were many games that stood out in his mind. 'Of course the Leinster final that we lost to Kilkenny in 1969 was special but we had some mighty county finals and also some great All Ireland club games. I enjoyed all the games'.

Barney's abilities as a first class hurler were rewarded in a variety of ways.

He was on the victorious Leinster Railway Cup teams of 1972 and 1973. He was Hurler of the Year in Toronto in 1968. In 1972 he was chosen as Offaly Hurler of the Year. In 1976 — the year he retired — he was chosen as man of the match after the county final. With his club St Rynagh's he won nine county senior hurling titles.

Was there a special factor that contributed to the Offaly breakthrough? 'There were always great players in Offaly but I believe that it was Brother Denis together with Dermot Healy — a Kilkenny man — wh came to coach the team that really made th difference. He made the players believe in themselves and out of that came the grea All Ireland victory of 1981.'

Does he see any difference betwee hurling when he played it and the gam today?

'Hurling was more physical and toughe in my playing days. Nowadays, the rule suit the forwards. The third man tackle i gone. Players are fitter and better traine now but I believe there were more hurlin skills in my time especially in the area o overhead hurling.'

Finally, I asked him if he ever looked bac with any regrets. 'My only regret is that w had the players good enough to win an A Ireland but teams like Wexford and Kilkenny were better trained and bette organised and so the county had to wai another decade before Offaly finally mad the breakthrough.'

It was a pity. Players like Barney Moyla deserved the reward of an All Ireland title

Born: 1952

"

To be asked to write in this book is a special honour and I would like to thank Brendan for giving me this opportunity to write in it.

GAA has been very special and very good for me, ever since I started to play with my club — Nemo Rangers in Cork. I first played with them when I was 14 years of age and I have been lucky to have had the success I had with them on the playing field. Apart from this success, there is and always has been something special about Nemo Rangers and their members. There is a special friendship between them, which is always as important as success, off the playing field. Growing up in Cork and playing underage with Nemo was something I will always cherish. In my early days playing with Nemo, they had Frank Cogan and Billy Morgan playing with Cork senior footballers. One of my main ambitions was to play with Cork and little did I think that I would later play with Frank Cogan and Billy Morgan on the Cork team that won the All Ireland in 1973. A lot of the friends I had in Cork played with Nemo Rangers and we played on the different teams from under 15 to senior. This was also the case with the school we

went to which was Colaiste Chriost Ri, which was the nursery for Nemo Rangers. Colaiste Chriost Ri is where I would have learned the skills of the game of hurling and football. This was of course because you had very dedicated trainers in school prepared to devote their spare time and knowledge to the teams in the school.

You had the likes of Brother Pius and Brother Bede and the main person that had so much to do with the success of the school was one Dick Tobin. One of the special wins was the Harty Cup final in 1968. This was a game that was played in Buttevant and one which we weren't given a chance of winning. And that special day for me was when we won the All Ireland football in 1970 when I was captain. There was something special about Colleges matches. You had a great build up with songs being learned, flags being made, training a number of days a week and great crowds at the matches themselves. I would have to say that the games played during my time in Colaiste Chriost Ri would go down as special and the most memorable time during my playing career.

I first played with Cork senior hurlers in the 1971/72 league and that match was in the Old Athletic grounds. That day I played on Babs Keating who was one of my heroes when I was growing up. I always remember getting a lift from Ossie Bennett to Urling-ford after that match. I was now stationed in Kilkenny as a member of the Garda Síochána and had yet to make the money to purchase a car. The first senior All Ireland I played in was 1972 against Kilkenny. This was a game that we appeared to have won with twenty minutes to go and eight points up but unfortunately, Kilkenny had other ideas. Between 1972 and 1983 I played many games with Cork in hurling and football. I was lucky enough to win four senior All Irelands but I also played in three that we lost and unfortunately that was against Kilkenny where I work.

I was very lucky and I have often said it, when you think of one of the greats of the game, Tony Doran, who gave so much to his club and county and has just one senior All Ireland.

In 1973 when Cork won the football final for the first time in 27 years, I was 21 years of age and I didn't appreciate it so much then as I do now. This was not the case when Cork won the three in a row in 1978 by beating Kilkenny in the final. That win is very significant now when you think of the fact that Cork have been beaten in three All Irelands since then by Kilkenny.

In my time playing with Cork footballers the defeat by Kerry in the Munster final in 1976 was the most significant defeat. Kerry went on to greater things and Cork football went back a lot. In the following year 1977, Cork were well beaten by Kerry and then the 'Adidas Affair' started and followed with the Cork team being suspended. Jimmy Barry Murphy and I were under a lot of pressure at the time because we were playing with the hurlers. This was a sad time for the GAA in Cork and one of the reasons for it was lack of communication between officials and players. Nowadays, you have sponsorship of our games, with a lot of money involved and names on jerseys. When you think of what happened over jerseys in 1976 with the Adidas crest on it, times certainly have changed.

The GAA have a great organisation in Cork but they didn't do themselves any good at that time and last year again with the Billy Morgan affair — a man whom I would regard as one of the most dedicated people ever to play our games and train our teams.

I certainly have enjoyed playing with Cork. I mainly played in the full-back line, a position where a player cannot afford to make a mistake and where a player certainly must concentrate on marking his man. The good thing now is that you don't have to keep the man out from the keeper — that is something which was no harm to have got rid of.

I would like to see the kicking of the sliotar to score, also being done away with.

Scores should be got with the hurley. I am now involved in under-age with O'Loughlin's GAA club. There can be great enjoyment got from training young lads. I would like to see more parents getting involved in this side of the GAA. Some are slow to do so because they may not have played the game or played very little of it. They should not be afraid to get involved because of this.

The standard of under-age hurling in Kilkenny is very strong. The reason for this is because of the dedication of the teachers and the clubs also put a lot of work into the under-age. The future of the game here is good but we cannot afford to relax and take it easy because nowadays the other sports are getting stronger and stronger. I would like to see more of the trend of counties employing full-time coaches — this can only help our game. I can see difficulties for rural clubs because of emigration and costs of running clubs. This problem is there now and I would hope that those in Croke Park would be taking notice of it and doing something about it. I would be afraid that the GAA would forget the importance of the grass roots of the organisation — which are the clubs.

I would also like to see the cost of attending matches kept as low as possible. Unfortunately, it has become very expensive of late and now the day of bringing a family to the All Ireland is gone — this is a pity. I would like to see our game which I have got so much from, going from strength to strength. This can be done with the dedication of people within the organisation and I hope this will always be the case.

Brian Murphy ”

Murphy! — the name is great in the annals of Cork hurling. It first appeared in 1893 when John Murphy captained Cork to All Ireland success over Kilkenny. The name Michael Murphy also appears on that team. In the second decade of the century the name appears regularly and three of the clan played in the final against Laois in 1915. Among the renowned names of the twenties was Sean Óg. He captained Cork in the three All Ireland finals of 1926, '27 and '28 — being successful on two occasions, 1926 and 1928. He is often referred to as the last of the horrendous full-backs. Martin Kennedy, the legendary Tipperary full-forward rated Sean Óg the best full-back he had seen — or encountered — playing the game. Dinny Barry-Murphy arrived on the scene in the twenties and adorned a Cork golden era with superb hurling at half-back and half-forward. He played in five All Ireland finals between 1926 and 1931 — missing out only in 1930 when Tipperary came out of Munster and went on to take the All Ireland title. He was successful on four occasions and had the honour of collecting the McCarthy Cup as captain in 1929.

Another Cork golden era dawned in 1939 and on that team was that stalwart right-full-back Willie 'Longpuck' Murphy. He was on the history making four in a row teams of 1941-44 — added a fifth medal in 1946 — and made his last All Ireland appearance in 1947 when Kilkenny stole the honours.

Gerald Murphy of Midleton kept the flag flying for the clan at midfield on the Cork All Ireland winning teams of 1952, '53 and '54. Denis Murphy was corner-back on the 1966 All Ireland winning Cork team which strangely enough is probably the least remembered of all victorious Cork teams. Denis together with Christy Ring and Billy Morgan, the great football goalkeeper and coach, were Brian Murphy's childhood heroes.

And that brings us to Brian Murphy. He ranks with the greatest of his clan. His path of glory is strewn with success and he must be one of the most decorated dual players of all time. It all began in his College days at Colaiste Chriost Ri — days that have very happy memories for Brian. 'I was probably more interested in the games than in the books. In 1968 we travelled to

Buttevant to play Limerick CBS in the Harty Cup final. We were rank outsiders. Limerick CBS had captured the previous four titles and had men of the calibre of Pat Hartigan in their ranks. We were hoping to do well. But we had a victory that leaves me with one of my most cherished memories. The same year we won the All Ireland colleges football final by defeating Belcamp OMI of Dublin. We repeated the football success in 1970. Again the final was at Croke Park and our opponents St Malachy's of Belfast. The one point victory 4:5 to 1:13 was very sweet. Being captain made it even sweeter'. His subsequent successes were as follows — All Ireland minor hurling 1969 and '70; All Ireland minor football 1970; All Ireland under 21 hurling 1971 and '73; All Ireland under 21 football 1971.

At senior level he had the following successes — All Ireland football 1973; All Ireland hurling 1976, '77 and '78. There were four National League victories in '72, '74, '80 and '81. Seven county senior football titles were won with Nemo Rangers between 1972 and 1983. The county successes led to All Ireland senior football club titles in 1973, '78, '82 and '84. No county senior hurling title came his way but he did have the compensation of an intermediate title in 1971. The honours list is remarkable and yet no matter what game or victory you talk about his mind keeps going back to his school days in Colaiste Chriost Ri. The memories and victories of those days will never leave him. They seem destined to remain indelibly imprinted on his mind. 'The build up in the school — the great atmosphere — the schoolyard meetings to get support going — the songs — the speeches — all contributed to the crescendo of excitement that was reached when victory was won.'

They flash upon that inward eye ...
And then my heart with pleasure fills

High among the highlights of an illustrious career, was the senior football victory of 1973 over Galway. It was Cork's fourth title and the first in 28 years since 1945. 'Cork in that period had some wonderful footballers and many fine teams but their record was terrible.'

Another special moment was the 1978 senior football All Ireland club victory over Scotstown of Monaghan when Brian had the honour of being captain. 'I can remember that day well. Snow was falling. It was difficult to see the guys at the far end of the field.'

Brian's most disappointing defeat in hurling was the 1979 All Ireland semi-final against Galway. It was lost on the score 2:14 to 1:13. 'We were heading for four in a row — hoping to emulate the great men of 1941 to '44. We had beaten Wexford in the finals of 1976 and 1977 — a little fortunate maybe in 1977 — the difference between victory and defeat can be a matter of luck. That day in 1977, Martin Coleman made a wonderful save from Christy Kehoe — and I was supposed to be marking Christy Kehoe. In 1978 we beat Kilkenny. Cork victories over Kilkenny in modern times are quite rare. That made the 1978

victory very special. Being resident in Kilkenny made it extra special and made returning to the city an easy and pleasant task. In my two decades in Kilkenny I have come to admire their hurling skills and players. When you think how we performed against, and lost, to Kilkenny in the finals of 1982 and '83, it's a matter for conjecture as to how we might have fared in the final of 1979. I was bitterly disappointed in 1983. I was confident going up and felt we could atone for the defeat of 1982. We were well prepared and everything seemed right beforehand. Kilkenny got crucial scores that day when they got a goal on either side of half time. When we had the aid of the strong wind in the second half, we were sending long attacking balls from the puckout right up behind the Kilkenny half-back line but the Kilkenny half backs supported by Frank Cummins, who kept dropping back from midfield, kept clearing their lines. We might have done better with shorter puckouts.'

Brian Murphy's playing career was spent in the full-back line where he played in all three positions. As a dual performer he was a magnificent defender in both codes. Had he a full-back line philosophy? 'Yes — you must mark tight. If you fail to get to the ball first, you must pressurise your opponent — harass him — stalk him. But you mustn't foul — some defenders foul too easily — fouling is the same as scoring for the opposition.'

Brian Murphy, who operated mainly at right-full-back was the kind of corner-back that goalkeepers and defences dream of. His style was quiet and unobtrusive. He did what every good corner-back should do — effectively marked his man — covered well — read the game — cleared intelligently — left no gaps to goal. His hallmark was dependability, consistency and sportsmanship. In the All Ireland final of 1976, when Tony Doran was threatening to cause havoc, Brian was moved to full-back where he put the shackles on what had been a rampant Tony Doran. He had the skills and the temperament to do it.

He is very conscious that the GAA and its

games have been very good to him. It brought him three trips to America. 'I would never have been there otherwise.' He travelled to Wembley to play tournaments. Above all he 'made many great friends.' Brian Murphy was a credit to the game — and to the name.

This is Brian's team from the men of his time.

Ger Cunningham
(Cork)

Fan Larkin	Pat Hartigan	Brian Murphy
(Kilkenny)	(Limerick)	(Cork)
Mick Jacob	Ger Henderson	Tadhg O'Connor
(Wexford)	(Kilkenny)	(Tipperary)

Frank Cummins   Gerald McCarthy
(Kilkenny)   (Cork)

Eddie Keher	Joe McKenna	Francis Loughnane
(Kilkenny)	(Limerick)	(Tipperary)
Charlie McCarthy	Ray Cummins	Michael 'Babs' Keating
(Cork)	(Cork)	(Tipperary)

After he had picked it, he stated the obvious — 'It wasn't easy.'

Born: 1939

"

I am very honoured to be asked to write this article on my playing days. I came from a farming family in Donoughmore with no hurling tradition.

Went to St Colman's College, Fermoy where I learned the skills. I was lucky to make corner-forward my Leaving Cert year 1956 on their Harty Cup team.

I won a Fitzgibbon Cup medal with UCC in 1958 and a mid-Cork junior hurling medal with Grenagh that year also. I was now working and living in the city and joined St Finbarr's, won two county medals 1965 and 1968; won one All Ireland 1966; one National League (captain) 1969; two Munster championships 1966 and 1969; two Railway Cup medals 1966 and 1969; All Ireland Longpuck 1965(approx).

Met some great players like Mick Ryan (Tipperary) — was finishing up with St Finbarr's when I started, Mick Roche, Jimmy Doyle and Babs Keating of Tipperary, Seamus Cleere, Martin Coogan and Fan Larkin of Kilkenny, Tony Doran, Hopper McGrath and Bobby Rackard of Wexford, Philly Grimes, Frankie Walsh, Johnnie O'Connor and Larry Guinan from Waterford, and Eamon Cregan and Joe McKenna of Limerick, Jimmy Smyth and Pat Cronin of Clare.

Christy Ring was the best player I ever played with or against. So many times the corner-forward would turn around to me after a score at the other end and say — only Ring would have scored it. His dedication and love of the game which was so evident in the training field, was tremendous. I used to travel with him in his car to the matches for about five years up to his retirement.

We ran up against some great Tipperary teams in the Munster finals in the sixties and were often humiliated. 1966 was our year — we got the breaks in Killarney against Limerick in the Munster semi-final. They scored a goal in the last few minutes when we had been two points ahead. None of our backline had heard the whistle so we

were glad when the referee pointed for a free. This game was notable for the display of Paddy Fitzgerald at left-half-back.

We were very much underdogs in the All Ireland against Kilkenny but from the moment Colm Sheehan drove home the first goal from a save from a 21 yard free from Fr Seanie Barry there was no stopping us. The hunger and will to win was so evident in that display.

1969 was the big disappointment. We beat Wexford in the National League final where there were tremendous displays by Willie Walsh and Charlie Cullinane. We beat Tipperary in the Munster final — the first time in the sixties this has happened. In the final against Kilkenny we were very hot favourites. About ten days beforehand Justin McCarthy, our centre-back was pillion passenger on Joe Murphy's motorcycle — one of our subs — on the way to training. A car reversed out of an avenue on the Rochestown Road and broke Justin's kneecap. Willie Walsh was moved back to centre-back in his place and gave an exhibition there on Pat Delaney but it weakened our forward line and this injury I believe, cost us the match.'

Denis Murphy   "

T his most modest and gentlemanly of players wore the number 4 jersey with rare distinction. He played hurling in the spirit that it should be played and sportsmanship and consistency were the hallmarks of his illustrious career. Not only was he never sent off but no referee had ever to either book or caution him. He was a calm, thinking and unobtrusive corner-back. In the tight he never flinched but his positioning, timing and reading of the game, enabled him to intercept many an attacking move and dispatch long well placed intelligent clearances downfield. It

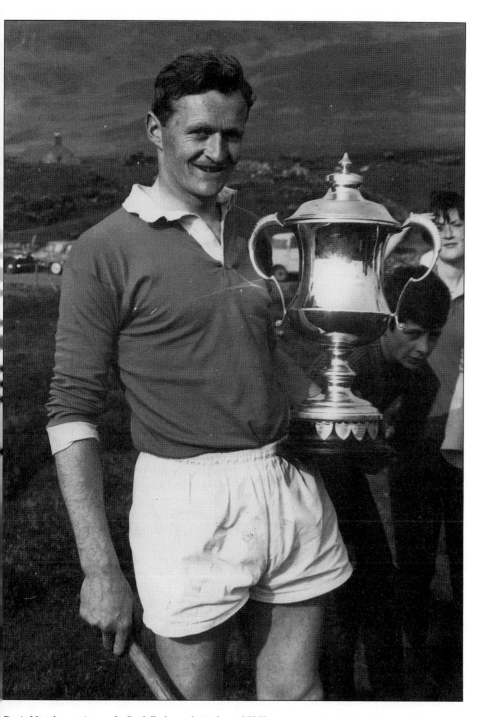

Denis Murphy — winner of a Puck Fada trophy in the mid 1960s.

was this capacity to intercept and cut off the danger that set him apart as a corner-back. Indeed, if a team from the sixties was selected it would be hard to find someone better at left full-back.

He belonged to one of Cork's leanest eras — a time when Tipperary delivered some crushing defeats as the following Munster final scorelines indicate

1961	Tipperary 3:6	Cork 0:7
1964	Tipperary 3:13	Cork 1:5
1965	Tipperary 4:11	Cork 0:5
1968	Tipperary 2:13	Cork 1:7

Tipperary had become a major obstacle to Cork progress but in 1966 a fast young Limerick team dispatched Tipperary in the first round, and when Cork met Limerick they shaded it by two points in a thriller. 'I didn't feel great that day but Paddy Fitzgerald in front of me, cut off every ball — I was glad. That victory over Limerick stands out as special.' Waterford were beaten in the Munster final and only Kilkenny now stood between Cork and Denis Murphy and All Ireland success. Cork hadn't won since 1954. They were hungry, eager and determined. But Kilkenny were favourites and perhaps that mantle was their downfall. For Cork there were two key factors in victory — three goals by their full-forward Colm Sheehan — and several magnificent saves by their goalkeeper Paddy Barry.

Despite the significance of breaking a twelve year losing spell this Cork team of 1966 is in many ways among the least remembered and talked about Cork teams. Perhaps it is because it is sandwiched in as a once off win between the glamorous three-in-a-row teams of the fifties and the seventies. As a selector Denis was closely associated with the latter.

Cork were back in the All Ireland final again in 1969 with Denis Murphy as captain. They buried the Tipperary bogey of the sixties in the Munster final when they won convincingly on the score 4:6 to 0:9 and they had earlier defeated them in the league campaign. Only Kilkenny now barred the way to another McCarthy Cup triumph. Having played against whatever wind there was in the first half Cork led at halftime by 2:6 to 1:6 and had the look of champions. Right from the second half throw-in Charlie McCarthy added a further point for Cork. How they only managed two further points for the rest of the game is hard to explain. But according to Denis it was in the last quarter that Kilkenny really turned on the style in a game in which Ted Carroll at corner-back had a magnificent hour. 'They are the artists I suppose.' It was a disappointment for Denis but nothing that his sporting and philosophical approach to every game couldn't readily cope with and put into context.

For a Cork man who spent a decade at top level his honours list is uncharacteristically bare. Yet it seemed to me as we spoke that medals didn't mean everything to Denis. 'I enjoyed playing with my club and county. Above all I particularly loved just going to the field and practising — attempting all the skills — pulling with and against the flying ball — the drop puck from the hand — the drop puck with and against the falling ball — the sideline cut that would rise and travel seventy yards — just pucking about and enjoying the thrill of it. I always took a special pride in my hurley. It had to feel right in my hands and the balance had to be right. I was meticulous about choosing it. A hurley becomes part of you and when it gets broken you can become quite upset.' He took a calm unruffled approach to the game and believed firmly in good sportsmanship. 'In my career I got one broken finger and three stitches — not bad I suppose — but then I didn't hit too many people either. Only once did I get the butterflies. It was at Limerick in the early sixties in a game against Tipperary. The sun was blazing — the crowd was huge — the gates had been broken down. The white shirted crowd seemed to be right on top of you and the pitch seemed small. I felt the tension.'

He retired in 1969 at the age of 30 and many would have felt it was a bit premature. Did he regret missing a Munster and All Ireland medal in 1970 and another Munster medal in 1972? 'There is a time to go at the top. Missing the additional honours caused me no regrets. I felt the timing was right. You're not a machine — there comes a day when someone will get three goals off of you and then ...'

Two personal achievements have meant a lot to him — Puck Fada champion in the mid-sixties on a course that follows the route of the legendary Setanta — and a green jersey (number 4) in 1966 presented at a dinner in The Gresham and sponsored by *Gaelic Sport* — the equivalent then of the present All Star awards.

I met Denis at the premises in Páirc Chriostóir Uí Rinn — officially opened by Peter Quinn, President of the GAA, on 23 May 1993. Total capital outlay including purchase and development amounted to £1.3m. It is a magnificent complex and an acquisition of which Cork County GAA Board can be extremely proud.

His team selection from the men of his era is as follows.

John O'Donoghue (Tipperary)

Jimmy Brohan (Cork)	Austin Flynn (Waterford)	Denis Murphy (Cork)
Seamus Cleere (Kilkenny)	Mick Ryan (Tipperary)	Tony Wall (Tipperary)
	Mick Roche (Tipperary)	Ned Wheeler (Wexford)	
'Babs' Keating (Tipperary)	Willie Walsh (Cork)	Jimmy Doyle (Tipperary)
Phil Grimes (Waterford)	Liam Dowling (Cork)	Christy Ring (Cork)

Having chosen the team he made the following comments — 'Centre-back Mick Ryan will be a strange choice — he was finishing up as centre-back with St Finbarr's when I joined them — I believe he was the best I saw there. I have not found a place for Eddie Keher, Frankie Walsh, Jimmy Byrne, Gerald McCarthy, Joe Salmon, Bobby Rackard, Martin Coogan, Liam Devaney, Jimmy Smyth, Theo English, Pat Delaney, Tom Cheasty, Tom Neville, Tony Doran, Tony O'Brien (RIP), Jim Treacy, Larry Guinan or Fran Whelan.'

Born: 1955

successes.

My best memory of my own playing days is to have been part of the three-in-a-row team of '76, '77 and '78. Since the forties it has always been a target to put two or three All Irelands together and this also proves the real worth of a team. What means most to me now about the GAA is the friends I made throughout the country and wherever I go I find somebody always wants to talk hurling and discuss prospects for future years. I am now involved in coaching both in my own club and with Cork minor hurlers and I hope in some small way to repay the game of hurling for all that I got from the game both on and off the field.

99

An rud a beirtear sa cnámh, is deacair scarúint leis sa bhfuil

66

I suppose it is inevitable that most boys born in Cork from the age of four or five years of age are going to have a hurley put in their hands at some stage. Obviously a great number of them do not partake much more. Some go on to play at various levels for either club or county. The lucky few like myself can go on to realise what was for me, from as far back as I can remember, the only ambition I can recall and that is to play in an All Ireland final wearing the red and white of Cork. The family's long involvement in Gaelic games also ensured that one would at least, play hurling and football and ability after that would dictate at what level. My grandfather and granduncle both won All Ireland medals in 1919 against Dublin and my granduncle Dinny of course captained Cork to win All Ireland honours in 1929.He also played in the famous final of 1931 against the 'old enemy' Kilkenny and often told me about the great players like Sean Óg Murphy, Eudi Coughlan, Lory Meagher and many more. My late father John won two county medals with St Finbarr's and also won a junior All Ireland medal in 1940. With a family history like that there was never much chance of getting big headed or carried away with brief

Few players have been as fortunate as Jimmy Barry-Murphy and it is probably true to say that he has been unsurpassed as a dual performer. He was highly gifted and richly talented in both hurling and football and played for his county in both codes at minor, under 21 and senior levels. Being a native of Cork provided him with the scope and opportunities for success, not available to players in other counties. Jimmy is very conscious of this.

Victory and honours flowed in abundance right through his career. In football there was All Ireland senior honours in 1973 at the age of 19. And for him it was a dream debut that produced telling scores at psychological moments — a goal within three minutes of the start to settle a team that hadn't won a football title since 1945 — a brilliant goal within eight minutes of the final whistle that clinched victory.

There followed All Star awards in 1973 and 1974 — four Railway cup successes in a row from 1975 to 1978 inclusive — National League honours in 1980 and an All Ireland club title with St Finbarr's the same year.

The hurling honours include ten Munster titles, five All Ireland titles and five All Star awards. Incredibly, he never won a Railway cup hurling medal. 'I wasn't picked that often but then I wasn't really interested in playing winter hurling.' The list also includes Oireachtas and National League victories and All Ireland club titles in 1975 and 1978 at the expense of the Fenians (Kilkenny) and Rathnure (Wexford). I pondered aloud on the diverse nature of all the medals. 'I don't place much store on medals. At the end of the day they don't count for much. The number of honours doesn't mean anything. Don't gauge anyone by that. It's how you present yourself and play on the day that really counts.'

The hurling background was strong. Hurling for Jimmy was inevitable. The most famous name in the family tree is of course his granduncle Dinny Barry-Murphy. He starred with Cork teams at half-back and half-forward during one of Cork's greatest eras. He has been described as a complete hurler and played in five All Ireland finals between 1926 and 1931 — missing out only in 1930 — winning on four occasions. His other love was greyhounds. Jimmy has inherited this too. It is quite possible that in a different environment Jimmy might have been a soccer superstar. He signed up for Cork Celtic in 1972. 'I only played five or six games. I didn't fancy it much. It probably improved my ball control.'

Of all the honours won the three in a row in hurling from 1976 to 1978 was the one which in retrospect meant most. 'It established so many friendships. There must have been a dozen of the same players on all three teams. The most satisfying aspect of the three in a row was the 1978 win over Kilkenny. They have the Indian sign on us so that win gave me great satisfaction. We had beaten Wexford in 1976 and '77 and the win over Kilkenny in 1978 gave our three in a row a seal of real merit.'

Jimmy's most humbling experience was his failure as captain to lead Cork to victory in 1982 and 1983 against Kilkenny. 'It was a good lesson — a humbling lesson. It made me take stock and think of the many great players who never won an All Ireland or indeed never even had the privilege of parading around Croke Park. It made me reflect too on how lucky I was to have been born in Cork.'

He sees hurling as a simple game where players should 'think about what they are doing.' He sees the 'guy who thinks about his mates and creates scores as, as important as the scorer.' Johnny Clifford used instil into them the importance of keeping the ball in play instead of going for impossible scores from difficult angles and driving the ball wide. Jimmy believes that every young hurler should be made watch over and over again the final seconds of the drawn Kilkenny/Wexford Leinster final of 1993. It was a classic in composure under pressure. Let's recall the scene. The seconds are ticking away and Wexford who had played some wonderful hurling over the hour and particularly in the first half are holding on to a one point lead and attacking. They have the ball at the Railway goal and out near the Cusack Stand. A ball that ought to have remained in Wexford possession is lost and collected by Simpson at corner-back — sent unerringly to Bill Hennessy who beats his man and dispatches the ball with speed to Adrian Ronan — with controlled urgency he beats his man and sends a radar-like pass to Eamonn Morrissey — there is no hesitation as he too beats his man and sends over the equaliser which was followed by the final whistle. The entire movement from Simpson all the way to Morrissey was executed with clocklike precision and with supreme hurling confidence and artistry that drew a game against the odds.

Jimmy always enjoyed playing at full-forward. 'I loved being in around the square. If you are prepard to wait and keep your patience your chance will come. You can destroy a back's day. A forward need only be lucky once. A back needs to be lucky all the time.'

He always enjoyed playing against Kilkenny because 'they are the ultimate in hurling.' He liked the games against Tipperary because of the 'fabulous atmosphere'. 'I played minor, under 21 and senior championship matches against Tipp and never lost.' And then he adds with a sense of pride — 'very few Cork fellows can say that.'

The name Jimmy Barry-Murphy is now a household word in Cork and all hurling circles. He was an opportunist and played the percentage game. He rarely if ever became embroiled in the intensely physical. He was a thoughtful player with a penchant for the quick snappy score. He conserved energy. He was a visionary and had the patience to wait. When a chance — indeed a half chance — arose, he pounced. He then made it look easy. But that was because he was a master of the basic skills and the simple things. At all times he played the ball. He was the personification of good sportsmanship.

Here is how sports correspondent Kevin Cashman once described him, 'The man. One of the all time greats. Matchless intelligence and composure. Predatory stalker and finisher of scores. Ability to hit the "Killer" pass was unique until the advent of Joe Cooney. Guides and inspires all around him.'

Pat Nolan receiving the Echo Cup after winning the County title in 1963.

"

I have many happy memories of the great game of hurling, the game that I love. I made a lot of good friends throughout the country from playing the game.

The greatest game I played in was the 1962 All Ireland final. I think it was one of the greatest finals ever, a game we did not deserve to lose.

I suppose I was lucky to be playing at a time when Wexford were winning titles, when I think of all the great Wexford players since 1968 who never won an All Ireland medal. We loved to win but if we were beaten it wasn't the end of the world.

My proudest moments were when we won the All Irelands and National Leagues and captaining my club Oylegate-Glenbrien to win the Wexford Senior championship in 1963. I think the game of hurling is not as exciting as it was before the rule changes. Most referees seem to blow a fair shoulder nowadays. One of the great thrills of the game was the tussle around the goal. That

Born: 1937

is now gone and you can't tackle the goal-keeper. Goalkeepers today seem to be a protected species. My favourite county to play against was Tipperary, great sportsmen, the same in victory or defeat.

My only wish now is to see Wexford win an All Ireland soon.

Pat Nolan **"**

He burned the hurleys — all four of them. That memory takes Pat back to the days of his early youth. His father who was a great hurling enthusiast had gone to Enniscorthy and brought home four new hurleys. The rest of the day was spent hurling and as dusk fell they were sitting on a stone outside the house feeling quite exhausted. John decided he would have one last puck before calling it a day. It was a fateful decision. The ball went flying through the window. Ash was turned to ashes.

Dawn broke the following morning and though Pat and his three brothers didn't know it then remorse had replaced retribution His father set off for Enniscorthy again and returned with four more hurleys. Hurling enthusiasm had triumphed — the game was worth more than a pane of glass.

His father's enthusiasm found concrete expression in the fact that there was always available to the local club a playing pitch on his farm holding. And when it was necessary to rotate the crops and till the playing pitch the goalposts were uplifted and removed to another field.

Pat, the second of four brothers, remembers as a twelve-year-old standing between the goalposts and the grown ups played backs and forwards and peppered him with shots. Thus did he learn to train the eye, sharpen the reflexes and get down to the ground ball — the achilles heel of

213

many a goalkeeper.

Like many a youngster he had a hurling hero — the stylish Jimmy Langton of Kilkenny. And when he played with his peers he would announce he was Jimmy Langton while others assumed the name of Nicky Rackard or some other folk hero of the day or perhaps yesteryear.

He played county minor in 1954 and 1955 and graduated to senior ranks in 1956 and as sub goalie won his first All Ireland medal in the great triumph over Cork. On Easter Sunday of that year he got his baptism of fire to senior hurling when in a challenge game against Limerick he picked the ball out of the net six times. 'There was nothing I could do about it. Limerick were flying and the shots were coming from all angles.' When Pat played well his father would never mention the game. 'When he did choose to discuss it I always knew there was something he was unhappy about — some message he wanted to get across — but there was never a word of criticism.'

In a career that lasted seventeen years at top level — he was Wexford's longest serving goalkeeper, probably their greatest, and the only Wexford man to win three National Hurling League medals — some memories stand out above all others.

1960 conjures up moments of nostalgia — it was his first All Ireland win. On that first Sunday in September Wexford defied the odds and confounded the critics with a most convincing 2:15 to 0:11 win over hot favourites Tipperary. They took a firm grip on the game from the start and never let go — Padge Kehoe had an early goal from a free about thirty yards out — Billy Rackard at centre-back was hurling splendidly and containing Liam Devaney — John Nolan at left-half-back was superb on Jimmy Doyle — the second half opened with the elusive 'Hopper' McGrath scoring Wexford's second goal. Pat kept a clean goal for Wexford and was fronted by Nick O'Donnell — one of the great full-backs of hurling. 'I worked with Nicko at Roadstone for twenty years. We played in factory leagues together. I remember as he got older he used to play in goal in those league games

and I used to play full-back. Nicko I believe could have played anywhere. He had great anticipation — could give the impression of being slow — but was always in the right place at the right time.'

The game of greatest regret was the 1962 All Ireland final. Again the opposition was Tipperary. Within two minutes Tipperary were two goals up. 'That is one game I would love to play all over again — and win it this time. That day Nicko was unwell and an altercation with a steward as he came onto the pitch — he wanted to bring his son out with him — caused Nicko to return to the dressing-room to regain his composure. No doubt all these factors combined to contribute to the very short puckout — it hardly went more than 25 yards — by Nicko that led to Tipp's second goal. It all happened so quickly and yet I nearly saved it. I got the hurl to the ball — it deflected and hit the goalpost and went into the net — nine times out of ten it wouldn't have gone in. By halftime we were back in the game — a goal down — but Billy Rackard was playing with a broken bone in his hand. Then came the move that won and lost the game. Mackey McKenna having gained possession came in from the Cusack stand side — well out the field — in a kind of an arc and cut through the centre — parted to Tom Ryan who finished to the net.' It all ended with only two points separating the sides 3:10 to 2:11 — and Tipperary knew they were fortunate.

1968 brought another All Ireland confrontation with Tipperary. 'If we were unlucky in 1962 we had our share of good fortune in 1968 — especially in the first half. We were very fortunate to be only eight points behind at halftime — Tipp were all over us — we were playing badly. I can remember in that first half a close in shot from the corner by Babs Keating. It rebounded from a reflex save off my hurl — McLoughlin met it and this time it hit the middle of the handle of my hurl — out again to where it was doubled on by Mackey McKenna — hit me on the chest and was cleared. If your luck is in, it's in — if it isn't as in 1962 —

well, it isn't. My full-back that day was Eddie Kelly. He hasn't always got the credit he deserved. He was a man of great physical strength and it was very easy play behind him. Switches made that day worked well and paved the way for victory in the second half.'

Pat's club, Oylegate-Glenbrien was always very special to him and one of his proudest days was when he captained them to their only county title in 1963. Special in that campaign were the victories over the highly rated St Aidan's and Rathnure teams on the path to the final.

Let us now look at what sportswriters had to say from time to time about Pat.

In a league semi final against Limerick in 1969 won by Wexford on the score 2:5 to 1:6 a sportswriter wrote as follows: 'Wexford's hero of the hour was custodian Pat Nolan. Nolan displayed wonderful courage between the posts, particularly in the second half and his saves from Eamon Cregan were right out of the top drawer.'

In June 1970 the following appeared in *Gaelic Sport* — 'There are goalkeepers and goalkeepers — of whom some get their full meed of praise and some are so sound that press and public alike seem, after a while, to more or less take them for granted, and Wexford's Pat Nolan is one who immediately springs to mind in the latter class. It is no exaggeration to say that during his ten years with the county to date he has probably won more matches for Wexford than any other player who ever wore the purple and gold.'

After victory over Limerick in the National League final of 1972/73 a report headed 'Prince of Keepers' went on to say 'let it be said here and now the one link between that game of fifteen years ago and last Sunday's, that prince of goalkeepers Pat Nolan, shone above all others in this torrid encounter.

His brilliant performances for the county in the last twenty years are innumerable (indeed the Slaneysiders could not have beaten Kilkenny in the semi-final without him) but rarely has he showed such courage and split second reflexes under tremendous pressure as in this encounter'.

But his *piece de resistance* must surely have been his performance between the posts at Wembley in 1968. He admits it was his greatest ever display. Here is what the *New Ross Standard* had to say in June 1968. 'Biggest individual success was that of goalkeeper Pat Nolan. The Glenbrien man's praises have been sung for many years in these columns and Wexford followers have realised for years that he is the country's outstanding custodian.'

After the game in Wembley Nicky Rackard said to Pat that it was the greatest display of goalkeeping he had seen since the days of Paddy Scanlon of Limerick. No higher praise was possible.

In his own contribution Pat wrote, 'we loved to win but if we were beaten it wasn't the end of the world' — what a healthy sporting philosophy — what a lovely sentiment — from a wonderful goalkeeper and sportsman.

Pat, after some thought decided to pick the team hereunder, after changing it many times, from all the opponents of his hurling days.

Pat Nolan (Wexford)

John Doyle (Tipperary)   Pat Hartigan (Limerick)   Jim Treacy (Kilkenny)

Seamus Cleere (Kilkenny)   Mick Roche (Tipperary)   Denis Coughlan (Cork)

Des Foley (Dublin)   Joe Salmon (Galway)

Eddie Keher (Kilkenny)   Tom Cheasty (Waterford)   Jimmy Doyle (Tipperary)

Christy Ring (Cork)   Billy Dwyer (Kilkenny)   Phil Grimes (Waterford)

" "

I started playing camogie when I was twelve years old. I played on the street with boys and girls. It was pretty tough by times. One day this girl called me and asked if I would like to play for her club Celtic. I said I would. Three years later I played my first game for Dublin. I was fifteen years old when winning my first All Ireland. I went on to win thirteen All Irelands, fifteen Leinster titles and nine inter-provincial titles. My greatest thrill was winning the Caltex award for best player of the year in 1967. I was the first camogie player to win the award. My only regret was that my father died the year before. He would have got such a thrill out of this.

I lived in the same parish as Kevin Heffernan. His sisters all played for Celtic. He would give us advice before the game. He would say to me you should score three goals today. I got to the stage that I would

be afraid to approach him if I didn't. I think the game has got too serious. We all like to win but young players should try to enjoy their game more and not take it so hard when they lose a game.

The game hasn't changed much. I think it has got a bit more tough. I would like to see more ground play. It really looks good when the ball is pulled on first time. Now always in hurling everybody lifts the ball. Some of the men can't hit the ball on the ground. I think this is a pity. I was sorry when they took away the top bar in camogie. There was more skill in the game when you had to put the ball under the bar. The sky is the limit now. Some people want to have fifteen aside. I would be against this because I don't think it suits girls. The game is getting too much like hurling and I can't see why we should change. It would not make for a better game.

I had some wonderful years in camogie. I

Una O'Connor with team-mate Eithne Leach

would like to see all young girls joining some club. You don't have to be a great player to enjoy the game. It's a great way to meet friends. I have met great friends over the years and they have made such a great difference to my life. I am still involved with my club Celtic and hope to be for a long time yet.

Una O'Connor. **"**

U na was the youngest of a family of eight and her mother died when she was eighteen. Given her talents it is hard to believe that she was the only member of the family that had any interest in sport. But what an immense difference it made to her life. It enriched it. She remembers very early in her career, having played a game, and following which mentors and players were gathered around her and making a fuss of her. 'It was the first time in my life I was made a fuss of. I felt special. I didn't realise I was good. I was just playing a game I enjoyed. It gradually began to dawn on me that this was something I could do better than most.' In those young days innate camogie talent was unfolding and Una — fortified by training and practice — nurtured by her mentors and senior team mates — blossomed into one of the all time greats of camogie. She had a tremendous turn of speed in the sprint and according to a Cork admirer 'would waft away from you and as you chased she would part with the ball without you realising it. She had all the skills.'

Throughout her career she was a prolific scorer. In a Leinster championship game against Wexford she scored 10:2. Not surprisingly, it has never been equalled. In her first All Ireland she scored three goals. Her trainer said well done and Kathleen Mills said to her 'I will help you — I will bring you along.'

'Kathleen was brilliant to me. When I first joined she got me into a corner and said if you see me get the ball, go down to the left-corner-forward position — that's where the ball will be laid. Being young I didn't follow her advice in the beginning but I quickly learned she was right and began to score regularly from her passes. In my early years I played in the half-forward line but when Sophie Brack, who was a great full-forward, retired, I moved into her position. I got the best out of my play in there. I scored more goals at full-forward than any place else.'

Her father who was a native of Kildare, never missed a game she played. He was very proud of her. His interest in her camogie career meant a great deal to Una. None of the rest of the family attended her games. But strangely enough they were in Croke Park for the final of 1957 against Antrim — the year Una was dropped. Entering the last quarter Antrim were ahead. The family and some of the club colleagues began to chant — Bring on Una, Bring on Una. 'I replaced an injured girl with about ten minutes to go. I got more ball than I would have got for a whole game. I saw an opening and passed the ball that brought the winning goal in a two point victory. 3:3 to 3:1. The following day the paper said that the genius Una O'Connor should have been on for the whole match. Dad was very proud.'

Winning thirteen All Irelands gave Una many moments to cherish. As always the first, won in 1953 was special. Her introduction in the last ten minutes of the 1957 final was fairytale stuff. Captaining a winning team in successive years in 1963 and 1964 was a great honour. Between 1957 and 1966 she set a record that may never be equalled when she won ten All Ireland titles in a row. In all those years she was a leading scorer and played a key role in the Dublin successes. In 1966 Sean O'Duffy who was always closely linked with camogie, approached Una at her place of work in Johnson Mooney & O'Brien and said to her that if she won the 1966 title she would get the Caltex award. Well win the title they did with a two point victory over Antrim 2:2 to 0:6 and Una became the first camogie player to receive the coveted Caltex award. 'There I was in the company of Ollie Walsh (hurling), Christy O'Connor (golf), Fred Teidt (boxing) and many others. I felt in awe. It was a wonderful night and Jack Lynch presented the trophies.'

I was surprised to learn from such an outstanding forward that her favourite position was fullback. Her opportunity to play there came in a Leinster championship game against Wexford in 1975 when she was persuaded to make a comeback and she gave a sterling display that matched her best forward performances.

Una feels the standard has gone down, particularly in Dublin where players are playing too many games — such as soccer and football. She feels Dublin could win a junior title if they concentrated specifically on that grade and that such a win would give them confidence for the future.

Una has very special words of praise for their trainer Nell McCarthy, a Cork lady. 'She was brilliant. You did what she told you. She taught us discipline. You had to dress properly and give of your best at all times. One evening she whistled us into the centre of the pitch and said — Go home you are not doing your best. We went home, we never questioned her.'

Her club Celtic is extremely special to her. It was they who spotted her talent the first day. It was there she made such lifelong friends as Eithne Leech, who won eight All Ireland medals, Rita White and Ann Carey who each won a junior All Ireland medal. It was club activity that enriched and has continued to enrich her life. It was for her club she scored the most satisfying goal of her career. 'It was a league game against Austin Stacks. The game was in the closing seconds and we were trailing by two points. Kitty Murphy took a sideline ball which she floated into the goalmouth. I put up my hand and palmed it in flight to the back of the net.' Celtic had the honour of being the first club to win the All Ireland club in 1964. 'I got six stitches in that final.' At present she is a committee member of the club and is involved with the younger players.

If Una was a young player at the present time she says she would want to emulate Angela Downey of Kilkenny.

This is her team. As she picked it she kept saying, 'I'm leaving off loads of players.' And when it was selected she announced. 'These are world beaters.'

	Eileen Duffy (Dublin)	
	Mary Sinnott (Wexford)	
Alice Hussey (Dublin)	Margaret O'Leary (Wexford)	Kathleen Lyons (Dublin)
Kathleen Mills (Dublin)	Ann Carroll (Kilkenny)	Liz Garvan (Cork)
Angela Downey (Kilkenny)	Noreen Duggan (Cork)	Judi Doyle (Dublin)
	Una O'Connor (Dublin)	

Born: 1884

When Sean O'Kennedy, a native of New Ross played for Wexford in the 1910 All Ireland Hurling final against Limerick, he was probably the finest full-back in the country. At six foot tall and weighing fourteen stone, he was a commanding figure. He had leadership qualities that benefited all those around him. When Limerick threw everything into a second half rally that threatened to carry the day it was the strength and fitness and stamina of Sean that played a key part in bringing Wexford its first hurling title. It was close 7:0 to 6:2. But close ones are often the sweetest.

In his student days Sean hurled in Dublin and had as a contemporary that great Cork-man P.D. Mehigan — better known to many as 'Carbery' — who hurled with Cork and was later famous for his writings on Gaelic games.

As well as being an outstanding hurler Sean was also an accomplished oarsman and a highly talented footballer. After the hurling success of 1910, football came to the fore in Wexford and the reputation of

Sean O'Kennedy soared. To him more than any other one man was due the football success of the 1913 to 1918 period — six Leinster titles in a row and four All Ireland titles in a row 1915-1918. Injury kept Sean out of the 1918 campaign. He was captain in the years 1915, 1916 and 1917 — the only man to captain a team to three successive All Ireland victories in either hurling or football. The mantle of captain is some-times seen as a personal honour and carried out in a passive role. But not so with Sean. He was a natural leader of men and endeared himself to his colleagues and associates.

He could read a game superbly and quickly spot any weaknesses in the opposition. He could inspire at halftime and his judgement when making switches won many a match. In the days when he trained Wexford teams he often cycled distances of seventy miles to fulfil a labour of love.

In common with many young men of his day he was involved in the political activities of the time. In 1915 and

subsequent years he took part in the Sinn Féin movement. This led to periods of imprisonment. For a number of years his health suffered but time proved to be a healer and he fully recovered.

'Carbery' had this to say of him. 'His enthusiasm, his buoyant humour, his wonderful strength, skill and endurance; his cool scheming brain to see scoring opportunity, his unselfish feeding of men better placed; his direction of training and tactics after he retired — all put Sean O'Kennedy on a plane apart.'

In a signal honour his name and that of all his 1910 colleagues — including the late Mick Neville of Castlebridge, born in 1887, who featured in *Giants of the Ash* — is commemorated on a Memorial Stone located in the church grounds in Castlebridge Co Wexford.

A photograph of the memorial is reproduced below.

Senior VIII — 1910. Winners of the Ros Mhic Treoin challenge cup, New Ross. Standing: T.J. O'Kennedy, D. Keating, M. O'Connor, W. Harding. Sitting: M. Roche, P. Forristal, M. Sheehan (cox) J. O'Kennedy, P. Roche

Below: Memorial at Castlebridge to the Wexford hurling champions 1910

Born: 1928

Roads. Hurling was introduced to the Athleague area in or around 1905/06 by a Patrick O'Sullivan — a national school teacher from Co Cork.

In 1913 the county team defeated Galway to win the Connaught Senior Hurling title. This was mainly powered by Athleague players who had been nurtured, coached and trained by the same 'Master' O'Sullivan. Some years later, the master was transferred to my local school in Brideswell to where he introduced hurling to the area. By the time I came along as a school goer, hurling was in full swing in our end of the parish and nobody kicked a football at all. The other end of the parish, football was and still is, the predominant game.

I vividly remember in my days in the national school bringing my hurley to school every Monday morning and back again on Friday evening. Each pupil interested in the game did likewise. During the week the 'Master' would have us all out hurling on the little playground at lunch break. And often he would demonstrate to the class — out on the floor — the skills of hooking, blocking, tapping, doubling with the hurley stick. It could be regarded as part of the school curriculum. He was the man that gave me my first love for hurling and to this day I am grateful to him for that. May I add he was an outstanding educationalist as well.

A few years after leaving the national school and my training ground, I became involved in my first game of hurling. It was the year after the war had ended. Yes there was a sigh of relief throughout the country but still many of the hardships lingered on. Rationing of fuel and food was still with us. Transport was difficult. Ponies and traps, bicycles, and the odd 'crock' of a car were still the most common ways of getting from one place to another.

Yes, it was the year of my first county final. It was a Roscommon county final. The game was hurling and the club Four

66

To me hurling is the best and finest field game I have ever seen or watched on TV.

Very few sports are as skilful or as graceful as hurling played at the highest level. It surely is poetry in motion. Everything about it I am particularly fond of — the clash of the ash — the ball flying at high speed through the air — the wrist work — the speed of thought and action — the bodily contact and the abundance of scores from all angles and directions.

In my youth I loved playing and practising it. Nowadays, I love watching it. To nearly all followers of the GAA I am known basically as a footballer — having played at senior level with my county over a long number of years.

Being born and reared in a county which is regarded as a football stronghold down through the years, I have often been asked where did my love and fondness for the game of hurling come from. To answer the question, I must go back to my schooldays and recap on a sequence of events which more or less explain the position. Hurling in Roscommon has been confined to a few parishes bordering on the Galway boundary — mainly Athleague and Four

Roads. Earlier in the season, that great hurling enthusiast — Johnnie Mee, had brought us to play minor football for his club. At half time in the minor game, would you believe it, I joined in a hurling puck about. Johnnie quickly spotted I could handle a hurley and that is how I came to play hurling for Four Roads.

The 1946 final was played in Knockcroghery. I travelled by bicycle from my home to Four Roads and from there to the county final. Many went by pony and trap — others cycled. I doubt if many went by car — if they did someone must have pushed them. Petrol was impossible to get. Of the match itself I don't remember very much. What I know is we won by a point. I can recall the joy, the thrills and the excitement of winning my first county final. It was one of my great moments on a hurling field.

To this day I believe the club is the foundation stone on which the Association is built and it is the closest unit of individuals that can be got in any community. It has always been a pleasure and privilege to play for my native parish. I only hope and pray we do not lose sight of the importance of the role of the club in the Association at large. Nowadays there is a lot of hype and publicity about the All Irelands, tickets, All Stars.

Growing up as an early teenager in the mid-forties was entirely different than it is today. World War 2 was raging across Europe and even though we maintained our neutrality its affect could be seen and felt throughout rural Ireland. At that time social, cultural and sporting facilities were at a minimum. Communication was mainly by word of mouth. The battery wireless — never called a radio — with the golden voice of Mícheál O'Hehir was the big attraction to look forward to every Sunday. He was one of my childhood heroes — bringing the game to every remote part of rural Ireland. Other heroes of my youth were the great footballers of Galway and Mayo of the time — Bobby Beggs, Henry Kenny, Dinny Sullivan, Patsy Flannery and many others. Not every family was lucky enough to own such a 'high tech' piece of equipment. We would gather at the home of the owner, knowing that a step or word out of place and we'd be shown the door. There was always the air of uncertainty that the battery would 'run out' before the match. It was the age of no phones, no electricity and no running water. There were few cars available and those that owned them had precious little petrol to run them. Normal transport was the pony and trap or the bike. We weren't picked up by cars at the house to take us to play the football or hurling match. In fact, we often had to cycle to the game, play the match and cycle back home again. But we had our own fun and above all, we had a most enjoyable and happy youth. As a pastime we played hurling and football in the local field at my own house. We played from morning to dusk. The evenings after a long day at the hay or in the bog, we would spend again in the playing field. We played for the love of the game. We pucked about the hurling ball from one end of the field to the other. We didn't wait for the trainer to come before we started. More often than not, there was no trainer. I often wonder do present day players get the same enjoyment out of training as we did out of practise. Is it too geared up for winning All Irelands?

Gerry O'Malley 99

The village all declared how much he knew;
'Twas certain he could write and cipher too:
Lands he could measure, terms and tides presage
And even the story ran that he could gauge.

The attributes of Goldsmith's Village Schoolmaster did not include hurling but fortunately for Gerry O'Malley, his teacher 'Master' O'Sullivan, loved and promoted the game. From him he learned the skills at an early age. It is understandable therefore that hurling was his first love. So it is fitting that after football glory had abandoned and deserted him, hurling provided him with honours and recognition as the final curtain fell on his playing days.

The name Roscommon will conjure up, for a certain age group, feats on the football field in the first half of the forties when names like Jimmy Murray, Phelim Murray, Bill Carlos, Brendan Lynch, Eddie Boland, Donal Keenan, Bill Jackson and Frankie Kinlough — to mention but some — spelt magic. And in his youth Gerry O'Malley basked in the reflected glory of these god-like heroes. But the love of hurling, imparted from 'Master' O'Sullivan had taken a grip that would never let go.

And so Roscommon — even though where hurling was concerned, has always been in the cinderella category — produced in the person of Gerry O'Malley a hurling giant — 'who tasted of no reward'. He had a great pair of hands. He was a rallying force that inspired colleagues. He had stores of stamina. His commitment and dedication were of the highest order and he had leadership qualities. In his twenty years of hurling he would have won an abundance of honours if he had been born in Tipperary, Cork, Waterford, Wexford or Kilkenny. And who knows he might have been a second Willie John Daly or a Bobby Rackard or a Philly Grimes.

In 1962 he captained Roscommon in the parade around Croke Park as they faced Kerry in the senior football final. He was hoping to emulate the great performances of the 1943 and 1944 teams when they defeated Cavan, after a replay and Kerry, respectively. And he was hoping too to erase the memory of 1946 when Roscommon were leading Kerry by six points with about as many minutes to go — and Kerry got two goals — and drew — and only clinched a four points victory in the replay in the very closing stages. 'Did you know that in the 1946 drawn game Jimmy Murray the captain went off injured with about ten minutes to go? Roscommon looked certain winners. Those attending his facial injury were careful to wash away all the blood so that he would look well and presentable when he went up to receive the cup' — 'the best laid schemes of mice and men ...'

Sadly for Gerry, 1962 brought defeat and disappointment. He retired early in the second half with an injury and was hospitalised. 'I was like *The Man from Clare* that day — just about the same age — Father Time had taken its toll.'

So let's now return to Gerry the hurler. He was selected on the Connaught Railway Cup hurling panel several times between 1954 and 1964 and had the honour of playing in 1954, '60 and '61. In the first of these encounters they played Munster. It is interesting to look at the Munster lineout which was full of hurlers of the highest calibre — many of them now legendary.

Tony Reddin (Tipperary) / Gerry O'Riordan (Cork), John Lyons (Cork), John Doyle (Tipperary) / Jimmy Finn (Tipperary), Pat Stakelum (Tipperary), Matt Fuohy (Cork) / John Hough (Tipperary), John Kiely (Waterford) / W.J. Daly (Cork), Josie Hartnett (Cork), Seamus Bannon (Tipperary) / Jimmy Smyth (Clare), Derry McCarthy (Limerick), Christy Ring (captain) (Cork).

'As I walked into Croke Park on 21 February 1954 I felt an unusual feeling carrying the hurley. I was very apprehensive. Even though I had played Fitzgibbon Cup hurling with UCG in the company of Josie Gallagher, Jim Brophy, Seanie Duggan and others, I felt I was now walking onto a new level. I was on trial. And remember, in the fifties the Railway Cup was a very prestigous competition that drew large crowds. The medals were treasured.' Were you happy with your performance? 'Well, I had my hands full in coping with John Hough — Joe Salmon was on John Kiely. I would describe my performance as negative. I tried to neutralise John Hough and keep him from doing damage rather than indulge in open play. I didn't play as I would like to have played. My main assets were speed, stamina and fitness.'

Gerry is a great believer in team spirit and co-operation. He takes the view that it is the duty of established players to encourage and support younger ones. He places great emphasis on sportsmanship. With him it comes before winning and before medals.

Where young players are concerned, he would like to see their games non-competitive. 'Let them first learn the skills — then play the matches — get the feel of what it is like to be part of a team — playing the ball — teaching themselves to enjoy playing on a team — not putting emphasis on winning. Competitive hurling is soon enough at minor level.'

In 1965 Gerry was 37 years of age. The sands of time were running out as he set forth with Roscommon junior hurlers in the championship. Kerry fell at the semi-final stage. In the home final they triumphed over Armagh 'where I hurled freely and with abandon at centrefield.' Here is an excerpt from a report in the *Armagh Observer* dated 18 September 1965.

Gerry O'Malley did the damage. Never have I seen one man dominate an All Ireland final as Gerry O'Malley did last Sunday's game at Croke Park. Let's face it Armagh had no answer to the brilliant Roscommon man. This Connaught inter-provincial hurling and football star was in unbeatable form and his stick work must rate him among the all time hurling greats, not too far behind men such as Christy Ring, Mick Mackey and Nicky Rackard.

A legend in his own county and province O'Malley showed us all the craft and vitality that have made him one of the outstanding figures on Gaelic fields over the past fifteen years.

In the final they accounted for Warwickshire. It was close 3:10 to 2:11. Roscommon were now All Ireland champions and Gerry O'Malley was proud of the achievement. 'But you need victory at a higher level to generate enthusiasm and really promote the game. You need hurling in the schools if you are to really foster the game. This is so evident in the traditional hurling counties. You might have noticed in my written contribution that I always referred to the ball. We never used the word sliotar — unlike the hurling strongholds.'

Gerry's last game of hurling was the Roscommon county senior final of 1968. 'I made it known beforehand that this would be my last game. Even though I scored two goals that day Tremane beat us by four points — 5:3 to 3:5. When the final whistle blew I was chaired off the field by the Tremane players.' Thus ended the career of a great sportsman. So let us recall for a moment his first football game with his native Roscommon — a game he has never forgotten. 'It was a cold November day and we were playing Kerry in a tournament game in Croke Park. I was in the half-forward line — young and full of energy and enthusiasm. I was chasing everything right into the end line. In the Kerry full-back line were Paddy Bawn Brosnan and Joe Keohane. After a couple of my sorties one of them — I forget which — kicked his heel into the soft ground at the fourteen yards line and drew a line parallel to the goal. He then looked at me and said, 'Young man, don't tempt the Lord.' Was he smiling Gerry? 'There wasn't a sign of a smile.'

Gerry picked the team he would like to have captained from the men of his era from eight counties. 'I could have picked several teams — dare I put my name among these greats.'

Seanie Duggan (Galway)

Bobby Rackard (Wexford)   Nick O'Donnell (Wexford)   Jim Treacy (Kilkenny)

Tom McGarry (Limerick)   Pat Stakelum (Tipperary)   Phil Grimes (Waterford)

Joe Salmon (Galway)   Gerry O'Malley (Roscommon)

Josie Gallagher (Galway)   Mick Roche (Tipperary)   Jim Langton (Kilkenny)

Jimmy Smyth (Clare)   Nick Rackard (Wexford)   Christy Ring (Cork)

'I didn't see Mackey play — he was before my time — otherwise he would be on my team.'

Paddy Phelan on his Confirmation day with his sister Biddy.

Born: 1910

Paddy was one of a family of ten — six girls and four boys — Paddy was the second youngest.

As I write (February 1993) the only surviving member is his sister Biddy — in her eighty-eighth year.

Paddy was born on 16th September 1910 and Biddy revealed that her father wrote all their dates of birth in a little notebook which she still has.

Life in those days in Ireland was for the vast majority simple and frugal, and the Phelans were no exception. Their enjoyment and amusement centred around the game of hurling. Biddy used to play in goal and stopped the ball with her skirt. It used to drive Paddy mad and he used run her out of the goal.

The photograph accompanying this article shows Paddy on his confirmation day in 1921 with his sister Biddy.

Paddy was a Freshford man but he made his name with famed Tullaroan. Limerick's Mick Mackey always spoke in glowing terms about Paddy Phelan's superb hurling skills — pronouncing the name 'Failin'. His silken brilliance blended beautifully with the varied skills of the many hurling artists that comprised the talented teams that Kilkenny produced in the 30's.

Paddy played in goal for Leinster against Munster in the Railway Cup final of 1930 and it was over a year later when he first played for his county. He was a stylist and a hurler to his fingertips. He was a first class striker who needed little or no space in which to turn. He was blessed with speed, stamina and skill. From play and placed balls he was deadly accurate. His anticipation was exceptional and as a consequence he always appeared to be in the right place. But none of this was by accident. He put in hours and hours of practice — striving for perfection in every facet of the game. Above all he was a wonderfully sporting player. Those of us who had not the privilege of seeing him play can however today see a reflection of his hurling genius in the performances of his grandnephew D.J. Carey in the black and amber of Kilkenny.

He played in the three famous finals of 1931 — in the forwards — later he was to become an outstanding half-back. He played on thirteen successive Railway Cup finals and was victorious on four occasions. He won two County titles with Tullaroan. His All Ireland victories number four — in 1932 when Clare went under by one goal — in 1933 when Johnny Dunne's famous goal denied an emerging young and dashing Limerick side — in 1935 when under the masterly generalship of Lory Meagher, firm favourites Limerick lost by one point in a thriller played in a downpour — in 1939 when in thunder and lightning and rain, an up and coming Cork side lost by a last minute point as Jimmy Kelly sealed it for Kilkenny. Paddy also won eight Leinster titles and one National League.

Paddy retired from the inter-county scene in 1942. He died on 8th September, 1971 at the relatively young age of 61.

As a half-back he will always rank with the immortals of the game and in the Centenary team of 1984 he was honoured with the left-half-back position.

Beyond this place of time and tide,
Beyond this hour of woe,
There is a bourn in Paradise,
Where all the hurlers go.
And there in pride they're goaling.
As they race across the sod
To thrill our dead forefathers
On the level lawns of God.

I never saw Nicky Rackard of Killanne and Wexford hurl but I do have memories of him — daring and dashing — strong and sporting. These memories have their origin in the voices of Mícheál O'Hehir and Mícheál O'Muircheartaigh. They go back to the mid forties when as a youngster in Limerick his name used to ring bells of hope in our hearts. You see we were aware that Cork's indian sign on Limerick was beginning to take a deep grip. We used to look around wondering who could conquer

Born: 1922

Cork. In the forties, they were supreme in Munster. Maybe Wexford could do the trick. We became fans of Nicky Rackard and Wexford. Mick Mackey was his idol, hero and inspiration. He set about modelling himself on him and attempted to emulate his style and approach. He could absorb punishment and smile at defeat. He was a sportsman supreme.

Nothing better illustrates this than the closing moments of the 1950 Leinster final against Kilkenny at Nowlan Park. Nicky gained possession and headed goalwards. Paddy 'Diamond' Hayden, the Kilkenny full-back decided that no legimate option was open to him to avert a certain goal so he grounded Nicky with a trip. From the resultant free the 'Rackard Special' was saved. Kilkenny won 3:11 to 2:11. After the final whistle Nicky held forth the hand of

Nicky Rackard (right) poses with his rival Christy Ring.

and friendship to 'The
...s a gesture that typified his
...orting encounters.
...one yard frees were known as
...pecials' and were usually fol-
...the waving of the green flag. We
...ed at his strength in the final against
...ary in 1951 and were sad to see him
... But we felt he would be back. It took
...ttle while — until 1954 in fact. By then
...e had become the great hope of the model
county just as John Kelly the Boy from
Killanne was in another century in a
different field.

He ran riot against Antrim scoring seven
goals and as many points. Cork must surely
fall in the final. But the big Wexfordman
had one of his most frustrating hours on
John Lyons and recorded only one point
from play. The final score was Cork 1:9
Wexford 1:6. Nicky had played centre-
forward for Leinster in 1943 when youth
was on his side. In 1950 he played Railway
Cup hurling and football finals with Leinster but failed in both to Munster and Ulster
respectively. *'Time the subtle thief of
youth'* was now working against him and
the chances of All Ireland success were
receding. But in the late Autumn of his
career the honours came — All Ireland
success against Galway in 1955 — the
crowning glory when Cork fell in 1956.

The apollo-like Nicky had a big heart and
a gregarious personality. He had great
strength but he had a weakness too.
Alcoholism caused him much suffering. He
eventually triumphed over it and crusaded
against it.

'Cúchulainn's Son' is a tribute to Nicky
Rackard, composed by Tom Williams and
sung by McMurrough. From four verses I
have chosen eight lines that appeal to me:

The challenge of an ancient game
Brought glory glory to your name

The hand that held the stick of ash
And the man who led with style and dash

The last parade was sad and slow
The last oration spoken low

An Ash tree toppled when you died
And scattered seeds at random.

He died young — much too young.
But the memory of the gentle giant still
lives with me just as it was in my childhood
days.
So as to get a deeper insight into this great
sportsman, I spoke with his brother Billy.
The following pages reveal to us much
about this hurling giant.

'Nicky was the eldest brother of five boys
— I was the youngest — a gap of eight
years. Contrary to what people may
surmise, I feel that such an age gap can
provide a more objective vision than that
offered to those closer in years.
He was an earlier developer unlike his
brothers. Nicky at seventeen was powerfully built and never appeared to have the
frame of a gangly youth.
Everyone in the Parish and in our little
village felt there was something special
about him. He was blessed with phenome-
nal strength and the feeling was that he was
destined to do something great. When he
took the role on horseback of 1798 hero
John Kelly in the celebratory pageant of
1938, the feeling was that had he been
around in Kelly's time, he too would have
been a well remembered rebel. Although in
1938 Wexford hurling was in the doldrums,
there was still a passionate love of the game
throughout the county and followers were
keeping a hurling weather eye out for any
young man who would show that something above the ordinary. This, Nicky
amply demonstrated by his displays for
Kieran's College, Kilkenny which was one
of the top hurling nurseries in the country.
His performances in the College colours
were more than sufficient to cause a flutter
in the hearts of Wexford hurling followers.
They just could not wait for this young man
to grow up. This he did to their satisfaction
and he gave sparkling performances in his
late teens and early twenties now wearing
his beloved purple and gold colours.
Wexford followers had no doubt that he
was destined for stardom.

228

If those who only saw Nicky as a burly full-forward in the mid-fifties could have witnessed his displays at midfield and centre-forward with a no hope Wexford team against Kilkenny and Dublin during the early and late forties, they would be greatly surprised at not just his hurling ability but also his athleticism. Here was a young man who won long jump and high jump youth titles, a great midfielder, excellent overhead striker and a speedy hitter of any type of ground ball. No stopping and lifting — yes a totally different player to the now burly full-forward. This transformation whilst effective in play saddened a lot of people including myself. No doubt the excessive drinking habits which were not known at the time were taking their effect.

He developed a reluctance to train and his student days in the Dublin Veterinary College were not conducive to keeping peak fitness. Although he lacked his earlier pace, his strength, allied to his fanatical desire, always with minimum frills, to stitch one of his pile drivers in the back of the net, made him a very dangerous forward for any opposition. Now at full-forward and in retrospect only half fit, his scoring achievements would still make him an almost automatic selection on any 15.

One wonders what he would have been like minus a drink problem and fully fit. Here I should mention that to me Nicky possessed a quality that belongs only to the truly great forwards — I'm referring to goal post obsession (yes he was a goal post addict). Let him loose for a split second and he was firing one at them. Great forwards go on the field to be marked, not to mark. Nicky was certainly in this mould. Play him in the back line — never! Preventing forwards from scoring was a far too mundane negative occupation — much more exciting to be the trigger that set a green flag waving — he was truly in the forward mould.

It has been said by many that he used get a lot of hardship playing at full-forward. Anyone who understood the game would know that this was self inflicted. When he lost his speed, he, with a view to getting clear used invite a challenge — which he generally won — with the opponent who hit him being driven back sufficiently to leave a gap for Nicky's assault on goal. He did not relish an opponent who backed away from him or played him technically. He preferred an opponent to give him hardship and challenge.

In spite of all his problems there was one abiding factor of motivation that kept him going. He felt Wexford could at last, with the men he had around him, bring home the McCarthy Cup. As he knew he would be a huge part of it he felt he must do something about himself and his fitness. He opted out of the fast lane and took the pioneer total abstinence pledge. This had the desired effect and although he never regained his earlier athletic figure he was now ensuring that he would be part of that Wexford team which was to bring such glory to the county. For those three years or so, he played brilliantly in the full-forward position and in fact established a scoring record that lasted for years until finally surpassed by the great Eddie Keher. That part of Nicky's life is well documented and it's not my desire to elaborate on it, but I would like to try and give some idea of what sort of person I felt he was.

Nicky, apart from his sporting prowess, came in contact with a lot of people especially through his veterinary practice. I believe it is true to say he was well liked and had a winning way with people. He loved a good party and would light up the room with his broad smile. He adored a sing song and given the right situation he was usually the catalyst for such an event. He had a reasonable singing voice but had a firm belief that the best performer was not necessarily the life of the party. He had a way with people which always ensured that the party had a joyous run.

Horses were a great passion in his life and during his latter years when on the straight and narrow he had noteable success in Point to Points and on major race courses. It has been said that he could have gone to the top as a race horse trainer, but alas as we sadly know, when in his early fifties it

all came to an abrupt end.

Nicky was never particularly concerned about his own property and was also noted for his willingness to help out a financially cramped individual, which usually happened on race courses. He was a soft touch.

Not being concerned about his own property prompts me to tell you this little story. As a teenager he took charge of a horse belonging to my father, which he was to prepare and ride in the local Point to Point. We all went as a family. I being considerably younger, was with my mother at the parade ring, full of family pride. I watched as the riders came out. Suddenly my mother exploded. 'My God I'll kill him when I get him home!' she announced. For his racing colours he was wearing, (need I say without her permission) the inner part of her most prized twin set, which now was considerably stretched. The evidence was conclusive — it was obvious to her that he had rummaged through her private bedroom chest of drawers without her permission and she was not pleased, but that was Nicky. He would get away with it.

The horse gave us all a good run and later on that evening he switched on his broad grin which had the desired effect on his now calm mother.

Nicky's life was to me epitomised in the close-in or 21 yards free. It was all or nothing. Some of his gambling exploits are well remembered. He once pulled off a coup with a horse in Ballinrobe — he had £400 on at 33 to 1. The bet with the help of a lot of his buddies was placed in small amounts across the country in bookie shops. Nothing was on course which as you know kept the odds as desired. Winnings were a tidy £13,000. However, as I once read — horse players don't die rich — and I have reason to believe his losses at a later stage may have put the bookies well in front.

Nicky had a lovely wife and family. He was also the proud owner of a fine farm in North Wexford. It looked that in his late forties he had finally sorted his life out. He was a member of the AA and as we know was doing heroic work for people in all walks of life who had drink problems. Some of the stories that are still coming on stream are quite incredible. You could phone him from Donegal looking for help. He would immediately drop everything to cover any distance at any time to give you that so essential moral uplift.

Everything was going his way. He appeared to be reclaiming lost ground, making up for a lot of mistakes in his life and then it happened.

I met him one day in summer and he was wearing a scarf around his neck. He dismissed my obvious question. His family were curious but again he dismissed everyone's foreboding. He was in fact condemned to death with one year to live. Nobody knew. He still didn't complain and eventually he died in Vincent's — a decimated human being — a victim of that awful scourge we all know so well. In his prime he was 15 stone. He was now 4. The staff in Vincent's said he was the easiest patient they ever had to deal with.

His funeral cortege was akin to a state funeral right down to Bunclody, ample testimony not just to his sporting prowess but mostly to the humanitarian work he had done in the ranks of the AA. He was 53. Flowers from friends he had helped, especially those with drink problems, came from every county in Ireland and the sheer volume of them was an incredible sight. Nicky was finally at peace.'

In 1984 a national poll produced the following centenary team — with Nicky at full-forward.

	Tony Reddin (Tipperary)	
Bobby Rackard (Wexford)	Nick O'Donnell (Wexford)	John Doyle (Tipperary)
Jimmy Finn (Tipperary)	John Keane (Waterford)	Paddy Phelan (Kilkenny)
	Lory Meagher (Kilkenny)	Jack Lynch (Cork)
Christy Ring (Cork)	Mick Mackey (Limerick)	Jimmy Langton (Kilkenny)
Jimmy Doyle (Tipperary)	Nick Rackard (Wexford)	Eddie Keher (Kilkenny)

Christy RING   1940-1963   Glen Rovers & Cork

To live in hearts we leave behind,
is not to die

Born: 1920

He succeeded Limerick's Mick Mackey as the High King of hurling. His reign lasted longer. He was Cork's greatest hurler and there is a school of thought that would rate him the greatest ever. He vies with Mick Mackey for that honour. But in reality it matters not. There is no equation that will ever produce an indisputable answer. They both scaled the heights of Everest in the hurling world.

Many others reached great heights too but fell short of the achievements of the two supremos. Hurling was Christy's whole life. It absorbed his entire thought process. His remarkably high level of fitness the whole year round contributed in no small way to his greatness.

His career is dotted with records and achievements of all kinds. He amassed the incredible record of eighteen Railway Cup medals stretching from 1942 to 1963 inclusive — a feat unlikely ever to be equalled. He had the honour of being the third captain ever to lead his county to three All Ireland successes in 1946, 1953 and 1954. The honour first fell to Mikey Maher of Tipperary before the turn of the century, and later to 'Drug' Walsh of Kilkenny during their golden era of 1904-1913. Christy was also the first hurler to win eight All Ireland medals. Only John Doyle of Tipperary subsequently equalled that. As a

Christy Ring (centre) with two other greats, Johnny Ryan, Tipp (left) and Mick Mackey, Limerick (right).

hurler Christy was always supremely confident — dedicated and skillful — fanatical and intense — powered with a burning passion — a never ending threat to all defenders.

As a person he could be very shy and reserved — remote and retiring — but as a friend his loyalty and generosity knew no limits.

He played his first game for his native Cork in a league match against Kilkenny in 1939. His last game with Cork was in 1962 and with Munster in 1963. When he died on 2nd March, 1979 at the relatively young age of 58 the hurling world was stunned.
'Brón ar an mbás ni féidir a shéanadh Leagann se úr is críon le chéile'.

At his graveside many a former friend and foe shed a silent tear and no doubt recalled again some dazzling deeds of yore.

Perhaps, his dramatic goal after a fine solo run in the closing stages of the replayed Munster final of 1944 against Limerick that denied the Shannonsiders another draw.

Or his solo run coming up to halftime in the All Ireland final against Kilkenny in 1946 that split their defence and finished with the ball in the net

Or Limerick two goals clear in the last quarter of the Munster final of 1956 and looking good as Christy was getting no freedom from Donal Broderick — and then it happened — three goals and one point in less than ten minutes

Or that day in November 1959 — aged 39 — when he scored six goals and four points against Wexford at the Athletic Grounds in Cork

Or his three goals in the last quarter in the county semi-final of 1962 against Imokilly — aged 42 — that paved the way to victory.

Or — or — or !

I called on his brother Willie John at Cloyne. They had a very close relationship and this is what he had to say about a brother he idolised.

'Christy started hurling at a very early age. The Cloyne hurling pitch was located behind the house where he lived. He always took his training very seriously and I spent

hours daily training and advising him. It was no problem to him to spend four or five hours at a time in the hurling field. This was not just pucking around the field. It was first time pulling on the ground — doubling on the ball in the air — sideline cuts — frees and anything else he felt needed attention. Relaxing played no part in Christy's mind while training and he would always practise from both the left and the right.

He played juvenile with Cloyne from an early age and while playing these matches his ability and skills were recognised by many. Throughout his life he was a non-smoker and a non-drinker and this together with his policy of keeping fit, greatly helped his performances.

From the moment he put on his Cork jersey in 1937 as a sub in the minor All Ireland final in Killarney, he was totally committed to the Cork jersey — there were no half measures. He played as hard in a tournament game as in an All Ireland final.

He always felt saddened when hurlers he played with or against retired from the game. A deep sadness used descend on him when the greats passed away and if at all possible he would be in attendance at the funerals.

He was Cork's freetaker throughout his career and there was no such thing as semi-penalties in his day. Six players lined the goalmouth as he prepared to send a bullet-like shot. When he went for a goal I can never recall him missing.

During his career he played in all six forward positions and also played at centre-field. He won a minor All Ireland at half-back in 1938 and came down that day to take a 21 yards free which he slammed to the net. He didn't indulge in too much solo running and he always took the view that a solo run should finish up with a score.

Christy's responses to comments and situations revealed a mental sharpness. One day while playing for Cork he broke away from his opponent and scored a goal. On his way back to his position he made his jubilation clear to his opponent. His opponent warned him about the jubilation and said he could have blown his head off.

Christy told him it wouldn't have mattered — he'd have scored the goal anyway. He was asked one day what he thought of a player and whether he thought he was quick on the ball or not — his reply was that he had seen quicker. As he advanced in years a priest came up to him and complimented him on a great game he had played the previous year and enquired as to when he was going to give it up. Christy said when I know all about it — then I'll give it up. He was asked one day what was the hardest man to be on and his answer was the man that wouldn't play the ball.

Before a big match he would never practise taking a free and when asked why not his reply was when the ball is thrown in that's the time I must put them over — practice is too late now. When Christy was captain he would make his own switches on the field. I only saw two others do that — Eudi Coughlan of Cork and Mick Mackey of Limerick.

He had a heart of gold. He regularly visited patients in hospital. He was a religious man and Mass played a big part in his life — he attended every morning if possible. He listened to the daily problems of people and would personally take the matter to the local TD and wouldn't take no for an answer. These people cried when he died.'

Willie John then showed me an article on Christy written by a friend Fr Bernie Cotter SMA who was a teammate in the late fifties. Here is an extract which deals in considerable detail with the hurling skills of Christy. 'A golfer plays a variety of shots with a selection of different clubs. Ring had an enormous repertoire of strokes: the strong forearm drive at goal, travelling with torpedo-like trajectory; the drop puck; the sideline cut — often of prodigious length; the overhead flick; the short-arm unhookable, stabbing shot putting over points from a ruck; the lethal knee-high double; the first time pull along the carpet spraying passes to the left or right corner from the centre-forward position; the open shouldered, full-blooded swing on the dropping ball; the over-hand lob from the wing, arching with deadly precision, like a lofted bowl to the edge of the square. All of these were executed off either hand with the one hurley, but with a virtuosity which defied the limitations of the ash-stick.'

His name lives in hurling lore and Cork has honoured him by naming a bridge across the Lee — 'The Christy Ring Bridge'. And a bronze statue honours him in a special way in his native Cloyne.

This is what the sculptor Yann Goulet RHA said, 'When I started to think of designing a memorial to Christy Ring, I kept in mind that the bronze statue 9 foot high will stand in his native town for hundreds and hundreds of years, an eternal and everlasting tribute to this great hurler.

The Christy Ring, whose memory I will perpetuate in bronze, will be the perfect athlete that he was in his youth, strong, but elegant like the Appollos of the Greek Mythology or Michael Angelo's David, men never marked by the passing of time.

In Christy Ring we had the typification of an ideal Irish athlete and it is as such that he should be remembered by the future generations. His determination, the pride for the game he loved, his nobility will be the main characteristics that I will try to depict, not forgetting his great physical strength allied with the agility and delicate balance of movement of a ballet dancer.'

Born: 1943

66

Where I came from, to play hurling was the most natural thing. It was the topic at school, work, the creamery, and above all after last Mass on Sunday when many a heated argument was commonplace. My father was a big influence and gave on-going encouragement — so also was school teacher, Clareman Tom Nealon. However, for me it was local neighbour Jimmy Henzey who did most and played a big part in any success the game gave to me. Having said that I'll always believe the single biggest influence on the youth of this country was one Mícheál O'Hehir. It was he that turned the Croke Park light in all our little hearts and filled us with an ambition that would sustain and remain. We all owe him a huge debt of gratitude. Long may it be the great game it is for in my view our nation would be the poorer without it.

Mick Roche. **99**

Down the years Tipperary has produced some great centre-half-backs. Working up from the thirties you had John Maher, Pat Stakelum and Tony

Wall. Each was a master centre-back — each had a different style. Then came Mick Roche. He was in their class — he too was different — and his versatility gave him added value. Despite outstanding displays at centre-half-back he hated playing there. But more about that later on.

His interest in hurling began at a very early age and was actively encouraged by his father Dan who adored the game and won a junior All Ireland with Tipperary in the twenties. 'My father was the driving force. I can remember him in the winter nights — he was a carpenter by trade — knee deep in shavings in the kitchen making hurleys for us. My mother didn't want us to play at all. She wanted us to do our homework. Then my father would push back the kitchen table to throw in the ball. I don't know how we didn't drive our mother demented.'

His earliest memory centres around a Dublin/Wexford Leinster championship game at Nowlan Park — 'Bill Walsh with a bandage on his head was the Dublin star. I remember the Wexford team in the parade — so many of them so big — blondie Ned Wheeler and the Rackards and Nick O'Donnell and Padge Kehoe. They must have been the physically biggest team ever to line out for any county.' He was in Thurles in 1956 for the Cork/Limerick final. 'I was sitting on the sleepers on the sideline near the town goal. Ring was being held scoreless by Donal Broderick. Time was running out for Cork. Then he seemed to move out off Broderick — and then he got three goals. No one else could have saved the day. "Sweeper" Ryan was umpire. He was a bit slow going for the flag for what I think was the second goal. Ring ran in — grabbed the flag — threw it over the bar and said put up the thing. I remember as well Willie John Daly's hurling at centre-back on Dermot Kelly that day. It was aggressive — intimidation at its best.'

He had his heroes too in those youthful years — 'Philly Grimes of Waterford who was a most complete player. I saw lots of clashes between Mount Sion and Erin's Own. Frankie Walsh of Waterford travelling like lightning down the wing and doubling first time on the ball on the run. Ollie Walsh in a game against Wexford at Walsh Park, Waterford in 1956 on a most miserable evening -with a wet ball — and saves that had to be seen to be believed. Barney Moylan of Offaly was another player I loved to watch.' Looking back now over his era he singles out Eddie Keher and Jimmy Doyle as being on a plain apart — 'Players who possessed an innateness that could make a full chance out of a quarter chance.' He laments the enforced early departure of Pat Hartigan from the hurling scene 'because the game needed players of his skill and character.'

The River Suir divides Carrick-on-Suir and Mick grew up on the 'Waterford' side in the parish of Carrickbeg. Even though geographically in Tipperary they played in the Waterford championship. This is where Mick won his first medal — a Waterford county minor title in 1959 — a victory and a medal that is still very special. He got a trial in the half-forward line for Waterford minors in 1960 and incredibly didn't make the team. But even if he did, it is doubtful if he would have played for Waterford. 'My father took over then. He had been a founding member of Carrick Davins and he encouraged me to join his club.'

Mick obliged and in 1961 played with a Tipperary minor team that lost to Kilkenny in the final. From then on for over a dozen years hurling followers were treated to all that was best in hurling from the stick and person of Mick Roche — natural ability, anticipation, delightful stick work, confidence, foresight and sportsmanship. In 1963 he won an intermediate title. And yet it was a title that might have eluded him but for the intervention of intermediate trainer Jim Stapleton. It was half time in the senior Munster final at Limerick between Waterford and Tipperary. Tipperary were in trouble. Mick was a sub and as Paddy Leahy passed Mick he told him get ready for the second half. 'I took off my short coat — no track suit in those days — delighted to be going on. As the team came back onto the field I prepared to join them and was grabbed by the shoulder by Jim Stapleton. Who told you to play — you'll ruin the intermediate team he said to me and with that frogmarched me off. At the time it was a humiliating moment.'

In 1964 as well as winning an under 21 title he took his place at midfield — where he was to give majestic and memorable displays on a Tipperary combination that was one of the finest the hurling world has seen — strong in defence, superb at midfield, deadly in attack. He recalled the training sessions they used have in Thurles. 'We used to play ten-a-side games — the hurling was great — the sessions were treated like All Ireland finals. You had to be dedicated because there were so many good players looking for places. I remember the clashes between Tony Wall and Larry Kiely — two army men — no mercy. And then there was Theo English at midfield. To me Theo was a father figure. I looked up to him. Not since the days of Tom & Willie Wall of Carrick did a South Tipp man play with Tipp. Theo who was there since the fifties paved the way for the likes of Babs Keating and myself. Coming to train he would say to me — listen here Mick if you think you are going to get fit up here you are mistaken. You must train at home. Have the ground work done. Only the finishing off is done up here.' Mick found no difficulty with this. He had spent all the spare time of his youth practising hurling skills. He even remembered getting up at six in the morning to train before going to work — and enjoying it. It was the result of a code of discipline learned from Jim Henzey in his juvenile and minor days — an ex-army man and neighbour with a great knowledge and passion for the game. 'If he had asked us to climb a mountain we would do it.'

In 1967 Tony Wall retired after the All Ireland final and Mick became a centre-back by default. 'We met Kilkenny in an Oireachtas game in Thurles. The team was only finalised in the dressingroom. Paddy Kenny, a senior selector and a founding father of Carrick Davins, who was a big influence on my hurling career, asked me to play at centre-back. I told him I hadn't a clue about the position. 'We are stuck. Stop the gap for today'. he said. 'I got such a roasting from Claus Dunne — I think he scored about nine points — that I took a dislike to the position and it remained with me till I retired. I never again got playing for Tipp in my favourite position of mid-field. I loved midfield. You had lots of options — it was less onerous than in defence — you could go where you liked — what you needed was stamina.' From 1967 onwards he was Tipp's centre-back and those who saw his displays in 1968 against Wexford in the All Ireland final and in 1971 against Limerick in Killarney in the Munster final, will wonder how displays of such splendour could fail to erase from his mind his dislike of the position.

You had an unlucky captaincy! 'I was a magpie.' He left it at that. He won every honour in the game including an All Star at centre-back in 1971, the year of inception. But the honour and glory of leading Tipperary to All Ireland victory eluded him twice. In 1967 Kilkenny ended a forty five year wait when they toppled Tipperary 3:8 to 2:7. The following year a resurgent Wexford denied him by two points 5:8 to 3:12. In 1968 some saw him as Man of the Match in the final and Hurler of the Year overall but when it came to the Texaco Award the sports editors gave the nod to Dan Quigley of Wexford. Incidentally Mick doesn't agree with Man of the Match awards and such things, taking the view that it takes fifteen players to win a game. He wouldn't object however to the hurlers themselves nominating a player of the year.

For the greatest moment — the most memorable game and victory — the game he would love to play all over again — he nominated the Munster final of 1971 against Limerick in Killarney. All the drama and tension and controversy and splendour and swaying fortunes were packed into that eighty minutes. Down two goals at half time they finished the second half with John Flanagan sending over the forty first score of the game from far out for a one point victory almost on the call of time to make the scoreboard read Tipperary 4:16 Limerick 3:18.

The only disappointment of significance was for a club team mate Steve Cleary.

'There were too many good times to be disappointed, especially when I think of the number of great players who didn't win much. Steve was a long serving club member who had won no award. He was the kind of dedicated clubman who would line out even if he had two broken legs. We reached the county final of 1965 and met Thurles Sarsfields — probably the best team in the land at the time. It would be Steve's last game before retiring. With time up scores were level and Steve got posses-sion — went for the winning point — only to see the ball shave agonisingly wide of the post. We lost the replay. My heart bled for him. Victory would have been better than twenty All Irelands to him.'

Mick retired at 31. There was more left in him. 'But I wasn't enjoying training any-more. I was losing the zest for the game. In my job I was travelling sixty thousand miles a year. Between that and playing tournament games and championship games it wore you down. Anyway I didn't enjoy playing in the mud and rain of winter. I felt 'twas time to go'.

Nowadays Mick looks forward to his social meetings with Johnny Ryan Tipperary defender of the thirties and forties. Over a drink Johnny reminisces about bygone days and 'battles long ago'. And he talks about times and social conditions that are fading memories. He talks with a love and a passion and an appreciation of the great game and the men who played it. Mick doesn't have words to describe Johnny's passion for the game and his vivid recollections. That's why he's enraptured. 'Johnny Ryan is special. I'm lucky to have known him. I look forward to meeting him. Occasionally I hanker for Carrick but while Johnny is alive I'm de-lighted to be here in Horse & Jockey.'

Born: 1882

Jack Rochford was a household name in the early glory days of Kilkenny hurling.

He was born on 24 April, 1882 and baptised in Freshford Church on 26 April, 1882. His father was a journeyman tailor — later to become a master tailor. Jack followed in his footsteps.

It isn't widely realised that the GAA was twenty years old before Kilkenny won their first All Ireland title in 1904. It heralded a golden era.

Jack was a key figure in that golden era and reaped a rich harvest of honours winning seven All Ireland medals between the years 1904 and 1913.

Jack was an automatic choice for the fullback berth and throughout his career filled it with great distinction. His fame spread all over the land. Each passing year added to his stature.

In the 1904 final his many fine clearances were a feature of the one point victory over Cork. He was to the fore again in the 1907 final — one of the greatest — played at Dungarvan on 21st June, 1908 — twenty seven scores — changing fortunes — sparkling hurling — won with the last puck of the game, when Jimmy Kelly pointed following a double on a dropping ball delivered by the Piltown star John Anthony.

He was rock-like in the 1909 final against Tipperary when Kilkenny scored 4:6 and Tipperary were held goalless — scoring twelve points. In 1912 and 1913 against Cork and Tipperary respectively he rose to heroic heights in a superb Kilkenny defence. The Noresiders were back again in 1916 to contest the final. Jack disagreed with the team selection — refused to play — and it is said threw his hurley and togs into the River Liffey in disgust.

In the ten year span from 1904-1913 Kilkenny's remarkable run of victories created a hurling record that has never since been equalled.

It was the era that made the names of Tullaroan and Mooncoin famous. For those were the days when parish pride and glory often took precedence over county and on occasions province.

Six of the titles were won with the seventeen aside lineout and in 1913 Jack won his seventh medal in the first fifteen aside championship.

In 1911 after a venue dispute Kilkenny got a walkover from Limerick — the only one in the history of the game.

Four of the All Ireland victories were over Cork teams. Indeed, it would seem that Kilkenny established their hoodoo over the rebel county in those early days.

The 1905 title was initially won by Cork on the score 5:10 to 3:14 but following an objection by Kilkenny a replay was ordered and Kilkenny won well 7:7 to 2:9. — the only occasion such a circumstance arose at All Ireland final level.

In 1904, 1907 and 1912 the titles were won by a margin of just one point — the scores reading 1:9 to 1:8, 3:12 to 4:8 and 2:1 to 1:3 respectively.

Many of his contemporaries are still household names in the hurling world —

Sim Walton, The Doyles, The Graces, John T. Power, John Anthony, Dan Kennedy and Matt Gargan, to mention but a few.

Jack was a staunch full-back — oozed confidence and had an outgoing personality.

Many stories surround his career such as the day in 1907 against Offaly when he told his goalkeeper John T. Power of Piltown that he would have to have two drinks before the game or else he would be no good at hurling. And then there is the story of those who used to rise him by telling him that he wasn't really that great a full-back because he always met bad full-forwards. But Jack's reply was a classic. 'I was great' he used to say. 'I met very good full-forwards — I made them look bad.'

Jack was widely mourned when he died.

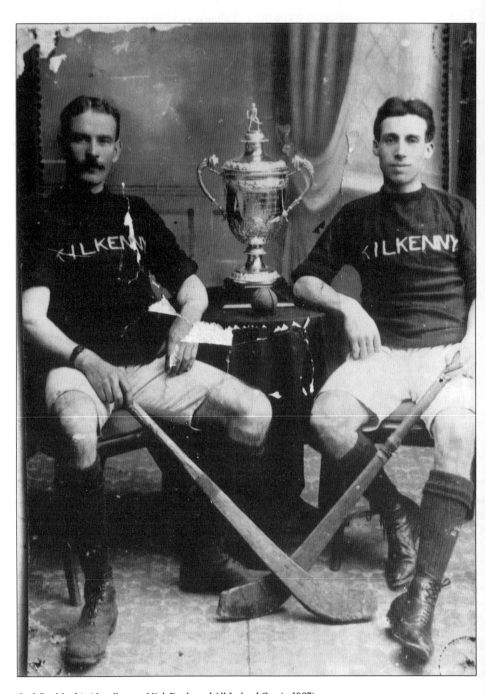

Jack Rochford (with colleague Mick Doyle and All Ireland Cup in 1907).

240

P. Connor of Collinstown, Leixlip expressed his feelings in verse. I have chosen two of the nine stanzas.

His heart was stout, his mind was quick,
And hurling cleanly all the way,
A sportsman on and off the field,
Kilkenny weeps for him today.
It was in defence he had no peer,
He to the ball was never led,
Like lightning flash he'd spring to clear,
Now all is hush, for Jack is dead.
Consistency to him was glued
In every game I saw him play,
He shone out like Aladdin's lamp
We've never known him fade away.
He'd finish fresh the hardest hour
When staying powers from some had fled,
His lion heart has ceased to beat,
Yes, all is hush, for Jack is dead

I went in search of a more intimate picture of Jack and got it through his youngest daughter Marie. Here is how she affectionately remembers her father.

'When asked if I would like to write down my memories of my father for *Hurling Giants* I felt honoured and delighted mainly for his sake and also because somebody remembered him. Dad was born in 1882 and passed away in 1953. So for a whole week I went back in my mind more than half a century and I recalled so many happy memories of him that I felt I had returned to a time that is long since gone and it was a nostalgic, albeit at times a sad experience.

My father was about 50 years old when I was born. I was the last and therefore the youngest of the family. I was his favourite child and he always called me "Little Ma". I only knew him for a short twenty years and I loved him very much. I am so glad that I was able to look after him in his final years when his health began to fail. However, I remember him best as a fine man, over six feet tall, about twelve stone weight, very athletic-looking, dark-haired and sallow-skinned. He always sported a small moustache. He was distant with other people but the two of us got on very well.

He talked to me about everything and he was my best friend.

I didn't know for a long time how great a hurler he was until I noticed getting into the matches free of charge and I always got up on the stand. To me he was very kind — he never forgot my birthday. He was always well dressed; of course he was a qualified tailor as was his father before him.

Dad told me that the Rochfords came to Ireland with Strongbow (c. 1170) and were granted land in the province of Meath. In those days they were called de Rochfort and so Rochfort Bridge Co Westmeath was their territory. Around 1690 the Rochfords came to Three Castles Co Kilkenny and on 24th April, 1882 my father was born — the same year as Eamon de Valera. Jack grew up there — hurled with Tullaroan as a boy and later with others formed a senior club in Three Castles.

As time went by I gathered from him and from others that he was a man of many talents. He was a graceful dancer and an accomplished concertina player. Not alone was he a great hurler, he also excelled at cricket, tennis and golf. Lady Desart held him in high esteem and he travelled regularly to Cork to play cricket for her team. At one stage he was on his way to America but she actually burned his ticket in order to keep him in Kilkenny.

Before I talk about his hurling years I'd like to say he was an all round sportsman, anti-ban and believed that sport should be played only for the love of it. To him each game had its own special skill and players should develop the necessary skills and use them to benefit the game. He admired sportsmanship, style, skill and artistry, but he had no time for dirty play. He felt that the GAA ban polarised the situation in not being able to have the freedom to play all games.

He won seven All Ireland medals playing at full-back for Kilkenny and felt honoured in his time to be one of the four Kilkenny players to have won seven All Irelands. The others were Drug Walsh, Dick Doyle and Sim Walton and he considered them great. I spent many summer holidays with the

Doyles of Mooncoin, the Walshs and the Anthonys of Piltown. He held John Anthony in such high regard that he asked me to name my first son John Anthony Butler. Of course I granted his wish. As the years went by he admired the following hurlers for their skills, sportsmanship, artistry and style — Lory Meagher, Paddy Phelan, Mick Mackey, Christy Ring and Nicky Rackard.

He brought me everywhere to matches both big and small. I met Mícheál O'Hehir on his only broadcast from Nowlan Park. I also met many of the great hurlers of the forties and fifties including those previously mentioned. Terry Leahy, scorer of the winning point in 1947 wrote regularly to my father when he went to New York and always said there was no gold in the streets of New York.

I accompanied my father on a visit to the "Diamond" Hayden who was in hospital. My father fell against the railings on the way into St.Luke's and consequently two great Kilkenny full-backs ended up in hospital together.

He often spoke of the early days when he was a trainer, selector and general nurse to the team. He also liked to recall training the boys in Artane to hurl during his time in Dublin. I remember too the many requiems held in our house when Kilkenny lost a match. He loved to go to juvenile matches or such like or to throw in the ball. "They are the future greats," he would say.

My Dad was a very religious man. He went to Mass every morning and he always wore his scapulars. I have them still. That might explain why he gave away most if not all his All Ireland medals to priests who went abroad. One of those medals he gave to Archbishop McGrath and that medal is the top of a tabernacle key somewhere in Australia.

Dr Peter Birch, late Bishop of Ossory said to Dad he felt honoured to have sat in the same desk as he did years previously in Clinstown NS.

A few years before he died a group of Americans with Kilkenny and Three Castle connections asked him to bring them on a tour of his childhood places. He brought them to Three Castles, Tulla and up the old road to Tullaroan. It was about ten miles. "Many a time we walked that journey to play a match," said Dad. The Americans were awe-struck and dumbfounded. "The men of those days were made of great stuff. They were great men," he continued.

He missed two All Irelands the last one being 1953 and it was evident that he was failing. I was with him most of that time and looked after him bringing him the few things he liked. He told me I had a heart of gold but I knew where that gold came from. He passed away on 17th October, 1953.

Next day Carbery (P.D.Mehigan) sports correspondent for the *Irish Times*, both a contemporary and great admirer of Dad, wrote about him and the sports page had a black border around it.

Hurlers, friends, and it seemed to me all Kilkenny, came first to St Canice's Church for the funeral and again the next day as the coffin with a black and amber jersey on top made its final journey back to his native Three Castles where he was laid to rest in Tulla graveyard longside his father and mother.

I never saw such a huge crowd at a funeral and burial.

I'm glad and also sad to have brought back all the happy memories. I always wear the two handmade gold rings that Dad gave me. They were his mother's engagement and wedding rings. Those along with many old photographs are constant reminders to me of someone very dear and very special — my father — Jack Rochford.'

The name Tom Semple will always be associated with hurling and Old Thurles Blues. He led them to All Ireland wins in 1906 and 1908 having earlier won his first All Ireland medal in 1900. He captained them to county successes in 1904, 1906, 1907, 1908, 1909 and 1911. He ranks among the great wing-forwards the game has known. He used to say that the key attributes required to be a successful hurler were skill, speed and speed of action on the ball.

Standing six foot three, he has been described as a born leader — a man that players and colleagues respected and responded to. 'Carbery' described him as 'a deer of a man and a glorious striker of the ball.'

Born: c.1880

What is your fear boys whilst Semple is with you,
That gallant old captain who leads in the fray?
Why should you doubt when you think of the past, boys?
That one word 'Dungourney' ought all trouble allay

These stirring lines were penned after a famous victory in Tipperary town in the Munster final of 1909 over Dungourney of Cork led by the renowned Jim Kelliher. Even though Thurles Blues were All Ireland champions Dungourney were favourites and confirmed this rating by leading 1:6 to 1:2 at halftime.

But Semple spoke at the break. His message echoed the ancient Gaelic warcry — Beir bua agus Beannacht. And the second half brought forth from his men reserves of courage and effort and fury — and victory in an epic contest on the score Tipperary 2:10 Cork 2:6. Tom led by example and scored the goal that put Thurles Blues and Tipperary into the lead and on the road to victory.

After his playing days he became a very able administrator. He added to his reputation for leadership and administrative ability in 1926 when he personally planned and oversaw the stewarding arrangements for two epic Cork/Tipperary encounters after a first game had to be abandoned due to overcrowding that led to encroachment onto the pitch.

He died in 1943.

It is fitting indeed that the wonderful stadium in Thurles — a stadium that has probably seen more great hurling games than any other arena — should in 1968 have been named after the legendary Tom who was a member of the first working committee set up to develop it into a proper GAA field in the early years of the century.

Surrounded by Offaly men Mark Corrigan, Brendan Birmingham and Johnny Flaherty, Skehan defies the odds and clears.

Born: 1944

"

Bennettsbridge when I was growing up was a very small parish with a small population but with one of the best club hurling teams in Ireland. Hurling was a must for all young lads growing up there.

I remember that great team of the 50s and 60s training every night of the week and Sunday mornings. The hurling field would be black with players — and how things have changed — nowadays, you would be lucky if you could get players or club teams to go to the local hurling pitch to train two nights a week.

As a young lad I used to go to the hurling field every evening in the summer and watch the team training and hope to get a few pucks of the ball or maybe if they were playing a game of backs and forwards you might get the job of pucking the ball in to them. When there would be too many players for backs and forwards they would play full length of the pitch so if you were pucking the ball in to the backs and forwards at the time you would have to go on the other goal. That's really how I started to play on goal.

The main aim for every young lad living in Bennettsbridge at that time was to play for the local team and wear the green and gold jersey. Bennettsbridge at that time was a household name in hurling circles and used to play in matches all over Ireland. When you established yourself on the Bridge team your next aim was to wear the black and amber.

At that time in Bennettsbridge, and I suppose it was no different in any other small country parish, there wasn't a lot for young people to do in the summer evenings only to play some sort of sport. With hurling so strong in our parish the thing to do was to play the game of hurling. Parish community spirit and loyalty to the club was of a very high standard. They had a great following at all times and the excitement around important matches and indeed championship matches was very

high. Bennettsbridge at that time were winning so much outside and inside the county that every team they played were anxious to beat them.

I started playing with Bennettsbridge on the under 16 team when I was 13 years old and played minor club at 14. I played on all club teams from there on. I played senior at 16 and won my first senior county championship in 1962. In 1962 I played minor for Kilkenny and won the All Ireland that same year. In 1963 I was a sub to goalkeeper Ollie Walsh on the Kilkenny team that won the senior All Ireland.

I played and captained the 1972 Kilkenny winning team. It was my first senior All Ireland to play in and to captain it was a bonus. After that I played with the county until April 1985 when I retired.

In those years I won nine All Ireland senior titles, eleven Leinster titles, four Oireachtas, three leagues and one minor — also six county titles, seven All Stars, four B & I awards, one Texaco award, two Man of the Match awards in the 1972 and 1982 All Irelands, several Sport Star of the Week awards and many others. During my playing days I made friends in all the counties we played and on trips to USA and Railway Cup matches.

To be good at any sport you must train hard and be very dedicated. I have a lot to be grateful for, for the GAA and enjoyed every minute of it.

"

Noel Skehan

The love for the game lingers on. This year (1993) he undertook the incredible workload of managing the Thomastown intermediate team which only fell at the final hurdle after a campaign that lasted eight months — the county junior team that reached the All Ireland final where it failed to Clare — the Leinster

Railway cup team which he guided to success.

He was reared in an atmosphere in the Parish of Bennettsbridge that lived and breathed hurling. It was much easier to be absorbed into the game than to escape from it. There were lots of heroes to look up to and to emulate. Among them was his uncle Dan Kennedy who gave many sterling displays for Kilkenny in the forties.

Noel won a minor All Ireland with Kilkenny in 1962. Between then and the Spring of 1985 when he retired he won trophies and awards on a regular basis. He togged out for eleven All Ireland senior finals — the first in 1963 — the last in 1983. He missed out in the finals of 1964 and 1966 due to a neck injury. He was sub goalie to his cousin Ollie Walsh on four occasions — played in seven finals and won six. His brilliance is reflected in seven All Star awards — a figure that has yet to be exceeded.

He belongs to the top bracket of goalkeepers and ranks with the greatest since the foundation of the GAA. When he stood on the goal line and looked out at the opposing team he never feared any forward or forward line. He had supreme confidence in his own ability to deal with anything that came his way.

His backs knew that too and it added a further dimension to their own individual performances. His dazzling brilliance was on many occasions worth a kings ransom to Kilkenny. So often it was the difference between victory and defeat in close finishes and evenly contested — and sometimes not so evenly contested — games outfield.

He played 'a little handball' and a great deal of squash — a game at which he excelled and reached inter-provincial standard. His commitment and dedication to the game of hurling was total. It was a case of practice, practice, practice and still more practice. This together with his squash playing all added up to a lynx-eyed goalkeeper of cat-like agility, allied to superb anticipation and concentration. Often indeed, did he break the heart and spirit of opposing forward lines. He could

be venturesome too. In the All Ireland final of 1973 against Limerick he sallied forth from goal in the second half and soloed onwards to midfield. Limerick folk worried that he was about to launch a successful attack. Kilkenny supporters feared that a swift counter attack would find their net unguarded. Neither materialised.

He played in the days when backs held out the forwards 'and a lot of fouling went on and the goalkeeper could be heavily tackled and "bet" into the net.' He also played when the rule changes eliminated the third man tackle and gave much more protection to the goalkeeper. 'It gave a fairer crack of the whip to the forwards too. I was glad to see the handpass goal done away with.' One of Noel's pet aversions is the taking of the penalty whereby the taker runs up to the ball — throws it as far ahead as he can and then strikes from well within the 21 yards line. 'The thing kills me — I can't understand it. The ball should be struck from a standing position on the 21 yards line. The key thing is where the ball is struck from. After all in soccer and gaelic the penalty has to be struck from where the ball is placed. If the goalie steps outside the square when pucking out he is penalised'. Noel sees this as an unfair inconsistency. He would also like to see a system introduced that would measure the standard of performance of referees, linesmen and umpires — and he feels that umpires should have a far greater involvement in the game.

In a career that spanned three decades there were many highlights. Noel has chosen three. 'The greatest team performance I ever played in was the Leinster final of 1973 when we beat Wexford by ten points in a high scoring game. Generally in any game a few players are off form but on that day everyone was on song. It was the greatest team display I have ever seen.'

He has very special memories of the 1972 All Ireland final. 'I was captain that day. It was the first All Ireland final I took part in. About mid-way through the second half Con Roche sent in a ball from about ninety yards. I looked up and watched it as it sailed over my goal at the Canal end. I think it left us trailing by eight points. I felt that was it. I felt very downhearted. I just grabbed the ball and pucked it out with a feeling of complete indifference as to where it was going or how far it was going. Around that time Keher was brought out from the corner to the wing and Martin Coogan came on at right-full-back. In less than fifteen minutes we were in the lead and the next thing is I am going up on the Hogan Stand to collect the cup having won by seven points.' Noel doesn't have any words to describe the change in his feelings from the nadir of despondency he encountered as Con Roche's point sailed over the bar to the zenith of esctasy that engulfed his entire being as he headed to collect the McCarthy Cup.

Noel's third memory is the 1982 All Ireland final with Cork again the opponents. 'We went into that final as complete underdogs — no one gave us a chance — and we won by such a fine score 3:18 to 1:13 — unbelievable. I was on my game that day.' Well he certainly was. Cork lay seige to the Kilkenny goal — particularly in the second half. Time and time again they sought goals with points there for the taking. They sprayed shots from all angles. But Skehan mocked their efforts with wonderful goalkeeping. He was everything a last line of defence should be — a citadel, a fortress, a castle, an inspiration. Aptly indeed do the following lines from *Macbeth* describe his superb performance that day:

'Our castle's strength
Will laugh a siege to scorn'.

Kilkenny had so many outstanding men in the two decades Noel spent with the team that he decided to select his team entirely from the men he played against.

	Noel Skehan (Kilkenny)	
Brian Murphy (Cork)	Pat Hartigan (Limerick)	Teddy O'Connor (Wexford)
Tom Cashman (Cork)	Mick Jacob (Wexford)	Iggy Clarke (Galway)
	John Connolly (Galway) Gerald McCarthy (Cork)	
Jimmy Doyle (Tipperary)	Ray Cummins (Cork)	Eamon Cregan (Limerick)
Charlie McCarthy (Cork)	Tony Doran (Wexford)	Jimmy Barry-Murphy (Cork)

JIM STAPLETON of Thurles, Co Tipperary, had the honour of being the first All Ireland senior hurling winning captain, when he led Tipperary to victory in the 1887 Championship. See above pages 11-13.

Born: 1919

be to play the game for the love of the game and to play a sporting game. As the years go by, the memories linger on and are more important than the medals. If I had a special wish it would be to see my native Wexford win either a senior hurling or senior football title — long overdue.

Samuel Thorpe 99

66

If I could have my life all over again I would still want to play soccer and football but most of all that great game of hurling and relive those great days.

I saw the great Limerick team of the 30's and early 40's. Mick Mackey was the greatest hurler I ever saw. I also saw that great Cork four in a row team. Men on that team that I admired were — Willie Campbell — a beautiful hurler — also Alan Lotty, Jack Lynch, Jim Young and Christy Ring.

I regret that I missed the glory days of Wexford hurling. It would be a special honour to have been part of the team that brought home the McCarthy Cup to the Slaneyside. My advice to the youth would

Wexford in the 40's and 50's produced a remarkable number of dual players who performed with distinction at the highest level in both hurling and football.

One of those was Sam 'Wilkie' Thorpe. But mark him down as a triple performer because he also played soccer with distinction. He joined the Irish Army in 1938 and was part of a group that was posted to Spike Island after the British Evacuation on 11th July, 1938. He remained on in Co Cork until 1945. It was during this time that his soccer talents came to the surface. He played League of Ireland football with Cork United in 1943/44 and he had the honour of being presented with his FAI Junior Cup Medal by Oscar Traynor when the Spike Island Army team beat Drogheda United in the final in 1944. ' Wilkie' who has a great sense of humour added that 'it was of course a great honour for Oscar Traynor too.'

He got his first taste of top class competition in 1937 when he played in the All Ireland minor football final for Wexford against Cavan — victory went to the men of Breffni.

'Wilkie' told me that despite his soccer fame — probably not as widely reported then as it would be now — he was never suspended although he did have one close call. That was in 1945 when Slaney Harriers of Enniscorthy played Galbally Farmers in the Junior Football final in

Wexford Park. An objection was lodged on the grounds that he had played soccer with Cork United. The Cork County Board was written to and word came back as follows — 'There was a Thorpe here who played soccer with Cork but we don't know what Thorpe it was.' With insufficient proof, the objection failed.

'Wilkie' played his first senior hurling game for Wexford against Waterford at New Ross in 1945. He played his second last Leinster final against Dublin in Nowlan Park in 1952. It was a game that the hurling world expected Wexford to win after their great showing in 1951. But Wexford were shocked by Dublin and when Jim Prior the Dublin captain had received the Leinster Cup, he remarked to 'Wilkie' that three of the Dublin panel hadn't bothered to travel, having said 'there isn't a team in Ireland that would beat that Wexford team today.'

I first heard of 'Wilkie' Thorpe when I listened to the 1950 Leinster final between Wexford and Kilkenny in Cleary's Pub in Herbertstown. I was taken that day by the style of the Wexford men. I was captivated by the display of Sam 'Wilkie' Thorpe. His name caught my fancy. There was a ring of chivalry about it — it matched his hurling.

The autumn of his hurling career had set in when his native Wexford came to life as a hurling force. Yet he left his mark. He had the ideal temperament for the big occasion. It was as if he could take it in his stride. His philosophy was good — 'it never bothered me who I was playing on — I was probably the fittest man in Co Wexford — never heard of hamstrings or torn ligaments in my day — I was always reading the game and I always kept my eye on the ball even when the play was far away from me. I was always trying to anticipate where the ball would come so as to be positioned that bit closer to it when I would have to run for possession with my opponent.'

On the morning of a big match he would walk his greyhounds around Vinegar Hill and later with a relaxed mental attitude, turn his thoughts to the hurling contest. Bobby Rackard told me that if he had to choose two half-back flankers, they would be Jim English and 'Wilkie' Thorpe. 'With them you could establish a great understanding' and then he added, 'Wilkie was a great man for the big occasion and for destroying reputations. His relaxed and unflappable temperament coupled with his confidence in his own ability and his fear of no opponent, enabled him to do this.'

'Wilkie' was disappointed that he didn't share in Wexford's All Ireland glory in 1955. His departure from the county scene in 1953 was perhaps a little premature. He was still a very fit man and Wexford with more astute and experienced management might have used his talents up to 1955.

He got his first taste of top class hurling when as a spectator, in the early forties, he saw the Cork/Limerick clashes of those days. 'Those were the greatest games of hurling I have seen. The Cork and Limerick teams of those days were magnificent and they made a lasting impression on me. Willie Campbell was a lovely stylish hurler. Jim Young was versatile — could play half-back or half-forward. Ted Sullivan at full forward for Cork was always thundering in on the goalkeeper. I saw him go in on Paddy Scanlon in the Limerick goal one day. You must remember that Scanlon as often as not did not catch a ball — just doubled on it as it came in. Well on this occasion as well as clearing the ball he took the cap off Ted Sullivan's head. There was of course Christy Ring. I played football with him with Midleton.

Great men on the Limerick team apart from Paddy Scanlon were Jackie Power and Paddy Carroll, Paddy Clohessy at centre-back, Timmy Ryan at midfield — and in the full-forward line Paddy McMahon, the 'Kildimo thresher'. And of course, the greatest of all Mick Mackey. He was the greatest hurler I saw playing — he had everything and I'll tell you a thing he used to do because I saw him at it. The ball would be down at the far end of the field and Mick would be roaming about and the first Corkman he would pass — it could be Johnny Quirke or Jim Young — he would jostle with a good hefty shoulder — just to let them know he was around — a kind of gamesmanship. I saw their father 'Tyler' on the pitch in Thurles too urging on his sons. Micka Brennan of Cork — Lord rest him — would tell you all about it.'

Reverting to his own playing days 'Wilkie' said 'there was one man you couldn't mark and that was Jim Langton of Kilkenny because he wouldn't stay with you and everytime you'd look around he was gone — neither could you upset him.

Another Kilkennyman I played on was Terry Leahy and I must confess he gave me a lesson in hurling. After the match I said to myself 'Terry Leahy if I ever play on you again it will be different but I never got a chance because he went off to America.

There were three Waterford men I had great admiration for — Vin Baston, Christy Moylan and Willie Barron.'

Finally, I asked, 'Are you known as Sam or Wilkie?' 'If anyone called me Sam I wouldn't respond. I have always been known as "Wilkie" and this is how it happened. When I was very young there was a gardener at The Rectory called Mr Wilkie. However, I spent more time in the garden helping myself to apples than Mr Wilkie. The result was that my pals used to say when they saw me coming — "here comes Wilkie the gardener." The name stuck. I became known as 'Wilkie' Thorpe.'

His team reads as follows.

Paddy Scanlon (Limerick)

Andy Fleming (Waterford)   Nick O'Donnell (Wexford)   Billy Rackard (Wexford)

Wilkie Thorpe (Wexford)   Bobby Rackard (Wexford)   Jackie Power (Limerick)

Ned Wheeler (Wexford)   Jim Morrissey (Wexford)

Christy Ring (Cork)   Mick Mackey (Limerick)   Tim Flood (Wexford)

Micka Brennan (Cork)   Nicky Rackard (Wexford)   Paddy McMahon (Limerick)

Martin White with a Kilkenny Hall of Fame award.

"

During my hurling career I made many great friends and comrades. I suppose my comrades on the field should get first place and I think the team-spirit developed with them was a great influence during my lifetime. I made many great friends especially team-mates but I think those from other counties made a very lasting impression so much so that, it was the beginning of lifelong friendships.

Most of those have gone to their great reward but the memory still lasts and we still speak of them as if they are still with

Born: 1909

us. I think my time in games was worthwhile if only to know and remember such very good friends.

I was lucky to come on the hurling scene in Kilkenny in 1931 when such experienced players as Lory Meagher, Ed Doyle, Mattie Power, Paddy Larkin, Pete O'Reilly, Martin Power and Tommy Carroll were still playing and young players such as Paddy Phelan, Jimmy Walsh, Jack Duggan, Dan Dunne and Jack Fitzpatrick were coming to begin a fruitful era in the hurling life of the county. All their skills and experience were wanted to cope with the great teams of other counties.

Martin White **"**

A t the time of writing Martin White is the only surviving member of the great 1931 Kilkenny team that participated in three memorable final games before going under to Cork in the second replay. At times now he feels like Oisin i ndiaidh na Féinne. It was a piece of hurling history that may never be repeated. It was his first season in senior hurling — having played junior with Kilkenny in 1930 — and he only took part in the first drawn game — 'the selectors decided they wanted a more experienced player to cope with Cork's star centre-back Jim O'Regan. I'd have liked another go on him. We lost Dick Morrisey through injury — it took him four years to recover — and that was a severe blow because Dick who was also a very fine hockey player was a most astute forward. We might have won the second day if Lory Meagher hadn't to retire injured with broken ribs and if Madden the Cork cornerback hadn't to retire injured after an accidental stroke across the forward from Mattie Power. Cork brought on George Garrett, one of the best corner-backs and half-backs that I have ever seen and he proceeded to subdue Mattie.'

I then recalled for Martin, an incident in the second game — told to me by Pat Stakelum — and recounted for Pat, on the occasion of a visit to Tommy Carroll, who was in action for Kilkenny in that game. 'The scores were level and time was running out. Kilkenny were awarded a close in free. I stood over the ball to take it. I couldn't miss. Anyone would have scored it. Jim O'Regan the Cork centre-back was standing too close and the referee was putting him back. By the time I was ready to take the free Lory Meagher had arrived on the scene. I stepped back. No one would stand over a free with Lory the King and the peak cap. He bent to lift and strike but two broken ribs from an earlier clash hindered his movement — he failed to rise the ball. Full time followed. The result is hurling history.'

There was great concern in Kilkenny about Lory's injury. If he wasn't on the third day many Kilkenny supporters would not have travelled — they knew Lory's worth. The selectors were well aware of the feelings in Kilkenny and arranged for Lory to be seen boarding the train with his hurley and boots — but there was of course no prospect of playing. The ruse led to criticism afterwards among supporters.

After the second draw a suggestion was made in some quarters that a half medal be presented to the players of both teams. The idea died and Martin told me that it had its origin in the fact that two Parle brothers from south Kilkenny — who were outstanding oarsmen — drew the world rowing championship. The result — a half medal each to the participants.

Martin played his last game with Kilkenny in the 1938 Leinster final when they were beaten in a replay by Dublin. Business matters then took him to Cork where he became associated with the Blackrock Club. In the years 1931-1938 he won many honours in an era that saw Kilkenny produce some brilliant combinations and outstanding hurling artists in several positions. He was proud to be among them.

As a teenager in 1926 he saw the men of those days being walked on the roads as part of their training programme. Even then he wondered at the wisdom of such an activity for men who came mainly from the land and spent their days walking the land and following horses. He can remember pouring milk into the lid of milk churns to give them a drink as they passed by his home.

He recalled too that when he won a county senior championship with Tullaroan in 1930 he had as a team mate Dick Grace — one of Kilkenny's greats of earlier years — who won an All Ireland with Kilkenny the year Martin was born.

After Martin had written his piece for me a few gentle tears fell from his eyes. 'Don't mind me I get a bit sad when I think of all the colleagues who have gone and the memories they bring back. I'm a bit soft that way.'

It was interesting to travel with him through his All Ireland successes and hear about some of those colleagues. 'In the 1932 final against Clare I played at full-forward on Pa "Fowler" McInerney. He was a big man — at that time 39 years of age — surely one of the oldest, if not the oldest, to have ever played in an All Ireland final. I was a chap of 23 — to me 'Fowler' was an elder statesman of the hurling field. As such I was a little in awe of him as I always had respect for older people. I remember that morning going to Mass and saying to Paddy Larkin I never thought to shave. Lory Meagher turned and said, "leave it on you boy — you'll look tougher." "Fowler's" job was to protect his goalkeeper Tommy Daly and keep me out. I finished the hour with two goals in a 3:3 to 2:3 victory. "Fowler" was unhappy. He maintained I was in the square for at least one of them. The following morning in a barber's shop he brought it up again. I didn't say anything out of respect. Paddy Phelan was sitting in the corner and he didn't say anything either. I must admit that Clare were most unlucky. They had a fine team with some wonderful hurlers such as Tommy Daly in goal, "Fowler" McInerney, John Joe Doyle, Larry Blake, Tull

The clash of the ash — opponents in the 1933 final (Kilkenny v Limerick) in an incident during a strenuous game.

Considine and Jim Holohan. Did you know that one Sunday in the mid thirties the Railway authorities sent an engine and one carriage from Dublin to Thurles so that Jim Holohan could line out with his native Clare in a championship match?'

The following year 1933 Kilkenny contested a great final with a young and talented Limerick team. It was the day Johnny Dunne playing on Mickey Cross scored the vital and only goal of the game in the second half. The final score was Kilkenny 1:7 Limerick 0:6. No wonder Kilkennymen of the next generation used to say 'why was

Mickey Cross when he saw what Johnny Dunne.'

Martin collected his second All Ireland medal. The prize for the 1933 win was a trip to America in 1934 — 'the treat of a lifetime'. Here is how An-tIománaidhe described the 1933 final in the *Kilkenny People*. 'Victory for Kilkenny and the All Ireland hurling title! What a vibrant phrase! How it thrills us! It has flashed its message North and South. It reverberates from the hills of gallant Tullaroan; it re-echoes softly along the gentle slopes of the Suir in grand old Mooncoin. Yes, Kilkenny's idols are undethroned; Kings of the hurling world they reign supreme. The grand ideal has been realised; the implicit confidence, the unswerving loyalty of thousands of ardent supporters has not been misplaced. Tradition has been maintained, nay, embellished. The "Black and Amber" flag waves in triumph along the banks of the Nore conveying its joyous message of Kilkenny's tenth All Ireland victory. Every Gael in the country for whom the swish of the camán holds a thrill worships at the shrine of the nation's greatest hurlers, thrice crowned champions within the brief space of a year.

The memorable and inspiring scenes at Croke Park on Sunday, the greatest day the GAA has ever had, are beyond adequate description. It seems almost futile to attempt to clothe in words that mighty manifestation of the strength and enthusiasm of the Gael. The 1933 All Ireland hurling final presents a panorama of splendour which leaves one almost breathless with amazement. Picture it!

Forty five thousand spectators a vast sea of faces, surrounding the pitch. The stands, sidelines and enclosures literally choked with cheering thousands and yet thousands more clamouring vainly for admission. It is a record attendance; it smashes all previous ones. Never before has the Association witnessed such a spectacle of almost awe-inspiring magnitude.

And, then, how can one convey an adequate impression of the mighty hurling drama enacted on Croke Park's green sod — that terrific battle between Kilkenny, the champions and Limerick, the challengers? Never before has the headquarters of the GAA seen such a great battle of hurling giants — sixty minutes of desperate conflict, dazzling speed, flashing camáns, splintering ash; thirty vigorous, manly combatants leaping through the air, crashing together in ceaseless conflict, striking like demons, fighting wildly for supremacy with a singular tenacity of purpose, returning blow for blow in grim silence, neither asking nor giving quarter, every ounce of strength in those wonderful bodies given in

a heroic effort to secure the nation's greatest prize. The very ground trembles from the mighty cheering of the assembled thousands, ever urging their idols, their hopes, on to greater efforts. Then, oh joy of joys! comes victory for grand old Kilkenny; victory for the gallant hurlers from the Noreside as the vast crowd repeats its tribute of 1932 and hails the all-conquering champions as the greatest team of a decade — Ireland's greatest camán wielders.'

In 1935 Kilkenny and Limerick again contested the final. In atrocious weather conditions the two teams served up a classic. Kilkenny kept the ball on the ground aided by the occasional flick at which Kilkenny are so adept and Lory Meagher was masterly. With time almost up and the scoreboard reading Kilkenny 2:5 Limerick 2:4, Limerick were awarded a 21 yards free. Surely a draw — did Mick Mackey go for a point? 'The ball was wet and heavy and some say that Mick went for the point but the ball didn't rise sufficiently high and was cleared by Kilkenny. Somehow, I think he went for the winner and if he did he shouldn't. Maybe Mick didn't know it but Jimmy O'Connell the goalkeeper, was a champion handballer. The entire full-back line of Paddy Larkin, Peter O'Reilly and Peter Blanchfield were all handballers of considerable ability. It meant they had a great eye and good hands — hard to get a goal. If the point was taken it would have been a draw — who knows what would have happened in the replay?'

'I had my hands full for the entire hour in 1935. I began off on Mickey Cross at left-half-forward — Mickey was among the best half-backs and ground strikers the game has known. I was switched to corner-forward on Mick Kennedy — the Tipperary man who starred so many times with his adopted Limerick and there has never been a closer corner-back in the game. In the second half I was switched to centre-forward on Paddy Clohessy — one of the outstanding centre-backs of the thirties and hurling history — I'd rather have him with me than against me. He was a great striker of a ball. There was venom in his hurling

— he had a great will to win. 'Twas a tough hour. All three are now gone, God be good to them. I remember Mickey Cross telling me that in his early days he played a few games with Limerick in his bare feet — he didn't have boots.'

After such a famous victory it was inevitable that some Noreside Bard would put pen to paper. Here is a verse that describes a few moments from that stirring encounter

A grand stroke by Locky
Hurtles towards the square.
Martin White flicks out his hand
To catch it will he dare?
Yes! he turns around and strikes
A hard one for the poles
And even the great Scanlon
Could not save that goal of goals.

Martin feels that hurling was more fun in his day. 'There was less pressure. The season can now be too long. The media publicity is an added burden.' He sees other changes too. 'There is more carrying and running with the ball — much too much at times — where does it lead? — often nowhere. Better make the ball do the work — save energy. There is less ground hurling and more is the pity. I miss the overhead and centrefield play — Lory Meagher of Kilkenny and Timmy Ryan of Limerick were masters of overhead striking. The lighter ball now lands nearer the half-back line than midfield. In my day everyone manned his position and minded his own territory and there was more first time hurling. When I see the light boots now I often think of the heavy leather ones we used to wear — almost half way up ones legs — and the leather cogs as well. I remember one day in New Ross when Dick Cantwell in goal pucked the ball out — it was doubled on in mid air by Lory Meagher and Willie "Wedger" Brennan doubled again to score a point without the ball hitting the ground.'

I invited him to pick his ideal team. 'I could pick one and then pick a couple of more to beat it. I could pick the Kilkenny half-back line of Ned Byrne, Padge Byrne and Paddy Phelan and say beat that. At the same time I could name the great Limerick half-back line of Mickey Cross, Paddy Clohessy and Garrett Howard and say beat that — and I could go on and on.'

I first met Martin at the Lory Meagher Heritage Launch at the Newpark Hotel in Kilkenny on Monday 25th May, 1992. He told me he was the fourth oldest living medal holder — the others being Jim Power the Galway full-back of the 1923 victory — Garrett Howard who won his first medal with Limerick in the 1921 championship — and 'Fox' Collins the Cork left-corner-back in the 1929 triumph. Among those present were many stars of yesteryear. Jack Lynch of Cork who officially launched the programme — John Joe Doyle and Mick Falvey of Clare who played in the 1932 final — Jimmy Coffey who won All Ireland honours with Tipperary in 1937 — Garrett Howard of Limerick — and indeed many others too.

Martin was fit and well despite his difficulty with his hips. At one stage in the exchanges of banter it looked as if himself and John Joe Doyle were about to challenge each other to a sprint but instead they settled down to a tranquil discussion on clashes from the past — now adorned by nostalgia.

Like to the summer's rain;
Or as the pearls of morning dew,
Ne'er to be found again.

For their names are treasured apart,
And their memories green and sweet
On every hillside and every mart,
In every cabin, in every street.

Stephen Gwynn, 'A Song of Defeat'

Prayer before a Game

O Lord I offer you this game.
To you, I offer my playing
As a prayer, and Lord I
will put my heart into it too.
More important than
the test of my limbs today
will be my behaviour during
the game, hence, O Lord,
help me to avoid vanity
if I do well, resentment
at being beaten, and all
feelings of revenge, anger
and jealousy. At the same
time, O Lord I want to win
so help me give of my very
best, and may my best be
good enough.

Amen.

256

HURLING GIANTS:

THE STATISTICS

Statistics on the Giants

	Born	County	Club	Era	All-Ireland Medals	National League (1926-)	Railway Cup (1927-)	County Titles	Provincial Titles	All Star Awards (1971-)
Ciaran Barr	1964	Antrim	O'Donovan Rossa	1984-94	-	-	-	1	5	1
Willie Barron	1914	Waterford	Dungarvan	1937-46	-	-	1	2	1	-
Paddy Barry	1928	Cork	Sarsfields	1948-64	3	2	4	2	4	-
Din Joe Buckley	1919	Cork	Glen Rovers	1939-47	5	2	-	8	5	-
Vincent Baston	1918	Waterford	Passage	1940-50	1	-	3	-	1	-
Richie Bennis	1945	Limerick	Patrickswell	1965-75	1	1	-	10	2	1
Johnny Callinan	1955	Clare	Clarecastle	1972-87	-	2	4	2	-	2
Pat Carroll	1956	Offaly	Coolderry	1977-85	1	-	-	2	4	2
Iggy Clarke	1952	Galway	Mullagh	1972-84	-	1	3	-	-	4
Sean Clohosey	1931	Kilkenny	Tullaroan	1953-63	2	1	1	1	5	-
Jimmy Coffey	1909	Tipperary	Newport & Ahane	1932-40	1	-	1	3	1	-
Martin Coogan	1940	Kilkenny	Castlecomer	1961-73	4	2	3	-	7	1
Tull Considine	1897(c)	Clare	Ennis	1917-33	-	-	4	6	1	-
John Coughlan	1898	Cork	Blackrock	1925-31	2	2	-	7	2	-
Eamon Cregan	1945	Limerick	Claughaun	1964-83	1	1	3	3	4	3
Frank Cummins	1947	Kilkenny	Blackrock	1966-84	7	3	6	6	10	4
Tommy Daly	1894	Dublin &Clare	Collegians & Tulla	1917-33	4	-	1	1	7	-
Pat Delaney	1955	Offaly	Kinnity	1974-89	2	-	-	5	6	1
Tony Doran	1946	Wexford	Buffers Alley	1967-84	1	2	7	11	4	1
Angela Downey	1957	Kilkenny	St Pauls	1972-94	12	-	-	20	13	-
Ann Downey	1957	Kilkenny	St Pauls	1973-94	12	-	-	20	13	-
Jimmy Doyle	1940	Tipperary	Thurles Sarsfields	1957-73	6	7	8	11	9	-
Jim English	1932	Wexford	Rathnure	1952-64	3	2	2	4	5	-
Leonard Enright	1952	Limerick	Patrickswell	1971-88	-	2	2	7	2	3

	Born	County	Club	Era	All-Ireland Medals	National League (1926-)	Railway Cup (1927-)	County Titles	Provincial Titles	All Star Awards (1971-)
John Fenton	1955	Cork	Midleton	1975-87	2	2	3	4	4	5
Liam Fennelly	1958	Kilkenny	Ballyhale Shamrocks	1981-92	3	4	-	9	6	4
Austin Flynn	1933	Waterford	Abbeyside	1955-67	1	1	2	-	3	-
Paddy Gantly	1919	Galway	Ardrahan & St Finbarrs	1945-49	-	-	1	2	-	-
Mick Gill	1899	Galway & Dublin	Ballinderreen & Garda	1922-32	3	2	1	6	3	-
Harry Gray	1915	Laois & Dublin	Rathdowney & Faughs	1934-49	1	1	1	8	5	-
Jimmy Gray	1929	Dublin	Na Fianna	1957-65	-	-	-	-	1	-
Sean Og Hanley	1872(c)	Limerick	Kilfinane	1890-1900	1	-	-	1	1	-
Pat Hartigan	1950	Limerick	South Liberties	1968-79	1	1	2	3	2	5
Conor Hayes	1958	Galway	Kiltormer	1979-90	3	1	4	3	-	3
Pat Henderson	1943	Kilkenny	Fenians (Johnstown)	1964-78	5	2	5	5	10	2
Brendan Hennessy	1938	Kerry	Ballyduff & New York	1955-76	-	-	-	2	-	-
Joe Hennessy	1956	Kilkenny	James Stephens	1976-88	3	4	1	3	6	5
Padraig Horan	1950	Offaly	St Rynaghs	1970-86	2	-	3	10	4	1
Willie Hough	1892	Limerick	Newcastle West	1913-29	2	-	-	2	3	-
Michael Keating	1944	Tipperary	Ballybacon-Grange	1964-75	2	2	2	-	5	1
Jim Kelliher	1880(c)	Cork	Dungourney	1900-14	2	-	-	?	7	-
Jimmy Kennedy	1926	Dublin &Tipperary	UCD & Kiladangan	1946-51	2	1	1	2	3	-
Mick King	1905	Galway	Castlegar & Galway	1923-35	-	1	-	-	-	-
Paddy Lalor	1926	Laois	Abbeyleix	1946-56	-	-	-	3	1	-
Johnny Leahy	1890	Tipperary	Boherlahan	1909-29	2	-	-	9	5	-
John Lyons	1924	Cork	Glen Rovers	1946-60	3	1	3	10	4	-
John 'T' Mackey	1883(c)	Limerick	Castleconnell	1901-17	-	-	-	1	2	-
Mick Mackey	1912	Limerick	Ahane	1930-47	3	5	8	15	5	1sp
PJ Mackey	1889	Wexford	New Ross	1907-16	1	-	-	2	1	-

	Born	County	Club	Era	All-Ireland Medals	National League (1926-)	Railway Cup (1927-)	County Titles	Provincial Titles	All Star Awards (1971-)
Mikey Maher	1870	Tipperary	Tubberadora	1890-1900(c)	5	-	-	3	5	-
Marian McCarthy	1954	Cork	SPPP & Eire Og	1970-91	8	-	-	5	20	-
Joe McDonagh	1953	Galway	Ballinderreen	1972-83	-	1	2	-	-	1
John McGrath	1928	Westmeath	Rickardstown	1950-65	-	-	1	3	-	-
Oliver McGrath	1938	Wexford	Faythe Harriers	1956-65	1	1	1	3	3	-
Joe McKenna	1951	Limerick	South Liberties	1971-85	1	1	4	4	3	6
Lory Meagher	1899	Kilkenny	Tullaroan	1926-36	3	1	2	5	6	-
Kathleen Mills	1923	Dublin	GSR	1941-61	15	-	-	?	20	-
Barney Moylan	1943	Offaly	St Rynaghs	1965-76	-	-	2	9	-	-
Brian Murphy	1952	Cork	Nemo Rangers	1972-83	3	4	1	-	8	2
Denis Murphy	1939	Cork	St Finbarrs	1959-69	1	1	2	2	2	-
Jimmy Barry-Murphy	1954	Cork	St Finbarrs	1974-86	5	2	-	6	10	5
Pat Nolan	1937	Wexford	Oylgate Glenbrien	1957-74	2	3	1	1	5	-
Una O'Connor		Dublin	Celtic	1953-76	13	-	-	4	15	-
Sean O Kennedy	1884	Wexford	New Ross	1907-23	1	-	-	2	1	-
Gerry O'Malley	1928	Roscommon	Four Roads	1946-65	-	-	-	6	-	-
Paddy Phelan	1910	Kilkenny	Tullaroan	1931-42	4	1	4	3	8	-
Nicky Rackard	1922	Wexford	Rathnure	1942-57	2	1	1	3	4	-
Christy Ring	1920	Cork	Glen Rovers	1940-63	8	4	18	12	9	-
Mick Roche	1943	Tipperary	Carrick Davins	1963-74	3	3	3	2	5	1
Jack Rochford	1882	Kilkenny	Three Castles	1902-16	7	-	-	2	9	-
Tom Semple	1880(c)	Tipperary	Thurles	1900-12	3	-	-	6	4	-
Noel Skehan	1944	Kilkenny	Bennettsbridge	1963-85	6	3	4	6	8	7
Jim Stapleton	1863	Tipperary	Thurles	1887(c)	1	-	-	?	-	-
Sam Thorpe	1919	Wexford	St Aidans	1945-53	-	-	-	6	1	-
Martin White	1909	Kilkenny	Tullaroan	1931-38	3	1	-	3	6	-

Where the Hurling Titles/Awards have gone — up to 1993 Final

COUNTY	Senior	Junior	Minor	Intermediate	Under 21	National League	All Stars
Clare	1	2	-	-	-	3	15
Cork	27	10	15	1	9	13	75
Kerry	1	2	-	-	-	-	-
Limerick	7	4	3	-	1	10	31
Tipperary	24	9	15	4	7	15	41
Waterford	2	2	2	-	1	1	5
Antrim	-	-	-	1	-	-	5
Down	-	1	-	-	-	-	1
London	1	5	-	2	-	-	-
Warwickshire	-	3	-	-	-	-	-
Galway	4	1	2	-	6	5	57
Roscommon	-	1	-	-	-	-	-
Carlow	-	-	-	1	-	-	-
Dublin	6	3	4	-	-	2	2
Kildare	-	2	-	1	-	-	-
Kilkenny	25	8	16	1	5	8	82
Laois	1	-	-	-	-	-	1
Meath	-	3	-	-	-	-	-
Offaly	2	2	3	-	-	1	22
Westmeath	-	1	-	-	-	-	1
Wexford	5	2	3	2	1	4	21
Wicklow	-	2	-	-	-	-	-

Senior began in 1887 (none in 1888)
Junior began in 1912
Suspended 1917-22 and 1942-45

Minor began 1928 Suspended 1942-44

Intermediate operated from 1961-73
Discontinued 1974-82 and incorporated in Div 3 of NHL.
Under 21 began 1964

All Ireland Hurling titles — Senior, Junior and Minor

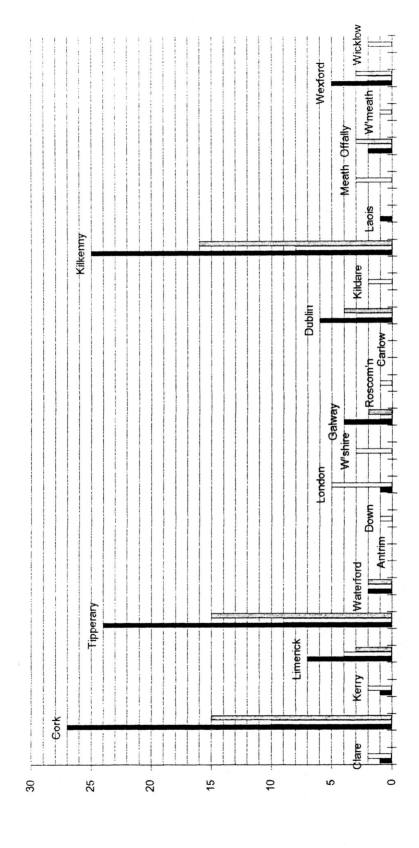

All Star Awards since inception in 1971 up to 1993

359 including 14 specials

	71	72	73	74	75	76	77	78	79	80	81	82	83	84	85	86	87	88	89	90	91	92	93	S	Total	% of Total
Clare	-	-	-	1	-	1	4	3	1	-	3	-	-	-	-	-	-	-	-	-	-	-	-	2	15	4
Cork	2	5	-	2	1	5	8	6	3	2	1	3	3	6	2	7	1	1	-	6	3	3	2	3	75	21
Limerick	2	2	5	3	-	-	-	1	1	3	3	-	1	2	-	-	-	-	-	-	1	2	-	3	31	9
Tipperary	3	1	1	-	1	-	-	1	2	1	-	-	1	1	1	1	4	4	6	2	7	1	1	2	41	11
Waterford	-	-	1	-	-	-	-	-	-	1	-	2	-	-	-	-	-	-	-	-	-	-	-	1	5	1
Galway	1	-	-	3	2	1	1	1	3	6	2	-	1	1	5	5	6	7	5	3	1	-	3	1	57	16
Antrim	-	-	-	-	-	-	-	-	-	-	-	-	-	-	-	-	-	1	2	-	1	-	1	-	5	1
Down	-	-	-	-	-	-	-	-	-	-	-	-	-	-	-	-	-	-	-	-	1	-	-	-	1	.5
Dublin	1	-	-	-	-	-	-	-	-	-	-	-	-	-	-	-	-	-	-	1	-	-	-	-	2	.5
Kilkenny	5	6	7	7	6	3	-	3	4	-	-	8	9	2	1	1	3	-	-	1	2	7	6	1	82	23
Laois	-	-	-	-	-	-	-	-	-	-	-	-	-	1	-	-	-	-	-	-	-	-	-	-	1	.5
Offaly	1	-	-	-	-	-	-	-	-	2	5	2	-	3	5	-	-	1	1	1	1	-	-	-	22	6
Westmeath	-	-	-	-	-	-	-	-	-	-	-	-	-	-	-	1	-	-	-	-	-	-	-	-	1	.5
Wexford	-	1	2	1	4	2	-	-	1	-	1	-	-	-	-	-	1	1	1	1	-	-	2	1	21	6
Number of Counties Honoured	7	5	4	6	6	5	4	6	7	6	6	5	5	6	6	5	5	6	5	7	6	6	6	8	359	100

All-Ireland and National League Winners

Year	Senior	Junior	Minor	Intermediate	Under 21	National League
1887	Tipperary *1*	-	-	-	-	-
1888	-	-	-	-	-	-
1889	Dublin *1*	-	-	-	-	-
1890	Cork *1*	-	-	-	-	-
1891	Kerry *1*	-	-	-	-	-
1892	Cork *2*	-	-	-	-	-
1893	Cork *3*	-	-	-	-	-
1894	Cork *4*	-	-	-	-	-
1895	Tipperary *2*	-	-	-	-	-
1896	Tipperary *3*	-	-	-	-	-
1897	Limerick *1*	-	-	-	-	-
1898	Tipperary *4*	-	-	-	-	-
1899	Tipperary *5*	-	-	-	-	-
1900	Tipperary *6*	-	-	-	-	-
1901	London *1*	-	-	-	-	-
1902	Cork *5*	-	-	-	-	-
1903	Cork *6*	-	-	-	-	-
1904	Kilkenny *1*	-	-	-	-	-
1905	Kilkenny *2*	-	-	-	-	-
1906	Tipperary *7*	-	-	-	-	-
1907	Kilkenny *3*	-	-	-	-	-
1908	Tipperary *8*	-	-	-	-	-
1909	Kilkenny *4*	-	-	-	-	-
1910	Wexford *1*	-	-	-	-	-
1911	Kilkenny *5*	-	-	-	-	-
1912	Kilkenny *6*	Cork *1*	-	-	-	-
1913	Kilkenny *7*	Tipperary *1*	-	-	-	-
1914	Clare *1*	Clare *1*	-	-	-	-
1915	Laois *1*	Tipperary *2*	-	-	-	-
1916	Tipperary *9*	Cork *2*	-	-	-	-
1917	Dublin *2*	-	-	-	-	-
1918	Limerick *2*	-	-	-	-	-
1919	Cork *7*	-	-	-	-	-
1920	Dublin *3*	-	-	-	-	-
1921	Limerick *3*	-	-	-	-	-
1922	Kilkenny *8*	-	-	-	-	-
1923	Galway *1*	Offaly *1*	-	-	-	-
1924	Dublin *4*	Tipperary *3*	-	-	-	-
1925	Tipperary *10*	Cork *3*	-	-	-	-
1926	Cork *8*	Tipperary *4*	-	-	-	Cork *1*
1927	Dublin *5*	Meath *1*	-	-	-	-

Year	Senior	Junior	Minor	Intermediate	Under 21	National League
1928	Cork 9	Kilkenny 1	Cork 1	-	-	Tipperary 1
1929	Cork 10	Offaly 2	Waterford 1	-	-	Dublin 1
1930	Tipperary 11	Tipperary 5	Tipperary 1	-	-	Cork 2
1931	Cork 11	Waterford 1	Kilkenny 1	-	-	-
1932	Kilkenny 9	Dublin 1	Tipperary 2	-	-	Galway 1
1933	Kilkenny 10	Tipperary 6	Tipperary 3	-	-	Kilkenny 1
1934	Limerick 4	Waterford 2	Tipperary 4	-	-	Limerick 1
1935	Kilkenny 11	Limerick 1	Kilkenny 2	-	-	Limerick 2
1936	Limerick 5	Westmeath 1	Kilkenny 3	-	-	Limerick 3
1937	Tipperary 12	Dublin 2	Cork 2	-	-	Limerick 4
1938	Dublin 6	London 1	Cork 3	-	-	Limerick 5
1939	Kilkenny 12	Galway 1	Cork 4	-	-	Dublin 2
1940	Limerick 6	Cork 4	Limerick 1	-	-	Cork 3
1941	Cork 12	Limerick 2	Cork 5	-	-	Cork 4
1942	Cork 13	-	-	-	-	-
1943	Cork 14	-	-	-	-	-
1944	Cork 15	-	-	-	-	-
1945	Tipperary 13	-	Dublin 1	-	-	-
1946	Cork 16	Kilkenny 2	Dublin 2	-	-	Clare 1
1947	Kilkenny 13	Cork 5	Tipperary 5	-	-	Limerick 6
1948	Waterford 1	Meath 2	Waterford 2	-	-	Cork 5
1949	Tipperary 14	London 2	Tipperary 6	-	-	Tipperary 2
1950	Tipperary 15	Cork 6	Kilkenny 4	-	-	Tipperary 3
1951	Tipperary 16	Kilkenny 3	Cork 6	-	-	Galway 2
1952	Cork 17	Dublin 3	Tipperary 7	-	-	Tipperary 4
1953	Cork 18	Tipperary 7	Tipperary 8	-	-	Cork 6
1954	Cork 19	Limerick 3	Dublin 3	-	-	Tipperary 5
1955	Wexford 2	Cork 7	Tipperary 9	-	-	Tipperary 6
1956	Wexford 3	Kilkenny 4	Tipperary 10	-	-	Wexford 1
1957	Kilkenny 14	Limerick 4	Tipperary 11	-	-	Tipperary 7
1958	Tipperary 17	Cork 8	Limerick 2	-	-	Wexford 2
1959	Waterford 2	London 3	Tipperary 12	-	-	Tipperary 8
1960	Wexford 4	London 4	Kilkenny 5	-	-	Tipperary 9
1961	Tipperary 18	Kerry 1	Kilkenny 6	Wexford 1	-	Tipperary 10
1962	Tipperary 19	Kildare 1	Kilkenny 7	Carlow 1	-	Kilkenny 2
1963	Kilkenny 15	London 5	Wexford 1	Tipperary 1	-	Waterford 1
1964	Tipperary 20	Down 1	Cork 7	Wexford 2	Tipperary 1	Tipperary 11
1965	Tipperary 21	Roscommon 1	Dublin 4	Cork 1	Wexford 1	Tipperary 12
1966	Cork 20	Kildare 2	Wexford 2	Tipperary 2	Cork 1	Kilkenny 3
1967	Kilkenny 16	Wicklow 1	Cork 8	London 1	Tipperary 2	Wexford 3
1968	Wexford 5	Warwickshire 1	Wexford 3	London 2	Cork 2	Tipperary 16
1969	Kilkenny 17	Warwickshire 2	Cork 9	Kildare 1	Cork 3	Cork 7

Year	Senior	Junior	Minor	Intermediate	Under 21	National League
1970	Cork *21*	Meath *3*	Cork *10*	Antrim *1*	Cork *4*	Cork *8*
1971	Tipperary *22*	Wicklow *2*	Cork *11*	Tipperary *3*	Cork *5*	Limerick *7*
1972	Kilkenny *18*	Kerry *2*	Kilkenny *8*	Tipperary *4*	Galway *1*	Cork *9*
1973	Limerick *7*	Warwickshire *3*	Kilkenny *9*	Kilkenny *1*	Cork *6*	Wexford *4*
1974	Kilkenny *19*	-	Cork *12*	-	Kilkenny *1*	Cork *10*
1975	Kilkenny *20*	-	Kilkenny *10*	-	Kilkenny *2*	Galway *3*
1976	Cork *22*	-	Tipperary *13*	-	Cork *7*	Kilkenny *4*
1977	Cork *23*	-	Kilkenny *11*	-	Kilkenny *3*	Clare *2*
1978	Cork *24*	-	Cork *13*	-	Galway *2*	Clare *3*
1979	Kilkenny *21*	-	Cork *14*	-	Tipperary *3*	Tipperary *14*
1980	Galway *2*	-	Tipperary *14*	-	Tipperary *4*	Cork *11*
1981	Offaly *1*	-	Kilkenny *12*	-	Tipperary *5*	Cork *12*
1982	Kilkenny *22*	-	Tipperary *15*	-	Cork *8*	Kilkenny *5*
1983	Kilkenny *23*	Cork *9*	Galway *1*	-	Galway *3*	Kilkenny *6*
1984	Cork *25*	Kilkenny *5*	Limerick *3*	-	Kilkenny *4*	Limerick *8*
1985	Offaly *2*	Wexford *1*	Cork *15*	-	Tipperary *6*	Limerick *9*
1986	Cork *26*	Kilkenny *6*	Offaly *1*	-	Galway *4*	Kilkenny *7*
1987	Galway *3*	Cork *10*	Offaly *2*	-	Limerick *1*	Galway *4*
1988	Galway *4*	Kilkenny *7*	Kilkenny *13*	-	Cork *9*	Tipperary *15*
1989	Tipperary *23*	Tipperary *8*	Offaly *3*	-	Tipperary *7*	Galway *5*
1990	Cork *27*	Kilkenny *8*	Kilkenny *14*	-	Kilkenny *5*	Kilkenny *8*
1991	Tipperary *24*	Tipperary *9*	Kilkenny *15*		Galway *5*	Offaly *1*
1992	Kilkenny *24*	Wexford *2*	Galway *2*	-	Waterford *1*	Limerick *10*
1993	Kilkenny *25*	Clare *2*	Kilkenny *16*	-	Galway *6*	Cork *13*
1994	Offaly *3*	Cork *11*	Galway *3*		Kilkenny *6*	Tipperary *16*

SPORTS BOOKS FROM WOLFHOUND PRESS

FOOTBALL CAPTAINS
The All-Ireland Winners
Brian Carthy

The greatest football book you'll ever buy. A unique portrait of fifty years of Gaelic football through the eyes of the players who captained the All-Ireland winning teams. Each captain who held aloft the Sam Maguire Cup from 1940 to 1993 gives his thoughts on sport and the game, memories of the glory days, reminiscences on his greatest team-mates and opponents, with facts, photographs, achievements and more.

Fully illustrated in colour and black and white, a magnificent record of Irish football.

ULSTER FOOTBALL AND HURLING
The Path of Champions
Jerome Quinn

The Sam Maguire Cup travelled to Down in 1991, to Donegal in 1992 for the first time ever, to Derry in 1993 and back to Down in 1994. Irish football has been taken by storm. *Ulster Football and Hurling* explores how the Ulstermen did it, the stories behind the scenes, the emotions experienced by these great players, managers and fans along the way both in hurling and football.

A beautifully produced book that explores, commemorates and celebrates the phenomenon that is Ulster GAA.

THE GREATEST HURLING DECADE
Nicholas Furlong

The sensational years of Wexford's hurling glory – the 1950s.

It was a mould-breaking decade for modern hurling, an era of revolution and sensation for Wexford and the teams they met in this explosion of hurling talent. Nicholas Fulong relives the epic games of the decade, portraying the fierce rivalries and great names — the Rackards, Floods, Foleys and Kehoes; Ring, Kehir, Salmon, Grimes, Stakelum, and many others.

The domination of Cork, Tipperary and Kilkenny was irrevocably challenged as Wexford, Clare, Limerick, Laois, Waterford, Galway, Dublin, Meath and Westmeath emerged into the mainstream. A riveting hurling memoir

THE HORSE IN IRELAND
Brian Smith

A complete illustrated account of the horse in Irish life through tradition, folklore, sport, work and play.

The Horse in Ireland is the book for anyone interested in horses and their role in folklore or tradition. From Tetrarch to Arkle and Early Mist to Dawn Run, from Fionn MacCumhail to the National Stud, this is the definitive story of the horse in Ireland.

THE STORY OF HANDBALL
The Game, the Players, the History
Tom McElligott

The story of this ancient and skilful game which prizes individual talent and technique — its history, players, partnerships, champions and championships, its rules, techniques and results. Illustrated with rare photographs, posters and programmes, many reproduced here for the first time.

GIANTS OF THE ASH
Brendan Fullam

'A great hurling book, *Giants of the Ash* has the nation's history woven into it. Conversation courses through the pages as it flows through the living body of the game.' *(Irish Times)*

Giants of the Ash by Brendan Fullam is the first in-depth study of the outstanding hurlers of the century. Seventy-nine of the greatest players including Christy Ring, Peter Cregan, John and Michael Maher, the Rackards and the oldest among them, John T Power.

'As you open the pages, you will hear again the roar of the crowds in Croke Park, the whirr of the flying sliotar and the unmistakable and unique sound of ash against ash.'

Write for our catalogue to:
WOLFHOUND PRESS
68 Mountjoy Square, Dublin 1